The New Testament Church

McMaster Divinity College Press
Biblical Studies Series

The New Testament Church
The Challenge of Developing Ecclesiologies

edited by

JOHN P. HARRISON

and

JAMES D. DVORAK

PICKWICK *Publications* · Eugene, Oregon

THE NEW TESTAMENT CHURCH
The Challenge of Developing Ecclesiologies

McMaster Divinity College Biblical Studies Series 1

McMaster Divinity College Press
1280 Main Street West
Hamilton, Ontario, Canada
L8S 4K1

Pickwick Publications
An Imprint of Wipf and Stock Publishers
199 W. 8th Av.e, Suite 3
Eugene, OR 97401

www.wipfandstock.com

ISBN 13: 978-1-60899-998-9

Cataloging-in-Publication data:

The new testament church : the challenge of developing ecclesiologies / edited by John P. Harrison and James D. Dvorak.

xxiv + 302 p. ; 23 cm. Includes bibliographical references and indexes.

McMaster Divinity College Press Biblical Studies Series 1

ISBN 13: 978-1-60899-998-9

1. I. Harrison, John P. II. Dvorak, James D. III. Title. IV. Series.

BV600 A1 N5 2012

Manufactured in the U.S.A.

Contents

Abbreviations

AB	Anchor Bible
AGAJU	Arbeiten zur Geschichte des Antiken Judentums und des Urchristentums
AnBib	Analecta Biblica
ANRW	*Aufstieg und Niedergang der römischen Welt*
ANTC	Abingdon New Testament Commentaries
ATR	*Anglican Theological Review*
BAR	*Biblical Archaeology Review*
BECNT	Baker Exegetical Commentary on the New Testament
Bib	*Biblica*
BNTC	Black's New Testament Commentaries
BT	*The Bible Translator*
CBQ	*Catholic Biblical Quarterly*
CTJ	*Calvin Theological Journal*
DJG	*Dictionary of Jesus and the Gospels*
EDT	*Evangelical Dictionary of Theology*
EvQ	*Evangelical Quarterly*
FRLANT	Forschungen zur Religion und Literatur des Alten und Neuen Testaments
FzB	Forschung zur Bibel
HNTC	Harper's New Testament Commentaries
HTR	*Harvard Theological Review*
HTS	Harvard Theological Studies
HvTSt	*Hervormde teologiese studies*
ICC	The International Critical Commentary
Int	Interpretation
IRT	Issues in Religion and Theology
IVPNTC	The IVP New Testament Commentary
JBL	*Journal of Biblical Literature*
JR	*Journal of Religion*

JSJ	*Journal for the Study of Judaism in the Persian, Hellenistic, and Roman Period*
JSNT	*Journal for the Study of the New Testament*
JSNTSup	Journal for the Study of the New Testament Supplement Series
JTC	*Journal for Theology and the Church*
KEK	Kritisch-exegetischer Kommentar über das Neue Testament
LNTS	Library of New Testament Studies
MNTC	Moffatt New Testament Commentary
NAC	New American Commentary
NCB	New Century Bible
NCBC	New Century Bible Commentary
NICNT	New International Commentary on the New Testament
NIGTC	New International Greek Testament Commentary
NIVAC	New International Version Application Commentary
NovT	*Novum Testamentum*
NovTSup	Supplement to *Novum Testamentum*
NRTh	*Nouvelle revue théologique*
NSBT	New Studies in Biblical Theology
NTL	New Testament Library
NTM	New Testament Monographs
NTOA	Novum Testamentum et orbis antiquus
NTS	*New Testament Studies*
PNTC	Pelican New Testament Commentaries
RB	*Revue biblique*
ResQ	*Restoration Quarterly*
RHR	*Revue de l'histoire des religions*
SANT	Studien zum Alten und Neuen Testament
SBL	Society of Biblical Literature
SBLDS	Society of Biblical Literature Dissertation Series
SBLSP	*Society of Biblical Literature Seminar Papers*
SBLSS	Society of Biblical Literature Semeia Series
SNT	Studien zum Neuen Testament
SNTSMS	Society for New Testament Studies Monograph Series
SNTSS	Society for New Testament Studies Special Studies
SNTW	Studies of the New Testament and its World
SP	*Sacra Pagina*

SUNT	Studien zur Umwelt des Neuen Testaments
SWJT	*Southwestern Journal of Theology*
TANZ	Texte und Arbeiten zum neutestamentlichen Zeitalter
TNTC	Tyndale New Testament Commentaries
TU	Texte und Untersuchungen
TWNT	*Theologisches Wörterbuch zum Neuen Testament,* edited by G. Kittel and G. Friedrich. Stuttgart, 1932–1979
TynBul	*Tyndale Bulletin*
WBC	Word Biblical Commentary
WMANT	Wissenschaftliche Monographien zum Alten und Neuen Testament
WUNT	Wissenschaftliche Untersuchungen zum Neuen Testament
ZNW	*Zeitschrift für die neutestamentliche Wissenschaft und die Kunde der älteren Kirche*

Contributors

William R. Baker is General Editor, Stone-Campbell Journal, Cincinnati, OH.

Allen Black is Professor of New Testament at Harding School of Theology, Memphis, TN.

James D. Dvorak is Associate Professor of Greek and New Testament, Oklahoma Christian University, Oklahoma City, OK.

George Goldman II is Associate Professor of Bible and Ministry at Lipscomb University, Nashville, TN.

John P. Harrison is Professor of New Testament and Ministry, Oklahoma Christian University, Oklahoma City, OK.

Christopher R. Hutson is Associate Professor of New Testament at Abilene Christian University, Abilene, TX.

Curt Niccum is Associate Professor of New Testament, Abilene Christian University, Abilene, TX.

Thomas H. Olbricht is Distinguished Professor Emeritus of Religion, Pepperdine University, Malibu, CA.

Olutola K. Peters is Professor of New Testament and Pastoral Studies at Emmanuel Bible College, Kitchener, Ontario.

Jeffrey Peterson is the Jack C. and Ruth Wright Professor of New Testament at Austin Graduate School of Theology, Austin, TX.

Stanley E. Porter is the President and Dean, and Professor of New Testament at McMaster Divinity College, Hamilton, Ontario.

Mark E. Rapinchuk is Professor of Philosophy and Religion at College of the Ozarks, Point Lookout, MO.

Eckhard J. Schnabel is Professor of New Testament at Trinity Evangelical Divinity School, Deerfield, IL.

Cynthia Long Westfall is Assistant Professor of New Testament at McMaster Divinity College, Hamilton, ON.

Introduction

SINCE THE HOLY SPIRIT came upon the disciples on the day of Pentecost, believers in Jesus have wrestled with the question, "How do we follow Jesus?" Or, as it is often asked today, "What does it mean to be the church?" Answering this question is no easy task. One reason it has been so difficult is because there is a multitude of complex questions that also need to be answered. For instance, what is the church? Did Jesus even intend for there to be a church? If he did, did he give it one mission or many? What are conditions in which believers should live together? What must they collectively know or believe? What practices must they observe? What practices are always inappropriate? What priorities should characterize them as a group? What relationship should the church have with those who don't believe in Jesus? How is unity to be defined? Who should lead the church? Who may not? What activities should the faithful engage in when they assemble? How should they discipline those whose behaviors are found unacceptable? These are only a few of the many questions associated with the study of "Ecclesiology."

The term "ecclesiology," simply put, is the study of the church. Those who ask ecclesiological questions seek to define what God wants his people to be, to believe, to do, to teach, and to become. Questions regarding the nature and function of the church are what the New Testament authors themselves addressed. Whether reading Paul calling the Corinthians to separate themselves from pagan idolatry, or Peter utilizing Israel's description as a holy priesthood to picture Christians, or James dispensing wisdom to various communities of Jesus followers, all New Testament authors deal with the issue of who Christians are and how they must act as a collective body. So ecclesiology is the study of the church in connection with a wide variety of others issues: ethics, Christology, soteriology, and eschatology, to name a few.

WHY IS EXPLORING NEW TESTAMENT
ECCLESIOLOGIES IMPORTANT?

Christian communities today face enormous challenges as they respond to new pastoral contexts and new teachings that attempt to redefine what churches should be. One of the many questions asked is, "How can churches proclaim the gospel of Jesus Christ in a postmodern culture that devalues any message that assumes exclusivity and privilege?" As church leaders seek assistance in redefining the nature and role of the church, they often appeal to several theological methods to construct an ecclesiology that is both instructive and relevant. The problem is that many methods do not recognize or interact with the diversity of ecclesiologies in the New Testament.

What the authors of the New Testament wrote about the church is foundational for many Christian traditions. These authors believed the followers of Jesus must think and behave in specific ways, and their instructions to believers then are formative for many church leaders now. But numerous Christian traditions have mistakenly assumed that the New Testament collectively presents a uniform picture of the structure, leadership, and sacraments that were practiced in the first century.[1] This is far from what is actually revealed when the New Testament books are explored individually. Certainly these books point to a unity shared by their communities. This unity is centered on the teaching that Jesus is the Christ, whom God has raised from the dead and has enthroned as Lord. They believed that they were living in the time prior to the age to come, when God's kingdom will be fully revealed and experienced by those who have put their trust in Jesus as God's messiah. Nevertheless, while these communities were unified in their belief in Jesus as the risen Christ, this unity did not translate into a uniform ecclesiology. This is why the present volume is needed. What is routinely overlooked and unrecognized is the variety of unique expressions within the New Testament concerning the identity and norms of Jesus' followers. The authors of the New Testament do not attest to any kind of comprehensive uniformity or a single indistinguishable pattern (where every assembly did exactly the same thing and saw themselves in exactly the same way) but rather they evidence a

---

1. This is what Ernst Käsemann called an *ecclesiologia perennis* ("Unity and Diversity in New Testament Ecclesiology," 290).

collage of rich theological insights into what it means to be the church.[2] By making church leaders aware of this diversity, it is our hope that they will no longer assume that their task is to find a single uniform description of the New Testament church but will look for New Testament ecclesiologies that are most relevant to the social and cultural context in which their community lives. This single volume of essays, written with the latest scholarship, highlights the uniqueness of individual ecclesiologies in the New Testament and their core unifying themes.

WHAT DOES THIS VOLUME CONTAIN?

John Harrison's "Matthew's Vision for the Community of Jesus' Disciples" explores six questions that sharpen the focus on the nature of Matthew's ecclesiology. After identifying the most probable location for Matthew's Jewish-Christian community, Harrison argues that they are primarily conceived of as the "assembly of the Lord" (the Hebrew Bible's *qahal Yahweh*) and ought to behave as *disciples* of Christ. As God's reconstituted Israel gathers to worship him, they also come to learn and obey the teachings of Jesus, God's anointed Son. The most significant activities described by Matthew that suggest what took place in these assemblies are teaching, prophecy, and prayer. Harrison concludes his overview of the Matthean community by pointing to the internal evidence that suggests Matthew's immediate audience was experiencing persecution from non-Christian Jewish authorities.

Mark Rapinchuk's chapter "Ecclesiology in the Gospel of Mark" operates from the standpoint that this Gospel does indeed reflect an understanding of Jesus' "church." He follows three lines of inquiry that provide a reconstruction of several ecclesiological features of the Markan community. The first feature is a model or philosophy of Christian leadership that finds its basis in Jesus' life and teachings rather than in leadership models in play in the first century Greco-Roman world. Next, Rapinchuk argues that Jesus' reinterpretion of Torah points to a distinctive feature of redefining the people of God. Finally, he contends that Mark portrays the church as those who place their faith in Jesus as Christ and are obedi-

---

2. The comprehensive and detailed book on ecclesiology by Ferguson, *The Church of Christ*, presents an excellent systematic theology of New Testament teachings on the church, but unfortunately it does not emphasize the diverse ecclesiologies of New Testament authors and may leave readers with the mistaken impression that this theology would have been held uniformly in some way by all the New Testament authors.

ent to God's will, as defined by Jesus. Whether they are Jews or Gentiles, God's true family is marked by the genuine commitment to Jesus of all believers and to his teaching to love God and one another.

George Goldman II describes the ecclesiology of Luke-Acts. Goldman sees three broad strands of Luke's ecclesiology that are most significant. One strand is the nature of the church—what Luke thinks the church is. He argues that Luke perceives the church not as a new Israel but as a renewed Israel. A key sign of this perception is the way in which Luke portrays early believers as devout Jews who believed Jesus brought about the redemption of Israel, thus fulfilling the promises of God. Further, nowhere does Luke undermine the hopes of pious Jews who long for the restoration of Israel. This emphasis notwithstanding, Luke envisions the church as an inclusive community. Portrayals of Jesus' identification with and ministry to those considered to be social outcasts as well as the inclusion of Gentiles in the church are significant contributors to an inclusive view of the church. Luke is also concerned with what the church does. On the one hand, he describes the church as a community of believers who commune together. Jesus gathered and broke bread with his disciples; the early church gathered and broke bread with one another. Further, they cared for one another by sharing their possessions to help the poor. Finally, Goldman emphasizes Luke's concern for leadership in the church. Leadership certainly consists of elders (cf. Acts 11:30) and other "leaders among the brothers and sisters" (Acts 15:22), but perhaps more important to Luke is that the church is led by the Holy Spirit. As Jesus was led by the Spirit (cf. Luke 4), so also is his church (cf. Acts 2).

Tom Olbricht contends that John's Gospel and the three epistles of John contain a distinctive ecclesiology that depicts in rich organic imagery several central concepts. While questions about the leadership and organization of the Johannine community cannot be clearly discerned from this literature, it is clear that the author understands that the life of the community is dependent upon God's love for them and Jesus' abiding presence with believers through the Holy Spirit, the way branches are dependent on a vine. The church is the "flock of God" and it is the central work of the church to bring individuals into the fold by motivating them to believe in Jesus. The church as God's flock comes into being because the Word has reached out to humanity and created a community of believers. The Johannine Epistles also attest to an understanding that the foundational activity of God is to create a *koinonia* through the life-giving word. A key characteristic that distinguishes this community as the authentic people of God is their demonstration of love to one another. It is a community that has to be unified around its common confession of Jesus as the Son of God. This unity is demonstrated by participation in two Christ-centered practices: baptism and the Lord's Supper.

Paul's letters to the Romans and to the Galatians are often discussed in tandem mainly because they share the common topic of justification or the righteousness of God. There is no doubt about the importance of this topic; however, it often so completely dominates scholarly treatments of these letters that other important topics receive less than satisfactory attention. Stanley E. Porter's essay revives scholarly dialogue on one of these neglected topics, namely, Paul's conception of "church" in Romans and Galatians. Porter marshals textual evidence to show that Paul conceived of the church as a grace- and faith-based community of believers that was focused upon the gospel. Because of God's gracious actions toward humans, the community of baptized believers gathered intentionally in order to preserve and promote the message of the gospel. The church organized and functioned much like a first-century family. It was an egalitarian community within which distinctions that separate (e.g., ethnic, socio-economic, gender) are all countermanded in order that all may be one in Christ as children of God. The church is Spirit-led and Spirit-empowered so that members may serve one another in mutually beneficial ways. Although questions about the church's organization or assembly practices are not the focus of Romans or Galatians, Porter correctly concludes that the church's nature is central to Paul's arguments about justification and the righteousness of God.

First Corinthians has long occupied a distinguished place in discussions of ecclesiology and, as Eckhard Schnabel demonstrates, there is good reason for this judgment. As a consequence of addressing the misguided beliefs and inappropriate behaviors manifest at Corinth, Paul's vision of "church" becomes apparent in the text. This happens in part through the use of metaphors or analogies, four of which Schnabel discusses in detail: the church as a plantation (3:5–9), a building (3:10–15), a temple (3:16–17), and a body (12:12–31). Of these, the body metaphor is likely the most well-known, and it may offer the greatest insight into Paul's understanding of the church in First Corinthians. Schnabel argues that this metaphor has as many as seven points of application to the congregation at Corinth. When taken together, these points project a grand vision of the church, which consists of a diverse number of people exercising a diverse number of functions yet who together, like a body, constitute a unity. In fact, it is the unity of all these diverse people and functions that exemplifies God's wisdom and power, thereby bringing him honor. Additionally, 1 Corinthians provides the clearest look into the meetings of the believers at Corinth. The careful analysis of the text by Schnabel results in a helpful profile of the most significant elements of their assemblies, including singing, teaching, prophetic messages, and communal meals.

Curt Niccum's essay "Heaven Can't Wait: The Church in Ephesians and Colossians" unfolds what he argues is the most mature ecclesiology in the entire New Testament. Niccum demonstrates that the author of these two Asian letters portrays the church as a political body and as Israel, God's bride. Ephesians chapter 2, in particular, stresses with the frequent use of σύν compounds an ecclesiology that recognizes the full inclusion of Gentile Christians into this Israel that now embodies the people of God. The Temple has now been replaced by Christ's crucifixion in terms of universal access to God. In addition to being a political body of a restored Israel, the church in Ephesians and Colossians is a Spirit-filled, cosmic community that is involved in an eschatological battle with spiritual forces. While a physical embodiment of this heavenly entity, the church devotes herself to such key practices as prayer, assembling for mutual edification, singing, baptism, and the exercise of spiritual gifts. Niccum concludes his survey of these two ecclesiologies by explaining several roles of ministry that existed in these churches, specifically apostles, prophets, teachers, and "shepherds."

The essay by Jeffery Peterson notes that constructing an ecclesiology from Philippians and Thessalonians requires the reader to focus on Paul's concern for specific issues in the lives of his converts in these two cities. Paul's instructions to individuals reflect what he assumed to be the true nature of Christian communities. From the Thessalonian correspondences the reader can observe that Paul conceives of these believers as a divinely chosen assembly in whom Israel's God is at work. They are now expected to live moral lives that are distinguished from their previous pagan behavior. Consequently, they experience a familial bond that connects them to one another locally and with the church in other places. This connection has physical implications, as there is an expectation that financial resources will be shared among believers. In addition to several moral exhortations, Paul urges the Thessalonian Christians to anticipate the same eschatological destiny. The ecclesiology of Philippians accentuates the believers as "saints" who enjoy a fellowship in the gospel and in grace. The saints are suffering for the gospel, as Paul is, but they are, nevertheless, the citizens of God's commonwealth, the heavenly polity. Paul exhorts these heavenly citizens to be unified in sharing the mind of Christ and to be obedient to the example of Christ who was faithful to God even when he was unjustly persecuted. Peterson stresses that the Philippian ecclesiology comes into sharp focus when Paul claims that the Philippians are "the circumcision" who worship by God's Spirit and put no confidence in the flesh. True circumcision, which defines the people of God, is a matter of keeping the will of God, which is accomplished by calling upon the Lord and confession of Jesus as the Christ. Doing so fulfills Torah's demands and defines those whom God saves.

Chris Hutson's essay helps readers obtain a more theologically formed interpretation of the ecclesiology in 1 and 2 Timothy and Titus. These letters are frequently cited by churches looking for biblical guidance in regards to Christian leadership and church polity. But as Hutson reminds readers, taking a piecemeal approach to these significant letters ignores what they indicate about the theological origin and mission of the church as the "household of God." In particular, Hutson explores the creedal formations in these letters, which he concludes stress God saving through Jesus *all* people, regardless of ethnicity or nationality. God is sovereign over creation and has formed a community that has experienced a "washing of regeneration" (i.e., baptism), is empowered with the presence of the Holy Spirit, and has become the future-orientated eschatological foundation and deposit of truth. It is equally crucial, Hutson reminds readers, that any use of these texts to construct a contemporary ecclesiology must do so by noting the social and historical circumstances in which these letters were written. He draws specific attention to such aspects as factionalism, criticisms from non-Christians, and (with regards to 2 Timothy) the experience of some official persecution. Hutson closes his essay by pointing out what the author likely assumed were the church organization and polity of his readers.

Despite the fact that many New Testament theologians do not think the letter to the Hebrews has much to offer in terms of ecclesiology, Cynthia Long Westfall's essay, "Left Behind? The Church in the Book of Hebrews," takes a much more optimistic view. There is an ecclesiology reflected in Hebrews, but only when one considers the context of the letter does it become very apparent. With substantial backing from the text, Westfall capably shows that the most salient contextual feature for grasping the author's ecclesiology is the sense of an impending crisis faced by this church. From the author's perspective, the impending crisis—one in which believers' lives may be in jeopardy—put the believers in danger of becoming hardhearted and falling away from faith in Jesus. As Westfall points out, this results in a very practical ecclesiology. The writer exhorts the believers to continue to meet together in order to care for and encourage one another in the face of struggle. They must submit to the leaders of the community who are responsible for maintaining the common foundation of faith upon which their community stands. What is more, they are not to remain static; they should be growing and maturing so the basic teachings of the faith do not need to be repeated. Based on these and a number of other features, Westfall concludes that the ecclesiology of Hebrews is strong and clear: the church is a community of believers who, in times of crisis and change, draw near to God and to each other to find the strength necessary to hold fast to the confession, to continued growth, and to mutual pastoral care.

Allen Black calls readers' attention to the pastoral concern of Peter as he delineates the significant aspects of the ecclesiology in 1 and 2 Peter. He demonstrates this pastoral concern by first recalling the significant images that are used in 1 Peter to describe the believing community. The church is, borrowing language found in the Old Testament for Israel, the community of God's elect and a chosen race. Like a pastor concerned for his congregation's self-image, Peter identifies their true status and honor before God. They are called by God and are his flock, his royal priests to serve the nations, and his holy temple. Black moves from these significant metaphors for the church's identity to describe the internal relationship Peter reminds his readers to have. Members of this persecuted community are to strengthen one another through mutual love, hospitality, and service. Their solidarity is all the more necessary because they are strangers and aliens in this world where they experience suffering. Black concludes his essay by highlighting two major aspects of the Petrine church's life. The first is Christian baptism, which Peter presumes his audience experiences as a spiritual cleansing and receiving of forgiveness of sins. The second is their experience with Christian leadership in the form of elders. Black then turns readers' attention to 2 Peter where ecclesiology is worked out in the context of severe false teachings that are tempting believers to immorality. Peter's major concern in this second letter is to remind the church that they are called to godliness and holiness, which are the expected qualities of God's family.

A New Testament ecclesiology that is often overlooked is the one provided by the Epistle of James. Unfortunately some scholars discount James as having nothing theologically to say at all. William Baker's essay "The Community of Believers in James" argues convincingly that such conclusions are ill-founded and that contemporary ecclesiologies are served tremendously if they engage the ideal of a Christian community that James describes in his letter. Baker assists readers in seeing a clear portrait of the Jacobean community. He contends that these Jewish Christians, who have yet to begin any significant evangelization of Gentiles, have been dispersed from their homes in Jerusalem and now live as Jesus followers outside the borders of Palestine. What can be seen clearly from this letter is an appeal to Christian communities who are spiritually conflicted, economically poor, socially harassed, and internally stressed with division and bitterness towards one another. James's appeal is that these communities return to the royal law of Jesus to love both those in the church and those who are outside harassing it. Also highlighted are the two most obvious practices these communities experienced: prayer and mutual confession of sins to one another. Congregational leadership comes from teachers and elders who pastor and disciple, but all members are urged to help admonish those believers who stray from the community. Though ecclesiological details may be more meager in James than in other epistles, the wisdom of James contributes uniquely to the variety of New Testament ecclesiologies.

The Apocalypse of John is nearly always excluded from discussions of ecclesiology, and when it is considered, the discussion is typically limited to what can be gleaned from the letters to the seven churches in chapters 2–3. This is quite unfortunate since, as Olutola K. Peters demonstrates, the Apocalypse reflects a comprehensive and cohesive understanding of the nature and function of the church. The church is portrayed as a community consisting of the redeemed. Peters shows how the Apocalypse is rife with texts describing Jesus as the one who loved the church and loosed her from sins through his blood. Jesus is therefore the foundation for the church's existence, but he calls her to holy living. The church is also portrayed as a community of the Spirit. However, as Peters shows, the church is not necessarily portrayed as a community constituted by the Spirit as in Acts, but as a community to whom and through whom the Spirit speaks: the community is consistently exhorted to listen to what the Spirit says and to respond positively, and the character and function of the community is symbolized by the two witnessing prophets (11:1–14) as those who speak for the Spirit. Perhaps most importantly, the Apocalypse of John portrays the church as the people of God, to which, Peters argues, the 144,000 is a significant reference. The Apocalypse culminates with the grand vision of the church as the bride of Christ, which provides a vision not only for what the church is currently, but for what the church will be: the holy and perfect people of God.

GRATEFUL ACKNOWLEDGEMENTS

For more than three years we have been engaged in this project from conception to completion. Completing the volume would not have occurred without the assistance and encouragement of a number of individuals who stood beside us. First, we would like to thank Dr. Stanley E. Porter, not only for accepting our book for publication in McMaster Divinity College Press's Biblical Studies series, but also for offering keen insights into the work very early on in the project. We are particularly grateful for Dr. Lois Dow at McMaster Divinity College Press for her careful copyediting skills and timely responses. You are a wonderful person and it was a joy to work with you. The editors at Wipf & Stock Publishers deserve our gratitude for their professionalism and patience throughout the entire process. Your interest in this volume both honored us and fueled every effort.

Of course an enormous thank you also goes out to the scholars who contributed to this volume. Thank you for instantly perceiving the purpose and merit of this volume and for providing your expertise and eloquence to help readers see the diverse and unique ecclesiologies represented in the New Testament. We are extremely grateful for your specialization, the time you sacrificed to share your knowledge, and the patience you demonstrated during the editing process. You are all colleagues extraordinaire!

Another sincere thanks goes out for the additional encouragement and support that came to us from the College of Biblical Studies at Oklahoma Christian University. In particular, thank you so much, Dr. Lynn McMillon, for agreeing to make resources available so we could secure assistance with formatting all the essays. Matt Dowling dedicated much time, effort, and the attention to style and formatting requirements that were needed; we feel very fortunate, Matt, to have had access to your talent and dedication.

Finally, the time and attention it took us over three years to complete this project meant that there were evenings, weekends, and summer days when we were away from our families. Words of gratitude fail to adequately convey how indebted each of us is to you. To John's family: Thank you Sharon, Joshua, and Stewart for understanding why I wanted so desperately to see this volume written and for encouraging me towards the finish line. I draw strength from you every day and love you with all my heart. To Jim's family: Thank you Celeste Joy, Sydney Rebekah, and Hagan James for your continued support, love, and grace as I pursue endeavors like this. I love each of you so very much.

John P. Harrison
James D. Dvorak
Oklahoma Christian University

BIBLIOGRAPHY OF THE INTRODUCTION

Ferguson, Everett. *The Church of Christ: A Biblical Ecclesiology for Today*. Grand Rapids: Eerdmans, 1997.

Käsemann, Ernst. "Unity and Diversity in New Testament Ecclesiology." *NovT* 6 (1963) 290–97.

1

Matthew's Vision for Jesus' Community of Disciples

John P. Harrison

MATTHEW'S GOSPEL WAS WRITTEN towards the end of the first century[1] for a community of Diaspora Jewish Christians[2] by a Jewish Christian trained in scribal practices.[3] This community of believers confessed Jesus as the Christ, the son of David, the son of Abraham,

---

1. I am presupposing a date of composition for Matthew between 65 and 100 CE. Matthew has used Mark, which most scholars believe was composed in the 60s. Allowing for enough time for the author to receive, edit, and add material, the date of Matthew's composition could still be prior to 70 CE. Several passages in Matthew (e.g., 22:7; 23:38; and 24:2), many scholars believe, show knowledge that Jerusalem and her Temple have been attacked severely. The argument is that the author was aware of this event and reflects that knowledge in Jesus' teaching. But these sayings are not so specific that a date of composition after 70 CE is the only option. Furthermore, there are a number of significant details about Jerusalem's suffering and destruction in 70 CE that do not appear in Matthew and must be taken into account. For arguments favoring a pre-70 date of writing, see Hagner, *Matthew*, 1:lxxiii–lxxv; Gundry, *Matthew*, 599–609; Nolland, *Matthew*, 16–17. For arguments for a post-70 CE date of composition see Davies and Allison, *Matthew*, 1:127–38; Witherington, *Matthew*, 28–29.

2. For the recent literature and problems in defining "Jewish Christianity" or "Christian Jews," see Verheyden, "Jewish Christianity."

3. It seems more probable that someone other than the Apostle Matthew wrote the Gospel. For the history of attributing this Gospel to the Apostle and arguments against doing so, see Davies and Allison, *Matthew*, 1:7–58. I do not believe that the author was a "rabbi," as Stendahl argued in *The School of St. Matthew*, but his interpretation of Jesus' life in light of Old Testament prophetic material suggests a sophisticated training that one might expect a scribe to possess. For convenience, in this essay I will use the name "Matthew" to designate the author.

1

who is the Son of the living God. Jesus fulfills the promises God made to Abraham to make him the father of a great nation. God fulfilled his promise by forming a people who recognize Jesus of Nazareth, the son of Abraham and David, as the Messiah who has risen from the dead. He is the Messiah whose kingdom and righteousness was anticipated by Israel's prophets and who is now coming into the world.

In addition to telling the story about God's actions in, through, and by Jesus, Matthew's Gospel points towards the author's vision of what the community of Jesus' followers ought to look like. The author composed his account when there were various Christian communities (e.g., Petrine and Pauline) and competing theologies (e.g., opponents of Paul) of what a Jesus-follower should believe and practice. By observing which details Matthew emphasizes in the construction of his story,[4] one may put together a portrait of certain ecclesiastical challenges he faced and the ecclesiastical vision he hoped his audience would adopt.

In order to provide a general overview of the "historical church of Matthew" or the direction he wanted them to move in, I will address six key questions: (1) Was Matthew's community primarily composed of Jewish Christians? An answer to this question will help indicate the general ethnic and cultural heritage of Matthew's immediate audience. (2) Where did Matthew's community live? If Matthew's community can be identified with a specific geographical location, any information about that location gives better insight into what social and political realities were faced by the community. (3) What image of the community dominates Matthew's ecclesiology? Answering this question will provide an overarching perspective of Matthew's ecclesiastical vision for his readers. (4) What points does Matthew want to stress when he uses the word "church"? No description of Matthew's ecclesiology would be satisfactory without observing Matthew's use of "church." While Matthew does not give a definition for "church," the word is defined, at least partially, as it is used in conjunction with Jesus' teaching. Noting what Jesus teaches

---

4. Scholars refer to this approach as the "redaction-critical" method. Though this method's use on Matthew was anticipated by others earlier (Schlatter in 1929, Bacon in 1930, and Bultmann in 1931), the first single treatment of Matthew using this method was by Bornkamm, "Die Sturmstillung im Matthäusevangelium." This method is routinely used to discover an author's literary intention, theology, and understanding of his community. Though valuable, the method is not fool-proof or a panacea. Nearly all competing reconstructions of Matthew's community use the redaction-critical method to arrive at their conclusions.

in the context where the word "church" occurs, it will be shown what Matthew believed is the nature of the church and the authority of its leadership. (5) What activities occurred in the assemblies of Matthew's churches? Here I am attempting to isolate in Matthew's Gospel those practices that the author assumed or expected his audience observed when they assembled to worship and receive instruction in their faith. Finally, (6) was Matthew's church persecuted, and if so by whom and why? If Matthew assumed his audience was experiencing persecution or that they would be, what he was anticipating can provide a better understanding about his vision for the community's relations to those who were hostile towards it. Answering these six questions will certainly not exhaust what can be said about Matthew's ecclesiology but it will provide a general portrait of the ethnic, social, and religious characteristics of the communities known by and a concern to the author.

WAS MATTHEW'S COMMUNITY PRIMARILY COMPOSED OF JEWISH CHRISTIANS?

A few notable scholars have argued that the author of Matthew was a Gentile Christian who wrote for Gentile Christians.[5] These scholars point out that God's rejection of Israel, which they argue is espoused in several places (Matt 8:12; 12:21; 21:1—22:14; 28:16–20), is a major theme in Matthew, and it is inconceivable that a Jew would have propagated such an idea as a means of exhorting other Jews towards faithfully following Jesus. Some have claimed that the author is too ignorant of aspects of first-century Judaism for the book to have been written by a Jew.[6] Still others have pointed out faulty reasoning used to argue for a Jewish-Christian audience so as to conclude that the best explanation of Matthew's origin is that he is a Gentile author writing to a Gentile audience.[7]

---

5. Clark, "Gentile Bias"; Strecker, *Der Weg der Gerechtigkeit*; Trilling, *Das Wahre Israel*; and Schulz, *Die Stunde der Botschaft*. Strecker and Trilling both argued that at an earlier time Matthew's community were Jewish Christians, but at the time of the composition of the Gospel the Christian audience was predominately made up of Gentiles.

6. Gaston, "Messiah of Israel." John P. Meier argued that statements like the one in Matt 16:12, which he believes does not recognize differences between the Pharisees and Sadducees, point to an author who was ignorant of Saducean teachings; see Meier, *Law and History*.

7. Nepper-Christensen, *Das Matthäusevangelium*.

However, these protests have failed to persuade the majority of Matthean scholars from the conclusion that Matthew was composed for Jewish Christians.[8] Matthew's particular use of the Old Testament, certain redactions of Mark's Gospel (e.g., Mark 7:1–23; 10:1–12), accounts of Jesus' positive statements about Torah and Pharisaic authority (Matt 5:17–18; 23:2), the pejorative use of the term "Gentiles" (Matt 6:7; 18:17), Jesus' instruction to his disciples to go only to the Jews (Matt 10:5–6), his teaching about the Temple tax (Matt 17:24–27), and the hope that disciples will not have to flee Jerusalem on a Sabbath (Matt 24:20) combine to leave the strong impression that Matthew was written for Jewish Christians who would appreciate and/or relate to these features. They signal the author's intention to encourage his audience, who still see themselves as the covenant people of Israel's God, to remain committed to their confession of Jesus as the Messiah and to follow Jesus' teachings. Matthew understood that Jesus did not teach his disciples to ignore Torah,[9] but rather his actions and teachings showed how to interpret it in order to excel in God's righteousness and be prepared to enter into God's kingdom.

While the predominately Jewish nature of Matthew's community appears self-evident, it was nevertheless a community that recognized that non-Jews could be included among Jesus' disciples and be incorporated into the people of God. God's promise is that the children of Abraham will bless the nations. Therefore the good news of the coming kingdom of God must be proclaimed to all people. Jesus' own life

---

8. The earliest recognition that Matthew was written to Jewish Christians was in the late second century by Irenaeus, *Haer.* 3.1.1. For a history of the scholarship up to the 1980s, which argues that Matthew was written for a Jewish Christian audience, see Stanton, "Origin and Purpose" 1916–21. Support for a Jewish Christian orientation can be found in Kümmel, *Introduction to the New Testament*, 113–14; Segal, "Matthew's Jewish Voice"; Nolland, *Matthew*, 17–18.

9. It is certainly not clear or proven that Matthew's emphasis on Jesus' teachings about Torah (e.g., Matt 5:17, 19) is intended as a specific rejection of Pauline Christianity. It has not been sufficiently demonstrated that Paul taught Jewish Christians that Jesus had abolished the law. It is true that Paul did not believe that Gentile Christians had to become Jews in order to be identified as God's people or that anybody could be justified by "works of the law." But these conclusions are a far cry from the position that Paul believed Jewish Christians did not have to concern themselves with Torah observance since Jesus had abolished it. Nowhere does Paul make such a claim. For recent debates on the possible relationships between Pauline and Matthean Christianities, see Stanton, "Origin and Purpose," 1908; Mohrlang, *Matthew and Paul*; Sim, "Matthew's Anti-Paulinism"; Sim, "Matthew 7.21–23"; Harrington, "Matthew and Paul."

shows that there are those who seek Israel's King from abroad (Matt 2:1) and outside of Israel (Matt 8:10). It is anticipated that those from the east and west will be welcomed to sit around the eschatological table with Abraham, Isaac, and Jacob to feast in the kingdom (Matt 8:11). Jesus' command to make disciples of all nations (Matt 28:19) shows that Matthew approved of a community that included both Jewish and Gentile believers. Whether or not Matthew's community was engaged in evangelizing Gentiles as the first Christians in Antioch did (Acts 11:20), the positive description of Gentiles expressing faith in Jesus (e.g., Matt 15:28) reflects the author's attitude that the community should welcome non-Jews who acknowledge Jesus as God's promised anointed king.

What is not clear about Matthew's openness to evangelizing Gentiles is what he believed Gentile converts were obligated to do. The Gospel shows no hint that Torah has been abolished by Jesus, but neither does it indicate that Gentile believers are expected to become Jewish (i.e., submit to circumcision) and obey Torah as Jewish Christians are.[10] It seems altogether possible that Matthew's community was made up of both Jews who kept Torah (as Jesus interpreted it) and Gentiles who practiced Jesus' teachings, except those that were obviously related to Jewish identity (e.g., Sabbath observance, food purity laws, Temple tax). Unfortunately, interpreters are left to speculate what specific advice Matthew would have given to his community when dealing with the types of conflicts and issues one might expect would arise with such a mixture of backgrounds (such as we see indicated in Paul's letter to the Romans).[11] In the end, Matthew's Gospel does not tell his audience.

---

10. Sim, "Christianity and Ethnicity," has argued that the author of Matthew would have expected Gentile males to be circumcised because his Gospel affirms the importance of Israel as God's elected covenant people who continue to follow the law. Sim contends that the reason circumcision is not mentioned in the commission to make disciples is because it was so obvious a requirement that there was no need to mention it, just as it was not mentioned as required for membership in the Qumran community. But an appeal to the absence of requiring initiates to be circumcised to join the Qumran community is not analogous since the latter did not initiate Gentiles. For a critique of Sim's arguments, see Riches, *Conflicting Mythologies*, 216–25.

11. For detailed discussions of Jewish and Gentile Christians in Rome at the time Paul wrote Romans, see Kümmel, *Introduction to the New Testament*, 309–10; Fitzmyer, *Romans*, 76–80; Dunn, *Romans 1–8*, xlv–liv. For the arguments against reading any sign of "Jewish Christianity" behind Paul's letter to the Romans, see Stowers, *Rereading*.

WHERE DID MATTHEW'S COMMUNITY LIVE?

The author undoubtedly had at least one specific community in mind that he hoped his Gospel would teach and help form.[12] But where did this community live?

Matthean scholars have suggested several locations for Matthew's immediate audience. The two places most often proposed are Antioch on the Orontes in Syria[13] and/or the neighboring areas of Galilee.[14] The conclusion that Matthew's community is in Syrian Antioch is most often based on five observations. First, in Matt 4:24, the author replaces Mark's "Tyre and Sidon" with "Syria." Second, in Jesus' discussion of the Temple tax (17:24–27), reference is made to a coin called a *stater* (v. 27), which was utilized only in Damascus and Antioch.[15] Third, Peter is a prominent figure in Matthew's Gospel and he was significantly active among the churches in Antioch (Gal 2:11–14). Fourth, Ignatius of Antioch (ca. 98–117 CE) appears to be the first person to utilize Matthew's Gospel.[16] Fifth, Antioch was a significant Hellenistic city with a sizeable Jewish population, and which played an important role in the evangelization of Gentiles (Acts 11:20–21).

Scholars who favor locating Matthew's community in the area of Galilee do so primarily on the basis of three observations. First, if

12. It is certainly possible and even probable, as Richard Bauckham and others have recently argued, that all four Gospels were written for a larger readership than a single geographically specific community. See Bauckham, *Gospel for All Christians*. My proposal, however, assumes that Matthew was at least familiar with one community in one specific location, which he hoped his Gospel would help shape.

13. This proposal was first suggested by Streeter in *The Four Gospels*, 500–23. It has been widely supported by scholars and more recently it has been advocated by Brown, *Churches the Apostles Left Behind*, 128; Hagner, *Matthew*, 1:lxxv; Gundry, *Matthew*, 609; Senior, *Matthew*, 82; Sim, *Gospel of Matthew and Christian Judaism*; Keener, *Commentary on the Gospel of Matthew*, 41–42; Carter, *Matthew and Empire*, 36–37; Slee, *Church in Antioch*, 118–22.

14. Schweizer, "Matthew's Church"; Overman, *Matthew's Gospel and Formative Judaism*, 158–59; Overman, *Church and Community in Crisis*, 16–19; Harrington, *Gospel of Matthew*, 9–10; Segal, "Matthew's Jewish Voice," 29; Saldarini, "Gospel of Matthew," 26–27; Gale, *Redefining Ancient Borders*, 15–30; Witherington, *Matthew*, 21–28.

15. Gundry, *Matthew*, 609.

16. E.g., Ign. *Eph.* 6:1; 17:1; Ign. *Phld.* 6.1; Ign. *Smyrn.* 1.1. The majority of Matthean scholars believe that Ignatius was aware of Matthew's Gospel in some form, but for a cautionary approach to the evidence of Matthean allusions in Ignatius's works, see Koester, *Synoptische Überlieferung*; Trevett, "Approaching Matthew."

Matthew's Gospel had been written in Antioch there would be more evidence of Pauline influence in the Gospel, since he was active in the city.[17] Second, this Gospel stresses the conflict that Jesus and his followers had (and likely would continue to have) with the Pharisees (Matt 9:11, 14, 34; 12:2–14, 24, 38; 15:1–12; 16:1–12; 19:3–9; 22:15). Since all literary evidence about the Pharisees points to the view that they were primarily active in Galilee and Jerusalem,[18] and since there is no evidence that they operated in Syrian Antioch, it is presumed that Matthew pays attention to this conflict with Pharisees because his community is in Galilee experiencing conflict with the same group. Third, it is argued, Matthew's Gospel focuses attention on Jesus' ministry in Galilee, especially Capernaum. The supposition is that the best explanation for why Matthew has this emphasis is because his audience lives in the same region.[19]

However, if Matthew's community lives in Galilee then some items are unclear. First, Sim argues that since Matthew's Gospel was written in Greek and since Aramaic was the predominate language of Jews in Galilee, if Matthew was written to Jewish Christians living in Galilee, even in the Hellenistic city of Sepphoris, there should be evidence that it was written in Aramaic.[20] What Sim does not take into account, however, is that there is ample literary and epigraphic evidence to show that Greek was used prevalently in Galilee.[21] Therefore Matthew's initial readers could have been Jewish Christians living in Galilean cities where

17. Kilpatrick, *Origins*, 130.

18. Saldarini, *Pharisees, Scribes and Sadducees*, 291–97; Horsley, *Sociology and the Jesus Movement*, 73–74.

19. Some of the scholars who argue for the Galilean theory attempt to identify specific Galilean cities where Christians could have been brought into a Jewish court. While cities such as Tiberias, Capernaum, and Bethsaida have been suggested, the most likely city would have been Sepphoris since it was wealthy, cosmopolitan, and had a large number of conservative Jews. See Overman, *Matthew's Gospel and Formative Judaism*, 159, and Gale, *Redefining Ancient Borders*, 57.

20. Sim, "Social and Religious Milieu," 23. Eusebius's famous quotation of Papias's claim that Matthew put the words (of Jesus) in an ordered arrangement in the Hebrew language (Eusebius, *Hist. eccl.* 3.39.16) does not refer to an earlier Hebrew or Aramaic version of our Gospel of Matthew. For a detailed treatment of Papias's statement, see Bauckham, "Papias on Mark and Matthew."

21. Porter argues, on the basis of literary and epigraphic evidence, that a significant portion of Galileans, especially those living in cities, used Greek as their primary language. See Porter, "Did Jesus Ever Teach in Greek?"

Greek was the primary language that united the entire community of disciples. A second unclear item is the existence of early Christianity in Galilee after the Jewish War in the late 60s. It can be asked, after the devastating effects of that war, would there be much of a community to whom Matthew could write?[22] Isn't it more likely that the Gospel was written to a larger audience? A third unclear item is the lack of reference to the Jewish War in Matthew. If Matthew's Gospel had been written to Jewish Christians in Galilee who lived either during the late 60s or after the Jewish War, would not the Gospel have referenced the conflicts with Rome that caused great suffering in that region? The only hint in Matthew that the author might have been aware that Jerusalem had been attacked is the description of a burned city in Jesus' parable of the wedding feast (Matt 22:1–10).[23] However, this reference is too oblique to point sufficiently to a Galilean provenance.

For these last two reasons, the most persuasive proposal is that Matthew's community lived in or in close proximity to Syrian Antioch. As one reads Matthew's Gospel, it is important to keep this urban setting in mind. Jesus' teachings regarding such issues as Roman imperialism, poverty, wealth, persecutions, and even healing diseases, take on new significance once it is postulated that Matthew's "church" is primarily a Jewish-Christian community in Antioch obeying and contextualizing what Jesus taught on these and other subjects.[24] The geographical location of a church alerts the interpreter to the social factors that are effecting how that community's understanding of itself (i.e., it ecclesiology) is shaped and expressed.

22. Sim asks a similar question. He argues that it is unlikely that Matthew could have been written by someone living in Galilee after the war. See Sim, "Social and Religious Milieu," 24. My point is, if such devastation makes Galilee an unlikely place *in which* the Gospel was written, is it not also less likely that such a place is the location *to which* the Gospel was written?

23. The reference to burning a city (v. 7) is not substantial enough to conclude that Matthew is aware that Jerusalem has been destroyed by fire, since the language used here fits with other descriptions of city destruction (Josh 6:21–24; Judg 1:8; 18:27; 20:48; 1 Macc 5:28; Josephus, *Ant.* 12:329; *J.W.* 3:132–34; *T. Jud.* 5:5–6).

24. For more on reading Matthew with a view of the social dynamics in Syrian Antioch, see Stark, "Antioch."

WHAT IMAGE OF THE COMMUNITY DOMINATES MATTHEW'S ECCLESIOLOGY?

Caution should be exercised about describing anything as "Matthew's ecclesiology." It has been noted repeatedly that Matthew's Gospel, while certainly shaped by a deep concern for the behavior and discipline of those in Jesus' church, does not contain a clearly worked out ecclesiology.[25] However, in the Gospel one description of Jesus' followers is detectable that reflects an important element of whatever ecclesiology the author may have had. Matthew's Gospel repeatedly describes Jesus' followers as "disciples" (μαθηταί).[26] Jesus the Messiah is the "Teacher" (διδάσκαλος, Matt 23:8, 10) and his community is comprised of learners and doers of his teachings. Disciples are made when individuals are baptized in the name of the Father, Son, and Holy Spirit and taught to obey everything that Jesus has commanded (Matt 28:19). But it is not enough to hear what Jesus has taught. True disciples must have "ears to hear" (Matt 11:15; 13:9, 15, 16, 43), which leads them not only to understand those teachings but put them into practice. If they do so, then in the end they will be found righteous and obedient to Jesus their master (Matt 7:26; 24:45–51; 25:14–30; 28:20).

The significance of the concept of being a disciple is also seen in the Evangelist's use of the tradition that Jesus called individuals to follow him and learn from him (Matt 9:9; 11:28–30; 16:24). While Jesus does not say, "Come be my disciple," the idea that he called people to literally follow him as he traveled to proclaim the gospel suggests that these followers were a community of learners who heard his teachings and were willing to obey them. But Matthew is not interested in describing the past only. Behind these references to calling followers and behind many of the references to Jesus' disciples is Matthew's own perception that his community is called by Jesus to follow, learn from, and obey him.[27]

However, to conclude that Matthew equated being Jesus' disciple only with learning and obeying his teachings fails to recognize how Matthew uses Jesus' instructions to disciples to broaden the concept.

25. Bornkamm, "End-Expectation," 38–39.

26. For examples of Matthew's use of μαθηταί, see Minear, "Disciples and the Crowds."

27. Barth, "Matthew's Understanding of the Law," 105–12; Luz, *Studies in Matthew*, 131–32. Riches, *Conflicting Mythologies*, 183 n. 1, argues that Matt 13:52; 27:57; 28:19 clearly show that the author wants his readers to identify themselves with the disciples.

Matthew 10 provides important insights into Matthew's understanding of what is involved in being Jesus' disciple. Several instructions in the Gospel's second major discourse (10:1—11:1)[28] indicate that the author expects Jesus' disciples to evangelize. Just as the Twelve were instructed to evangelize and heal, Matthew's audience is instructed to preach Jesus' message that "the kingdom of heaven is near," exorcise unclean spirits, and heal various sicknesses (10:1, 7).[29] Being a disciple, therefore, is more than simply receiving teachings. It involves sharing God's message and healing others. Chapter 10 also warns that as the disciples share God's message they will face persecutions and trails (10:16–33). Since none of the Twelve appeared before governors and kings prior to Jesus' resurrection,[30] the author saw these warnings as fitting for Jesus' post-Easter disciples who are experiencing such things. A disciple is also a learner who must confess Jesus as the Christ before Jews and Gentiles (10:32). Proclaiming Jesus as the Messiah is as much at the heart of what it means to be Jesus' disciple as is learning his teachings.

The importance of being a disciple can also been seen when Matthew often replaces Mark's references to the "Twelve" with the term "disciples."[31] After naming the Twelve in chapter 10, Matthew uses the definite article with μαθηταί to refer specifically to the Twelve or certain members of the group.[32] Jesus' teachings to the Twelve (e.g., 13:24–30;

---

28. The five major discourses of Jesus in Matthew's Gospel are (1) Sermon on the Mount, chs. 5–7; (2) Mission, ch. 10; (3) Parables, ch. 13; (4) Discipleship (or more accurately Leadership), ch. 18; and (5) Eschatology, chs. 24–25.

29. Luz notes that in Matthew's Gospel (contra Mark 6:12, 30) it is not reported that the disciples actually go out or come back to Jesus, because Matthew sees this instruction as actually being fulfilled by the post-Easter disciples (Luz, *Studies in Matthew*, 118).

30. Is Matthew alluding to the Apostle Paul?

31. However Luz states that there was already a pre-Matthean tendency to identify Jesus' larger circle of disciples with the Twelve, so Matthew is not "historicizing" Jesus' post-resurrection disciples with the Twelve as Georg Strecker and others have proposed. See Luz, "Disciples," 117. For Strecker's thesis, consult his *Der Weg der Gerechtigkeit*.

32. For instance, in Matt 17:6 the author uses οἱ μαθηταί to refer to Peter, James, and John. For a fuller treatment of Matthew's distinctive use of οἱ μαθηταί, see Martinez, "Interpretation of οἱ μαθηταί." In every Matthean text after ch. 10, any reference to "the disciples" (οἱ μαθηταί) refers specifically to Jesus' apostles. The word "disciple" can refer to the apostles, as the opening and closing verses of the "missionary discourse" show (Matt 10:1 and 11:1). Prior to ch. 10, "disciples" refers to unspecified people who follow and seek to learn from Jesus. There is no use of the term "the disciples" (with the article) before ch. 10. But after ch. 10 the use of the definite article before "disciples"

18:6–35; 24:42—25:46) often function as instructions to those responsible in the community for the physical and spiritual welfare of Jesus' followers. Church leaders are first and foremost "disciples." They too continue to learn and put into practice what Jesus taught.

WHAT DOES MATTHEW EMPHASIZE WHEN HE USES THE WORD "CHURCH" (MATT 16:13–20; 18:15–20)?

In Matthew 16 and 18, the author records sayings that illustrate some of the distinctive elements in Matthew's ecclesiology. As is often noted, Matthew is the only Gospel that actually uses the word ἐκκλησία (usually glossed "church" in English). It is found once in 16:18 and twice in 18:17. The word appears in two contexts in which there are several key points Matthew wants to stress.

The first emphasis in chapter 16 is that Jesus identified the disciples as *his* "church," which he is building. By the word "church" (ἐκκλησίαν), Matthew understands Jesus to imply that his disciples will have a self-understanding of themselves as Yahweh's (the Lord's) distinct people.[33] Since Matthew and his community were familiar with the Septuagint, it is instructive to note that the LXX translators used ἐκκλησία for the Hebrew qhl ("assembly" or "community").[34] This word occurs in several situations when Israelites are assembled or called to assemble in order to praise the Lord and to hear and pledge allegiance to the Lord's commands.[35] While the LXX, Luke, and Paul all proclaim that the church

suggests that Matthew has in mind either the specific group of twelve or some members of the group who were introduced to the reader in 10:1–4.

33. Hagner, "Holiness and Ecclesiology," 42, notes that if this statement goes back to the historical Jesus then he could also have used either the Aramaic words *'edah* (= Greek συναγωγή) or *kenishta*.

34. This translation most often occurs in 3 Kings and 1 and 2 Chronicles. Nolland states that qhl is most often translated in the LXX as ἐκκλησία but sometimes is rendered with συναγωγή (*Matthew*, 672–73). Also, note the use of ἐκκλησίαν κυρίου in the Septuagint's rendering of Deuteronomy 23. It this chapter, legislation describes who can and who cannot be counted among God's people (Deut 23:1–3, 8). In Matthew 16 and 18, Jesus identifies those who are in his church who submit to Peter's interpretation of Torah. Weren, "Ideal Community," 178, observes that in the Septuagint, qhl depicts Israel as "a nation or religious community."

35. For examples, see LXX Neh 5:13, 8:2, Ps 39:9 (40:9), 67:26 (68:26). Matthew may very well see his community as the counterpart to the gathered Israelites in the Exodus story as did the authors of 1QM 4:9–10 and 1QS^a (1Q28) 2:4 for his community (Nolland, *Matthew*, 673 n. 353).

is God's,[36] Jesus can still claim the church as his because he is God's anointed king through whom God reigns over his church and through whom God operates his presence with his people.[37]

A second emphasis in Matthew 16 is that the community of Jesus will not be destroyed. After Peter's confession of Jesus as the Christ, Jesus tells him (v. 18b) that the "gates of Hades" (πύλαι ᾅδου) "will not overpower it" (οὐ κατισχύσουσιν αὐτῆς). The interpretation of these words has been debated extensively. The best reading of Jesus' promise takes into account the social and political realities of Matthew's community (a community that, as will be argued below, was experiencing persecution), which takes the "gates of Hades" as a general reference to death. Since Jesus has overcome death by his own resurrection, death will not overcome those who belong to him. Matthew does not perceive Jesus as promising that individuals who confess him as Christ will never be killed. On the contrary, Matthew is quite aware that some may even lose their lives for Jesus' sake (Matt 10:39). Instead, Matthew understands Jesus' words to give hope to his church by claiming that despite the death of any disciple, all disciples will overcome death. In the end, all of them will prevail against death and find life.

A third emphasis in chapter 16 (which is also found in chapter 18) is the stress on Peter's authority, and possibly the authority of those whom the community would have identified as the Twelve, to determine for the church how to interpret and obey Torah. Jesus promises Peter, "I will give you (singular) the keys of the kingdom" (16:19). Regardless of how one interprets the pun of Πέτρος ("Peter") and πέτρα ("rock"), it is clear that Peter holds the key. He unlocks the way to the kingdom by showing the church how to interpret Torah and obey it accurately. Peter's role as the authoritative interpreter of Torah is indicated in Jesus' statement of "binding" (interpreting what Torah requires) and "loosing" (interpreting what Torah allows) in 16:19 and 18:18. Peter and the other apostles have learned from Jesus how to interpret Torah to discern what is and what is not permissible to do. Now he, along with the others, will interpret for Jesus' followers what God calls his people to do in compliance to his commands.[38]

36. LXX Deut 23:2–4, 9; 1 Chr 28:8; Neh 13:1; Mic 2:5; and in the New Testament, Acts 20:28; 1 Cor 1:2; 10:32; 11:22; 15:9; 2 Cor 1:1; Gal 1:13.

37. Nolland, *Matthew*, 673.

38. Powell, "Binding and Loosing," especially 443–44. For arguments that by "bind-

Matthew 18 is the fifth discourse and is often labeled as a discourse on "Community Order."[39] It should be seen more accurately as a discourse on church leaders, since the chapter opens with Jesus addressing a question of "the disciples" about who is the greatest in the kingdom of heaven (v. 1). As noted earlier, after the introduction of the Twelve in chapter 10, Matthew uses "the disciples" to refer specifically to the apostles or a portion of them (i.e., Peter, James, and John) and they are used as representatives (or "prototypes") of church leaders who have taken on the responsibilities of instructing and disciplining the church as the apostles had done in the previous generation.[40] If this is the case, then chapter 18 shows that Matthew expected the community leaders to exercise their authority over the community by humbling themselves (18:4). They should not be preoccupied with their own honor as community leaders but instead show concern for the "little ones" in the community who are sinning. They should not behave in ways that lead these other disciples to sin (18:6–7) but should show due diligence to rid their own lives of sin (18:8–9). They must not show contempt for these "little" disciples, but if one gets lost through sinning, they should take the initiative and go after that disciple and restore them (18:10–14). If a disciple who has sinned will not listen to the leader after being admonished, the leader must not use their authority to cast the unrepentant believer out of the community immediately. Instead, the leader should humbly submit to a process that involves confirming, through the testimony of at least one other witness (as Torah requires in Deut 19:15), that the action was

---

ing" and "loosing" the pre-Matthean Jesus would have had in mind the authority of the apostles to exorcise demons, see Hiers, "'Binding' and 'Loosing.'"

39. Bornkamm, "Authority to 'Bind' and 'Loose'"; Thompson, *Matthew's Advice*, 251–58, helpfully notes that the overall tenor of the chapter is proverbial rather than prescriptive. This insight should be kept in mind by congregations who look to this passage when dealing with their own internal disciplinary issues.

40. For additional arguments and discussion that advocate this understanding of Matthew's use of "the disciples" as "prototypes" of church leaders, see Thysman, "Communauté et directives éthiques." For a rejection of this identification of "the disciples" with "church leaders," see Schweizer, "Matthean Church," 216. I agree with Schweizer that Matthew's Gospel does not mention "presbyters" or "bishops," but Matthew knows of individuals, whether they be prophets (itinerate or permanently located), teachers, scribes, or sages, who will provide authoritative teaching and discipline to other disciples in the period after the apostles and their appointed representatives are gone. In Matthew chs. 18, 24, and 25, the author is directing Jesus' teachings to those who exercise the role of instructing and disciplining believers.

sinful. Then, if the disciple is still unrepentant, the leader should take the case before the church (18:15–17). It is the local community, rather than a single leader or a group of designated leaders, that hears the case and renders a judgment about the individual's innocence or guilt. Leaders, who are symbolized by Peter, are also warned to humbly and willingly forgive the erring disciple who repents of sinning against them and they are to do so as often as their forgiveness is requested (18:21–35).

One final important concept emphasized in chapter 18 is the belief that Jesus' spirit is present with the community's leaders when they seek to determine what Torah identifies as unlawful behavior when they are accusing a disciple of sin (18:18–20). It has often been observed that by identifying Jesus as "Emmanuel" at the beginning of the Gospel (Matt 1:23) and closing it with Jesus' promise to the Eleven that he will always be present with them until the end of the age (Matt 28:20), Matthew intends to communicate that God is with his people in the presence of Jesus. While this contributes to Matthew's overall understanding of the community as possessing the spirit of the risen Jesus, of particular note is that this "Messiah-presence" occurs when church leaders are exercising congregational discipline. This point is made explicit in 18:20 when Jesus promises his disciples to be "with you" (μεθ' ὑμῶν).[41] What is not clear, however, is what exactly Jesus' presence with church leaders is supposed to accomplish. Is it merely to sanction their judgment as to what will be "bound" (i.e., required) or "released" (i.e., permitted)? Is it to provide spiritual guidance so that they will know what to bind and loose? Is it something else? Matthew's Gospel does not make it clear.

WHAT ACTIVITIES OCCURRED WHEN MATTHEW'S CHURCHES ASSEMBLED?

Evidence certainly does not exist in Matthew's Gospel for us to be able to describe in detail what the author's community did when they assembled as Jesus' church. However, I want to highlight three specific activities: teaching, prophecy, and prayer.[42]

---

41. This point has been stressed by Frankenmölle, *Jahwebund und Kirche Christi*, 7–83. He also correctly connects this concept of the presence of Jesus with his disciples to the concept of God's guiding and sustaining presence with his covenant people Israel. For Matthew, God is still with his covenant people through the spirit of Jesus who is present with his followers.

42. I did not include the Lord's Supper as one of the activities of the Matthean

In light of the importance of discipleship in Matthew's Gospel, it stands to reason that Matthean churches must have been served by teachers. Even if the community refrained from calling them "rabbis" or "teachers" (Matt 23:7–10), the assembly most likely gathered together to hear the reading of Scripture and the teachings of Jesus as well as to receive admonition and instruction regarding how to obey God's will as revealed through Torah, the prophets, and Jesus. While the exact method of instruction cannot be identified, it is reasonable to suppose that disciples were instructed in a familiar pattern of teaching and memorization that characterized Jewish pedagogy.[43]

In addition to teaching via common pedagogical methods, the community experienced the activities of prophets.[44] Jesus teaches his disciples, "He who receives a prophet because he is a prophet shall receive a prophet's reward" (10:41). The idea of "receiving" refers to the practice of offering hospitality to itinerant prophets.[45] These Christian prophets probably saw the nature of their ministry as resembling that of Jesus' itinerant ministry, especially since Jesus saw himself as a prophet (13:57). Matthew's community knew itinerant Christian prophets must be welcomed and in their assemblies they would gather to hear what they came to proclaim. However, there was also the danger that some would come to the community engaged in prophesying and exorcisms but their deeds were not righteous (Matt 7:15–23). These were "false prophets." They were "false," not in the sense that their prophecies did not come true or that their teaching was not correct doctrine, but in the

churches because, while the Gospel certainly attests to Jesus' Last Supper (26:26–29), Matthew's version closely follows Mark's and as such contains nothing that makes it clear that the meal would be reenacted regularly, as is suggested in Luke 22:19 with the words "Do this in remembrance of me."

43. It is often pointed out that the arrangement of much material in Matthew's Gospel appears concerned for mnemonic use, which would lend itself to pedagogical activities.

44. The nature of biblical prophets and prophecy is multi-faceted. By "prophets," Matthew is referring to individuals who claim to speak a message from God or Jesus that they received directly from them. These messages may have contained predictions (such as the one from Zechariah about John the Baptist in Luke 1:68–70 or the ones from Agabus in Acts 11:28; 21:10) or they may have been more general exhortation or warning. For more on the scope of biblical prophetic utterances, consult Heschel, *Prophets*, and Brueggeman, "Prophets."

45. *Did.* 11:1—13:1 also exhorts believers to offer hospitality to itinerate Christian prophets.

sense that they were not producing in their own lives the righteousness
that is expected of disciples. Though they can claim to have prophesied,
performed exorcisms, and done many mighty works in Jesus' name,
they must be rejected because they are doing what is lawless (οἱ ἐργαζό
μενοι τὴν ἀνομίαν).[46] Jesus does not recognize them nor will he welcome them into God's kingdom. His rejection implies that the disciples
should also decline to recognize their prophecies and exorcisms as abili-
ties given by Jesus.

In addition to the prophecy occurring in the assembly, certain
prophets were to have a more public role, for Jesus was sending them
to those who would reject them (23:34).[47] Some would be scourged,
others would be harassed and forced from town to town, and others
would be crucified. Those who rejected Jesus' prophets were like those
among Israel's leaders who rejected and murdered the prophets God
sent throughout Israel's history. God will hold accountable those who
reject Jesus' prophets.

Finally, I want to take note of two teachings of Jesus about prayer
and what they might suggest about prayer in the Matthean assemblies.
The first teaching might lead some interpreters to conclude that these
disciples would not have prayed in their assemblies. In Matt 6:5–6, Jesus
admonishes his disciples to pray in one's "inner room" rather than in
the synagogues or in public areas. However, it is highly improbable that
Matthew or his audience took this saying as an absolute condemnation
of praying in public or praying in assemblies. They would have understood Jesus' saying as a rebuke using hyperbole (as is done in v. 3 with
almsgiving), aimed against praying publicly in order to be admired. This
saying would neither be seen as a prohibition of praying in synagogues
nor of participating in prayers among the general public.[48] The main re-

46. Later Christian writers also admonished believers to inspect the ethical lives
of those who claimed to be legitimate prophets of Jesus (*Did.* 11:7–12; *Herm. Mand.*
11:7–16).

47 It is not necessary to argue, as Schweizer does ("Matthew's Church," 151), that
Matthew has changed into a present tense (ἀποστέλλω), "I am sending," what was
originally a future tense (ἀποστελῶ), "I will send," in order to stress that Jesus is presently sending Christian prophets out to the opponents of Matthew's community. The
present indicative is occasionally used to describe an action that will take place in the
future (e.g., John 11:11; 1 Cor 16:5). Either way, Matthew's community would clearly
expect the risen Jesus to communicate in their context via prophets.

48. According to Acts 2:42, Jesus' disciples in Jerusalem were committed to "the
prayers" (ταῖς προσευχαῖς), which probably refers not to praying in general but to the

striction Matthew's churches would have taken from these words is that those who pray among the assembled disciples should do so without looking for praise for their piety.

The conclusion that Jesus was not prohibiting public prayers is made even more evident by his second teaching, which follows immediately after the first one. In what is commonly called "the Lord's Prayer" (Matt 6:9–13) Jesus' words appear to have elements reflecting a liturgical setting. The fact that Jesus says "All of you pray like this" (οὕτως προσεύχεσθε ὑμεῖς) shows the disciples are given a model (or the very words) that they are to pray with one another. The corporate nature of the prayer is emphasized throughout by means of plural first person pronouns: "our Father" (v. 9), "Give us" (v. 11), "forgive us our debts as we ourselves have forgiven our debtors" (v. 12), and "do not lead us . . . but deliver us" (v. 13). The overall impression is that the prayer was either already part of a liturgy or Matthew desired it to be in his audience's liturgy. But whether they were familiar with it or not, Matthew uses it to further identify the community as a group who worship God as the Father, Sustainer, and Deliverer of his people.[49] It seems altogether reasonable that Mathew included this prayer because he intended it to be prayed verbatim in the liturgy of churches, just as the author of the *Didache* taught that it should be (*Did.* 8:3–11).

WAS MATTHEW'S CHURCH PERSECUTED AND IF SO WHY?

There are several extensive statements in the Gospel where Jesus warns his disciples that they could or will face persecution for the sake of "righteousness" or because of him (Matt 5:10–12; 10:16–33; 23:34–36).[50] Jesus' blessing on those who will be persecuted acts as an exhortation to Matthew's community to remain steadfast in their allegiance to Jesus and his teachings. These warnings also anticipate that the disciples would experience persecution from other Jews.

---

daily public Jewish prayer times. See Haenchen, *Acts of the Apostles*, 191.

49. For arguments that the Lord's Prayer in Matthew shows non-Matthean elements that point to a prayer that was already in use by Matthew's audience, see Luz, *Matthew 1–7*, 370; Strecker, *Sermon on the Mount*, 110, 123, 210 n. 57; Carter, "Recalling the Lord's Prayer."

50. For a detailed study of these passages and other less extensive references in Matthew's Gospel to the persecution of Christians, see Hare, *Theme of Jewish Persecution*.

The conflict between Jesus' disciples and non-Christian Jews is often described as an internal Jewish dispute,[51] which raises the question of whether Matthew's community still considered themselves Jewish. While several argue that Matthew's community saw itself as separated from "official Judaism,"[52] it was argued earlier that they saw themselves as the covenant people of God, obeying Torah—as Jesus interpreted it—and submitting to the authority of God's Messiah, who had taught them how to live righteously in preparation for the arrival of God's kingdom. The inclusion of Jesus' teaching on the Temple tax is most understandable if Matthew's readers still saw themselves as connected to Judaism. While some Jewish authorities may have cast certain disciples of Jesus out of their synagogues, there is no evidence that indicates all non-Christian Jewish communities in Antioch had separated themselves from all of Matthew's community so that no interaction between Matthean churches and non-Christian Jews continued. If such were the case, the polemic against non-Christian Jews would certainly have been more pronounced and encompassing.[53]

Nevertheless, tension between Matthew's community and some powerful non-Christian Jews did exist. Matthew's perspective is that certain Jews were responsible for Jesus' death and took upon themselves God's judgment for their action (Matt 27:25). He uses the word "Jews" (Ἰουδαῖοι) in Matt 28:15 in a manner that suggests to some that he is not one.[54] In Jesus' parable of the vineyard (Matt 21:33–46), Jesus prophesies that God will take his kingdom away from the Jewish authorities and give it to a nation that will produce the type of righteousness that is supposed to be associated with God's kingdom.[55] In Matthew, Jesus

51. Overman, *Matthew's Gospel and Formative Judaism*; Saldarini, *Matthew's Christian-Jewish Community*; Sim, *Gospel of Matthew and Christian Judaism*; Harrington, "Matthew's Gospel: Pastoral Problems and Possibilities," 66–69.

52. Stanton, *Gospel for a New People*, 113–45; Luz, *Matthew 1–7*, 52–56; Weren, "Matthean Community," 53, 58; Gundry, "Responsive Evaluation"; Hare, "How Jewish is the Gospel of Matthew?"; Riches, *Conflicting Mythologies*, 202–25; Hagner, "Matthew: Christian Judaism or Jewish Christianity?"

53. Brown, *Churches the Apostles Left Behind*, 134 n. 183.

54. Nolland correctly cautions against reading Ἰουδαῖοι in this way, stating, "given the strongly Jewish stamp that Matthew has placed on his Gospel materials and given his evident hopes for a significant Jewish turning to the Christian faith, it seems unlikely that he would allow 'the Jews' to become a designation that excluded his own group" (Nolland, *Matthew*, 1258).

55. It is more accurate to recognize Matt 21:43 and 27:25 as having an "anti-Jewish

warns his disciples that "they" (the non-Christian Jewish opponents of Jesus' disciples) will flog them "in their synagogues" (Matt 10:17).[56] This last saying suggests that Matthew's community is still in some manner connected to the authority of the local synagogue leaders who perceive them as misleading other Jews and therefore due to be punished, even to the point of bringing members of Matthew's community to Gentile authorities and killing Christian prophets, sages, and scribes (Matt 23:34). It may even be that some of the opponents were relatives of members in Matthew's community and would persecute Jesus' disciples to the point of driving them out of "the villages of Israel" (Matt 10:21–23). These indicators of serious tension between Jesus' disciples and local Jewish authorities are best explained by placing Matthew's audience within an internal Jewish dispute where parties are trying to identify what constitutes legitimate expressions of Jewish faith.

Matthew's community continued to interact with the larger Jewish population in Antioch. They were perceived by certain Jewish leaders as a social threat to the integrity of the Jewish community because of their allegiance to Jesus, whom authorities in Jerusalem crucified, yet through whom, the Christian Jews say, God is present with his people. It is because of their allegiance to this crucified Messiah that Matthew's community is not welcome in at least some synagogues.

---

authorities" tone rather than anachronistically mischaracterizing it as an "anti-Jewish" tone, as does Segal ("Matthew's Jewish Voice," 23), since the author of Matthew was Jewish, his audience was Jewish, and his Messiah was Jewish.

56. A great deal of Matthean scholarship has pointed out that the additional occurrences of the phrase "their synagogue(s)" (συναγωγὴ αὐτῶν) in Matt 9:35; 10:17; 12:9; and 13:54 and "your synagogues" (συναγωγαῖς ὑμῶν) in Matt 23:34 imply that the author knows his community has already begun holding their own religious assemblies. But more than this conclusion is difficult to support. It is not clear that the phrase indicates that the Jews in Matthew's community thought that they had been "excommunicated" from Jewish synagogues. This conclusion was argued by Kilpatrick, *Origins*, 111, on the basis of the *birkath ha-minim* (the rabbinic curses on heretics), which some scholars have seen as an allusion to Christians. John's Gospel seems aware of Christians being excommunicated from synagogues (John 9:22), but Matthew does not. It seems unlikely that a complete separation from non-Christian Jewish synagogues had occurred and Matthew still retains a Jesus saying that acknowledges Pharisaic authority to interpret Torah (Matt 23:2). Therefore, it remains a possibility that Matthean Christians, even after 70 CE, attended both Christian assemblies and non-Christian synagogues.

CONCLUSION

I have argued, therefore, that Matthew's community was primarily made up of Jewish Christians living in or near Syrian Antioch. As God's assembly, they are committed to instruction from Jesus, God's anointed Messiah. He is risen from the dead but he is present in spirit with his people and ensures that his people will never be destroyed. The community is served primarily by teachers and prophets who instruct and discipline the community in the ways of righteousness so that they might enter into God's kingdom. When they assemble they listen to the reading and interpretation of Torah, the prophets, and the teachings of Jesus, and they are exhorted to obey these so that their righteousness might exceed that of Jewish religious authorities and so that they might glorify God. While many of them experience ostracism from the larger Antiochean Jewish community, Jesus' disciples come together and with one voice pray to God as their Father, Sustainer, and Deliverer from all evil. Matthew envisions a community who would learn from Jesus how to live righteously and prepare for the arrival of God's kingdom on earth.

FOR FURTHER STUDY

Balch, David, ed. *The Social History of the Matthean Community: Cross-Disciplinary Approaches*. Minneapolis: Fortress, 1991.

Bornkamm, G., G. Barth, and H. J. Held, eds. *Tradition and Interpretation in Matthew*. London: Westminister, 1963.

Gundry, Robert. H. *Matthew: A Commentary on His Handbook for a Mixed Community under Persecution*. Grand Rapids: Eerdmans, 1994.

Hagner, Donald. "Holiness and Ecclesiology: The Church in Matthew." In *Holiness and Ecclesiology in the New Testament*, edited by Kent Brower and Andy Johnson, 40–56. Grand Rapids: Eerdmans, 2007.

Overman, J. Andrew. *Matthew's Gospel and Formative Judaism: The Social World of the Matthean Community*. Minneapolis: Fortress, 1990.

Schweizer, Eduard. "Matthew's Church." In *The Interpretation of Matthew*, edited by Graham Stanton, 138–70. IRT 3. Philadelphia: Fortress, 1983.

Sim, David C. *The Gospel of Matthew and Christian Judaism: The History and Social Setting of the Matthean Community*. SNTW. Edinburgh: T. & T. Clark, 1998.

van de Sandt, Huub, and Jürgen K. Zangenberg, eds. *Matthew, James, and Didache: Three Related Documents in Their Jewish and Christian Settings*. SBLSS 45. Atlanta: SBL, 2008.

BIBLIOGRAPHY

Barth, Gerhard. "Matthew's Understanding of the Law." In *Tradition and Interpretation in Matthew*, edited by G. Bornkamm, G. Barth, and H. J. Held, 58–164. Philadelphia: Westminster, 1963.

Bauckham, Richard. *The Gospel for All Christians: Rethinking the Gospel Audiences*. Grand Rapids: Eerdmans, 1997.

———. "Papias on Mark and Matthew." In *Jesus and the Eyewitnesses: The Gospels as Eyewitness Testimony*, 222–28. Grand Rapids: Eerdmans, 2006.

Bornkamm, Günther. "The Authority to 'Bind' and 'Loose' in the Church in Matthew's Gospel." *Perspective* 11 (1970) 37–50.

———. "End-Expectation and Church in Matthew." In *Tradition and Interpretation in Matthew*, edited by G. Bornkamm, G. Barth, and H. J. Held, 15–51. Philadelphia: Westminister, 1963.

———. "Stilling of the Storm in Matthew." In *Tradition and Interpretation in Matthew*, edited by G. Bornkamm, G. Barth, and H. J. Held, 52–57. Philadelphia: Westminster, 1963. Originally published as "Die Sturmstillung im Matthäusevangelium." *Wort und Dienst*, Jahrbuch der theologischen Schule Bethel 1 (1948) 49–54.

Brown, Raymond. *The Churches the Apostles Left Behind*. New York: Paulist, 1984.

Brueggeman, Walter. "Prophets." In *Reverberations of Faith: A Theological Handbook of Old Testament Themes*, 158–61. Louisville, KY: Westminster John Knox, 2002.

Carter, Warren. *Matthew and Empire: Initial Explorations*. Harrisburg, PA: Trinity Press International, 2001.

———. "Recalling the Lord's Prayer: The Authorial Audience and Matthew's Prayer as Familiar Liturgical Experience." *CBQ* 57 (1995) 514–30.

Clark, K. W. "The Gentile Bias in Matthew." *JBL* 66 (1947) 165–72.

Davies, W. D., and Dale Allison. *Matthew*. 2 vols. ICC. Edinburgh: T. & T. Clark, 1988.

Dunn, James. *Romans 1–8*. WBC 38A. Dallas: Word, 1988.

Fitzmyer, Joseph. *Romans*. AB. New York: Doubleday, 1993.

Frankenmölle, H. *Jahwebund und Kirche Christi*. Neutestamentliche Abhandlungen N. F. 10. Münster: Aschendorff, 1974.

Gale, Aaron M. *Redefining Ancient Borders: The Jewish Scribal Framework of Matthew's Gospel*. London: T. & T. Clark, 2005.

Gaston, L. "The Messiah of Israel as Teacher of the Gentiles." *Interpretation* 29 (1975) 25–40.

Gundry, Robert. *Matthew: A Commentary on His Handbook for a Mixed Church under Persecution*. 2nd ed. Grand Rapids: Eerdmans, 1994.

———. "A Responsive Evaluation of the Social History of the Matthean Community in Roman Syria." In *Social History of the Matthean Community: Cross-Disciplinary Approaches*, edited by David Balch, 62–67. Minneapolis: Fortress, 1991.

Haenchen, E. *The Acts of the Apostles*. Oxford: Blackwell, 1971.

Hagner, Donald. "Holiness and Ecclesiology: The Church in Matthew." In *Holiness and Ecclesiology in the New Testament*, edited by Kent Brower and Andy Johnson, 40–56. Grand Rapids: Eerdmans, 2007.

———. *Matthew*. 2 vols. WBC 33A–B. Dallas: Word, 1993–1996.

———. "Matthew: Christian Judaism or Jewish Christianity?" In *The Face of New Testament Studies: A Survey of Recent Research*, edited by Scot McKnight and Grant R. Osborne, 263–82. Grand Rapids: Baker, 2004.

Hare, Douglas. "How Jewish is the Gospel of Matthew?" *CBQ* 62 (2000) 264–77.

―――. *The Theme of Jewish Persecution of Christians in the Gospel according to St. Matthew.* SNTSS 6. Cambridge: Cambridge University Press, 1967.

Harrington, Daniel J. *The Gospel of Matthew.* Collegeville, MN: Liturgical, 1991.

―――. "Matthew and Paul." In *Matthew and His Christian Contemporaries*, edited by David Sim and Boris Repschinski, 11–26. Edinburgh: T. & T. Clark, 2008.

―――. "Matthew's Gospel: Pastoral Problems and Possibilities." In *The Gospel of Matthew in Current Study*, edited by D. E. Aune, 63–73. Grand Rapids: Eerdmans, 2001.

Heschel, Abraham. *The Prophets: An Introduction.* I. New York: Harper & Row, 1962.

Hiers, Richard. "'Binding' and 'Loosing': The Matthean Authorizations." *JBL* 104 (1985) 233–50.

Horsley, Richard. *Sociology and the Jesus Movement.* New York: Continuum, 1994.

Keener, Craig S. *A Commentary on the Gospel of Matthew.* Grand Rapids: Eerdmans, 1999.

Kilpatrick, G. D. *The Origins of the Gospel according to St. Matthew.* Oxford: Oxford University Press, 1946.

Koester, H. *Synoptische Überlieferung bei den apostolischen Vätern.* TU 65. Berlin: Akademie Verlag, 1957.

Kümmel, W. G. *Introduction to the New Testament* (originally *Einleitung in das Neue Testament*), translated by H. C. Kee. Nashville: Abingdon, 1975.

Luz, Urlich. *Matthew 1–7.* Continental Commentaries. Minneapolis: Augsburg, 1989.

―――. "The Disciples in the Gospel according to Matthew." In *Studies in Matthew*, 115–41. Grand Rapids: Eerdmans, 2005. Originally published as "Die Jünger im Matthäusevangelium." *ZNW* 62 (1971) 141–71.

―――. *Studies in Matthew.* Grand Rapids: Eerdmans, 2005.

Martinez, Ernest R. "The Interpretation of οἱ μαθηταί in Matthew 18." *CBQ* 23 (1961) 281–92.

Meier, John P. *Law and History in Matthew's Gospel.* AnBib 71. Rome: Biblical Institute, 1976.

Minear, Paul. "The Disciples and the Crowds in the Gospel of Matthew." *ATR*, Supplementary Series 3 (1974) 28–44.

Mohrlang, R. *Matthew and Paul: A Comparison of Ethical Perspectives.* SNTSMS 48. Cambridge: Cambridge University Press, 1984.

Nepper-Christensen, P. *Das Matthäusevangelium—ein judenchristliches Evangelium?* Aarhus: Universitetsforlaget, 1958.

Nolland, John. *The Gospel of Matthew.* NIGTC. Grand Rapids: Eerdmans, 2005.

Overman, J. Andrew. *Church and Community in Crisis: The Gospel according to Matthew.* The New Testament in Context. Valley Forge, PA: Trinity Press International, 1996.

―――. *Matthew's Gospel and Formative Judaism: The Social World of the Matthean Community.* Minneapolis: Fortress, 1990.

Porter, Stanley. "Did Jesus Ever Teach in Greek? A Look at Scholarly Opinion and the Evidence." In *Studies in the Greek New Testament: Theory and Practice*, 139–71. Studies in Biblical Greek 6. New York: Peter Lang, 1996.

Powell, Mark Allan. "Binding and Loosing: A Paradigm for Ethical Discernment from the Gospel of Matthew." *Currents in Theology and Mission* 30 (2003) 438–45.

Riches, John K. *Conflicting Mythologies: Identity Formation in the Gospels of Mark and Matthew.* Edinburgh: T. & T. Clark, 2000.

Saldarini, Anthony J. "The Gospel of Matthew and Jewish-Christian Conflict in the Galilee." In *The Galilee in Late Antiquity*, edited by L. I. Levine, 23–38. Cambridge, MA: Harvard University Press, 1992.

———. *Matthew's Christian-Jewish Community.* Chicago: University of Chicago Press, 1994.

———. *Pharisees, Scribes and Sadducees in Palestinian Society.* Wilmington, DE: Michael Glazier, 1988.

Schulz, S. *Die Stunde der Botschaft: Einführung in die Theologie der vier Evangelisten.* Hamburg: Furche-Verlag, 1967.

Schweizer, Eduard. "Matthew's Church." In *The Interpretation of Matthew*, edited by Graham Stanton, 149–77. 2nd ed. Edinburgh: T. & T. Clark, 1995.

———. "The Matthean Church." *NTS* 20 (1974) 216.

Segal, Alan. "Matthew's Jewish Voice." In *Social History of the Matthean Community: Cross-Disciplinary Approaches*, edited by David Balch, 3–37. Minneapolis: Fortress, 1991.

Senior, Donald. *The Gospel of Matthew.* Interpreting Biblical Texts. Nashville: Abingdon, 1997.

Sim, David. "Christianity and Ethnicity in the Gospel of Matthew." In *Ethnicity and the Bible*, edited by Mark G. Brett, 171–95. Biblical Interpretation 19. Leiden: Brill, 1996.

———. *Gospel of Matthew and Christian Judaism: The History and Social Setting of the Matthean Community.* SNTW. Edinburgh: T. & T. Clark, 1998.

———. "Matthew 7.21–23: Further Evidence of Its Anti-Pauline Perspective." *NTS* 53 (2007) 325–43.

———. "Matthew's Anti-Paulinism: A Neglected Feature of Matthean Studies." *HvTSt* 58 (2002) 767–83.

———. "Reconstructing the Social and Religious Milieu of Matthew: Methods, Sources, and Possible Results." In *Matthew, James, and Didache: Three Related Documents in Their Jewish and Christian Settings*, edited by Huub van de Sandt and Jürgen K. Zangeberg, 13–32. SBLSS 45. Atlanta: SBL, 2008.

Slee, Michelle. *The Church in Antioch in the First Century C.E.: Communion and Conflict.* JSNTSup 244. London: Sheffield Academic, 2003.

Stanton, Graham N. *A Gospel for a New People: Studies in Matthew.* Edinburgh: T. & T. Clark, 1992.

———. "The Origin and Purpose of Matthew's Gospel: Matthean Scholarship from 1945 to 1980." In *ANRW*, II, 25, 3, edited by H. Temporini and W. Haase, 1889–1951. Berlin: de Gruyter. 1985.

Stark, Rodney. "Antioch as the Social Situation for Matthew's Gospel." In *The Social History of the Matthean Community: Cross-Disciplinary Approaches*, edited by David L. Balch, 189–205. Minneapolis: Fortress, 1991.

Stendahl, Krister. *The School of St. Matthew and Its Use of the Old Testament.* Philadelphia: Fortress, 1968.

Stowers, Stanley. *A Rereading of Romans: Justice, Jews, and Gentiles.* New Haven, CT: Yale University Press, 1994.

Strecker, G. *Der Weg der Gerechtigkeit.* FRLANT 82. Göttingen: Vandenhoeck & Ruprecht, 1962.

———. *The Sermon on the Mount.* Nashville: Abingdon, 1988.

Streeter, B. H. *The Four Gospels: A Study of Origins.* London: Macmillan, 1924.

Thompson, W. G. *Matthew's Advice to a Divided Community: Matthew 17:22–18:35*. Rome: Loyola, 1970.

Thysman, R. *Communauté et directives éthiques: La catéchèse de Matthieu*. Recherches et synthèses, Sect. d'Exégèse 1. Gembloux: Duculot, 1974.

Trevett, Christine. "Approaching Matthew from the Second Century: The Under-used Ignatian Correspondence." *JSNT* 20 (1984) 59–67.

Trilling, W. *Das Wahre Israel*. SANT 10. 3rd ed. Munich: Kosel, 1964.

Verheyden, Joseph. "Jewish Christianity, a State of Affairs: Affinities and Differences with Respect to Matthew, James, and the Didache." In *Matthew, James, and Didache: Three Related Documents in Their Jewish and Christian Settings*, edited by Huub van de Sandt and Jürgen K. Zangenberg, 123–35. SBLSS 45. Atlanta: SBL, 2008.

Weren, Wim J. C. "The History and Social Setting of the Matthean Community." In *Matthew and the Didache: Two Documents from the Same Jewish-Christian Milieu?*, edited by H. van de Sandt, 51–62. Assen: Van Gorcum, 2005.

———. "The Ideal Community according to Matthew, James, and the Didache." In *Matthew, James, and Didache: Three Related Documents in Their Jewish and Christian Settings*, edited by Huub van de Sandt and Jürgen K. Zangeberg, 177–200. SBLSS 45. Atlanta: SBL, 2008.

Witherington, Ben III. *Matthew*. Smyth & Helwys Bible Commentary. Macon, GA: Smyth & Helwys, 2006.

2

Ecclesiology in the Gospel of Mark

MARK RAPINCHUK

WHEN ONE UNDERTAKES TO study a topic like ecclesiology in the New Testament documents, there is a temptation to limit consideration to texts in which related terms appear. For example, one could examine the literature for every occurrence of the term "church" (ἐκκλησία; *ekklēsia*) and synthesize these data into a doctrine of ecclesiology. But such an approach would be misguided. The absence of a specific term does not warrant the conclusion that the concept it represents is likewise absent.

New Testament authors frequently provide important information and teaching about key theological concepts without use of specific or technical terminology (e.g., the immutability of God, divine aseity, etc.). Thus, the absence of the term ἐκκλησία (*ekklēsia*) in Mark's Gospel is not sufficient to support the conclusion there are no ecclesiological ideas and principles present in this text. We can learn much about Mark's[1] view of the church through reading his record of the life and ministry of Jesus of Nazareth.

It has become commonplace to recognize the Gospels as products of Christian communities. This is not to deny that a single author played the primary, perhaps exclusive, role in the composition of the Gospel. Rather, it acknowledges that the challenges, concerns, and contexts of

---

1. The name Mark will be used to identify the author of the Gospel in keeping with long-standing tradition. For discussion of authorship, attribution, and related matters, see Carson and Moo, *Introduction*, 92–99.

26

the communities played a formative role in the composition of the text.[2] In light of this observation, it seems reasonable to suggest that, through careful study of the text, the reader might discern those principles and ideas that were considered significant by the author and his community. Furthermore, when considering the words of John (20:30–31), one may conclude that the evangelist selected material for a particular purpose.[3] We can learn much about these implied purposes through careful study and consideration of the recorded teaching, actions, and events. Although ecclesiology is not explicitly discussed and is not likely to be considered a major theme of Mark, I suggest that in this Gospel there are several principles and insights relevant to the concept of ecclesiology.

Discussions of ecclesiology are complicated by questions about Jesus' intentions regarding a "church." Consider the position of N. T. Wright:

> Did Jesus intend to found a "church"? The question is hopeless. Of course he didn't; of course he did. The way the oft-repeated question puts it is impossibly anachronistic: it makes Jesus sound like a pioneer evangelist of the nineteenth century, throwing previous denominations to the winds and building his own tin tabernacle. Worse, it implies, almost with a sneer, that Jesus could hardly have envisaged the church as we know it today, or even as it has been for most of the last two thousand years; and that therefore the church stands condemned, untrue to its founder's intentions.[4]

Later Wright observes:

> The evidence points, I suggest, towards Jesus intending to establish, and indeed succeeding in establishing, what we might call cells of followers, mostly continuing to live in their towns and villages, who by their adoption of his praxis, his way of being Israel, would be distinctive within their own communities. . . .

---

2. E.g., Marshall, "Church," 122; Kee, *Beginnings of Christianity*, 113–16.

3. John explicitly informs the reader that he chose material for the purpose of demonstrating that Jesus is the Christ, the Son of God (John 20:31), and that he did not record all of Jesus' sayings and deeds (21:25). One may observe evidence of a similar approach in the redactional activity of the Synoptic authors. For a discussion of this claim, see Carson, "Redaction Criticism." For an explanation of this material from a perspective that does not accept literary dependence, see, e.g., Linnemann, *Is There A Synoptic Problem?*

4. Wright, *Jesus and the Victory of God*, 275.

> The praxis that went with the kingdom-story cannot, then, be reduced to terms either of individual "ethics" or of the individual response to grace. The whole point of it is that it demarcated Jesus' people as a community; scattered through various villages, maybe, as indeed some of the Essenes may have been, but a community none the less.[5]

Thus, according to Wright, Jesus did intend to establish a continuing presence, a community that embodied and enacted his way of being the people of God. Yet questions remain. How would this community appear? What identifying characteristics would the cells display? Was there to be strict uniformity of polity and praxis? As we consider the ecclesiology of Mark, several such questions seem relevant.

It may prove beneficial to discuss Markan ecclesiology by considering some of the following questions. First, what is the leadership model or philosophy of the "true church"? To answer this question we will consider the material recorded in Mark that may provide information relevant to developing a model or theory of leadership. When Jesus speaks to issues of leadership, we will assume this reflects, at least in some way, the view of leadership accepted by Mark's community. We can then construct a model that reflects the concerns of the Markan community.

A second question relates to the theology of the "true church." The theological beliefs and commitments of a community are an essential aspect of its ecclesiological understanding. These beliefs serve to distinguish one group from another. Those who viewed themselves as [the?] "true" followers of Jesus would likely assume their theological perspective to be the theology of the "true church."

If, as seems reasonable, Jesus' early followers thought of themselves as faithfully preserving, preaching, and practicing his teaching, then we may learn their perception of theological truth by examining the teaching recorded in "their" Gospels. The theology of Mark's community is expressed by the material present in the Gospel.[6] Therefore, later readers may be justified in thinking that the theology present in Mark represents his community's understanding of theological truth.

---

5. Ibid., 276–77.

6. This does not mean, of course, that Mark or his community fabricated teaching in order to validate their own perspective. Rather, it acknowledges that all records of another's teaching are necessarily selective and that decisions regarding inclusion are likely influenced by personal or community concerns.

Third, we will examine the composition of the "true church." Does Mark's account provide any insight into the social and ethnic make-up of the community? How restrictively or exclusively did Mark understand the concept of "true church"? Put differently, did Mark think there was only one way of being a true follower of Jesus and did this require association with a particular community?

WHAT IS THE LEADERSHIP MODEL OR PHILOSOPHY OF THE "TRUE CHURCH"?

There are several texts that appear relevant to this topic, but we will focus attention on only a few. One might well begin with Mark's record of Jesus' assessments of the Pharisees, Sadducees, scribes, and chief priests. The rejection of Jesus by these groups, together with the undesirable character traits enumerated in the text, would suggest that they function as negative role models. Leaders of the Jesus community are to be different.

> As he taught, he said, "Beware of the scribes, who like to walk around in long robes, and to be greeted with respect in the marketplaces, and to have the best seats in the synagogues and places of honor at banquets! They devour widows' houses and for the sake of appearance say long prayers. They will receive the greater condemnation. (Mark 12:38–40)[7]

In this brief statement we find several grounds for criticism of the scribes. First, they like to walk around in long robes. This is much more than a criticism of fashion. The "long robes" distinguished the scribe from others.[8] Wearing these in public could easily be interpreted as a shameless attempt to draw attention to one's piety[9] (cf. Matt 6:5). Here Jesus denounces this desire for praise and honor based on perceived piety. The next three indictments (they like to have salutations in the market places, the best seats in the synagogue, and the places of honor at banquets) are all related to prestige and status. Jesus is denouncing the all-too-common desire for public recognition and deference to one's position. These scribes made it a point to insist on their "rights and

---

7. Unless otherwise noted, Scripture references are from the NRSV.

8. Lane, *Mark*, 439–40; Brooks, *Mark*, 202.

9. For a helpful introduction to the concepts of honor and shame, see Malina, *New Testament World*, 25–50.

privileges" and to make sure that everyone acknowledged their authority and education.

As often happens, leadership models were adopted from the prevailing culture. Self-promotion and desire for public prestige and status were commonplace in Greco-Roman culture.[10] The religious leaders of Judea were not immune to the effects of this cultural influence. But Mark and his community understood leadership to be different. Unlike many of the contemporary religious leaders with whom they were all very familiar, the leaders of the Jesus community were not to be concerned with status and public recognition. For those in the Jesus community, cultural models were to be redefined.[11] The foolishness of seeking public approval in place of God's approval was to be avoided. The wise leader was not concerned with reputation based on a fabricated public persona.

Furthermore, leaders of the new community were to be concerned with the welfare of those in need. Unlike those condemned by Jesus, who took advantage of the poor (Mark 12:40), the leaders of the Jesus community were to help meet the needs of those they led. Leadership was not intended to be exploited for one's personal gain. The shepherd cares for the sheep; he does not exploit them.[12]

In what might be called the paradigmatic leadership passage, Jesus confronts the ambition and pride of his disciples in order to correct their corrupted sense of leadership.

> James and John, the sons of Zebedee, came forward to him and said to him, "Teacher, we want you to do for us whatever we ask of you." And he said to them, "What is it you want me to do for you?" And they said to him, "Grant us to sit, one at your right hand and one at your left, in your glory." But Jesus said to them, ". . . to sit at my right hand or at my left is not mine to grant, but it is for those for whom it has been prepared." When the ten heard

---

10. Savage, *Power through Weakness*, 19–53. Although Savage is concerned with describing the social context of Corinth, his extensive documentation from Greco-Roman literature indicates the widespread reality of the attitudes and practices identified.

11. The reconception of cultural expectations extended beyond leadership models. For example, in chapter 10 alone Jesus addressed distorted understandings of marriage and divorce (10:2–12). He also elevated the status of children (10:14–16) and corrected misconceptions about material wealth and spiritual blessing (10:17–31).

12 Throughout the Gospels, Jesus' denunciations of the religious leaders calls to mind texts such as Ezekiel 34, in which the contrast is made between shepherds who exploit and plunder the people and the good shepherd who will minister to them for their benefit.

this, they began to be angry with James and John. So Jesus called them and said to them, "You know that among the Gentiles those whom they recognize as their rulers lord it over them, and their great ones are tyrants over them. But it is not so among you; but whoever wishes to become great among you must be your servant, and whoever wishes to be first among you must be slave of all. For the Son of Man came not to be served but to serve, and to give his life a ransom for many." (Mark 10:35–45; see also 9:33–37)

Here again we see an important reconception of leadership. The true leader, according to Jesus, is not one concerned with power or privilege. The terms used to describe those who ruled over the Gentiles (κατα– κυριεύουσιν and κατεξουσιάζουσιν) have strong negative connotations.[13] These are not neutral terms of political or administrative oversight. They express a distinct sense of tyrannical domination.

Rather than taking the lead from such oppressive and abusive models of leadership, Jesus teaches that godly leadership requires selfless service. Unlike the pagan rulers, and unlike their Jewish counterparts, the leaders of Jesus' community were to be characterized by servanthood. The Son of Man did not come to be served, but to serve. How could his community leaders do anything else?

The leadership of the Jesus community was to be identifiable by its humility. It was, after all, Jesus' community, not the community of Peter, John, or any other leader. This may be illustrated by Mark's account of Peter's messianic declaration at Caesarea Philippi. All three Synoptic Gospels record this conversation between Jesus and the disciples regarding his identity (Matt 16:13–20; Mark 8:27–30; Luke 9:18–20). Yet Mark does not include Jesus' statement about Peter and the rock upon which the church would be built. This omission is suggestive. If tradition is correct in taking Mark, at least to some degree, to be based on Peter's recollections, the silence of Mark on this point is significant.[14]

13. This is especially true of κατεξουσιάζουσιν, which is defined as "to gain or exercise complete dominion over; to gain dominion over, or gain possession of" in LSJ, 924.

14. Of course, Luke makes no mention of this either. But the absence of this in Mark is more intriguing. I admit this is speculative, but given the traditional association between Peter and Mark, the absence of Jesus' statement about Peter as the rock upon which the church would be built (Matt 16:18–19) begs for some explanation.

The model of leadership we discern from Mark was at odds with the first-century religious leadership that Jesus so often confronted. It was also contrary to the prevailing practices of Greco-Roman rulers. Mark's Gospel calls for a different approach altogether. Biblical leadership is not self-centered or self-promoting. It seeks the good of the other.

WHAT IS THE THEOLOGY OF THE "TRUE CHURCH"?

The intent of Jesus' teaching cannot be reduced to the creation of a new religion. Indeed, he was redefining what it meant to be the people of God, yet he did so within the context of the story of God's covenant with Israel.[15] God had committed himself to the promises he had made to Abraham, Isaac, Jacob, Moses, David, and so on. Included in these promises were those made to the people of Israel. Jesus came, at least in part, to fulfill these promises and to call the people back to God. However, this call required a revised understanding of Israel and its purpose and place in God's plan. This redefinition involved many, even most, aspects of Israel's identity and way of life. As followers of Jesus, Mark and his community would have been situated within this story of promise and fulfillment.

As Howard Clark Kee observes:

> Since the new covenant community pictured in Mark was so deeply conscious of itself as heir to the promises made to Israel, it could not merely brush aside the distinctive features of Jewish piety. What should the attitude of the church be toward Sabbath observance, fasting, prayer, dietary laws, eating a meal with those who are ritually or religiously impure? Each of these issues is addressed by Jesus in the Markan gospel.[16]

Although some may object to the suggestion that the church became the "new" Israel (Wright prefers the term "true Israel"), it seems inescapable that Mark understood that the life, death, and resurrection of Jesus required a radical redefinition of what it meant to be faithful to God. For example, when Jesus is confronted with the question regarding fasting (Mark 2:18–22), he responds with two important comments. First, he says it makes no sense for the friends of the bridegroom to fast

---

15. On this, see Wright, *New Testament and the People of God*; Wright, *Jesus and the Victory of God*.

16. Kee, *Beginnings of Christianity*, 113.

while the bridegroom is still with them. Second, he responds with the parable of the new wine skins. In this enigmatic response, he seems to be saying that a new way of relating to God has come; old forms are no longer functional.[17]

One can observe similar redefinitions of Sabbath observance. In Mark 2:23–28 Jesus maintains that the Sabbath was made for people, not people for the Sabbath. The conception and purpose of the Sabbath, as a day of rest and re-creation, had been lost. What had been intended as a day for the benefit of people had become a burden on many. As well-intentioned as the oral tradition governing the Sabbath may have been, the teaching of the Pharisees and scribes had made the Sabbath less about benefit to people and more about meticulous religious observance. Jesus dramatically makes this point when he asks, "Which is lawful on the Sabbath: to do good or to do evil? To save a life or to kill?" (Mark 3:4). If people had properly understood the Sabbath as a day of rest for the benefit of people, they could not possibly see a conflict between the Sabbath and Jesus' act of healing. Yet the religious leaders, here represented by the Pharisees, took offense at this gracious action. How could they possibly take offense at the physical restoration of one in need of healing? It could only be because they had a corrupted understanding of the Sabbath. Jesus redefines this understanding.

A redefinition of piety is seen in Jesus' comments about hand washing and defilement (Mark 7:1–23). Apparently the religious leaders of Jesus' day had come to see the problem of purity and defilement as primarily concerned with external factors. As long as one was careful to avoid external contamination, one was deemed to be clean. With such an understanding, meticulous observance of ritual purification, hand washing, ablutions, and so on, would be of great significance.

Unfortunately, such an emphasis on external contamination had the effect of making people ignore the true problem. Rather than understanding externally caused ritual impurity as a symbol of the real problem—impurity caused by sin—too many had come to see the external as the real problem. Jesus corrects this misunderstanding and redefines purity and defilement by teaching that the real problem of defilement is caused by one's heart (7:15–23). Meticulous observance of the regulations of ritual purity completely misses the point.

---

17. Ibid., 115.

In this same passage, Jesus responds to his disciples' question about his parable,

> Then do you also fail to understand? Do you not see that what-
> ever goes into a person from outside cannot defile, since it enters,
> not the heart but the stomach, and goes out into the sewer?

The comment "Thus he declared all foods clean" appears to be a parenthetical addition by Mark[18] to make the point that Jesus had rede-fined the basis for defilement even in the area of dietary law. No longer were they to think that food made one unclean or impure. They were to recognize that the real problem of sin and impurity was a matter of one's heart or inner attitude.

Jesus expresses another significant theological reconception in his exchange with a scribe (Mark 12:28–34). When the scribe asks Jesus which of the commandments is the greatest, Jesus responds,

> The first is, "Hear, O Israel: the Lord our God, the Lord is one;
> you shall love the Lord your God with all your heart, and with
> all your soul, and with all your mind, and with all your strength."
> The second is this, "You shall love your neighbor as yourself."
> There is no other commandment greater than these.

In his response, Jesus articulates two "commandments" as the foundation of the law and the prophets (cf. Matt 22:40). In distilling the Hebrew Scriptures down to these two commandments, Jesus establishes a basis upon which his community will function.[19] The people of God will be defined by living out these two commands that capture the es-sence of the Torah. The covenant community of Jesus will now be guided

---

18. This translation is found, with slight differences, in major translations like the RSV, NRSV, NIV, NASB, NJB, ESV, HCSB, and the New American Bible for Catholics. The Greek text reads καθαρίζων πάντα τὰ βρώματα (*katharizōn panta ta brōmata*) and includes this as part of Jesus' question. This would suggest something like, "do you not know that nothing from outside that goes into a man is able to make him unclean, because it does not go into his heart but into his stomach and goes out into the latrine, making all foods clean?" Garland suggests that the variant καθαρίζον would affirm that the food has become clean through the process of elimination in accordance with the tradition of the Pharisees (see his discussion in *Mark*, 275–76). But he also notes that in either case, Jesus' point is the same: what one takes into one's body is not the real source of impurity. If food is what defiles a person, why do the Pharisees say it is not regarded as unclean when it winds up in the latrine? Jesus' answer is that defilement comes from somewhere else. See Garland, *Mark*, 276. See also Brower, "Holy One," 70–73.

19. See McKnight, *Jesus Creed.*

and governed by these two commands. This new covenant was not established by the death of bulls and goats (i.e., the traditional sacrificial system), but by the sacrificial death of Christ (Mark 14:24).

The oral tradition was rejected and the written Torah was reinterpreted by Jesus. In light of the recorded teaching on issues such as fasting, hand washing, Sabbath observance, dietary laws, etc. and the significant redefinitions and reconceptions of these practices, one might reasonably expect the Markan community to have a distinctive appearance and praxis.

WHO ARE THE "TRUE CHURCH"?

Any discussion of Markan ecclesiology would seem to require consideration of the community's composition. Who would be accepted as part of the people of God? Did the Markan community accept or reject the "boundary markers" of the first-century religious establishment with which Jesus interacted?

It would seem, given the number of instances recorded, that Jesus intended also to redefine the understanding of fitness for participation in the community of God. His acceptance of "sinners and tax-collectors," demonstrated by his participation with them in table fellowship (Mark 2:16–17), required a radical rethinking of eligibility for inclusion in the "true Israel."[20] In a culture where meals were an important means of establishing, maintaining, and even challenging social status, Jesus chose to eat with people that the respectable religious community routinely excluded. His acceptance of "sinners" as meal partners was an explicit act of inclusion and reconciliation of the "unrighteous" and an implicit rejection and judgment of the status quo. Jesus used meals to illustrate and enact the grace of God's rule and to challenge the exclusivism and pride of the religious establishment.[21]

In a similar way, Jesus received those who were defiled by their physical illness or disability. Jesus healed a wide range of maladies. Still, these healings were more than a return to physical wholeness. They also involved community or social restoration. For example, in Mark 1 we read of Jesus' encounter with a leper (Mark 1:40–45). Leprosy was a physical illness (and the term covered a wide range of skin disorders)

---

20. See the discussion in Brower, "Holy One," 64–70.
21. See Bartchy, "Table Fellowship"; McKnight, *Jesus Creed*, 33–41.

that had significant social and communal consequences. Lepers were excluded from the community; they were required to live "outside the camp" (Lev 13:46). Only after healing and purification (Lev 14) could they experience social restoration.

When Jesus heals the leper, he is also restoring the man to his social group, both family and community. Jesus instructs the man to offer the appropriate offerings as a testimony to his healing, making it possible for him to experience complete social restoration. But it should be noted that Jesus accepts him even before the process of restoration is completed. Jesus touches the leper (Mark 1:41). This touching is not necessary for the healing, so it would seem to have significance for some other reason, namely, as a sign of acceptance.[22]

The inclusiveness of the Jesus community extended beyond ethnic boundaries. Mark 7:24–30 records Jesus' encounter with the Syrophoenician woman. This woman approaches Jesus with a request for the healing of her daughter. Jesus responds that it would be improper to take food from the children in order to give it to the dogs. This response would seem to be in concert with the Jewish attitude toward Gentiles as "outsiders," however, such an interpretation of Jesus' words may be premature. Three factors suggest that Mark intended this exchange to be ironic.

First, tradition accepts that Mark's community had a significant Gentile presence. It would be odd for Mark to record this saying if it were simply to be taken at face value. Why would he offend his community for no purpose? A second factor is the quickness of Jesus' "change of perspective." The woman offers a clever reply and Jesus immediately "changes his mind." This would suggest the change was not so dramatic. Finally, the location of this account is instructive. This pericope is located immediately after Jesus' discussion about defilement in which he makes the point that defilement is not an externally caused problem. The text moves from dialogue about *unclean food* to a dialogue with an *unclean person*.[23] Jesus explicitly redefines purity with respect to food and implicitly redefines it with respect to people. So the stage is set for the inclusion of non-Jewish people in the Jesus community.

---

22. This theme of Jesus' acceptance of the unacceptable is further demonstrated by his healing of demoniacs (Mark 1:21–28; 5:1–20; 9:14–29) and the woman with the hemorrhage (Mark 5:25).

23. Brooks, *Mark*, 120.

Mark presents Jesus as reconfiguring the membership of God's people. Old expectations, limitations, and boundary markers are being rejected or redefined. Perhaps the most surprising change occurs in Mark 3:31–35, when Jesus redefines his "family."

> Then his mother and his brothers came; and standing outside, they sent to him and called him. A crowd was sitting around him; and they said to him, "Your mother and your brothers and sisters are outside, asking for you." And he replied, "Who are my mother and my brothers?" And looking at those who sat around him, he said, "Here are my mother and my brothers! Whoever does the will of God is my brother and sister and mother."

In a culture where family ties were among the most significant social relationships, Jesus completely redefined what it meant to be part of his "family."[24] Malina and Rohrbaugh describe the significance of both the biological family and the fictive kin group:

> In antiquity, the extended family meant everything. It was not only the source of one's honor status in the community, but also functioned as the primary economic, religious, educational and social network. Loss of connection to the family meant the loss of these vital networks as well as loss of connection to the land. But a surrogate family, what anthropologists call a fictive kin group, could serve many of these same functions as a biological family.[25]

Membership in Jesus' "family" (fictive kin group) was not based on physical descent, but on obedience to God's will. If Jesus' own mother and siblings did not automatically qualify to be members of his "family" (i.e., the people of God), no one could claim automatic membership. The true family would be defined by one's faith relationship to Jesus—by living in accordance with God's will. Presumably Mark would have viewed his community as "brothers and sisters" of Jesus. Any other group that likewise lived in accordance with God's will would also be part of the family.

The inclusive nature of the Jesus community is also emphasized by the incident recorded in Mark 9:38–41:

> John said to him, "Teacher, we saw someone casting out demons in your name, and we tried to stop him, because he was not fol-

---

24. See Barton, "Family," 226–29; Malina, *New Testament World*, 94–121.

25. Malina and Rohrbaugh, *Gospel of John*, 88–89.

> lowing us." But Jesus said, "Do not stop him; for no one who does
> a deed of power in my name will be able soon afterward to speak
> evil of me. Whoever is not against us is for us. For truly I tell you,
> whoever gives you a cup of water to drink because you bear the
> name of Christ will by no means lose the reward.

John reports an encounter to Jesus, in which the disciples meet a man who is casting out demons in Jesus' name. They rebuke the man because "he was not following us." Jesus replies that they should not forbid him because "he that is not against us is for us" (see also Luke 9:49–50). John appears to think that one must be part of a particular group (i.e., "one of us") in order to be a legitimate follower of Jesus. Jesus uses very inclusive language to reject this understanding. There is, it would appear, a great deal of room under the umbrella of "whoever is not against us."

It is worth noting that both Matthew and Luke record the more restrictive saying, "whoever is not for us is against us" (Matt 12:30; Luke 11:23). When we survey the data, we find Matthew records only the more exclusive version (Matt 12:30), Luke records both the inclusive (Luke 9:49–50) and exclusive (Luke 11:23), and Mark records only the more inclusive statement (Mark 9:38–41). This, I suggest, is in keeping with Mark's understanding of the new people of God. The new people of God is identified by relationship to Jesus, not to any particular ethnic, social, or traditional group. All are welcome, although not all accept the invitation.[26]

CONCLUSION

What might one conclude about Mark's ecclesiology from this brief survey? Although Mark does not present explicit ecclesiological instruction as in Matthew's Gospel (18:15–20), there are suggestive "bits and pieces" that allow the reader to construct an understanding of Mark's view of the church. Markan ecclesiology incorporated a model of leadership based on humility and service. The community leaders were not to govern with a heavy hand. Rather, they were to serve the community. Leaders were expected to work for the benefit of others, rather than for personal selfish gain. One aspect of the "true church" would be this model of servant leadership.

---

26. See also, Brower, "Holy One," 68–75.

Mark's ecclesiological conception extended beyond polity. There were theological considerations as well. The church was to embrace the teaching of Jesus, which included important redefinitions and reconceptions of theological themes. For example, purity and defilement were no longer associated with external causes such as food or contact with the "wrong" type of person. The real problem (sin) was rooted in the heart of each person. Fitness (or righteousness) was now defined in terms of one's commitment to Jesus, not to observance of Torah (either written or oral).

The church was to act in accordance with the "Jesus Creed." The commands to love God completely and to love others rightly were to guide the life and practice of the Jesus community, the "true Israel."

Finally, membership in the community was determined not by ethnic affiliation, social class, or economic status, but by faith in Jesus. The community was open and inclusive. For example, in Mark's view Gentile Christians were not required to observe Jewish food laws. All were welcome, if only they would commit to living as Jesus called them to live.

There is room for diversity within this conception of the church. There would be unity of purpose (to love God and one's neighbor), even though there is no requirement for a uniformity of appearance or expression.[27] A true follower of Jesus is defined by his or her commitment to Jesus, not association with any particular group (Mark 9:38–41).

In Mark we see an ecclesiological conception that has room for a wide range of people and practices. No rigidly defined structure is present in Mark's account. Instead, we find material suggesting an openness to diverse expressions of faithfulness to Jesus. The "true" church is comprised of those who are restored to God through the redemptive work of Jesus and who are committed to living out his command to love God and to love others.

BIBLIOGRAPHY

Bartchy, S. Scott. "Table Fellowship." In *DJG*, edited by Green et al., 796–800. Downers Grove, IL: InterVarsity, 1992.

Barton, Stephen C. "Family." In *DJG*, edited by Green et al., 226–29. Downers Grove, IL: InterVarsity, 1992.

Brooks, James. *Mark*. NAC. Nashville: Broadman, 1991.

27. Omanson, "Church," 232.

Brower, Kent E. "The Holy One and His Disciples: Holiness and Ecclesiology in Mark." In *Holiness and Ecclesiology in the New Testament*, edited by Kent E. Brower and Andy Johnson, 57–75. Grand Rapids: Eerdmans, 2007.

Carson, D. A. "Redaction Criticism: On the Legitimacy and Illegitimacy of a Literary Tool." In *Scripture and Truth*, 119–42. Grand Rapids: Baker, 1992.

Carson, D. A., and Douglas J. Moo. *Introduction to the New Testament*. 2nd ed. Grand Rapids: Zondervan, 2005.

Garland, David E. *Mark*. NIVAC. Grand Rapids: Zondervan, 1996.

Kee, Howard Clark. *The Beginnings of Christianity: An Introduction to the New Testament*. New York: T. & T. Clark, 2005.

Lane, William L. *The Gospel according to Mark*. Grand Rapids: Eerdmans, 1974.

Linnemann, Eta. *Is There A Synoptic Problem? Rethinking the Literary Dependence of the First Three Gospels*. Grand Rapids: Baker, 1992.

Malina, Bruce J. *The New Testament World: Insights from Cultural Anthropology*. Atlanta: John Knox, 1981.

Malina, Bruce J., and Richard L. Rohrbaugh. *Social-Science Commentary on the Gospel of John*. Minneapolis: Augsburg Fortress, 1998.

Marshall, I. Howard. "Church." In *DJG*, edited by Green et al., 122–25. Downers Grove, IL: InterVarsity, 1992.

McKnight, Scot. *The Jesus Creed: Loving God, Loving Others*. Brewster, MA: Paraclete, 2004.

Omanson, Roger L. "Church." In *EDT*, edited by Walter A. Elwell, 231–33. Grand Rapids: Baker, 1984.

Savage, Timothy B. *Power through Weakness: Paul's Understanding of the Christian Ministry in 2 Corinthians*. SNTSMS 86. Cambridge: Cambridge University Press, 1996.

Wright, N. T. *Jesus and the Victory of God*. Minneapolis: Fortress, 1996.

———. *The New Testament and the People of God*. Minneapolis: Fortress, 1992.

3

The Church in Luke-Acts

GEORGE GOLDMAN II

IN ANY COURSE ON exegesis students learn the danger of interpreting the New Testament writings as systematic theological treatises. Rather, what we have are occasional documents—written for specific audiences at specific times for specific reasons. Though Luke's narrative is broad and wide-ranging, its content is surely more determined by the circumstances of his audience than by his desire to set out a comprehensive guide for the universal church.[1] Nevertheless, every occasional document reflects something of a writer's broader mindset and theology. What can we learn about Luke's ecclesiology by reading "between the lines" of his two volume work?[2]

Some may mistakenly assume that Luke's vision for the church of his day is more fully reflected in Acts than in his Gospel. After all, Acts deals directly with "the church age" whereas the Gospel is about the ministry of Jesus, which some may view as merely a prelude to the church. However, such an approach wrongly minimizes something Luke assumes—the significance of the example and teaching of Jesus for the church. Jesus' purpose was to preach about the kingdom of God. "I must proclaim the good news of the kingdom of God to the other cities also;

---

1. Luke's audience seems to be predominately made up of Gentile Christians. As we will see, Luke pays great attention to the Gentile mission and the status of Gentiles in relation to Israel. See also the arguments in Fitzmyer, *Luke*, 1:57–59.

2. For a brief defense of the common authorship of Luke-Acts, with Luke as author, see Fitzmyer, *Acts*, 49–51.

for I was sent for this purpose" (Luke 4:43).[3] This "kingdom" preaching was not just about some future rule of God, nor was it about God's rule in a heavenly realm far removed from day-to-day activities on earth. The kingdom is about God's will being done on earth, as it is already being done in heaven (Luke 11:2).[4] Thus, Jesus' kingdom teaching is teaching for the life of the church.

At Acts 1:21–22, Luke's own narrative emphasizes the importance of Jesus' ministry and teaching for the "church age." In order for someone to take Judas's place as apostle, that person had to be a witness to the entirety of Jesus' ministry, from his baptism until his ascension. This means that what Jesus did and taught before his resurrection was still relevant to what it meant to be the church of God.[5] Therefore, this summary of Luke's ecclesiology will look at both of Luke's volumes, the Gospel and Acts.

THE CHURCH IS A RENEWED ISRAEL

It is beyond dispute that one of Luke's major concerns is to connect the new Christian movement with God's people Israel. What is disputed is the exact nature of the connection. In this section it will be shown that, for Luke, the church is not a "new Israel" in the sense that the Gentile church has replaced Israel. Rather, Luke sees the church as a "renewed Israel," still connected to God's plans for the world manifested in the hopes and promises made to Israel in the Old Testament.[6]

3. Unless otherwise noted, all quotations are taken from the NRSV.

4. See also Luke 11:20 ("But if it is by the finger of God that I cast out the demons, then the kingdom of God has come to you") and 17:21 ("The kingdom of God is among you"). For a good discussion of the "now and not yet" aspect of Jesus' preaching of the kingdom of God, see Ladd, *Theology of the New Testament*, 54–67.

5. Tannehill, *Narrative Unity*, 2:23. Strange, "Jesus-Tradition," rightly notes the surprising absence of references to Jesus' teachings and life in Acts to support the practices of the church, e.g., the inclusion of the Gentiles in Acts 15. Though Luke does not make such connections explicit, common themes between the Gospel and Acts make clear Luke's intention to base the church's actions on Jesus.

6. An article by Jacob Jervell, in his *Luke and the People of God*, has become the classic statement of this position. Jervell's further argument that for Luke early Jewish Christians were still *obligated* to keep the "old" law needs modification. Luke's concern was to show that the law, rightly interpreted, leads one to recognize Jesus as Messiah. However, the ministry of Jesus and the bestowal of the Spirit do take the law out of its former central place in the relationship of God to his people. See Turner, *Power from on High*, 354–55, and Blomberg, "Law in Luke-Acts."

First, in both his Gospel and Acts, Luke emphasizes that key participants in his narrative were not just Jews, but devout Jews. Zechariah and Elizabeth lived "blamelessly according to all the commandments and regulations of the Lord" (Luke 1:6). Simeon was "righteous and devout, looking forward to the consolation of Israel" (Luke 2:25). Anna worshipped in the temple day and night (Luke 2:37). The crowd in Acts 2 was composed of "devout Jews" from every nation (Acts 2:5). Many priests in Jerusalem became believers in Jesus (Acts 6:7). Even at a much later stage in the narrative, the leaders of the church in Jerusalem report that there are thousands of Jewish believers and "they are all zealous for the law" (Acts 21:20). Paul's baptizer, Ananias, is called "a devout man according to the law and well spoken of by all the Jews living there [in Damascus]" (Acts 22:12). Why is it so important to Luke to note that these early believers were devout Jews?

In Luke's theology, Jesus brought about the redemption of Israel. Granted, this redemption looked different from what many Jews expected, but Luke is concerned to show the connections between the new Christian movement and the promises and hopes of Judaism. Mary sings about God fulfilling his promises to Abraham through her son Jesus (Luke 1:54–55).[7] Zechariah sees in Jesus the one who will save Israel from their enemies in fulfillment of the promises made to the Jewish ancestors (Luke 1:68–75). Nowhere does Luke explicitly dash the hopes of the pious Jews in his narrative who long for the restoration of Israel.[8] Like other New Testament authors, Luke shows how Jesus and the church fulfill Old Testament prophesies (Luke 3:4–6; 4:17–21; Acts 2:16–21; 15:15–18). The church is not a stand-alone entity. It fulfills the plans of God from long ago. The day of Pentecost in Acts 2 did not create a brand new story. Rather, it began a new chapter in a very old story.

---

7. Mary's song is reminiscent of Hannah's song (1 Sam 2:1–10), which also emphasizes God's faithfulness to his people.

8. Tannehill, "Israel in Luke-Acts," takes this to mean that these hopes take a tragic turn in Luke-Acts with the final scene being the rejection of the gospel by the Jews in Rome (Acts 28:23–28). It is better to understand the promises as fulfilled, albeit in an unexpected way, in the ministry of Jesus and those Jews who did believe. Bruce, "Eschatology in Acts," 53, states: "When [Luke] wrote, he knew that the son of David had not overthrown the Gentile oppressors or established national independence for Israel. Yet the promises on which those hopes were based were not forgotten in the early church: their fulfillment was recognized and proclaimed. But it was a fulfillment on a plane other than what formerly had been envisaged. The promises made to the house of David were fulfilled in the resurrection and exaltation of Jesus, the Son of David."

After Jesus rose from the dead, Luke tells us that Jesus spent forty days teaching his disciples about the "kingdom of God" (Acts 1:3–8).[9] The disciples ask Jesus if this is the time when he will restore the kingdom to Israel, that is, the time when Israel will rule as a nation. The question itself is not out of line. The conjunction of the kingdom of God, an order not to leave Jerusalem (the hub of Jewish kingdom expectation),[10] and the promise of a baptism in the Spirit would naturally heighten the disciples' expectations. These are all elements of Old Testament prophecies about what will happen when Israel is restored.[11] If Jesus had simply answered this query with a "yes" or "no," theological discussion of the relationship of the church to Israel would have been greatly simplified! Instead, Jesus tells them that it is not for them to know the timing of the restoration.[12] He then goes on to "answer" their question by saying that they will be empowered by the Holy Spirit to be his witnesses to the ends of the earth.

Some interpreters think the worldwide nature of this mission serves to counteract the parochialism of the disciples' question that focused on Israel as a nation.[13] However, the bestowal of the Spirit and the worldwide mission are not *alternatives* to Israel's restoration, but rather the *means* by which the restoration is accomplished. Indeed, as already noted, the kingdom of God had been inaugurated in the mission of Jesus (Luke 4:21—"Today this scripture has been fulfilled in your hearing"). Now it is time for the disciples to experience the Spirit as Jesus has *already* experienced him.[14] It is time for them to play their role in fulfilling

9. Bruce, *Book of Acts*, 32, makes the plausible suggestion that Jesus needed to relate the recent events of his crucifixion and resurrection to the earlier message of the kingdom. The disciples' question in v. 6 provides a narrative way of clarifying this important topic for Luke's readers. So Tannehill, *Narrative Unity*, 14.

10. Chance, *Jerusalem*, 5–18.

11. E.g., kingdom: Dan 2:44; Jerusalem: Isa 2:1–4; Spirit: Joel 2:28.

12. In his answer, Jesus switches from the singular ("time," χρόνῳ) used in the question to the plural phrase "times or seasons" (χρόνους ἢ καιρούς). This may suggest that Israel's restoration will be part of a larger process and not happen at a certain point of time. See Jervell, *Apostelgeschichte*, 115.

13. Marshall, *Acts of the Apostles*, 60; Stott, *The Spirit, the Church, and the World*, 41; and especially Maddox, *Purpose of Luke-Acts*, 106.

14. Turner, *Power from on High*, 318–47. Again, Pentecost is not a brand new beginning, but "more of the same." This is also implied in a possible translation of Acts 1:1. In Luke's first book, he related what Jesus "*began* to do and teach" (TNIV). In Acts, Jesus is still active and teaching through his Spirit in the disciples. In favor of giving "began" its

God's promises to Israel. One goal of Israel's restoration was to be a witness to the nations.[15] Though the final restoration remains a part of the future that only God knows, the gift of the Spirit and worldwide mission are integral parts of the process.

As Luke's narrative shows, the Gentile membership of the church was increasing. Ambivalence toward practice of the Law is evident within Luke and Acts (e.g., the Sabbath controversies of the Gospel and the circumcision controversy in Acts). Still, Luke thinks it is important for Christians to understand that they are part of God's centuries-old plan for expanding his kingdom in the world.

THE CHURCH IS LED BY THE SPIRIT

As Jesus was directed by the Spirit in Luke, so shall his followers be in Acts. All of the Gospels associate the Spirit with Jesus at his baptism (Matt 3:16; Mark 1:10; Luke 3:22; John 1:32–34). Luke emphasizes Jesus' empowerment by the Spirit before and after the temptation account (4:1, 14). Luke also highlights the Spirit in the synagogue scene at Nazareth (4:18). Several other characters in Luke's Gospel are said to be filled with the Spirit in some way (John the Baptist, Mary [in a special way], Elizabeth, Zechariah, and Simeon). There is also a promise that Jesus will baptize his followers with the Holy Spirit (3:16; 24:49), that the Father will give the Spirit to those who ask (11:13), and that the Holy Spirit will teach the disciples what to say when on trial (12:12). What role does the Holy Spirit play, then, for Jesus' followers in Acts?

The pouring out of the Spirit at Pentecost marked a new era. Before Pentecost, as some Old Testament narratives indicate, the Spirit was indeed active, though typically for leaders and rulers.[16] To be sure, Jesus was guided by the Spirit. But at Pentecost, God poured out his Spirit in an expansive way upon those who believed in Jesus. Peter promised this

---

natural force, instead of taking it as the Greek version of an Aramaic helping verb, see the arguments in Barrett, *Acts*, 1:66–67.

15. The wording of Acts 1:6–8 contains strong allusions to the servant songs of Isaiah (32:15; 43:10–12; 49:6). "To the circle of disciples falls the vocation of the Isaianic servant, to raise up Jacob and to restore the remnant of Israel. . . . [Jesus' answer in 1:7–8] is not a denial of an important future for 'Israel,' but a change of emphasis from Israel's kingship to her task as servant bringing the light of God's salvation to the nations" (Turner, *Power from on High*, 301).

16. E.g., kings (2 Sam 23:2; Ps 51:11), prophets (2 Kgs 2:9), and leaders (Num 11:25; Deut 34:9). See Turner, *Holy Spirit*, 4.

same gift to those who repented and were baptized (Acts 2:38). Because of its status as a turning point, Pentecost does have some unique elements. The symbols of wind and fire are not mentioned in later accounts. Though the disciples in Acts 2 speak in tongues, which here appear to be foreign languages, such activity is not mentioned in every conversion story.[17] Sometimes the Spirit is associated with baptism (2:38) and at other times with the laying on of hands (8:17–18). Some conversion accounts do not even mention the bestowal of the Spirit (8:36–39; 16:31–34). In the Cornelius account the Spirit even comes *before* baptism (10:44–48). If one is looking for a stable pattern, it is not to be found in Acts.[18] One can assume from the overall Lukan narrative that disciples will be like Jesus in being baptized and receiving the Spirit.

In several places Luke attributes more specific activities to the Spirit. The Spirit directs people to go on specific missions, to do specific tasks (8:29; 10:19; 13:2; 20:28), and also keeps Paul from going certain places (16:6–7). But it seems as though this Spirit direction was not always easily discernable.[19] In Acts 15:28 the Holy Spirit partnered with the Jerusalem leaders in a decision not to require circumcision for Gentiles, but that conclusion only came about after quite a bit of discussion and argument. Paul feels bound by the Spirit to go to Jerusalem (20:22), though he says he does not know exactly what will happen to him there, only that prison and hardships await him. Paul thinks he may even die in Jerusalem, though that turns out not to be true (21:13). Indeed, Paul's friends advise him *through the Spirit* not to go (21:4). Agabus predicts through the Spirit that Paul will be bound in Jerusalem, and Paul's companions and friends once again deduce from this that Paul should not go (21:10–12).[20] When Paul adamantly insists on going

17. Speaking in tongues is only mentioned in Acts 2, 10, and 19. There is no indication that Luke expected every believer to manifest this gift. For a fuller discussion see Turner, *Holy Spirit*, 221–27.

18. "Luke is not interested in constructing a self-consistent theory of sacraments" (Johnson, *Acts*, 57).

19. *Pace* Brown, *Churches*, 68: "Thus every essential step in this story of how witness was borne to Christ from Jerusalem to the ends of the earth is guided by the Spirit, whose presence becomes obvious at great moments where the human agents would otherwise be hesitant or choose wrongly."

20. Indeed, Agabus's prophecy does not exactly fit with the "fulfillment" in Luke's later narrative. Paul is not bound by the Jews and handed over to the Gentiles, but is "saved" from the Jews (who would have preferred to handle the situation themselves without an arrest) by being taken into custody by the Gentiles. Agabus's prediction

to Jerusalem, these friends accept his decision and take it as God's will. It appears that even though Luke depicts many people as being guided by the Spirit, he does not expect that the Spirit's direction will always be absolutely clear or comprehensive for everyone involved.[21] It is possible for Spirit-guided disciples to have trouble distinguishing their own desires for Paul's safety from what God is trying to reveal through them, the difficult calling Paul received to endure suffering in imitation of his master, Jesus.

When Paul gets to Jerusalem, the leaders of the church ask him to join with some who have made a vow, to show his loyalty to the Law (21:20–26). This plan to placate the Jews backfires, as it leads to Paul's arrest.[22] Though God is able to use Paul's imprisonment to advance the gospel, it is doubtful that this is the outcome James and the Jerusalem elders had in mind. This is yet another illustration that, according to Luke's narrative, the Spirit does not give the church comprehensive insight about how to achieve her intended goal. Rather, in Luke's portrayal, the Spirit works in combination with human decisions.

THE CHURCH IS AN INCLUSIVE COMMUNITY

Luke goes out of his way to show how disparate groups were involved with Jesus. Whereas the Pharisees and teachers of the law criticized Jesus for eating with tax collectors and sinners (e.g., Luke 5:27–32; 15:1–2; 19:7), Jesus so identified with outcasts that he himself could be accused of being a glutton and drunkard, a friend of tax collectors and sinners (Luke 7:34). For Luke, a community of Jesus followers may often be accused of associating with the wrong kinds of people.[23]

---

might be stated in a way to make it parallel with predictions of Jesus' treatment in the Gospel (Luke 9:44; 18:32). See Béchard, "Disputed Case against Paul," 241. The Jews at least are the cause of Paul's being arrested by the Gentiles. See Bock, *Acts*, 638.

21. Indeed, being led by the Spirit is not incompatible with disputes. Paul and Barnabas, both described at times as being led by the Spirit, have a dispute so great that they have to go on separate mission trips (Acts 15:36–41).

22. "Undoubtedly the plan, as described in Acts, misfired. That is, the demonstration proposed by James was ill adapted to its purpose" (Barrett, *Acts*, 2:1013). Although Luke cannot detail every event that happened, it is curious that there is no mention of the response to Paul's arrest on the part of the church in Jerusalem. Thompson suggests Luke is using the Jewish Christians as a negative example because they do not reach out to help Paul in this instance. See Thompson, *Keeping the Church in Its Place*, 231–34.

23. Though it is not clear that women should be classed with social outcasts in the

Luke's Gospel also has several positive accounts about Samaritans (10:33—parable of the Good Samaritan; 17:11—a Samaritan returns to thank Jesus). These encounters set up the narrative in Acts, where the gospel is spread to Samaritans as a first step to the Gentile world (Acts 8). These converts become the first people in the narrative to receive the Spirit outside the nation of Israel.[24]

Of course the biggest sign that Luke believed the church to be an inclusive society is his attention to the addition of Gentiles. At the very beginning of Luke's narrative, Simeon declares the goal of Gentile inclusion (Luke 2:32). This goal is reiterated by Jesus himself when he says that forgiveness of sins will be preached to all nations in the name of the Messiah (Luke 24:47).[25] Peter has to be taught that uncircumcised Gentiles are legitimate recipients of the gospel, and he finally gets the point (Acts 10).[26]

The major actor in accomplishing this goal is Paul. Paul is told from the beginning of his commission that he will be God's witness before the nations (Acts 9:15; 22:21; 26:17, 20). Paul's common practice is to go to the Jews first, but he always ends up turning to the Gentiles (e.g., 13:46; 18:6). Acts ends with the hopeful note that "they will listen" (28:28). The picture that Luke gives of what churches are like is of racially diverse groups who are united by the universal gospel of the kingdom.

The narrative of Acts does not ignore some of the difficulties that come with such inclusivity. In Acts 6:1–7, after Luke has described a Spirit-filled Jerusalem community that has one heart and mind and shares all things in common, he notes a dispute between the Hellenistic and Hebraic Jews. The specific occasion revolved around a distribution of food, but the underlying issue was that the Hellenistic Christians be-

---

first-century world, and Jesus is never criticized in Luke for associating with women, in Luke's narrative women get special attention as followers and supporters of Jesus' ministry (8:2–3; 10:38–42; Acts 1:14). This may be part of Luke's theme of fulfillment of prophecy, such as the "sons and daughters" of Joel 2 and Isaiah 40–66. See Black, "Women in the Gospel of Luke."

24. Barrett, *Acts*, 1:413.

25. In Greco-Roman culture, it was important to tie innovative practices to the founder. Balch argues Luke ties the acceptance of foreigners into house churches to Jesus' own practice as well as to predictions of the Old Testament prophets. See Balch, "ΜΕΤΑΒΟΛΗ ΠΟΛΙΤΕΙΩΝ," 140.

26. "Much of the tension in Luke's narrative from this point on [Acts 8] has to do with . . . humans trying their best to catch up to God's action in the world" (Johnson, *Acts*, 150).

lieved their culture was being overlooked. Luke's narrative shows that prejudice is not an issue that God's people can ignore or leave unattended.

The inclusion of Gentiles without circumcision becomes the biggest community issue in Luke's narrative (Acts 15). Luke is concerned both with what this episode says about the make-up of the community and with how the dispute is reconciled. Johnson helpfully notes four points in the community discernment process that can serve as a Lukan model for dispute resolution.[27] First, all voices are heard and an emphasis is placed on narratives of God's activity. Peter, Paul, and Barnabas tell of their experiences, which the entire community then evaluates. Second, they notice that God can work in unexpected ways, and use the experience of Gentile inclusion as a key to unlock possibly new interpretations of Scripture.[28] Third, extensive conflict and debate are valid and even necessary parts of the process. The insistence of the Pharisees on circumcision forced the church to articulate more carefully the basis of salvation on faith. Fourth, the community gives its consent. The issue is not totally settled until the "whole church" (15:22) agrees and the decision is disseminated and taught among all those concerned, who communicate their agreement back to the "mother church" (15:27, 30–34). Despite the problems that come with the inclusion of diverse believers, in Acts the church finds a way to bring the good news of the kingdom to Jew and Gentile alike.

THE CHURCH HELPS THE POOR

From the beginning of Luke's Gospel, in Mary's song, God acts on behalf of the poor and against the wealthy (Luke 1:52–53). John the Baptist tells his disciples with two shirts to share with those who have none, and to do the same with their food (Luke 3:11). Jesus was anointed to share good news with the poor (Luke 4:18).[29] Luke includes sayings and stories in his Gospel in which Jesus tells his followers to give to the poor

27. Johnson, *Acts*, 271–72, 279.

28. The citation from Amos in 15:16–18 follows a line of interpretation in the LXX that differs from the Hebrew. For more detail, see Bauckham, "James and the Gentiles."

29. The "good news" or "gospel" includes matters of social justice, not just the forgiveness of sins. This is seen in Luke 7:22. The blind regain sight, the lame walk, the lepers are cleansed, the deaf hear, the dead are raised, and the poor hear the gospel. "Hearing the gospel" must mean more than having sins forgiven in order to match with the healings in the list. It means the poor hear the good news that they will become blessed, also in material terms!

(11:41; 12:33; 14:13; 19:1–10, all found only in Luke). The main point of the parables of the Shrewd Manager and the Rich Man and Lazarus (Luke 16), found only in Luke's Gospel, is that Jesus' followers should be concerned for the poor.[30]

Luke clearly shows that the church in Acts lived out this central teaching of Jesus. In Acts, the early Christians in Jerusalem sell their possessions in order to give to those in need (2:45; 4:32–37).[31] Once the Spirit has been poured out, the community devotes itself to the apostles' teaching, fellowship, the breaking of bread, and prayer (2:42). From the context, this "fellowship" would include the sharing of material possessions. As Krodel notes, "What we do or do not do with our material possessions is an indicator of the Spirit's presence or absence."[32] The subsequent narrative shows that the church in Jerusalem will continue to include members with a range of socio-economic status, some with property (12:12) and some in need (24:17), but there is still a fundamental principle that "there will, however, be no one in need among you" (Deut 15:4).[33]

Barnabas serves as an example of one who uses his possessions properly (4:36–37), as do Dorcas (9:36–39), and the church at Antioch (11:29–30). Ananias and Sapphira try to appear more generous that they really are, and so are notably struck down (5:1–11). The seven ministers appointed in Acts 6 show their spiritual gifts by serving widows.[34] Simon

30. See as well the material from Mark that Luke has changed to emphasize this theme, noted in Fitzmyer, *Luke*, 247–48. "No other NT writer—save perhaps the author of the Epistle of James . . . speaks out as emphatically as does Luke about the Christian disciple's use of material possessions, wealth, and money" (p. 247).

31. Barrett, *Acts*, 1:168, suggests they were motivated by an imminent expectation of the parousia, but the only motivation mentioned in the text is care for the poor (so Bock, *Acts*, 153). Many commentators note that Luke's description of the early Christians' sharing of goods is similar to Greek ideals of community and friendship as found, e.g., in Aristotle and Plato. (See esp. Mitchell, "Social Function of Friendship"; Sterling, "Athletes of Virtue"). Also important is the allusion to the ideal picture of an obedient Israel (Deut 15:4) in Acts 4:34—"there was not a needy person among them." This furthers Luke's theme of the restoration of Israel.

32. Gerhard Krodel, *Acts*. Minneapolis: Augsburg, 1986, 95, as cited by Blomberg, *Neither Poverty nor Riches*, 161.

33. Blomberg, *Neither Poverty nor Riches*, 165.

34. Luke often uses "authority over material possessions as a symbol for spiritual authority. . . . The transfer of spiritual power (through the laying on of hands) is symbolized by the taking on of 'table service' (as it was for Jesus and the Twelve)" (Johnson, *Acts*, 111).

the Sorcerer is condemned for being greedy (8:20). Paul works hard with his hands so that he can take care of himself and others, citing a saying of Jesus, "it is more blessed to give than to receive" (20:35). Paul brings gifts for poor Jews in Jerusalem (24:17).

The hospitality shown to traveling missionaries in Acts can also be mentioned in this regard (16:15, 34; 21:4, 7, 16–17; 27:3). Especially picturesque is the reciprocity shown by the Philippian jailor, who, after his baptism, cares for Paul and his fellow workers (16:31–34). This is a concrete example of the social implications of the gospel. "To know God means that others are treated with care." [35]

It could be that, for Luke, the important goal was not so much to make the churches of Acts a pattern for future churches to follow in terms of acts of ritual worship, but to show that Jesus himself is the pattern to be followed. Luke's emphasis on taking care of the needy provides a compelling example of Jesus' teachings lived out in concrete situations. [36]

THE CHURCH BREAKS BREAD

Luke's Gospel describes Jesus participating in the usual acts of worship done by the Jews of his day (4:16; 5:16; 22:7–8). After Jesus' ascension into heaven, Jewish Christians in Jerusalem continue going to the temple to pray and to preach (Luke 24:53; Acts 2:46; 3:1; 5:12, 20–21, 42). Interestingly, Luke does not give any detailed picture of the worship practices of the early church. [37] However, one ongoing practice that gets a modicum of attention in Acts is the practice of breaking bread, or the "Lord's Supper."

Like the other Synoptic Gospels, Luke records Jesus' "institution" of the "Lord's Supper" on the night that he was betrayed (Luke 22:7–38). [38]

---

35. Bock, *Acts*, 543.

36. Luke's audience presumably included more "middle class" Christians than was typical of early Christian churches. "It seems likely that Luke wanted to show that Jesus challenged affluent spirituality and saw the kingdom of God in a holistic way, with practical sharing being just as important as spiritual gifts and experience" (Wenham, "Purpose of Luke-Acts," 86).

37. Jeremias's view that the four elements that characterize the Jerusalem church in 2:42 "describe the sequence of an early Christian [worship] service" (*Eucharistic Word*, 118–21) has not gained many adherents. It seems better understood as a general summary of the communal life of the early Jerusalem church. So Fitzmyer, *Acts*, 269.

38. However, Luke is the only Gospel to contain the admonition to "do this in remembrance of me" (22:19). "With the command to repeat the meal when Jesus is no

This meal with the disciples should be seen as the climax of Jesus' earlier table fellowship. Jesus uses times of eating as teaching opportunities for the disciples (5:27–32; 7:36–50; 9:10–17; 10:38–42; 11:37–54; 14:1–24; 19:1–10; 22:7–38; 24:13–53).[39] Then, during the last supper, Jesus takes the normal elements of the Passover celebration and gives them a new meaning. Jesus says that he will not eat with them again until it is fulfilled in the kingdom of God (22:16). Jesus is likely referring here to the eschatological messianic banquet. However, just three days later we see Jesus at a meal with some disciples, and they recognize him in the breaking of the bread (24:30–31). In some sense Jesus' death and resurrection have already brought in the kingdom of God.[40] The meals in Acts are also meals in the kingdom. Jesus is continually recognized in the breaking of bread. An examination of the meals in Acts fills in Luke's picture of the breaking of bread as a ritual for the church.

In Acts 2 Luke describes the early Christians in Jerusalem devoting themselves to the apostles' teaching and also to fellowship, which included the breaking of bread (2:42). Every day they broke bread in their homes and ate together (2:46).[41] Does this refer to a ritual meal like the Lord's Supper or is it just a regular meal?[42] Given Luke's descriptions of Jesus' table fellowship in his previous volume, it is likely that these meals would take on a special significance given the resurrection of Jesus and the establishment of the kingdom.[43] These are now kingdom meals. Though there is a difference between the Eucharist and "normal" meals, Luke likely sees a religious significance to this early sharing of meals together.[44] Fitzmyer summarizes Acts 2:42–47 well: "Luke has included

---

longer visibly present, the pericope becomes the foundational story and theological explanation for the early church's continuing practice of 'breaking bread' as recorded in Acts" (Hahn, "Kingdom and Church," 309).

39. See Hicks, *Come to the Table*, 53–81.

40. Hahn, "Kingdom and Church," 307–9.

41. Ferguson, *Church of Christ*, 239–40, suggests that the "every day" of Acts 2:46 may apply only to the meeting in the temple and not to the "breaking bread." However, it seems more likely that "daily" goes with all the elements in the verse, because it mentions taking food, which would have been done every day.

42. Ibid., 259, rightly suggests that after the Last Supper, every blessing of the bread before a meal would bring back memories of Jesus for the disciples.

43. So Johnson, *Acts*, 58; Hahn, "Kingdom and Church," 319; and Hicks, *Come to the Table*, 88–93. Bock, *Acts*, 154, thinks it simply refers to a regular meal.

44. "Luke does not make a concrete distinction between eucharistic activity and a common meal, which suggests to the readers that the meals together among the believ-

this description of early Christian life as an ideal that he would desire to be characteristic of all Christians. It may be an idyllic description, but it highlights the elements that should be part of genuine Christian life: harmony, reverent care for one another, formal and informal prayer in common, and celebration of the Lord's Supper."[45]

Luke's next mention of breaking bread is in Acts 20. The Christians at Troas met together on the first day of the week "to break bread." The mention of the timing of this story is not just an incidental reference.[46] The story is important because here is yet another resurrection on the first day of the week (cf. Luke 24:1), this time of Eutychus. After Eutychus is raised the group breaks bread and eats, being greatly comforted that the young man is alive again.

It looks like the practice of meeting to break bread at Troas was a weekly event. Breaking bread every day in Jerusalem was part of that community's sharing of all their possessions. Though Luke does not say specifically why Christians were now meeting on the first day of the week, all the narrative clues point to that being the day of resurrection.[47] It is clear from early church history that the first day of the week became the typical time for weekly Christian worship and the Lord's Supper.[48] Luke's depiction of the believers at Troas portrays them as gathering on the first day of the week to break bread in remembrance of Jesus. One may infer from this that, from Luke's perspective, breaking bread at their gatherings on the first day of the week was a significant event in the life of the Christian community.[49]

---

ers are characterized by the same gospel that the eucharistic ritual enacts. . . . The text *does* suggest to the reader that the coming of the promised Holy Spirit results in a communal bond among the believers that is evident in a close if not inseparable relationship between worship and social practices" (Thompson, *Keeping the Church in Its Place*, 49, emphasis original).

45. Fitzmyer, *Acts*, 269.

46. Hicks, *Come to the Table*, 93–97.

47. The first day of the week, the placement in an upper room (Luke 22:12; Acts 1:13), and the breaking of bread (Luke 24:30–35) are all "clear verbal pointers back to the resurrection of Jesus and the experience of his risen presence by the first disciples" (Johnson, *Acts*, 358).

48. The practice of meeting in order to take the Lord's Supper is evident in 1 Corinthians 11. Meeting on the first day of the week is referred to in 1 Corinthians 16. For a convenient collection of early church literature outside the New Testament, see Ferguson, *Early Christians Speak*, 67–79.

49. The only other time Luke mentions breaking bread is in the shipwreck narrative in Acts 27:35. There are several narrative elements that point to a eucharistic

THE CHURCH HAS LEADERS

Luke's narrative indicates that some believers played different roles within the churches. Of course, at the beginning, the apostles played the foundational role. Apparently, it was important to have twelve apostles who died "in the faith," since Judas, the "apostate," was replaced at the beginning of Acts (1:15–26) and there is no mention that James was replaced after his death (12:2). Why was it important to have twelve apostles who died "in the faith"? Having twelve apostles shows the continuing connection of the church to the twelve tribes of Israel.[50] Also, Jesus himself had promised that the twelve would eat and drink in his kingdom and sit on thrones judging the tribes of Israel (Luke 22:30). The two aspects of Jesus' saying, table fellowship and ruling authority, are at least partially fulfilled in Luke's narrative, which speaks of the apostles eating with the risen Lord (Luke 24:41–43; Acts 1:4, 10:41) and of their leadership in Jerusalem over the church, i.e., the renewed tribes of Israel (2:42; 4:35, 37; 5:2; 6:2–6; 8:14; 15:2).[51]

When complaints arise about the distribution of food, the Jerusalem church appoints seven men to "wait on tables" while the apostles focus on teaching (Acts 6:1–6). These men are not explicitly called deacons, but they perform a similar role to that of deacons in the later church.[52] This is the closest Luke comes to the distinction between elders and

---

interpretation of this story. "As far as language goes, this is more 'eucharistic' than any other passage in Acts" (Barrett, *Acts*, 2:1208). The context is one of salvation and the description of taking bread, giving thanks, and breaking it is identical to that of Jesus at the Passover meal in Luke. See Hicks, *Come to the Table*, 201–2. Although all of these terms could be associated with a regular meal as well, the parallel with the Last Supper does not seem accidental. Luke could have expressed himself differently.

50. "The fact remains that salvation is always destined first of all for Israel. That is why, of necessity, the Twelve, throughout all the history of the Church, and no matter what may be the numerical proportion of Jews and Gentiles among the believers, keep their same historical and eschatological significance. To lose sight of this fact, would be, for the Gentile Christians, to come to the hasty conclusion that God had rejected His people" (Menoud, "The Additions to the Twelve Apostles," 141–42).

51. See Clark, "Role of the Apostles," 174–77, and Ferguson, *Church of Christ*, 29.

52. "This is probably not the origin of the office of deacon. This title is never used of the group, nor is there evidence that these men do all the things that deacons did. However, the principle of designating a set of laborers for this kind of task is probably what led to the creation of this office at a later time" (Bock, *Acts*, 262). Though διακονεῖν and διακονία are used, the noun διάκονος is not. "It is impossible that anyone should set out to give an account of the origin of the diaconate without calling its first holders deacons" (Barrett, *Acts*, 1:304).

deacons that appears elsewhere in the New Testament (Phil 1:1; 1 Tim 3:1–13; Rom 16:1).

The church at Antioch had prophets and teachers, but no elders are mentioned there (13:1). In 11:26–27, Luke mentions that Paul and Barnabas taught in the church there for a whole year (cf. the apostles teaching in Jerusalem), and that prophets came down to Antioch from Jerusalem. Agabus, one of these prophets, predicted that a severe famine was coming (he also makes a prediction in 21:10–11). Philip, himself called an "evangelist," had seven virgin daughters who prophesied (21:8–9).[53] In 15:22 Judas and Silas are called "leaders among the brothers" and later they too are called prophets (15:32). Apparently the prophets were resident in churches but also would travel from time to time, sometimes giving messages about the future, or just encouraging and strengthening.[54]

Luke also mentions the role of elder several times. Until Acts 11:30, Luke uses the term to describe non-Christian community leaders. It would not be surprising if the early church copied this Jewish leadership role. In Acts 11:30, a gift of money is given to the elders of the church at Jerusalem, perhaps indicating their role of taking care of financial matters instead of the apostles.[55] Paul and Barnabas appoint elders over each assembly they have established on their first missionary journey (14:23).[56] Paul and Barnabas are also appointed to go to Jerusalem to see the apostles and elders there on the matter of circumcising Gentile believers (15:2, in Acts 6 only apostles are mentioned). Paul sends to Ephesus for the elders of the church there to meet him at Miletus (20:17), and in his speech he calls them overseers (20:28).[57] After his third mis-

---

53. This is the only use of the term "evangelist" in Acts. It describes well Philip's activities in 8:4, 12, 35, 40.

54. For further description of traveling prophets in the early church, and the problems they could cause, see *Did.* 11:3–12.

55. Barrett, *Acts*, 1:566. Luke's description of the church at Jerusalem implies that though there were several house churches in one city, the different communities made up one church with one group of elders. See also Acts 20:17; Malherbe, *Social Aspects of Early Christianity*, 70.

56. Though in reality, Luke elsewhere notes, it is the Holy Spirit who appoints elders (Acts 20:28). "The Holy Spirit is at work in the church choosing and preparing by his gifts those who are to be ministers" (Barrett, *Acts*, 2:974–75).

57. Fitzmyer, *Acts*, 679, says Luke "apparently saw no difference between their functions and regarded the titles as equal designations." See also Barrett, *Acts*, 2:975.

sionary journey, Paul goes to Jerusalem and sees James and "all" the elders (21:18). Luke's combination in church leadership of prophets and elders shows "that there is no essential incompatibility between a prophetic self-consciousness or a charismatic awareness, and ecclesiastical structure."[58]

Thus, Luke knew that the churches had various offices based on the needs of the church. The apostles served in Jerusalem, but even there the church also had elders. Luke's church hierarchy would, at least apparently, include apostles, elders, teachers, and prophets.

THE CHURCH AWAITS THE SECOND COMING

Lukan eschatology has been a subject of great debate in scholarship. Some think Luke anticipated an imminent return of Christ.[59] Others believe Luke had nearly abandoned any future eschatology and had replaced it with "the church age."[60] It is best to see an "inaugurated eschatology" in Luke. The church for Luke is already part of the messianic kingdom planned from long ago, but there are still events waiting to be fulfilled.

For Luke, the church is living in "the last days." These are the words Luke has added to the prophecy he quotes from Joel in Acts 2:17.[61] This phrase does not mean that the early Christians were now expecting the imminent end of the world. Rather, it means that the "future" time of prophecy had now arrived, the time of a decisive new era, the time of the messianic kingdom.[62]

Although the restoration of Israel and the time of the Messiah have begun, the church in Acts still awaits a final consummation. This is the part of Israel's restoration about which it was not for the disciples to know (Acts 1:7). Acts 1:11 shows that there still remains an expectation of a final End; it has not been entirely replaced by the "era of the Spirit." The bestowal of the Spirit is a present anticipation of the final

---

58. Johnson, *Acts*, 257.

59. Mattill, *Luke and the Last Things*.

60. Conzelmann, *Theology of St. Luke*.

61. Compare Luke's use of "in the last days" in Acts 2:17 to "then afterward" in Joel 2:28.

62. For more on the background of the phrase "in the last days" in the Old Testament, and Luke's intent to connect Joel's prophecy with Isa 2:2, see Goldman, "Contribution of Joel 2–3," 167–77.

consummation.[63] Jesus will come from heaven and restore everything, as promised by the prophets (Acts 3:21).[64] The parallel between Acts 2:38 and 3:19–20 indicates that the "times of refreshing" are connected with the gift of the Spirit. As in the Old Testament prophecies (Isa 32:15; 44:3–4; Ezek 36:26–27; 37:7–14; 39:29; Joel 2:28), the bestowal of the Spirit is part of a complex of events that bring refreshing for Israel. The restoration is ongoing and will end with the sending of the Messiah from heaven. In the meantime, Luke does not describe an inactive church that gazes at the skies waiting for Jesus to return, but rather one that through the Spirit engages in the mission he has already begun.

CONCLUSION

Luke's contribution to New Testament ecclesiology is unique in that he is the only writer to combine an account of Jesus' life and ministry with an account of the church that followed thereafter. What is noteworthy in these two accounts is that the church that Luke describes in Acts looks like the Jesus that was described in the Gospel. The most important aspects of the ecclesiology of Acts can be traced back to Luke's Gospel. Like Jesus, the church follows the leading of the Spirit, includes outcasts, helps the poor, and practices table fellowship. That is the best description of Luke's vision of what the church should be. One searches Luke's narrative in vain for detailed descriptions of worship practices and church organization. Rather, Luke describes the church as a community of believers in Jesus who continue what Jesus "began" to do and to teach—God's longtime kingdom purpose for human beings taking place on earth as it is in heaven.

---

63. "Luke sees the eschaton, expected by many first-century Jews, as having already occurred but as being still to occur. The End had happened in Calvary, Easter, and Pentecost; one need no longer fight for it, since it has already happened. At the same time, the End is yet to come, with the return of Jesus (Acts 1:11); history, including the history of Jesus' people as the renewed people of Israel's god, must continue, with all its ambiguities and puzzles" (Wright, *New Testament and the People of God*, 382).

64. The use of the plural in "times of refreshing" (3:20) and "times of universal restoration" (3:21, obscured in the NRSV) means that the refreshing and restoration are a process and not a single event.

FOR FURTHER STUDY

Blue, Bradley. "Acts and the House Church." In *The Book of Acts in Its Graeco-Roman Setting*, edited by David W. J. Gill and Conrad Gempf, 119–222. Grand Rapids: Eerdmans, 1994.

Giles, Kevin. "The Church." In *Dictionary of the Later New Testament and Its Developments*, edited by Ralph P. Martin and Peter H. Davids, 194–204. Downers Grove, IL: InterVarsity, 1997.

———. *What on Earth is the Church? An Exploration in New Testament Theology*. Downers Grove, IL: InterVarsity, 1995.

Hahn, Scott W. "Kingdom and Church in Luke-Acts: From Davidic Christology to Kingdom Ecclesiology." In *Reading Luke: Interpretation, Reflection, Formation*, edited by Craig Bartholomew, Joel B. Green, and Anthony C. Thiselton, 294–321. Grand Rapids: Zondervan, 2005.

Jervell, Jacob. *Luke and the People of God: A New Look at Luke-Acts*. Minneapolis: Augsburg, 1972.

Levison, John R. "Did the Spirit Withdraw from Israel? An Evaluation of the Earliest Jewish Data." *NTS* 43 (1997) 35–57.

Peterson, David. "The Worship of the New Community." In *Witness to the Gospel: The Theology of Acts*, edited by I. Howard Marshall and David Peterson, 373–95. Grand Rapids: Eerdmans, 1998.

Seccombe, David. "The New People of God." In *Witness to the Gospel: The Theology of Acts*, edited by I. Howard Marshall and David Peterson, 349–72. Grand Rapids: Eerdmans, 1998.

Thompson, Richard P. *Keeping the Church in Its Place: The Church as Narrative Character in Acts*. New York: T. & T. Clark, 2006.

Turner, Max. *Power from on High: The Spirit in Israel's Restoration and Witness in Luke-Acts*. Journal of Pentecostal Theology Supplement Series. Sheffield: Sheffield Academic Press, 1996.

———. "The Sabbath, Sunday, and the Law in Luke-Acts." In *From Sabbath to Lord's Day: A Biblical, Historical, and Theological Investigation*, edited by D. A. Carson, 100–57. Grand Rapids: Zondervan, 1982.

Wenham, David. "The Purpose of Luke-Acts: Israel's Story in the Context of the Roman Empire." In *Reading Luke: Interpretation, Reflection, Formation*, edited by Craig Bartholomew, Joel B. Green, and Anthony C. Thiselton, 79–103. Grand Rapids: Zondervan, 2005.

BIBLIOGRAPHY

Balch, David. "ΜΕΤΑΒΟΛΗ ΠΟΛΙΤΕΙΩΝ: Jesus as Founder of the Church in Luke-Acts: Form and Function." In *Contextualizing Acts: Lucan Narrative and Greco-Roman Discourse*, edited by Todd C. Penner and Caroline Vander Stichele, 139–88. Atlanta: SBL, 2003.

Barrett, C. K. *The Acts of the Apostles*. ICC. 2 vols. Edinburgh: T. & T. Clark, 1994.

Bauckham, Richard. "James and the Gentiles (Acts 15:12–21)." In *History, Literature, and Society in the Book of Acts*, edited by Ben Witherington III, 154–84. Cambridge: Cambridge University Press, 1996.

Béchard, Dean Philip. "The Disputed Case against Paul: A Redaction-Critical Analysis of Acts 21:27—22:29." *CBQ* 65 (2003) 232–50.

Black, Robert Allen. "Women in the Gospel of Luke." In *Essays on Women in Earliest Christianity*, edited by Carroll D. Osburn, 445–68. Joplin, MO: College, 1993.

Blomberg, Craig. "The Law in Luke-Acts." *JSNT* 22 (1984) 53–80.

———. *Neither Poverty nor Riches*. NSBT. Downers Grove, IL: InterVarsity, 1999.

Bock, Darrell L. *Acts*. BECNT. Grand Rapids: Baker, 2007.

Brown, Raymond E. *The Churches That the Apostles Left Behind*. New York: Paulist, 1984.

Bruce, F. F. *The Book of Acts*. NICNT. Grand Rapids: Eerdmans, 1988.

———. "Eschatology in Acts." In *Eschatology and the New Testament: Essays in Honor of George Raymond Beasley-Murray*, edited by W. Hulitt Gloer, 51–63. Peabody, MA: Hendrickson, 1988.

Chance, J. B. *Jerusalem, the Temple, and the New Age in Luke-Acts*. Macon, GA: Mercer, 1988.

Clark, Andrew C. "The Role of the Apostles." In *Witness to the Gospel: The Theology of Acts*, edited by I. Howard Marshall and David Peterson, 169–90. Grand Rapids: Eerdmans, 1998.

Conzelmann, Hans. *The Theology of St. Luke*. Translated by Geoffrey Buswell. Philadelphia: Fortress, 1961.

Ferguson, Everett. *Early Christians Speak: Faith and Life in the First Three Centuries*. Rev. ed. Abilene, TX: Abilene Christian University Press, 1981.

———. *The Church of Christ: A Biblical Ecclesiology for Today*. Grand Rapids: Eerdmans, 1996.

Fitzmyer, Joseph A. *The Acts of the Apostles*. AB. New York: Doubleday, 1997.

———. *The Gospel according to Luke*. 2 vols. AB. New York: Doubleday, 1981.

Goldman, George II. "The Contribution of Joel 2–3 to the Restoration of Israel Theme in Acts." PhD diss. Trinity Evangelical Divinity School, 2002.

Hahn, Scott W. "Kingdom and Church in Luke-Acts: From Davidic Christology to Kingdom Ecclesiology." In *Reading Luke: Interpretation, Reflection, Formation*, edited by Craig Bartholomew, Joel B. Green, and Anthony C. Thiselton, 294–326. Grand Rapids: Zondervan, 2005.

Hicks, John Mark. *Come to the Table: Revisioning the Lord's Supper*. Orange, CA: New Leaf, 2002.

Jeremias, Joachim. *The Eucharistic Words of Jesus*. Philadelphia: Fortress, 1977.

Jervell, Jacob. *Die Apostelgeschichte*. KEK. Göttingen: Vandenhoeck & Ruprecht, 1998.

———. *Luke and the People of God: A New Look at Luke-Acts*. Minneapolis: Augsburg, 1972.

Johnson, Luke Timothy. *The Acts of the Apostles*. SP. Collegeville, MN: Liturgical, 1992.

Ladd, George Eldon. *A Theology of the New Testament*. Rev. ed. Grand Rapids: Eerdmans, 1993.

Maddox, Robert. *The Purpose of Luke-Acts*. Göttingen: Vandenhoeck & Ruprecht, 1982.

Malherbe, Abraham J. *Social Aspects of Early Christianity*. 2nd ed. Philadelphia: Fortress, 1983.

Marshall, I. Howard. *The Acts of the Apostles: An Introduction and Commentary*. TNTC. Grand Rapids: Eerdmans, 1980.

Mattill, A. J. Jr. *Luke and the Last Things: A Perspective for the Understanding of Lukan Thought*. Dillsboro, NC: Western North Carolina Press, 1979.

Menoud, Philippe H. "The Additions to the Twelve Apostles according to the Book of Acts." Translated by Eunice M. Paul. In *Jesus Christ and the Faith: A Collection of Studies*, 133–48. Pittsburgh: Pickwick, 1978.

Mitchell, Alan C. "The Social Function of Friendship in Acts 2:44–47 and 4:32–37." *JBL* 111 (1992) 255–72.

Sterling, Gregory E. "'Athletes of Virtue': An Analysis of the Summaries in Acts (2:41–47; 4:32–35; 5:12–16)." *JBL* 113 (1994) 679–96.

Stott, John. *The Spirit, the Church, and the World: The Message of Acts*. Downers Grove, IL: InterVarsity, 1990.

Strange, W. A. "The Jesus-Tradition in Acts." *NTS* 46 (2000) 59–74.

Tannehill, Robert C. "Israel in Luke-Acts: A Tragic Story." *JBL* 104 (1985) 69–85.

———. *The Narrative Unity of Luke-Acts: A Literary Interpretation*. 2 vols. Minneapolis: Fortress, 1990.

Thompson, Richard P. *Keeping the Church in Its Place: The Church as Narrative Character in Acts*. New York: T. & T. Clark, 2006.

Turner, Max. *The Holy Spirit and Spiritual Gifts*. Peabody, MA: Hendrickson, 1996.

———. *Power from on High: The Spirit in Israel's Restoration and Witness in Luke-Acts*. Journal of Pentecostal Theology Supplement Series. Sheffield: Sheffield Academic Press, 1996.

Wenham, David. "The Purpose of Luke-Acts: Israel's Story in the Context of the Roman Empire." In *Reading Luke: Interpretation, Reflection, Formation*, edited by Craig Bartholomew, Joel B. Green, and Anthony C. Thiselton. Grand Rapids: Zondervan, 2005.

Wright, N. T. *The New Testament and the People of God*. Minneapolis: Fortress, 1992.

4

The Church in the Gospel and Epistles of John

T HE GOSPEL OF JOHN and the three Johannine Epistles have an ecclesiology, that is, a doctrine of the church. But that doctrine is not to
be located through looking up conventional terms. We must therefore
turn to other constructs and concepts.

The word "church" (used to translate *ekklēsia*) occurs 76 times in
the New Revised Standard Version, but in the Johannine writings the
word only occurs in 3 John 2. The word only occurs three times in the
Synoptic Gospels (i.e., Matthew, Mark, and Luke), all three in the Gospel
of Matthew: once at 16:18 and twice at 18:17. In the Synoptic Gospels
the church is often anticipated when referring to either the kingdom of
God or the kingdom of heaven. In these three Gospels these phrases
are employed 119 times, especially in the kingdom parables. The word
kingdom occurs five times in the Gospel of John and not at all in the
epistles. Jesus discussed the kingdom with Nicodemus. His statements
likely envision entering both into the church and the eternal kingdom.
"Jesus answered him, 'Very truly, I tell you, no one can see the kingdom of God without being born from above'" (John 3:3). Then again
in John 3:5 we read, "Jesus answered, 'Very truly, I tell you, no one can
enter the kingdom of God without being born of water and Spirit.'" The
three additional instances are found in John 18:36: "Jesus answered, 'My
kingdom is not from this world. If my kingdom were from this world,
my followers would be fighting to keep me from being handed over to

the Jews. But as it is, my kingdom is not from here.'" Jesus' references to kingdom in these statements seem to anticipate both the church and the eternal kingdom.[1]

In the Gospel of John the concept of the church is to be found in the phrase "children of God" (1:12; 11:52), and in the images of a "flock" (10:12, 16) and "branches" (15:5, 6). In the Johannine epistles the focus is upon the leaders and members of the churches (addressed as "children," "fathers," and "*adelphoi*") and upon the central role of the apostolic message as contrasted with a deviant message. Collectively, the Johannine materials provide no information about the qualifications of the leaders or officers, the nature of the organization, or the functions of the church. Rather the emphasis is placed upon abiding/remaining/dwelling in Jesus (John 15:4–7; 1 John 2:24, 27), his teachings (John 15:7), and his love (John 15:9, 10), and the role of the Holy Spirit in teaching (John 14:26; 1 John 2:20, 27). It is clear that the church is dependent upon its shepherd who is none other than Jesus Christ (John 10:11, 14, 16). He is the vine though whom the branches, that is, the people of God, are nourished (John 15:1–5). The church is dependent for its message and its works upon the *paraklētos* (John 14:16, 26; 15:26; 16:7), that is, the Holy Spirit.[2]

In the Johannine writings, the church consists of those communities of faith that preserve the words and works of Jesus Christ propounded from the beginning. As John 12:16 says, "His disciples did not understand these things at first; but when Jesus was glorified, then they remembered that these things had been written of him and had been done to him." Later Jesus urges his disciples to be his witnesses, saying, "You also are to testify because you have been with me from the beginning" (John 15:27). The author of 1 John admonishes the recipients, "Let what you heard from the beginning abide in you. If what you heard from the beginning abides in you, then you will abide in the Son and in the Father" (1 John 2:24). Central to what they had heard was that God

---

1. Because of a paucity of specific comments in the Gospel of John on the church, some scholars have concluded that John was little interested the church as an institution. This is the claim of Bultmann, *Theology of the New Testament*, 2:3–14, and Schweizer, "Concept of the Church." An opposing view is expressed by the major British commentator C. K. Barrett (*John*, 92–96). John P. Meier discusses the absence in a short essay and finds the presence of the church in the sheepfold and the vine and branches analogies (Meier, "Absence and Presence of the Church").

2. Schnelle, "Johanneische Ekklesiologie," gives special emphasis to the sending of the Son in mission, the Paraclete, the disciples, and the sacraments.

reaches out in love to human beings and expects them to reach out in love to their fellows. The love of God for the believers in the Son and their love for him trump any discussion of the ecclesiastical structure of the church, qualifications of leaders, or practical lists of rules for life. True doctrine resides in the Son coming in the flesh to exhibit his oneness with humankind. The Holy Spirit provides the assurance that the words and works of the Son are remembered. Jesus tells his disciples, "But the Advocate, the Holy Spirit, whom the Father will send in my name, will teach you everything, and remind you of all that I have said to you" (John 14:26). The author of 1 John makes a similar promise when he writes, "As for you, the anointing that you received from him abides in you, and so you do not need anyone to teach you. But as his anointing teaches you about all things, and is true and is not a lie, and just as it has taught you, abide in him" (1 John 2:27). In neither the Gospel nor the Epistles is there the proposal of Irenaeus that true doctrine must be handed down from teacher to student, that is, from John to Polycarp, to Ignatius, to Irenaeus. The guarantee is rather the Holy Spirit refreshing the memory.[3]

JOHN'S ECCLESIOLOGY AND THE CENTRAL MESSAGE OF THE JOHANNINE LITERATURE

Before looking at specific materials in the Gospel and the letters it is important to locate the church in the context of the theological centers of the Johannine writings. John has a definite grounding for the church in his perception of God, as imbedded in his Christology and pneumatology. In this regard, the theology of the church commences from a somewhat different foundation than that of the rest of the New Testament. In a recent essay on the theology of the Gospel of John, I wrote:

> After years of reflecting upon and teaching the theology of the Gospel of John, I have come to believe that a focal point permeates the Gospel and is introduced in the prologue, "In the beginning was the Word" (1:1). The importance of Jesus' words and the words of the disciples persists all the way through the Gospel into the epilogue in which Peter is told to "feed the sheep." It is through the word that the Son who is the Word brings eternal

---

3. Irenaeus, *Heresies* 4.20.3.

life to those who believe through his word and by the word of his "feeding" disciples.[4]

In the Epistles Christ is likely identified as the word of life (1 John 1:1), but otherwise "word" refers to his words (1 John 1:10; 2:5, 7, 14; 3:18).

These words and works of Jesus, sometimes identified as signs, go hand in hand to bring individuals to belief:

> Now Jesus did many other signs in the presence of his disciples, which are not written in this book. But these are written so that you may come to believe that Jesus is the Messiah, the Son of God, and that through believing you may have life in his name. (John 20:30–31)

A traditional view of the signs in the Gospel of John is that they number seven. This is based in part on the fact that the first two are numbered. These are as follows:

1. Turning water to wine, 2:11; first sign, in Cana

2. Healing the official's son, 4:54; second sign, in Cana

3. Healing at the pool, 5:1–15

4. Feeding the 5,000, 6:1–13

5. Walking on water, 6:16–21

6. Healing the blind man, 9:1–34

7. Raising Lazarus, 11:38–44.

To these Raymond Brown argues that an eighth sign must be added:

8. 8. The 153 fish, 21:1–14.[5]

I would argue, however, that the greatest sign is that Jesus was raised from the dead (John 20:1–18). Jesus himself identified his resurrection as a sign (John 2:18–22). In fact, I think it is clear that sometimes the words Jesus spoke were signs, for example, when he told Nathanael he saw him under the fig tree.[6]

---

4. Olbricht, "Word as Sign," 83. I have published two books on the Johannine writings: *Lifted Up*, and *Life Together*.

5. Brown, *Gospel according to John*, 1:525–32.

6. Olbricht, "Word as Sign," 84–85. I have worked out this point in some detail in Olbricht, "Theology of the Signs."

> When Jesus saw Nathanael coming toward him, he said of him, "Here is truly an Israelite in whom there is no deceit!" Nathanael asked him, "Where did you get to know me?" Jesus answered, "I saw you under the fig tree before Philip called you." Nathanael replied, "Rabbi, you are the Son of God! You are the King of Israel!" (John 1:47–49)

The story of the woman at the well in Samaria is another case of Jesus amazing people with what he knew about them. His prescience becomes a sign pointing to a reality beyond the immediate concrete entity at hand. Jesus began his conversation with the woman by making a comment on the water in Jacob's well. Beginning with a physical entity Jesus often redirected those with whom he came in contact to an analogically related heavenly reality. He offered the woman living water that would gush up to eternal life (John 4:14). The woman was not clear as to what that was all about, but when Jesus brought up her many husbands she was convinced that he was no ordinary Jew. She asked herself, then her own people, whether he might be the Messiah (John 4:25, 29). She served as a catalyst for their coming to faith (4:39).

THE FAMILY CREATED BY THE WORD

Those who came to believe in Jesus, in his words and his signs, became a part of the family of God, that is, the flock, or the church. Early on the Gospel John declares, "But to all who received him, who believed in his name, he gave power to become children of God . . ." (John 1:12). This same point is made in 1 John 5:1, "Everyone who believes that Jesus is the Christ has been born of God, and everyone who loves the parent loves the child." It is also implied in Jesus' comment to Nicodemus:

> Jesus answered, "Very truly, I tell you, no one can enter the kingdom of God without being born of water and Spirit. What is born of the flesh is flesh, and what is born of the Spirit is spirit. Do not be astonished that I said to you, 'You must be born from above.'" (John 3:5–7)

In my essay on the theology of John, I observed in respect to this foundational declaration that

> Jesus himself is the Word. His words and works declare that he came from God and is returning to God. Everything about the Son of Man discloses who he is and the character of his ministry

in the world. It is not surprising therefore that from John 1 to John 21 Jesus is placarded as the *Logos*, the revelatory word of God.[7]

It is through the Word—the Son—that the Father, Son, and Spirit reach out to humankind and create a community of faith. The desire of God to communicate with humankind through Christ is implied in various ways in the Gospel, and it is explicit in 1 John 1. The church in the Johannine writings is therefore a foundational society created by God who himself is community and creates a community of humans in communication and fellowship with the Son and the Spirit and with one another. The church exists because God is a God of love who desires fellowship.

First John was written to the members of the churches in the region around Ephesus after the Gospel of John. A crisis arose in these churches because of certain members who left (1 John 2:18, 19). Those departing claimed special insights regarding God and Christ as well as maintaining that they exercised a superior purity of life. They declared that God held himself and his Son apart from the material world. John wrote this letter, not so much to denounce the defectors and call them to repentance, but to bolster those who remained. Rather than retrenching into an inferiority complex, the loyal should exhibit the utmost confidence in the original message they received. The writer admonishes them, "Let what you heard from the beginning abide in you. If what you heard from the beginning abides in you, then you will abide in the Son and in the Father. And this is what he has promised us, eternal life" (1 John 2:24–25).[8]

The beginning of the epistle presupposes a God who reaches out in fellowship to the universe he has created and especially the humans made in his image. He has done this in a new and unique manner through the "word of life" (1 John 1:1)—a word of life heard, seen, and touched; therefore revealed. The Father and the "word of life" shared eternal life (1 John 1:2) and then revealed it to those first believers who saw and heard. As a result, the first believers were likewise incorporated into eternal life

7. Olbricht, "Word as Sign," 86.

8. Raymond Brown traces the Johannine community from the Gospel through the Epistles (Brown, *Community*). One can learn much from Brown's observations. I think, however, that the Johannine churches were less isolated from the other early churches than Brown supposes.

because they shared *koinōnia* with "the Father and with his Son Jesus Christ" (1 John 1:3). The "word of life" is therefore the Word who was in the beginning with God and was God (John 1:1)—Jesus Christ, the only begotten Son of God (John 3:16). God himself does not hold his creation at arm's length. Rather, he embraces it. The fundamental essence of God is *koinōnia*. God is a God who seeks fellowship.[9]

The first believers were drawn into the *koinōnia* with God through the "word of life." These disciples in turn reached out to extend this *koinōnia* to others, "so that you also may have fellowship with us . . . (1 John 1:3). Not only do the believers to whom this letter was written have fellowship with God, just as importantly they also have fellowship with one another. "But if we walk in the light as he himself is in the light, we have fellowship with one another . . ." (1 John 1:7). They form communities of faith strongly bonded in love. "God is love, and those who abide in love abide in God, and God abides in them. Love has been perfected among us in this . . ." (1 John 4:16, 17). The *koinōnia* and *agapē* of God and his Son are the fountainheads of fellowship in 1 John.

LOVE AS THE GATHERING POWER

The love of God for the Son and the love of both for those who believe is also fundamental. Because God is love, his children should love one another in word and deed. They manifest such love in fellowship (*koinōnia*), that is, in the church. The love (*agapē*) of God and of Christ is declared many places in the Johannine documents. Early in the Gospel, John declares, "For God so loved the world that he gave his only Son, so that everyone who believes in him may not perish but may have eternal life" (John 3:16). Later Jesus affirmed, "As the Father has loved me, so I have loved you; abide in my love" (John 15:9). Later, in chapter 17, Jesus stated,

> The glory that you have given me I have given them, so that they may be one, as we are one, I in them and you in me, that they may become completely one, so that the world may know that you have sent me and have loved them even as you have loved me. Father, I desire that those also, whom you have given me, may be with me where I am, to see my glory, which you have given me

9. I find the commentary of David Rensberger especially helpful (Rensberger, *1 John, 2 John, 3 John*).

because you loved me before the foundation of the world. (John 17:22–24)

In 1 John the author states:

Whoever does not love does not know God, for God is love. God's love was revealed among us in this way: God sent his only Son into the world so that we might live through him. In this is love, not that we loved God but that he loved us and sent his Son to be the atoning sacrifice for our sins. Beloved, since God loved us so much, we also ought to love one another. No one has ever seen God; if we love one another, God lives in us, and his love is perfected in us. (1 John 4:8–12)

The love of God and Christ was to be shared with those who believed and who comprised the church.

I give you a new commandment, that you love one another. Just as I have loved you, you also should love one another. By this everyone will know that you are my disciples, if you have love for one another. (John 13:34–35)

This is my commandment, that you love one another as I have loved you. No one has greater love than this, to lay down one's life for one's friends . . . (John 15:12–13)

I am giving you these commands so that you may love one another. (John 15:17)

The love of believers for one another is further affirmed in the Epistles:

Everyone who believes that Jesus is the Christ has been born of God, and everyone who loves the parent loves the child. By this we know that we love the children of God, when we love God and obey his commandments. For the love of God is this, that we obey his commandments. And his commandments are not burdensome. (1 John 5:1–3)

The new love commandment in the Gospel is repeated in 2 John:

But now, dear lady, I ask you, not as though I were writing you a new commandment, but one we have had from the beginning, let us love one another. And this is love, that we walk according to his commandments; this is the commandment just as you have heard it from the beginning—you must walk in it. (2 John 5–6)

The love of God in the death of Christ elicited overt acts of love on the part of believers for those within their community of faith:

> We know love by this, that he laid down his life for us—and we ought to lay down our lives for one another. How does God's love abide in anyone who has the world's goods and sees a brother or sister in need and yet refuses help? (1 John 3:16–17)

THE COMMUNITY OF THE DISCIPLES

The footings for the church were poured in the call of the disciples. Jesus attracted certain disciples of John the Baptist as he commenced his ministry and added to these (John 1:29–51; 4:1–3). The disciples play as prominent a role in John, or even more so, as in the other Gospels.[10] Jesus never showed up without his disciples present. After his resurrection he appeared only when the disciples were together. They, with Jesus present, constantly displayed *koinōnia*. As they scattered in later years they gathered together communities of believers just as Jesus had done. Jesus obviously intended for his disciples to plant churches wherever they went.

When Jesus attended the wedding in Cana his disciples were there too. As it says, "Jesus and his disciples had also been invited to the wedding" (John 2:2). They accompanied him to Jerusalem (John 2:22). He spent time with them in private as well as public: "After this Jesus and his disciples went into the Judean countryside, and he spent some time there with them and baptized" (John 3:22). It was they who did the baptizing, not Jesus: "Now when Jesus learned that the Pharisees had heard, 'Jesus is making and baptizing more disciples than John'—although it was not Jesus himself but his disciples who baptized—" (John 4:1–2). The time came when several disciples abandoned Jesus because of his teaching about his body and blood, but a number continued.

> Because of this many of his disciples turned back and no longer went about with him. So Jesus asked the twelve, "Do you also wish to go away?" Simon Peter answered him, "Lord, to whom can we go? You have the words of eternal life. We have come to believe and know that you are the Holy One of God." (John 6:66–69)

---

10. Schnackenburg, *John*, 203–17, especially emphasizes the role of the disciples in obtaining a perspective on ecclesiology in the Gospel.

As Jesus anticipated his departure he spent some of his last hours with the disciples. In his remarks to them it is clear that he anticipated that they would continue in fellowship with one another into the distant future. They were to wash one another's feet.

> After he had washed their feet, had put on his robe, and had re-
> turned to the table, he said to them, "Do you know what I have
> done to you? You call me Teacher and Lord—and you are right,
> for that is what I am. So if I, your Lord and Teacher, have washed
> your feet, you also ought to wash one another's feet. (John
> 13:12–14)

The disciples are prominent in the story of Jesus' closing days and after Jesus rose from the grave. The night Judas betrayed Jesus by iden- tifying him with a kiss, the disciples were alone with Jesus in a garden across the Kidron valley. Again after the death of Jesus the unbelievable occurred when Mary Magdalene saw Jesus alive. The disciples, astound- ed but hopeful, gathered in a room with the doors locked. Suddenly Jesus appeared among them and breathed upon them the Holy Spirit (John 20:19–23).

According to John, the final appearance of Jesus to the disciples was by the Sea of Tiberias after the large catch of 153 fish. Jesus employed this occasion to lay out procedures for the disciples. In the future there would be a flock of believers to feed. Apparently that of which Jesus spoke was the larger church made up of individual congregations. Peter was charged three times that if he loved Christ he was to feed the lambs, tend the flock, and feed Christ's sheep (John 21:15–17). The feeding may imply giving more than the words of the head shepherd, but certainly words are involved. In the section on the sheepfold, as we shall see, Jesus declares, "I have other sheep that do not belong to this fold. I must bring them also, and they will listen to my voice. So there will be one flock, one shepherd" (John 10:16). In 1 John also, the communities of faith existed because the disciples had shared the efforts of God and his Son:

> we declare to you what we have seen and heard so that you also
> may have fellowship with us; and truly our fellowship is with the
> Father and with his Son Jesus Christ. We are writing these things
> so that our joy may be complete." (1 John 1:3–4)

The efforts of Jesus of Nazareth are not designated for individual- ization and dissolution. Those who believe are to become the people of

God, the living church of the Lord Jesus Christ. The ideal leaders among the people of God are not so much administrators but teachers.[11]

THE FLOCK OF GOD

In chapter 10 Jesus first speaks of a sheepfold. Those who become his followers comprise a flock. Jesus envisioned what later was called the church, though only three times is the word church found in the Johannine writings, all in 3 John (verses 6 and 9). To enter the sheepfold one must enter by the gate, not climb in at some other point. The person who enters at some other location is "a thief and a bandit" (John 10:1). The entry into the church is therefore mandated. According to John 3:5, the entry comes about because of a birth from above accompanied by baptism.

> Jesus answered him, "Very truly, I tell you, no one can see the kingdom of God without being born from above." Nicodemus said to him, "How can anyone be born after having grown old? Can one enter a second time into the mother's womb and be born?" Jesus answered, "Very truly, I tell you, no one can enter the kingdom of God without being born of water and Spirit. (John 3:3–5)

This birth comes about, not by any human means. It is of God:

> But to all who received him, who believed in his name, he gave power to become children of God, who were born, not of blood or of the will of the flesh or of the will of man, but of God. (John 1:12–13)

The shepherd, no doubt Jesus himself, enters first (John 10:2). The gatekeeper opens the gate for him, apparently God the Father. The sheep hear the voice of the shepherd entreating them to enter. They recognize his voice as the Son. The shepherd knows his sheep and he calls them by name and leads them out to the succulent pastures. These are his own, those God has given him, and he goes ahead of them (John 10:4). The sheep follow him because they know his words and voice. They

---

11. Schneiders, "Raising of the New Temple," 355, writes, "It presents the Johannine understanding of the Church not as an institution replacing the departed Jesus, nor even as his commissioned representative or agent, but as the ongoing presence and action of Jesus in the world though his corporate body, the ecclesial community, which will salvifically reveal him as he revealed God."

have come to faith because of the proclamation of the signs: "But these are written so that you may come to believe that Jesus is the Messiah, the Son of God, and that through believing you may have life in his name" (John 20:31). The sheep will not follow the voice of strangers. The strange voices in contrast envision those who have departed from the churches of 1 John. They have interjected an alternate teaching from that of the apostolic voice.

> They are from the world; therefore what they say is from the world, and the world listens to them. We are from God. Whoever knows God listens to us, and whoever is not from God does not listen to us. From this we know the spirit of truth and the spirit of error. (1 John 4:5–6)

These first disciples did not fathom the ramifications of these statements (John 10:6) but they would come to do so.

Jesus thereupon proceeded to reiterate his statements. He declared that he was the gate for the sheep and those who came before him were thieves and bandits, but the sheep did not listen to them. Those who enter by Jesus will be saved. They are the ones who enter the kingdom by water and the Spirit. The classical hymn expresses the point well!

> The church's one foundation is Jesus Christ her Lord.
> She is the new creation by water and the word.
> From heaven he came and sought her to be his holy bride.
> With his own blood he bought her and for his life he died.[12]

Jesus came that those in the church will have "life, and have it abundantly" (John 10:10). The true shepherd protects the sheep with his very life: "I am the good shepherd. The good shepherd lays down his life for the sheep" (John 10:11). The false shepherd runs away when he observes the wolf approaching. The wolf thereupon proceeds to scatter the sheep. Compare the words of 1 John:

> As you have heard that antichrist is coming, so now many antichrists have come. From this we know that it is the last hour. They went out from us, but they did not belong to us; for if they had belonged to us, they would have remained with us. But by going out they made it plain that none of them belongs to us. (1 John 2:18–19)

---

12. Stone, "The Church's One Foundation."

Jesus declared that he would lay down his life for his sheep anticipating his death on the cross:

> For God so loved the world that he gave his only Son, so that everyone who believes in him may not perish but may have eternal life. (John 3:16)

Jesus further explained that his sheep, that is, his communities of faith, the church, would not be limited to Israel. Rather his flock would be worldwide: "I have other sheep that do not belong to this fold. I must bring them also, and they will listen to my voice. So there will be one flock, one shepherd" (John 10:16). Jesus lays down his life for all these others also as declared in John 3:16.

The launching of the Gentile mission is anticipated when Greeks seek out Jesus:[13] "Now among those who went up to worship at the festival were some Greeks. They came to Philip, who was from Bethsaida in Galilee, and said to him, 'Sir, we wish to see Jesus'" (John 12:20–21). When that occurred Jesus declared, "The hour has come for the Son of Man to be glorified" (John 12:23).

His glorification came when he was lifted up on the cross: "'Father, glorify your name.' Then a voice came from heaven, 'I have glorified it, and I will glorify it again' . . . 'And I, when I am lifted up from the earth, will draw all people to myself'" (John 12:28–32).[14] All are to be welcomed into the church of the living God. Third John carries on this theme:

> I have written something to the church; but Diotrephes, who likes to put himself first, does not acknowledge our authority. So if I come, I will call attention to what he is doing in spreading false charges against us. And not content with those charges, he refuses to welcome the friends, and even prevents those who want to do so and expels them from the church. (3 John 9–10)

From this shepherd and sheepfold analogy is it clear that the church is that community of faith that has come about because Jesus gave his life and because it listens to his voice alone. The leadership of the church is clearly spelled out. The first disciples derive their leadership from him. The only powers they possess are those he gave. The only message that

---

13. See especially Brown, *Gospel according to John*, 1:469–71.

14. I am impressed by several observations of O'Day, "John," e.g., "The cross thus makes sense of the double meaning of *anōthen*: To be born *from above* is to be born *again* through the lifting up of Jesus on the cross" (p. 552).

the church is to hear is that of the Lord Jesus Christ and the message given by those disciples reminded by the Holy Spirit of what he taught. The entry into the sheepfold, the church, is by water and by word.

THE CONTINUED RELATIONSHIP OF THE DISCIPLES

It is clear that Jesus anticipated that his disciples would maintain a close relationship with each other after his departure. In fact, it was to be a relationship that would last because it was to be a serving, loving relationship. Chapter 13 commences with the observation that "Jesus knew that his hour had come to depart from the world and go to the Father" (John 13:1). He gathered the disciples for a last meal in which he proceeded to wash their feet. The surprise is not that feet were washed. The washing of feet was an ingrained social custom. The surprise was who it was that washed the feet. He was one who "had come from God and was going to God" (John 13:3). It was he who should have been the recipient of foot washing, but here he was washing the feet of the disciples. Jesus' point was that in the future they would stay together, they would work together. They would form the backbone of the church. They would give deference to one another by washing each other's feet just as Jesus had washed theirs:

> So if I, your Lord and Teacher, have washed your feet, you also ought to wash one another's feet. For I have set you an example, that you also should do as I have done to you. Very truly, I tell you, servants are not greater than their master, nor are messengers greater than the one who sent them. (John 13:14–16)

These disciples were not to disband, for they were to be sent out into the world to bring others into the "sheepfold," that is, the church.

Jesus made it plain that upon his departure the disciples would not be able to follow, but we soon learn that they would not simply be left to their own devices. They could not follow Jesus out of the world (John 13:33). They were to remain with each other, bound together by love:

> I give you a new commandment, that you love one another. Just as I have loved you, you also should love one another. By this everyone will know that you are my disciples, if you have love for one another." (John 13:34–35)

THE HOLY SPIRIT ASSISTS THE GROWING
COMMUNITY OF DISCIPLES

Jesus clearly envisioned that his disciples would remain in community after his departure. Though he was leaving they would not be left alone to fend for themselves. The God-given presence of the Spirit would take his place forever:

> And I will ask the Father, and he will give you another Advocate, to be with you forever. This is the Spirit of truth, whom the world cannot receive, because it neither sees him nor knows him. You know him, because he abides with you, and he will be in you. (John 14:16–17)

They would not be without a place in the family of God: "I will not leave you orphaned; I am coming to you. In a little while the world will no longer see me, but you will see me; because I live, you also will live" (John 14:18–19).

Not only will the Advocate (*paraklētos*) be with them when Jesus departs, so also will the Father and the Son. They will make their home with those who believe: "Jesus answered him, 'Those who love me will keep my word, and my Father will love them, and we will come to them and make our home with them'" (John 14:23). It is the Holy Spirit who will remind the disciples of the words and works of Jesus. The Father will send the Spirit in the name of the Son: "But the Advocate, the Holy Spirit, whom the Father will send in my name, will teach you everything, and remind you of all that I have said to you" (John 14:26). The Advocate is present with the disciples so that they testify to the signs that Jesus did and thereby bring new persons into the community of faith, that is, the church:

> When the Advocate comes, whom I will send to you from the Father, the Spirit of truth who comes from the Father, he will testify on my behalf. You also are to testify because you have been with me from the beginning. (John 15:26–27)

The statement of Jesus to Thomas after he confessed that Jesus is the risen Lord also re-enforces the view that many additional persons would come to faith: "Thomas answered him, 'My Lord and my God!' Jesus said to him, 'Have you believed because you have seen me? Blessed are those who have not seen and yet have come to believe'" (John 20:28–29).[15] The Advocate will prove the world wrong about "sin and righteousness and judgment" (John 16:8). The Spirit will guide the disciples into all truth so that the church will have the authentic instruction:

> When the Spirit of truth comes, he will guide you into all the truth; for he will not speak on his own, but will speak whatever he hears, and he will declare to you the things that are to come. He will glorify me, because he will take what is mine and declare it to you. (John 16:13–14)

Jesus breathed the Spirit on the disciples after his resurrection and gave them the privilege of forgiving sins: "When he had said this, he breathed on them and said to them, 'Receive the Holy Spirit. If you forgive the sins of any, they are forgiven them; if you retain the sins of any, they are retained'" (John 20:22–23). In 1 John it is the fellowship of believers that provides the grounds for forgiveness of sins. We will come back to that later.

When one looks at 1 John it is clear that the work of the Spirit was not just with the first disciples, but with all those who later came to faith: "But you have been anointed by the Holy One, and all of you have knowledge" (1 John 2:20). They have abiding in them that which was from the beginning, that is, the words and works of Jesus (1 John 2:24). These second- and third-generation Christians who comprise the church also know the truth because of the Spirit:

> As for you, the anointing that you received from him abides in you, and so you do not need anyone to teach you. But as his anointing teaches you about all things, and is true and is not a lie, and just as it has taught you, abide in him. (1 John 2:27)

But they also have one of the first disciples among them, from whom they can hear the truth: "We are from God. Whoever knows God listens to us, and whoever is not from God does not listen to us. From this we know the spirit of truth and the spirit of error" (1 John 4:6).

THE VINE AND THE BRANCHES

Jesus employed the powerful analogy of the vine and the branches to depict the communities of faith that would result from the works of

---

15. On believing as the result of the "preaching of the word," see Beasley-Murray, *John*, 386.

the disciples. The Father "owns" a vineyard. Jesus is the true vine (John 15:1). The believers or the churches are the branches. They are sustained by their connection with the vine. The church is organically dependent upon Jesus Christ for its nourishment. The Father trims away the dead branches and prunes the healthy ones so that more fruit will be produced: "You have already been cleansed by the word that I have spoken to you" (John 15:3). The church is disciplined. This disciplining comes about as a result of the declarations of the Word:

> The law indeed was given through Moses; grace and truth came through Jesus Christ. No one has ever seen God. It is God the only Son, who is close to the Father's heart, who has made him known." (John 1:17–18)

The branches, however, must never lose their connection with the vine if they are to produce fruit: "Those who abide in me and I in them bear much fruit, because apart from me you can do nothing" (John 15:5).

The church consists of the branches connected to the vine, who is Jesus Christ. It is nothing apart from him:

> Whoever does not abide in me is thrown away like a branch and withers; such branches are gathered, thrown into the fire, and burned. If you abide in me, and my words abide in you, ask for whatever you wish, and it will be done for you. (John 15:6–7)

The church, because it is connected to Jesus Christ, is a community of love. It is comprised of the friends of Christ:

> This is my commandment, that you love one another as I have loved you. No one has greater love than this, to lay down one's life for one's friends. You are my friends if you do what I command you. I do not call you servants any longer, because the servant does not know what the master is doing; but I have called you friends, because I have made known to you everything that I have heard from my Father. (John 15:12–15)

The same connection of God, Christ, and the church is made in 1 John, in which the church is the body that is in fellowship with God and Christ and the members have fellowship with one another. Whereas in John 20:23 it is the disciples (the first believers) who are to dispense the forgiveness of sins, in 1 John the privilege is extended to all those who come together in fellowship. Since it was the ten (John 20:23) who received the Spirit, we might assume that they were the ones to administer forgiveness. But 1 John suggests that this privilege resides with the whole church. The church in fellowship is the place where forgiveness of sins occurs, although, of course, the real ground is the blood of Jesus Christ:

> If we say that we have fellowship with him while we are walking in darkness, we lie and do not do what is true; but if we walk in the light as he himself is in the light, we have fellowship with one another, and the blood of Jesus his Son cleanses us from all sin. (1 John 1:6–7)

It is for this reason that the sin unto death may well be leaving the fellowship of the body of Christ. This is a high doctrine of the church. The church in its fellowship provides the context for forgiveness. Those who have departed no longer are in touch with the place where sins are forgiven (1 John 2:18):[16]

> If you see your brother or sister committing what is not a mortal sin, you will ask, and God will give life to such a one—to those whose sin is not mortal. There is sin that is mortal; I do not say that you should pray about that. All wrongdoing is sin, but there is sin that is not mortal. (1 John 5:16–17)

One is not to pray that those who have left be forgiven. They are no longer in fellowship. This sin of leaving the fellowship cannot be forgiven outside the fellowship. Diotrophes negates the prospect for fellowship by expelling people from the church:

> I have written something to the church; but Diotrephes, who likes to put himself first, does not acknowledge our authority. So if I come, I will call attention to what he is doing in spreading false charges against us. And not content with those charges, he refuses to welcome the friends, and even prevents those who want to do so and expels them from the church. (3 John 9–10)

In the Johannine literature any disrupting of fellowship constitutes a sin.

JESUS' PRAYER FOR UNITY

For a number of scholars, the prayer of Jesus for the unity of his disciples (John 17) has the clearest ecclesiology found in the Johannine writ-

---

16. This conclusion first came to my attention when reading Marxsen, *Introduction to the New Testament*, 263. See also Rensburger in his commentary on 1 John.

ings.[17] Unquestionably this prayer anticipates that upon his departure Jesus' disciples will form a believing community or church in which love prevails.

The prayer begins with the declaration that God has given Jesus "authority over all people" (17:2). Jesus' stay on earth was to bring eternal life to all humankind through knowing the only true God and Jesus Christ whom God sent (John 17:2–3). Jesus prayed on behalf of those who have come to faith "so that they may be one as we are one" (John 17:11). Jesus anticipated that his disciples would continue after his departure as a close, growing community. While Jesus was with the disciples, he protected them so that none would be lost from God. Jesus had given the disciples God's word. He himself was the disseminator of that word (John 1:1–3, 14). To protect them from the world Jesus prayed that God would sanctify the disciples:

> Sanctify them in the truth; your word is truth. As you have sent me into the world, so I have sent them into the world. And for their sakes I sanctify myself, so that they also may be sanctified in truth. (John 17:17–19)

The future of the community or church is likewise anticipated:

> I ask not only on behalf of these, but also on behalf of those who will believe in me through their word, that they may all be one. As you, Father, are in me and I am in you, may they also be in us, so that the world may believe that you have sent me. (John 17:20–21)

We are reminded of Jesus' declaration to Thomas regarding those who would believe as the result of the testimony of first-hand witnesses and not because they actually saw the risen Christ face to face. The church of the Lord Jesus Christ is a community he loves and prays for (John 17:25).

BAPTISM

As mentioned previously, those who enter the kingdom and the church are born from above (John 3:3). They enter when they are baptized with the water and the Spirit: "Jesus answered, 'Very truly, I tell you, no one can enter the kingdom of God without being born of water and Spirit'"

---

17. Ferreira, *Johannine Ecclesiology*, focuses especially on John 17 as he lays out the ecclesiology of the Johannine writings.

(John 3:5). Jesus' disciples baptized as did those of John the Baptist (John 4:1–2). The one baptism is both of water and Spirit. The Spirit baptizes from above. Baptism in water is the believer's demonstration of faith and commitment. Water was involved in these early baptisms, that is, immersion, because according to John 3:23, John the Baptist "also was baptizing at Aenon near Salim because water was abundant there; and people kept coming and were being baptized."

Besides these occasional references to baptism, there is one other text in the Johannine literature that might provide insight into how this community viewed baptism. A few commentators see in 1 John entry into the church through baptism in water being declared:

> This is the one who came by water and blood, Jesus Christ, not with the water only but with the water and the blood. And the Spirit is the one that testifies, for the Spirit is the truth. There are three that testify: the Spirit and the water and the blood, and these three agree. (1 John 5:6–8)

Asking the question, "What did the author mean by stating that Jesus Christ 'came by water' (v. 6a)?" Martinus de Boer points out that the phrase "not in water only but in water and in blood" (v. 6b) is polemical and was probably directed towards the secessionists who did not confess Jesus (1 John 4:3).[18] The majority of commentators on the epistle would agree with this conclusion and have interpreted "came by water" to refer to Jesus' baptism and the coming in blood to refer to Jesus' crucifixion.[19] In this case, the secessionists are presumed to have held either a gnostic or docetic Christology that taught that the heavenly Christ descended on Jesus during his baptism and then departed prior to his passion and crucifixion. Other commentators have argued that not only in verse 8 but also in verse 6 "water" refers to Christian baptism and "blood" refers to the eucharist.[20] If this is the case, then the secessionists may have claimed that Jesus is received in Christian baptism but

18. de Boer, "Jesus the Baptizer," 88–89.

19. Bultmann, *Johannine Epistles*, 79–80; Bruce, *Epistles of John*, 118–19; Houlden, *Johannine Epistles*, 125–26; Marshall, *Epistles of John*, 231–32; Brown, *Epistles of John*, 576–78, 595–96; Smalley, *1,2,3 John*, 278.

20. Westcott, *Epistles of St. John*, 182. Bruce, *Epistles of John*, 120–21, and Marshall, *Epistles of John*, 237–38, allow this interpretation as a possibility. For two other less commonly held interpretations, including de Boer's arguments that "the one who came by water" means Jesus was a baptizer with water and the Holy Spirit, see de Boer, "Jesus the Baptizer," 91–100.

is not "received" or experienced in the eating the body and drinking the blood of Jesus in the Lord's Supper. While the interpretation of "water" as a reference to Jesus' own baptism is more persuasive, it is at least possible that the author had in mind the expectation of believers to "receive" Christ in their own baptism.

THE LORD'S SUPPER

Jesus promised to give filling bread to those who came to him (John 6:27). What is this bread he will give? Jesus continued speaking metaphorically, "For the bread of God is that which comes down from heaven and gives life to the world" (John 6:33). Again, what is this bread? Jesus made it clear that he was the one who had come down from heaven: "I am the bread of life. Whoever comes to me will never be hungry, and whoever believes in me will never be thirsty" (John 6:35). Furthermore, the bread that came down from heaven in the days of Moses, the manna, did not continue to satisfy, for those who ate of it hungered the next day. Jesus states, "I am the living bread that comes down from heaven. Whoever eats of this bread will live forever; and the bread that I will give for the life of the world is my flesh" (John 6:51).

It is at this point that Jesus made a controversial and alienating assertion, which is often understood as the Johannine theology of the Eucharist: "Very truly I tell you, unless you eat the flesh of the Son of Man and drink his blood, you have no life in you" (John 6:53). Almost immediately, however, Jesus made an even more astounding claim, unless it is understood in the light of the theme of the Gospel, that is, that Jesus is the Word and that he heals and saves by his word. Jesus declared after the disciples complained about the difficulty of accepting his statement about eating his flesh and drinking his blood, "It is the spirit that gives life; the flesh is useless" (John 6:63). This is to say, as I understand it, the everlasting life he gives is not as a result of a literal eating of his body and drinking his blood. Rather, it is the proclamation of his death and resurrection and the celebrating of his body and blood (which would have been proclaimed during the Johannine Eucharist as well as at other times) that bring about eternal life. His mighty salvific acts in his death and resurrection are appropriated through the words declared about them, not through the eating of the fleshly body and the drinking the literal blood. Jesus makes it clear that it is the words that he has spoken that bring eternal life: "The words that I have spoken to you are spirit and life" (John 6:63). Salvation comes through the pronouncing of the words of the one who is the Word: "But these are written so that you may come to believe that Jesus is the Messiah, the Son of God, and through believing you may have life in his name" (John 20:31).

CONCLUSIONS

In the Johannine literature the church is viewed from the perspective of its beginnings with God and Christ, and its continued sustenance by the Holy Spirit. It is an "organism" that reflects the characteristics of its founders. It is a community of love and fellowship. Entry into the community is through baptism, and the community continues to survive by the preaching of the word and eating the bread and drinking the fruit of the vine. These features are cast in the analogies of the shepherd and the sheepfold, and of the vine and the branches. The leaders of the church are those who teach what Christ taught and what the Holy Spirit brings to their remembrance. No effort is made in the Johannine literature to spell out the features of the church, the qualifications of the leaders, the character of their authority, or the specific lifestyle of the believers.

FOR FURTHER STUDY

Barrett, Charles Kingsley. *The Gospel according to St. John: An Introduction with Commentary and Notes on the Greek Text*. 2nd ed. London: SPCK, 1978.

Beasley-Murray, George Raymond. *John*. 2nd ed. Nashville: Thomas Nelson, 1999.

Brown, Raymond. *The Epistles of John*. AB 30. Garden City, NY: Doubleday, 1982.

————. *The Gospel according to John*. 2 vols. AB. Garden City, NY: Doubleday, 1966.

Culpepper, R. Alan. *The Gospel and Letters of John*. Nashville: Abingdon, 1998.

Keener, Craig S. *The Gospel of John: A Commentary*. 2 vols. Peabody, MA: Hendrickson, 2003.

O'Day, Gail R. "The Gospel of John." In *The New Interpreter's Bible*, 9:493–875. Nashville: Abingdon, 1995.

Pack, Frank. *The Gospel according to John*. 2 vols. Abilene: Abilene Christian University Press, 1984.

Rensberger, David. *1 John, 2 John, 3 John*. Nashville: Abingdon, 1997.

Roberts, J. W. *The Letters of John*. Austin, TX: R. B. Sweet, 1968.

Schnackenburg, Rudolf. *The Gospel according to St. John*. Translated by Cecily Hastings, Francis McDonagh, David Smith, and Richard Foley. New York: Crossroad, 1990.

———. *The Johannine Epistles: Introduction and Commentary*. New York: Crossroad, 1992.

Smith, D. Moody. *John*. Nashville: Abingdon, 1999.

BIBLIOGRAPHY

Barrett, C. K. *The Gospel according to John.* 2nd ed. Philadelphia: Westminster, 1978.

Beasley-Murray, George Raymond. *John.* 2nd ed. Nashville: Thomas Nelson, 1999.

Brown, Raymond E. *The Community of the Beloved Disciple: The Life, Loves, and Hates of an Individual Church in the New Testament.* New York: Paulist, 1979.

———. *The Epistles of John.* AB 30. Garden City, NY: Doubleday, 1982.

———. *The Gospel according to John.* 2 vols. AB. Garden City, NY: Doubleday, 1970.

Bruce, F. F. *The Epistles of John.* Grand Rapids: Eerdmans, 1970.

Bultmann, Rudolf. *The Johannine Epistles.* Hermeneia. Philadelphia: Fortress, 1973.

———. *Theology of the New Testament.* 2 vols. New York: Scribners, 1955.

de Boer, Martinus. "Jesus the Baptizer: 1 John 5:5–8 and the Gospel of John." *JBL* 107 (1988) 87–106.

Ferreira, Johan. *Johannine Ecclesiology.* Sheffield: Sheffield Academic, 1998.

Houlden, J. L. *The Johannine Epistles.* HNTC. New York: Harper & Row, 1973.

Marshall, I. H. *The Epistles of John.* Grand Rapids: Eerdmans, 1978.

Marxsen, Willi. *Introduction to the New Testament.* Translated by G. Buswell. Philadelphia: Fortress, 1968.

Meier, John P. "The Absence and Presence of the Church in John's Gospel." *Mid-Stream* 41 (2002) 27–34.

O'Day, Gail R. "The Gospel of John." In *The New Interpreter's Bible,* 9:493–875. Nashville: Abingdon, 1995.

Olbricht, Thomas H. *Life Together: The Heart of Love and Fellowship in 1 John.* Webb City, MO: Covenant, 2006.

———. *Lifted Up: John 18–21: Crucifixion, Resurrection and Community in John.* Webb City, MO: Covenant, 2005.

———. "The Theology of the Signs in the Gospel of John." In *Johannine Studies in Honor of Frank Pack,* edited by James E. Priest, 171–81. Malabu, CA: Pepperdine University Press, 1989.

———. "The Word as Sign." In *Preaching John's Gospel: The World It Imagines,* edited by David Fleer and David Bland, 83–91. St. Louis: Chalice, 2008.

Rensberger, David. *1 John, 2 John, 3 John.* Nashville: Abingdon, 1997.

Schnackenburg, Rudolph. *The Gospel according to St. John.* New York: Crossroad, 1982.

Schneiders, Sandra M. "The Raising of the New Temple: John 20:19–25 and Johannine Ecclesiology." *NTS* 52 (2006) 337–55.

Schnelle, Udo. "Johanneische Ekklesiologie." *NTS* 37 (1991) 37–50.

Schweizer, Eduard. "The Concept of the Church in the Gospel and Epistles of St. John." In *New Testament Essays in Memory of T. W. Manson,* edited by A. J. B. Higgins, 230–45. Manchester: Manchester University Press, 1959.

Smalley, S. S. *1, 2, 3 John.* WBC. Waco, TX: Word, 1984.

Stone, Samuel J. "The Church's One Foundation." In *Songs of Faith and Praise,* edited by Alton H. Howard, hymn 715. West Monroe, LA: Howard, 1996. [Reprinted from *Lyra Fidelium: Twelve Hymns of the Twelve Articles of the Apostle's Creed.* London: Parker, 1866.]

Westcott, B. F. *The Epistles of St. John.* Grand Rapids: Eerdmans, 1966.

5

The Church in Romans and Galatians

STANLEY E. PORTER

INTRODUCTION

ROMANS AND GALATIANS, as two of Paul's "major" letters, are often grouped together because they have a number of similarities.[1] The major one is that they have much to say about the notion of being justified or righteous before God—and discussion of this issue often dominates discussion of Romans and Galatians.[2] The book of Romans goes into significant detail in the body of the letter on what it means for sinful humanity, with or without the law, to be judged by God. The righteousness of God, though witnessed to by the Scriptures, is accessed

---

1. I do not attempt in this essay to survey all of the pertinent literature regarding issues not central to the topic of this essay. For issues regarding the Pauline letters as a whole, see McDonald and Porter, *Early Christianity*, 409–10.

2. Readers will note that I do not accept the so-called New Perspective on Paul (see ibid., 358–61). I note that much recent research has clearly shown the limitations, if not outright misunderstandings, of this perspective. For recent treatments of relevance in this regard, see Bird, *Saving Righteousness*; Carson, O'Brien, and Seifrid, eds., *Justification and Variegated Nomism*; Das, *Paul, the Law, and the Covenant*; Gathercole, *Where Is Boasting?*; Kim, *Paul and the New Perspective*; Koperski, *What Are They Saying about Paul and the Law?*; Rapa, *Meaning of "Works of the Law"*; de Roo, *Works of the Law*; Seifrid, *Christ, Our Righteousness*; Smith, *What Must I Do to Be Saved?*; Stuhlmacher, *Revisiting Paul's Doctrine of Justification*; Waters, *Justification and the New Perspective on Paul*; Westerholm, *Perspectives Old and New on Paul*.

through faith in Jesus Christ by those who believe.[3] The consequences of this justification include reconciliation and sanctification. The book of Galatians is almost entirely focused upon this topic. Like Abraham, those who have faith are reckoned as righteous by God. This righteousness, which comes through Christ as Abraham's seed and leads to spiritual life, exists apart from the law.

Apart from this commonality, however, there are many differences between Romans and Galatians. Paul had visited churches in the Roman province of Galatia, but he had never been to the city of Rome. The book of Romans can be fairly accurately dated and located, as being written in around AD 57 from Corinth, on Paul's second missionary journey. As for Galatians, scholars are still divided over whether it was written to north or south Galatia, and whether it was written at the end of Paul's first missionary journey (which requires the south Galatian or Roman provincial hypothesis), or whether it was written during Paul's second missionary journey, and around the time of writing of Romans—although the south Galatian view is overwhelmingly more probable.[4] As a consequence of the situation of writing to an un-visited church, Romans is a letter that is wide-ranging in its subject matter. In this letter to a church that he hopes to visit on his way toward a western missionary venture in Spain, Paul addresses such topics as the fallenness of humanity, the role of the Jewish law, various theological concepts noted above, the character of human desire, the role of the Holy Spirit, the future role of Israel in God's saving economy, and a variety of practical topics, such as gifted service, civil obedience, and conscience with regard to weaker Christians, among others. Galatians is more particularly addressed to a church in contemporary crisis, and so Paul focuses upon topics germane to that crisis. As a result, he places his comments within the context of his being an apostle to the Gentiles, including reference to his own Jewish background, his connections to the Jerusalem leaders, and his rebuke of Peter (Cephas) for reverting to Jewish practices not germane to Gentile believers. He then focuses upon the notion of justification, and the freedom in the Spirit that results and encourages spiritual fruit.

---

3. For defense of the so-called (but probably wrongly labeled) objective genitive, see Porter and Pitts, "Πίστις with a Preposition and Genitive Modifier."

4. See McDonald and Porter, *Early Christianity*, 411–13.

There has not been much scholarship recently written specifically on the nature of the church in Romans or Galatians.[5] Such articles as there are often focus upon tangential topics, and few are particularly insightful regarding the question of this chapter. In the light of the significant differences between Galatians and Romans, as well as some significant similarities, there are a number of common beliefs regarding the church that Paul draws upon in both letters that give an idea of his conception of the church. In some ways, these constitute fundamental beliefs that guide his discussion of the more prominent issues that occupy the bulk of these letters. I have selected four sets of key features and characteristics that help to define the nature of the church in Paul's letters to the Romans and to the Galatians.

THE CHURCH IN ROMANS AND GALATIANS

There are a number of ways in which the church in Galatians and Romans might be approached. However, on the basis of their common authorship, as well as thematic cohesion, the books of Galatians and Romans have a common conceptual framework regarding the church that I wish to explore. In this section, I wish to outline some of these common features.

What Is the Church according to Paul?

What does Paul envision as the defining characteristics of the church, at least as he talks about it in Galatians and Romans? The most important feature of the church as depicted in Galatians and Romans is that it is a grace- and faith-based community focused upon the gospel.[6] There are a number of important ideas contained within this definition, each of which merits some elucidation.

The first is that, in both Galatians and Romans, the church is seen as a community or an intentionally gathered group of those who are followers of Jesus Christ. Paul uses the term "church" (ἐκκλησία, *ekklēsia*) explicitly in both Galatians and Romans to refer to such a gathering.

---

5. See Oakes, "Made Holy by the Holy Spirit"; Martin, "Circumcision in Galatia and the Holiness of God's Ecclesiae"; Bockmuehl, "Is There a New Testament Doctrine of the Church?" Several older sources include: Seitz, *One Body and One Spirit*; Schweizer, *Church Order in the New Testament*; and Schnackenburg, *The Church in the New Testament*.

6. On the general notion of Paul's communities, see Banks, *Paul's Idea of Community*.

Though it is disputed by many, I believe that Jesus himself used the term "church" to label the community of his followers that he brought into existence (see Matt 16:16; cf. Matt 18:17), and this usage is the basis of Paul's employment of the term.[7] The word ἐκκλησία is a Greek term well suited to label such a body, as it indicated a group gathered for an explicit purpose, especially the body that gathered in community in Athens to expedite the business of the city. In Galatians, Paul writes to "the churches of Galatia" (Gal 1:2), and notes that they are distinct from the churches of Judea (Gal 1:22). In Romans, Paul does not address the letter to the churches in Rome, but in his closing greetings, he refers to those in other churches, such as Phoebe who is a member of the church at Cenchrea (Rom 16:1), the churches of the Gentiles (Rom 16:4), the church that meets in the home of Prisca and Aquila (Rom 16:5), all the churches of Christ (Rom 16:16), and the church presumably in Corinth hosted by Gaius (Rom 16:23). These references in both Galatians and Romans refer to specific groups of followers of Jesus Christ who are gathered together in particular locations, what is perhaps best labeled as instances of the local church. These churches probably met in the homes of local followers, presumably those with economic means to afford accommodations for such gatherings.[8] Gaius may have been one of those (cf. also Phlm 2). Paul frequently, not only in Galatians and Romans but also elsewhere in his letters, refers to local churches. There were a number of local churches in Galatia,[9] and probably a number in Rome as well.

Paul also recognizes, however, that local instances of the church are a part of a larger body, what he terms in Gal 1:13 "the church of God." In briefly recounting his autobiography, Paul notes that the Galatians had

7. On the authenticity of Matt 16:18, and even the possibility that Jesus delivered these words in Greek, see Porter, *Criteria for Authenticity,* 126–80, esp. 159–61. Even if Jesus did not use the Greek word ἐκκλησία, but used an Aramaic word, or if these words were put on his lips by later interpreters, the fact is that the word ἐκκλησία was chosen as the best Greek rendering of what Jesus was believed to have in mind. Paul clearly adopted this usage. Contra Dunn, *Theology of Paul the Apostle,* 537–38, but who provides his own arguments against his proposal; Schreiner, *Paul,* 331.

8. On the Pauline house churches, see Branick, *The House Church in the Writings of Paul*; Ascough, *Pauline Churches,* 5–9.

9. As indicated above, I believe that the dispute over whether Paul writes to north or south Galatia has been satisfactorily resolved, so that it is clear that Paul is addressing churches in the Roman province of Galatia, and probably the churches located in the cities that he visited on his first missionary tour.

heard of his former life as a persecutor of the church of God. As we know from elsewhere in the New Testament (note Acts 8:1–3 and elsewhere), Paul became a persecutor of the church by attacking individual churches—note that Acts 8:3 speaks of him decimating the church, entering house after house, probably local house churches. For Paul, the term "church" functions on two levels.[10] The term church represents both the inclusive community of all of those who are followers of Jesus Christ, and the various instances of the local communities as they gather individually. For Paul, one does not have one without the other, and those who are members of the church universal are only recognizable by their being parts of a church local.

The second feature of this community is that it is a grace- and faith-based community. In Romans, Paul does not address the letter to the "church" or "churches" in Rome, but addresses the letter to "those who are beloved of God in Rome, called saints." For Paul, the church is a community that is gathered on the basis of God's gracious actions toward humans. In Romans, he states that these people are "beloved" by God, and (as a result) called saints (Rom 1:7). For Paul, grace is God's unmerited gift to humans. As Moffatt in his classic and now neglected study says, Paul's

> powerful statement of [Christianity] as a religion of grace, or rather as the religion of grace, was due to his dominant conception of God bestowing undeserved favour and fellowship upon men. . . . he confines his attention to grace as originally manifested in Jesus the Lord and as verified in the experience of Christians who yield to God's gracious love and serve Him in the fellowship of the Church.[11]

This grace is then manifested in the death and resurrection of Jesus Christ, which enables justification, reconciliation, and sanctification—all of which are the results of God's gracious beneficence—and which allows Paul to call those who have received such a gift "saints."[12]

---

10. See Ridderbos, *Paul*, 328; contra Dunn, *Theology of Paul the Apostle*, 539–43, who sees development of the notion of a universal church only in the later Pauline letters.

11. Moffatt, *Grace in the New Testament*, 8, 9. See also Amiot, *Key Concepts of St. Paul*, 150–53.

12. See Morris, *The Apostolic Preaching of the Cross*, for a conspectus on these theological ideas.

The term "saints" is one that Paul uses in many of his letters to describe individual believers, not necessarily as part of any local church but as part of the church universal. He uses this term several times in Romans (1:7; 8:27; 12:13; 15:25, 26, 31; 16:2, 15), but never in Galatians.[13] The reason is apparently that the term "saints" conveys the sense that these are people settled within their relationship with God, whereas one of the major issues in Galatia is the unsettled basis and nature of that relationship. In Galatians, Paul must remind his readers that they were called by God by means of or through the grace of Christ (Gal 1:6, 15), this grace being something that was given to them and not earned or merited (Gal 2:9), that grace is what leads to righteousness (Gal 2:21), not their seeking to be justified by performing the law (Gal 5:4). In Romans, Paul goes so far as to make receiving grace from God tantamount to his own calling as an apostle (Rom 1:5). He further notes that grace, which is given from God (Rom 15:15), is the basis of righteousness (Rom 3:24), which comes about not through what one does, such as following the law, but only through faith (Rom 4:4, 16; 6:14, 15; 11:6). Whereas grace is God's unmerited gift that leads to one's right relationship with God, it is accessed, so Paul says, by means of faith. As already noted above, in Romans Paul makes a clear distinction between the free gift of grace (Rom 3:24; 5:15, 17) that comes only through faith (Rom 4:16; 5:2) and any attempts to gain it by means of the law. In fact, whereas it is God's grace that initiates the process of salvation (to use a term that encapsulates many of the theological metaphors that Paul uses for one's right standing with God), it is through faith in Jesus Christ that individual humans access this grace.[14] As Paul states, just as it was with Abraham whose faith was reckoned as righteousness (Rom 4:5, 9, 16), any righteous person can expect to live through faith (Rom 1:17). God's righteousness and the other salvific results come about through faith in Jesus Christ (Rom 3:22, 26; cf. v. 25; Rom 5:1; 9:30). Even more so in Galatians, Paul draws a clear line of demarcation that the righteousness that comes from God comes about through faith (Gal 2:16; 3:11), not through anything one does, including obeying the law (Gal 3:2, 5, 12).

The third and final element of this definition that I wish to explicate is the relationship of the church to the gospel. For Paul in Galatians and

13. For fuller treatment of the evidence, see Ridderbos, *Paul*, 330–31.

14. See Hatch, *Pauline Idea of Faith*. Faith is often discussed in terms of its mystical dimension. This does not necessitate a link to mystery religions.

Romans, it appears that not only is the church a grace- and faith-based community, but it is one intent upon preservation and promotion of the gospel.[15] For Paul, the gospel is the good news regarding the salvific effect of the death, resurrection, and expected return of the incarnate Jesus Christ. That is why Paul can say, with some understatement, that he is not ashamed of the gospel, as it is the power of God for salvation for all humanity (Rom 1:17). The gospel is both the foundational truth upon which the church rests, and the message that the church proclaims (e.g., in Rom 10:9: Jesus is Lord). Paul states that humanity is judged on the basis of the gospel (Rom 2:16), and whereas some are not obedient to it (Rom 10:16) and become God's enemies (Rom 11:28), he was designated and selected by it (Rom 1:1). Paul's concern with the Galatians is even stronger, because he fears that they have abandoned the gospel and are following another gospel (Gal 1:6, 7; 2:14) than the one that he proclaimed to them (Gal 1:11).

Although not mentioned above in the definition of the church, one issue that emerges in much contemporary thought is the relationship between the church and Israel.[16] Within Romans and Galatians, there is no doubt that there is much continuity seen by Paul between Israel and the church. In Romans, Paul illustrates throughout the book that the plight and situation of the Jewish people is the same as that of the non-Jew—that all people stand equally before God. Every person is without excuse, and subject to God's judgment (Rom 2:1). This prompts the question of whether the Jew has any advantage. Paul clarifies that there is the benefit of having received the "oracles" of God. In fact, more than that, the way of salvation is the same for Jew and Gentile, in the same way that Abraham was justified by faith, not by his own works (Rom 4:3, etc., citing Gen 15:6). Similarly, in Galatians Paul makes the point that Abraham was justified by faith, not by works (Gal 3:6, citing Gen 15:6), a pattern that he sees as determinative for every human being's

15. The centrality and fullness of the meaning of the gospel in Paul is discussed in Dunn, *Theology of Paul the Apostle*, 163–315. Cf. Nanos, *Irony of Galatians*, 284–96, who takes the opponents as non-believers, with implications for understanding their "other gospel."

16. I believe that this is an issue driven much more by a type of theology—in which the church entirely supersedes Israel on the basis of wishing to establish a type of unitary covenantal theology—than by the biblical evidence. However, I will attempt to address it on a biblical level.

relationship to God.[17] Being part of the faith community enables one to be Abraham's descendant (Gal 3:29). In Galatians, Paul depicts this line as continuing through Isaac, and in the end addresses those who are followers of Christ on the basis of faith, not works, as part of the "Israel of God" (Gal 6:16). This line of continuity, in which the basis of salvation is found in grace through faith in Jesus Christ, is present in both Galatians and Romans. However, this is not to say that all that might be said about Israel as a community of God's people has been taken over by the church.

In Romans, Paul makes clear that this may have been an implication that some could have drawn from what he says on the basis of a common means of salvation. To the contrary, even as he makes his argument he clarifies that there are still distinctives regarding Israel. He develops these further in Romans 9–11. He first distinguishes between the true and false descendants of Isaac (Rom 9:7–8), such that even within national Israel there are those who are God's people and those who are not. Paul's desire is still that there would be salvation for those Israelites who have been disobedient and have not followed as the true descendants of Isaac. Their way to salvation will be by faith, just as it is for all human beings. In this light, Paul can say that God has not rejected his people, those who are Israelites and physical descendants of Abraham (Rom 11:1), even though they have been disobedient, including killing the prophets. The olive tree—which represents Abraham or his true descendants, i.e., those saved through faith—represents those who have followed the obedient line, so that the disobedient have been broken off and the Gentiles who are obedient through faith have been grafted in. The reminder is to the Gentiles that their joining this plant is late and reversible. There is a time coming, Paul states, when the disobedient Israelites will come to faith in Jesus Christ and be re-grafted in (Rom 11:25).[18] Thus, Paul definitely entertains a future role for Israelites who are obedient in faith—their role has not been superseded by the church. This also makes sense of the phrase "Israel of God" with reference to the

17. For recent treatments of Abraham in Paul, see Hansen, *Abraham in Galatians*, esp. 97–139; Davies, *Faith and Obedience in Romans*, 143–72; and Longenecker, *Triumph of Abraham's God*, 117–46.

18. See, for example, Wagner, *Heralds of the Good News*, 219–305, esp. 276–80 and notes 193, 194, where he refutes Wright, *Climax of the Covenant*, 246–51; Barth, *People of God*, 29–49; and Childs, *Church's Guide for Reading Paul*, 178–93.

church—all of those who are obedient through faith are a part of the one tree, whether natural or grafted growth.

How Does This Community Function?

The second category for discussion is the internal working of this community, called the "church." The church as Paul understands it is a grace- and faith-based community focused upon the gospel. That is its external face as it is presented in Galatians and Romans. However, there is also an apparent internal constituency that Paul envisions.

Paul gives indications in both Galatians and Romans that he views the church as functioning in terms of fictive kinship, that is, there are a set of internal relations that in effect resemble the kinds of relations found in families.[19] In Galatians, Paul depicts this in several ways. The first is that he labels the church the "household of the faith" (Gal 6:10). The image here connotes a family structure in which the faith, probably as a body of belief, is safeguarded by the family, as their primary responsibility. This concept of the church as family is continued by the form of address that Paul often uses when he addresses his readers. He calls them "brothers [and sisters]" (ἀδελφοί; Gal 1:11; 3:15; 4:12, 28, 31; 5:11, 13; 6:1, 18). That this use is more than a mere formality is seen in two ways. The first is that Paul refers to those who are with him in similar terms (Gal 1:2). He uses this term for his traveling and missionary companions, and so there is nothing condescending about his addressing the Galatians in a similar way. The use of the term "brothers" draws those in the church at Galatia into the wider sphere of those who are "related" to Paul through their fictive kinship now become reality in Christ. The second is that Paul uses the address "brothers" at key places in his argument, especially when he wants to reinforce a line of connection between his readers and others within the believing community. For example, in Gal 4:28 and 31, Paul addresses his readers as "brothers" when he draws an equation between them and Isaac, with both as children of Abraham— however, believers are children not of the bondwoman Hagar but of the free woman Sarah. In Romans, Paul similarly uses the term "brothers" as a means of establishing fictive kinship within the Christian community. It is noteworthy that he uses this form of address especially in those sections of the letter where he is not engaging in as much theologizing. As a

---

19. See Hellerman, *Ancient Church as Family*, 92–126.

result, there is no use of this form of address in chapters 2–6 of Romans. The second observation regarding usage in Romans is that Paul calls his recipients "brothers" when he uses two particular forms of address. The first one is his "ignorance" formula. Paul reassures the Romans that he does not want them to be ignorant of certain things, and he reassures them by addressing them as "brothers" (Rom 1:13; 7:1; 11:25). Another formula he uses is in terms of a persuasion or beseeching formula. Again Paul reassures his readers by imploring them, while addressing them as "brothers" (Rom 15:14; 16:17).

One of the results of the creation of this fictive community is that there must be relationships within such a community. Paul addresses all of the recipients as "brothers," and with this address come other implications for their internal relationships. One of the major results is that, while Paul recognizes that there are differences inherent in any human association, he wishes to create an egalitarian community. In his letter to the Galatians, Paul addresses this situation head-on in 3:26–28, when he recognizes that the Galatian followers of Christ are "all children [literally, sons] of God through faith in Christ Jesus, for all of you who were baptized into Christ have clothed yourselves with Christ. There is neither Jew nor Greek, neither slave nor free, neither male and female, for you are all one in Christ Jesus."[20] I will return to the issue of baptism below, but within the context of the church (that is, the baptized community), Paul recognizes that all are "children of God." This comes about through their faith in Christ Jesus, and results in their being baptized. As a result, Paul says, within the believing community, such distinctions as ethnic ones, socio-economic ones, and gender-based ones—more categories than he needs simply for the issue of Jew and Gentile[21]—are all over-ridden, so that all are one in Christ. This is a great proclamation of egalitarianism within the community of believers. As Fee states, "both

20. The programmatic nature of this passage has been seen by Richardson, *Paul's Ethic of Freedom*, and Longenecker, *New Testament Social Ethics for Today*. For interpretation within a social-scientific context, but one that sees its egalitarian nature in terms of establishing a worldview, see Asano, *Community-Identity Construction*, 180–206. There are also those who take a far more limited view of the passage. For further discussion of the issues, see Beck and Blomberg, eds., *Two Views on Women in Ministry*, esp. 183–88, where one of the contributors, Thomas Schreiner, treats the passage from a complementarian perspective. This is not the place to enter into extended discussion of this passage, but this interpretation fails to appreciate the full significance of what it means to be "in Christ."

21. Fee, "Male and Female," 172.

the argument of Galatians as a whole and the specifics of this passage itself indicate that this text has to do with Paul's ecclesiology: what it means to be the people of God under the new covenant brought about through Christ's death and the gift of the Spirit."[22]

One does not find an equivalent statement within the book of Romans; however, there is a major passage that indicates that egalitarianism remains fundamental to Paul's conception of the church. One of the major strategies of those who wish to hierarchicalize is to draw distinctions on the basis of all sorts of what amount to incidental differences. As noted in the passage from Galatians above, some of the distinctions that might be used are fundamental ones, involving such things as ethnicity or gender. For Paul, these have no bearing in regard to one's being in Christ. In Romans, Paul is confronting a situation where there are distinctions apparently being made on the basis of religious belief and practice. He confronts these in Rom 14:1–15:13, the passage on the so-called "weak and strong."[23] Paul, speaking from the standpoint of those who identify themselves as the "strong," instructs others who conceive of themselves in this way. He clearly states that they are not to draw distinctions on the basis of such incidentals as their eating habits, their celebration of certain religious observances, or the like. What is the reason for this? Paul recognizes that some may be weaker or stronger in faith and freedom than others, but the point is that within the church one is not to make such distinctions and judge another—recognizing that each one of us has weaknesses for which we will be accountable to God. Instead we are to put no obstacle in another believer's way (Rom 14:13), but are to help those who are weaker (Rom 15:1), and accept them just as Christ has accepted us (Rom 15:7).

The Role of the Spirit and Gifts

In Paul's mind, at least as reflected in Romans and Galatians, the church is a community that continues to be led by the Holy Spirit, and exemplifies charismatic gifts. Whereas the church is constituted as a grace- and faith-based community, it continues to be governed and directed by the Holy Spirit. The result is the evidence of various Spirit-inspired gifts.

---

22. Ibid., 184.

23. On this passage, see Reasoner, *The Strong and the Weak*.

The Holy Spirit plays an important role in both Galatians and especially Romans. For both letters, the Spirit is seen to be instrumental in the life of the believer, both as an individual and within the larger Christian community.[24] In Galatians, Paul strongly emphasizes to his readers that they are Spirit-led people on the basis of faith, not works (Gal 3:2, 14), and that the Spirit continues to lead them (Gal 3:3), and it is this Spirit that cries out in our hearts, "Abba, Father" (Gal 4:6). In Galatians 5, Paul goes into greater detail regarding the work of the Spirit. This includes noting that it is the Spirit that makes us expectant of receiving confirmation of righteousness (Gal 5:5), by enabling us to live without succumbing to the desires of the flesh (Gal 5:16) or of the law (Gal 5:18). Similarly in Romans, Paul recognizes the crucial empowerment of the Holy Spirit, including the full empowerment of Jesus as "son of God" (Rom 1:4) and the resulting empowering love of God in the believer (Rom 5:5). For the believer, Paul notes that it is the Holy Spirit that enables the believer to live in a Spirit-filled way that leads to life, rather than according to the desires of the flesh (Rom 8:2, 4, 11, 14). For Paul, the Holy Spirit is clearly an active and live being, one that is distinct from God the Father and Jesus Christ the Son, but that is nevertheless active in the life of the believer empowering him or her for a life of righteousness (Rom 8:10).[25]

As a result, the community of believers who are led by the Spirit is a community that displays the gifts that the Spirit gives. Paul writes to the Romans that he wishes to come to visit them so that he might share some spiritual gift with them, in order to strengthen them (Rom 1:11). Paul notes that just as he might be a spiritual encouragement for them, they might be an encouragement to him, as they strengthen each other's faith (Rom 1:12). This mutual encouragement makes sense in the light of the fact that both Paul and his audience were followers of Jesus Christ who were being led by the Holy Spirit, and so had the empowering presence of the Spirit in their lives. We are not sure what these "spiritual gifts" might be to which Paul refers, although they may well be similar to those that he mentions in Romans 12. These gifts are mentioned in the context of the analogy of the body, in which there are many members

24. See Fee, *God's Empowering Presence*, esp. 469–71, 634; cf. Amiot, *Key Concepts of St. Paul*, 153–68; Childs, *Church's Guide for Reading Paul*, 113–22.

25. On the proto-trinitarian dimensions of Paul's theology, see Fee, *Pauline Christology*, esp. 586–93, who acknowledges (p. 63) borrowing the term "proto-Trinitarian" from me (Porter, "Hermeneutics, Biblical Interpretation and Theology," 97–127, here 122 n. 59).

of the one body, and thus there is diversity within the unity of the single body.[26] Paul singles out several particular gifts: prophecy, service, teaching, exhortation, giving, leading, and showing of mercy (Rom 12:6–8). Paul defines these gifts not in terms of their constituting official offices within the church, but in the context of their being given by God as gifts for the mutual benefit of the church. Similarly, in Galatians, at the end of his discussion of the work of the Holy Spirit, Paul itemizes the fruit of the Holy Spirit as love, joy, peace, patience, kindness, goodness, faithfulness, gentleness, and self-control (Gal 5:22–23).

Rituals and Practices: Baptism

A number of rituals and practices related to the church are mentioned in Galatians and Romans. Most of these are incidental to the nature and purpose of the church, or are rituals and practices that Paul is clearly refuting. The ones he refutes include circumcision, food laws, special feast days, and the like. However, there is one practice that Paul briefly, though clearly, depicts as related to the life of the church. This ritual is baptism.

There are two clear statements regarding baptism in the two letters, and the wording in Greek is very similar.[27] In Galatians, Paul mentions baptism only once, but he does so in conjunction with his important statement regarding the lack of hierarchy within the church. In Gal 3:23–28, Paul states that his audience, like those within the churches in Galatia, are all "sons of God" through faith in Christ Jesus. He then states that "for whoever of you is baptized into Christ, you are clothed with respect to Christ" (ὅσοι γὰρ εἰς Χριστὸν ἐβαπτίσθητε Χριστὸν ἐνδύσασθε; Gal 3:27). This sentence is part of a sequence that Paul develops from vv. 23–29. Before faith, "we" were under control of the law, so that the law served as a tutor to lead to Christ, so that we might be justified by faith, and no longer under a tutor. Then you are all "sons of God" through faith in Christ Jesus. Then baptism led to being clothed with Christ, and the resulting egalitarian relations. If you belong to Christ you are Abraham's descendants. This appears to be a chronologically based progression that describes both the macro-history of the Jews and Gentiles, and the micro-history of each individual who comes to faith

---

26. See Schreiner, *Paul*, 335–37.

27. On baptism in Paul, see Ridderbos, *Paul*, 400–406, who recognizes a close relation between the two passages treated below, and their fuller theological significance.

in Christ Jesus. Baptism in this sequence appears to be one of the necessary stages in the progression to "full membership" in the community of God, while not being equated with any of the other stages, such as faith and justification. In Rom 6:3, Paul states, in wording resembling that of Gal 3:27, ὅσοι ἐβαπτίσθημεν εἰς Χριστὸν Ἰησοῦν εἰς τὸν θάνατον αὐτοῦ ἐβαπτίσθημεν ("as many of us as were baptized into Christ Jesus were baptized into his death").[28] This statement too appears as part of a progression, but one that begins much earlier in the book. Paul first lays out the human predicament (Rom 1:18—2:29), then proposes the solution to the legal predicament in terms of justification by faith, including the place of Abraham (Rom 3:1—4:25) and the personal solution in terms of reconciliation (Rom 5:1–21), and then turns to living the life of one alive to Christ in Romans 6, before moving on to life in the Spirit. The place of baptism within this progression appears to be similar to the more compact depiction in Galatians. Baptism is a necessary stage within the progression to full incorporation into life in Christ, but to be distinguished from such other stages as justification and reconciliation. In both letters, however, it is clear that baptism is an important part of what it means to be fully initiated and incorporated into the faith community.

CONCLUSION: THE CHURCH IN PAUL'S LETTERS, ESPECIALLY ROMANS AND GALATIANS

Much more could be said about the church in Romans and Galatians. This could include discussing each of the elements above in far more detail—but that would become a full exposition of these two important letters. I have inevitably only been able to touch on several of the major factors that emerge in these two letters. A treatment such as this could also include discussing other features that are particular and peculiar to Galatians and Romans in relation to the church—but that would tend toward a full theology of Paul. In terms of this exercise, I think that it is important to note the several key features of the church in Paul as he discusses them in these two letters. These letters are not primarily concerned with the nature of the church as the community of faith-followers of Jesus Christ. Instead, the role of the church is one of the assumptions

---

28. Most take this statement as a literal statement, but a number of recent interpreters take it as metaphorical. For discussion, see Sabou, *Between Horror and Hope*, 94–109.

upon which Paul grounds the more pressing issues that he intends to discuss. Nevertheless, as I hope I have shown in this discussion, what Paul believes about the church as this grace- and faith-grounded community that is focused upon the gospel is foundational and fundamental to how he approaches a whole host of other issues. These other issues are often seen to be more important, and certainly garner far more discussion, than does the notion of the church. However, in their proper context, they are perhaps better seen as logical theological extensions of Paul's fundamental theology regarding the church.

FOR FURTHER STUDY

Ascough, R. S. *What Are They Saying about the Formation of Pauline Churches?* New York: Paulist, 1998.

Banks, R. *Paul's Idea of Community.* Rev. ed. Peabody, MA: Hendrickson, 1994.

Branick, V. *The House Church in the Writings of Paul.* Wilmington, DE: Glazier, 1998.

Brower, K. E., and A. Johnson, eds. *Holiness and Ecclesiology in the New Testament.* Grand Rapids: Eerdmans, 2007.

Hellerman, J. H. *The Ancient Church as Family.* Minneapolis: Fortress, 2001.

Ridderbos, H. *Paul: An Outline of His Theology.* Translated by J. R. de Witt. Grand Rapids: Eerdmans, 1979.

Schweizer, E. *Church Order in the New Testament.* Translated by F. Clarke. London: SCM, 1961.

Schnackenburg, R. *The Church in the New Testament.* Translated by W. J. O'Hara. London: Burns & Oates, 1974.

Seitz, O. J. F. *One Body and One Spirit: A Study of the Church in the New Testament.* Greenwich, CT: Seabury, 1960.

BIBLIOGRAPHY

Amiot, F. *The Key Concepts of St. Paul.* New York: Herder & Herder, 1962.

Asano, A. *Community-Identity Construction in Galatians: Exegetical, Social-Anthropological and Socio-Historical Studies.* JSNTSup 285. London: T. & T. Clark International, 2005.

Ascough, R. S. *What Are They Saying about the Formation of Pauline Churches?* New York: Paulist, 1998.

Banks, R. *Paul's Idea of Community.* Rev. ed. Peabody, MA: Hendrickson, 1994.

Barth, M. *The People of God.* JSNTSup 5. Sheffield: JSOT Press, 1983.

Beck, J. R., and C. L. Blomberg, eds. *Two Views on Women in Ministry.* Grand Rapids: Zondervan, 2001.

Bird, M. F. *The Saving Righteousness of God: Studies on Paul, Justification and the New Perspective.* Bletchley: Paternoster, 2007.

Bockmuehl, M. "Is There a New Testament Doctrine of the Church?" In M. Bockmuehl and A. J. Torrance, eds., *Scripture's Doctrine and Theology's Bible: How the New Testament Shapes Christian Dogmatics,* edited by M. Bockmuehl and A. J. Torrance, 29–44. Grand Rapids: Baker, 2008.

Branick, V. *The House Church in the Writings of Paul.* Wilmington, DE: Glazier, 1998.

Carson, D. A., P. T. O'Brien, and M. A. Seifrid, eds. *Justification and Variegated Nomism.* 2 vols. Grand Rapids: Baker, 2001, 2004.

Childs, B. S. *The Church's Guide for Reading Paul: The Canonical Shaping of the Pauline Corpus.* Grand Rapids: Eerdmans, 2008.

Das, A. A. *Paul, the Law, and the Covenant.* Peabody, MA: Hendrickson, 2001.

Davies, G. N. *Faith and Obedience in Romans: A Study in Romans 1–4.* JSNTSup 59. Sheffield: JSOT Press, 1990.

de Roo, J. C. R. *Works of the Law at Qumran and in Paul.* NTM 13. Sheffield: Sheffield Phoenix Press, 2007.

Dunn, J. D. G. *The Theology of Paul the Apostle.* Grand Rapids: Eerdmans, 1998.

Fee, G. D. *God's Empowering Presence: The Holy Spirit in the Letters of Paul.* Peabody, MA: Hendrickson, 1994.

———. "Male and Female in the New Creation: Galatians 3:26–29." In *Discovering Biblical Equality: Complementarity without Hierarchy,* edited by R. W. Pierce and R. M. Groothuis, 172–85. 2nd ed. Downers Grove, IL: InterVarsity, 2005.

———. *Pauline Christology.* Peabody, MA: Hendrickson, 2007.

Gathercole, S. J. *Where Is Boasting? Early Jewish Soteriology and Paul's Response in Romans 1–5.* Grand Rapids: Eerdmans, 2002.

Hansen, G. W. *Abraham in Galatians: Epistolary and Rhetorical Contexts.* JSNTSup 39. Sheffield: JSOT Press, 1989.

Hatch, W. H. P. *The Pauline Idea of Faith in Its Relation to Jewish and Hellenistic Religion.* Cambridge, MA: Harvard University Press, 1917.

Hellerman, J. H. *The Ancient Church as Family.* Minneapolis: Fortress, 2001.

Kim, S. *Paul and the New Perspective: Second Thoughts on the Origin of Paul's Gospel.* Grand Rapids: Eerdmans, 2002.

Koperski, V. *What Are They Saying about Paul and the Law?* New York: Paulist, 2001.

Longenecker, B. *The Triumph of Abraham's God: The Transformation of Identity in Galatians.* Edinburgh: T. & T. Clark, 1998.

Longenecker, R. N. *New Testament Social Ethics for Today.* Grand Rapids: Eerdmans, 1984.

Martin, T. W. "Circumcision in Galatia and the Holiness of God's Ecclesiae." In *Holiness and Ecclesiology in the New Testament*, edited by K. E. Brower and A. Johnson, 219–37. Grand Rapids: Eerdmans, 2007.

McDonald, L. M., and S. E. Porter. *Early Christianity and Its Sacred Literature*. Peabody, MA: Hendrickson, 2000.

Moffatt, J. *Grace in the New Testament*. London: Hodder & Stoughton, 1931.

Morris, L. *The Apostolic Preaching of the Cross*. 3rd ed. Grand Rapids: Eerdmans, 1965.

Nanos, M. D. *The Irony of Galatians: Paul's Letter in First-Century Context*. Minneapolis: Fortress, 2002.

Oakes, P. "Made Holy by the Holy Spirit: Holiness and Ecclesiology in Romans." In *Holiness and Ecclesiology in the New Testament*, edited by K. E. Brower and A. Johnson, 167–83. Grand Rapids: Eerdmans, 2007.

Porter, S. E. *The Criteria for Authenticity in Historical-Jesus Research: Previous Discussion and New Proposals*. JSNTSup 191. Sheffield: Sheffield Academic, 2000.

———. "Hermeneutics, Biblical Interpretation and Theology: Hunch, Holy Spirit or Hard Work?" In *Beyond the Bible: Moving from Scripture to Theology*, by I. H. Marshall, with essays by K. Vanhoozer and S. E. Porter, 97–127. Grand Rapids: Baker, 2004.

Porter, S. E., and A. W. Pitts. "Πίστις with a Preposition and Genitive Modifier: Lexical, Semantic, and Syntactic Considerations in the πίστις Χριστοῦ Discussion." In *The Faith of Jesus Christ: Exegetical, Biblical, and Theological Studies*, edited by M. F. Bird and P. M. Sprinkle, 33–53. Carlisle: Paternoster, 2009.

Rapa, R. K. *The Meaning of "Works of the Law" in Galatians and Romans*. New York: Lang, 2001.

Reasoner, M. *The Strong and the Weak: Romans 14.1–15.13 in Context*. SNTSMS 103. Cambridge: Cambridge University Press, 1999.

Richardson, P. *Paul's Ethic of Freedom*. Philadelphia: Westminster, 1979.

Ridderbos, H. *Paul: An Outline of His Theology*. Translated by J. R. de Witt. Grand Rapids: Eerdmans, 1979.

Sabou, S. *Between Horror and Hope: Paul's Metaphorical Language of "Death" in Romans 6:1–11*. Bletchley: Paternoster, 2005.

Schnackenburg, R. *The Church in the New Testament*. Translated by W. J. O'Hara. London: Burns & Oates, 1974.

Schreiner, T. R. *Paul, Apostle of God's Glory in Christ: A Pauline Theology*. Downers Grove, IL: InterVarsity, 2001.

Schweizer, E. *Church Order in the New Testament*. Translated by F. Clarke. London: SCM, 1961.

Seifrid, M. A. *Christ, Our Righteousness: Paul's Theology of Justification*. Leicester: Apollos, 2000.

Seitz, O. J. F. *One Body and One Spirit: A Study of the Church in the New Testament*. Greenwich, CT: Seabury, 1960.

Smith, B. D. *What Must I Do to Be Saved? Paul Parts Company with His Jewish Heritage*. NTM 17. Sheffield: Sheffield Phoenix, 2007.

Stuhlmacher, P. *Revisiting Paul's Doctrine of Justification: A Challenge to the New Perspective, with an Essay by Donald A. Hagner*. Downers Grove, IL: InterVarsity, 2001.

Wagner, J. R. *Heralds of the Good News: Isaiah and Paul in Concert in the Letter to the Romans*. Leiden: Brill, 2002.

Waters, G. P. *Justification and the New Perspective on Paul: A Review and Response.*
    Phillipsburg, NJ: P. & R., 2004.

Westerholm, S. *Perspectives Old and New on Paul: The "Lutheran" Paul and His Critics.*
    Grand Rapids: Eerdmans, 2004.

Wright, N. T. *The Climax of the Covenant: Christ and the Law in Pauline Theology.*
    Edinburgh: T. & T. Clark, 1991.

6

The Community of the Followers
of Jesus in 1 Corinthians

ECKHARD J. SCHNABEL

T HE FOLLOWERS OF JESUS in the church in the city of Corinth faced
difficult predicaments that resulted from their pagan past and from
their inadequate grasp of the consequences of their faith in the revelation of God's saving righteousness through Jesus Christ. Their struggles
provided the Apostle with the opportunity to elaborate on what it means
to be "the assembly of the people of God."

Paul had arrived in the city of Corinth in February or March of AD
50, preaching and teaching about Jesus, the crucified and risen Messiah,
Savior, and Lord (1 Cor 2:1–5; 15:1–7). Paul and his co-workers labored
in Corinth for over eighteen months, establishing a community of followers of Jesus (Acts 18:1–18).[1] After Paul left Corinth in September AD
51, the behavior of individual believers in the church provoked problems that prompted several Christians to contact Paul who was engaging
in missionary work in Ephesus at the time.[2] Paul wrote to the Christians
in Corinth in AD 54, clarifying the consequences of the gospel for followers of Jesus who lived in the midst of the social and cultural realities
of Corinth.

---

1. On the city of Corinth and the founding of the church in Corinth, see Schnabel,
Early Christian Mission, 2:1181–97.

2. Cf. Winter, *After Paul Left Corinth*, for a discussion of the causes of these problems in the church in Corinth.

The questions that he takes up in his first letter to the Corinthian believers are wide-ranging. Should the rhetorical praxis of contemporary orators be allowed to influence the way in which the church evaluates their missionaries, teachers, and preachers (1:1—4:21)? Should the prominent social position of a believer be a factor when the church leadership contemplates disciplinary action in the case of serious moral failure (5:1–13)? Should Christians continue to initiate civil litigation against others, even if the perceived opponents are fellow believers (6:1–11)? Can Christian men continue to frequent prostitutes, as they did before their conversion (6:12–20)? Is it acceptable to focus on one's own personal interests in times of crisis, even if this means that spouses are no longer treated as spouses (for example by refraining from sexual relations in order to avoid the conception and birth of children) and fiancées are being abandoned (7:1–40)? Can Christians accept invitations to banquets in pagan temples (8:1—10:33)? Can Christian men signal their high social position, as they did before their conversion, by praying *capite velato*, with their heads covered by their toga (11:1–4)? Can married Christian women pray without the traditional *palla* (stola) as head covering (11:5–16)? Can wealthy Christians ignore the material needs of fellow believers when they come together in the regular meetings of the church (12:17–34)? Do particular activities of Christians in the assemblies of the church, such as prophecy and speaking in unlearned languages, make these believers more prominent than others (12:1—14:40)? Is the expectation of a future resurrection of the body a necessary belief of Christians, in view of the general acceptance of the immortality of the soul in Greek thought (15:1–58)?

Paul's first letter to the Christians in Corinth demonstrates that the life of the church is determined by the message of Jesus Christ who died on the cross and who rose from the dead on the third day—a reality that affects both the faith and the life of the Jewish and Gentile believers. What do Paul's discussions tell us concerning the question what it means to be an *ekklēsia* of believers in Jesus Christ?

THE CHURCH IS THE ASSEMBLY OF THE PEOPLE OF GOD

Paul addresses the Corinthian believers as "the church of God that is in Corinth" and as "those who are sanctified in Christ Jesus" (1:2). The term *ekklēsia*, generally translated as "church," was used in the Greek world to designate the assembly of the free men of a city who were entitled to vote. In a more general sense it describes any public assembly. In this context, *ekklēsia* refers to the local assembly of the believers who gather to worship God and Jesus Christ.[3] At the same time, the phrase *ekklēsia tou theou* ("the church of God") is the Greek equivalent for the Hebrew term *qehal'el*, which is used in some early Jewish texts to describe the members of God's people who are called by God in the last days to serve him.[4] In this context, the phrase *ekklēsia tou theou* describes the people who confess Jesus as Messiah and Lord, the one who was sent by God in fulfillment of God's promises. The church is the assembly of Jewish and Gentile believers in Jesus Christ who constitute the people of God in the new covenant.[5]

In the phrase *ekklēsia tou theou*, the genitive *tou theou* ("of God") describes the Creator and the Owner of the church. The *ekklēsia* in Corinth was created by God as Jews and Gentiles came to faith in Jesus Christ. Since they came to faith in Jesus Christ through the power of God, who is effectively present in the proclamation of the gospel concerning Jesus Christ (1:24, 30; 2:4–5), they belong to God and Jesus Christ. Paul states this relationship explicitly in 3:23: "you belong to Christ, and Christ belongs to God." It is neither Paul nor other apostles or teachers who determine who belongs to the *ekklēsia tou theou*. It is God himself who called the members of the Corinthian church to give them life, righteousness, holiness, and salvation. Thus Paul asserts in 1:27–29: "God chose what is foolish in the world to shame the wise; God chose what is weak in the world to shame the strong; God chose what is low and despised in the world, things that are not, to reduce to nothing things that are, so that no one might boast in the presence of God."

Paul's theological understanding of the fundamental nature of the church is focused on the phrase "in Christ." It is as a result of the person, the life, the death, and the resurrection of Jesus Christ that the Corinthian believers who assemble in the "church of God" have been "sanctified" and declared to be "saints" (1:2). Their commitment to Jesus the Messiah (Greek *christos*) who died "for our sins" (15:3) means that

3. On the meaning of *ekklēsia* see Roloff, "ἐκκλησία," 1:411–12; Roloff, *Die Kirche im Neuen Testament*, 96–99; Banks, *Paul's Idea of Community*, 27–31; Ferguson, *Church of Christ*, 129–33.

4. See the Qumran texts 1QM IV, 10; 1QS[a] I, 25.

5. Of the 62 occurrences of the term *ekklēsia* in Paul's letters, 22 occur in 1 Corinthians, a fact that underlines the importance of the concept of the church for this letter.

they share in Jesus' death as a death of atonement. Since the death sentence that sin had pronounced against them had been carried out in Jesus' death on the cross, the Corinthian believers find that Jesus and his death have become the "source of life" for them, a new life that consists in "righteousness and sanctification and redemption" (1:30). This is why Paul's message as a missionary is focused on Jesus the crucified Messiah (1:23; 2:2).

The description of the Corinthian congregation as "the church of God" provides a theological interpretation of the reality of people from different ethnic and social backgrounds meeting together to worship the one true God. The church is not simply a gathering of like-minded people who have decided to spend time together regularly. The church is the community of God's people created by God's initiative in the last days to redeem fallen humanity, a new people consisting of Jews and Gentiles (1:18–25, 26–31; cf. 7:18–19; 12:13). The identity of God's people is no longer connected with ethnic origins, or with circumcision and obedience to the Mosaic Law, but with the sovereign power of God who sanctifies all who believe in Jesus Christ.[6] The church is the community of God's people whose lives have been transformed by the message of a crucified Messiah and Lord who has risen from the dead and who is present in the church through his Spirit.

Paul's conviction that the *ekklēsia* of believers in Jesus Christ is the people of God of the new covenant is the basis for the exposition in 1 Corinthians 3 that describes the church as a plantation, a building, and a temple. In the Old Testament and Jewish tradition, these metaphors have their place in the description of Israel as God's people.[7]

THE CHURCH IS GOD'S "PLANTATION"

Paul compares the congregation in Corinth with a plantation: "I planted, Apollos watered, but God gave the growth" (3:6).[8] The reference to planting and watering is an image of the establishment and the consolidation of a congregation of believers in Jesus Christ. The metaphor may be an echo of the song of Isa 5:1–7 in which Israel is described as God's vine-

---

6. Cf. Kraus, *Volk Gottes*, 160–71.

7. Ibid., 171–84.

8. For metaphors of vegetation in the New Testament, cf. von Gemünden, *Vegetationsmetaphorik*.

yard.[9] The metaphor of a plantation is a traditional description of the congregation of God's people.[10] If Paul indeed alludes here to Isa 5:1–7,[11] he points out that the congregation of Jewish and Gentile followers of Jesus Christ constitutes the true people of God.

Paul uses the metaphor of planting and watering in the context of his argument in 3:5–9 to make the point that he and Apollos are "farm hands" who are hardly relevant objects of competitive quarrels about prestige and status. They are both laborers whose work is necessary for the growth of the plantation (v. 8). As laborers in God's field, they are God's servants, and it is God alone who gives growth (vv. 6–7).

The metaphor of the plantation is part of Paul's larger argument that the evaluation of the teachers of the church on the basis of human or "secular" criteria contradicts the status of believers as mature spiritual people who have grown from infants to maturity (3:1–4). Paul deplores the fact that he cannot speak to the Corinthian Christians as believers who are controlled by the Spirit; this is not possible because they continue to be focused on "the flesh," i.e., on purely human values and criteria. Their behavior is childish, not worthy of mature adults (v. 1). They still need to be fed milk, like newborn babies or sick people,[12] rather than solid food (v. 2). The focus on personalities that are deemed prominent and the focus on public expressions of personal loyalty to particular teachers produce quarrels and rivalries in the church (1:10–17). Such behavior is the manifestation of secular values that they should have left behind (3:3–4) as they grow into maturity (3:1–2) as God's plantation (3:5–6).

9. Cf. Williams, *Wisdom*, 243–49.

10. Cf. Isa 60:21; 61:3; Jer 1:10; 2:21; 18:9; 24:6; 1QS VIII, 5; XI, 8; 1QH VI, 15; VII, 18–19; VIII, 5–26; CD I, 7. For the metaphorical use of "planting," cf. Isa 5:7; 60:21; 61:3; Ezek 17:1–8; 34:29; Wis 4:3–5; *Jub.* 16:26; *1 En.* 10:16; 84:6; 93:2–10; Matt 15:13; 20:1–5; Mark 4:1–20; Rom 11:16–24. Cf. Fujita, "Metaphor of Plant."

11. Williams, *Wisdom*, 243–49.

12. Artemidorus, *Oneirocritica* 1.16 speaks of adults who need milk "if they cannot tolerate food (*trophē*) on account of an illness." On Paul's reference to milk, cf. Gaventa, "Mother's Milk."

THE CHURCH IS GOD'S "BUILDING"

The second metaphor Paul uses to illustrate the nature of the congregation of the followers of Jesus is the construction of a building (3:10–15).[13] The description of the church as God's building takes up the traditional description of Israel as God's building in the Old Testament and in Jewish writings.[14] The following observations help us to understand this metaphor.[15]

First, the "building" has been established as a result of God's grace (v. 10) and thus belongs to God (v. 16–17: the building is "God's temple"). The church does not belong to an apostle or to a teacher but to God alone. Since Paul calls himself a "skilled master builder" or "architect" (v. 10), it is significant for his discussion in the larger context that in antiquity buildings were linked with the names of clients, and rarely with the names of architects.[16] The building does not belong to the architect but to the person(s) who sponsored the building.

Second, the focus of the metaphor is not on the individual Christian but on the congregation. The personal pronoun "you" in the formulation "you are God's temple" (v. 16) is plural. What is being built is the *ekklēsia* into which the individual believers are inserted.[17]

Third, as regards the church in Corinth, it was Paul who had laid the foundation of the building. Paul describes his function as *sophos architektōn*, as a "skilled master builder" (v. 10).[18] This phrase indicates that the building in view is not a private house but a monumental build-

13. The metaphor of building construction echoes two Old Testament texts. The phrase *sophos architektōn* "skilled master builder" (v. 10) occurs once in the Greek Bible (Isa 3:3); both 1 Cor 3:10 and Isa 3:3 speak of wisdom and of judgment with regard to the leaders of God's people. The materials gold, silver, and stone (vv. 12–15) are also mentioned in connection with Bezalel, who was filled with the Spirit of wisdom, skilled as an architect, and appointed to build the tabernacle (Exod 35:31–32 LXX). Cf. Williams, *Wisdom*, 257–300; Beale, *Temple*, 245–52; Ciampa and Rosner, "1 Corinthians," 703.

14. Cf. Jer 1:10; 31:4 (LXX 38:4); 33:7 (LXX 40:7); 48:7; for Qumran, cf. 1QS XI, 8–9; 1QH VI, 24–28; VII, 8–9; CD III, 19; for metaphor of God's building with the metaphor of planting, cf. Jer 1:9–10; 24:6; 31:27–28; 42:10; 45:4; Ezek 36:36; 1QS VIII, 4–10; 1QH VI; Philo, *De cherubim* 98–106; *Quis rerum divinarum heres sit* 116; *De praemiis et poenis* 139; *Legum allegoriae* I, 48.

15. It was not before the fourth century that Christians erected separate buildings for their activities; cf. White, *Social Origins*.

16. Only approximately thirty Roman architects are known by name.

17. Kitzberger, *Bau der Gemeinde*, 282–83.

18. Cf. Shanor, "Paul as Master Builder."

ing (a temple, a council building, a basilica, a theater, a multi-storeyed building). Cities and wealthy citizens who commissioned building projects hired an experienced *architektōn*, a master builder who had a knowledge of geometry, mathematics, and the art of drawing, who was competent in judging manual skills and knowledge, and who was able to estimate costs and to organize, coordinate, and supervise the work of the stonemasons, carpenters, mosaic layers, and merchants.[19] After the building commission of the city or the private sponsor had drawn up the building specifications and determined the cost of the building project, the architect prepared the building design, planned the logistical implementation, and organized the construction process. The foundation of a building was not only the first part of the building to be constructed, but also the decisive part, as it determined both the size and the weight of the structure. Paul the "skilled master builder" traveled from city to city and proclaimed the gospel of Jesus Christ, leading Jews and pagans to faith in Jesus, establishing congregations of followers of Jesus to whom he taught the content of God's revelation in Israel, in Jesus Christ, and in the teachings of the apostles.

Fourth, Paul describes the foundation of the building (the church) in terms of the gospel of Jesus Christ: "that foundation is Jesus Christ" (v. 11). The foundation of a building is laid only once. This means that the "fundamental" message of God's initiative of granting salvation through the life, death, and resurrection of Jesus Christ cannot not be reversed, canceled, or countermanded.

Fifth, the construction of the building, i.e., of the church, is still in progress. The building is not finished once the church has been established (by Paul, AD 50–51), or once teachers such as Apollos are active in the church (between AD 51 and 54), or once the Corinthian Christians read Paul's letter (in AD 54). The "building" of local churches that a missionary has established in the past is continued by other teachers in the present and in the future (v. 10). Once a church has been established, it needs further development. A foundation without the continuation of consistent building activity makes no sense. When Paul left Corinth, the

---

19. For a job description of an architect in a Roman city, see Vitruvius, *De architectura* 1.1–18. For the responsibilities of the architect in the Greco-Roman world, cf. Höcker, "Architect"; see also Höcker, "Building Trade"; Höcker, "Construction Technique."

"building" of the church was not finished; others needed to continue the work. The building activity continues until the day of judgment (v. 13).

Sixth, the workers who continue to build the church "must choose with care how to build on it" (v. 10). Paul insists that the teachers of the church cannot have an indifferent attitude regarding their work. Authentic church work must be carried out with care and competence. In particular, the "upbuilding" of the church must be carried out in correspondence with the foundation that has been laid. This means that the worship, the preaching, the teaching, and the other ministries in the congregation must be consistent with the apostolic proclamation of the gospel of Jesus Christ, the crucified and risen Messiah and Savior (v. 11, cf. 1:18–2:5).

Seventh, ignoring the foundation has fatal consequences (vv. 12–15, 17). When Herod I rebuilt the temple in Jerusalem, he disregarded the existing foundation and erected the monumental building on newly dug foundations. The result was that "in the course of time this dropped as the foundations subsided."[20] Jesus Christ, the crucified and risen Savior and Lord, is the indispensable foundation of the church. When the "building activities" comply with the fundamental truth of the gospel, which is focused on "Jesus Christ, and him crucified" (2:2), the church will prosper. When the church leaders disregard the truth of the gospel of Jesus Christ, seeking new foundations, the building will collapse and the church will cease to be an authentic *ekklēsia* of the people of God. Paul mentions six building materials, beginning with the most expensive and ending with the least expensive: gold, silver, precious stones,[21] wood, hay, and straw (v. 12). It is striking that he does not mention stones (limestone) or fired bricks, common building materials used in the construction of the walls; the latter seem to be presupposed, as gold, silver, and marble were used in the decorations of a building. Wood was an indispensable building material, used in roof- and load-bearing constructions and in interior features such as doors and windows. Hay and straw were used for the roughcast and plasterwork. If Paul thinks of specific buildings,

---

20. Josephus, *Jewish Antiquities* 15.391. In the time of Nero, Agrippa II attempted to underpin the part of the temple that had sunk, cf. Josephus, *Jewish War* 5.36. Cf. Richardson, *Building Jewish*, 262–63.

21. The "precious stones" are probably a reference to costly marble. In the nearby city of Athens the celebrated Pentelic marble was quarried until the late Roman period. On the occurrence, techniques, transportation, and costs of marble, cf. Schneider, "Marble."

the reference to gold, silver, and precious stones implies the building of a palace or an opulent villa; the reference to wood, hay, and straw suggests cheap wooden houses or huts.[22] Paul's point is not that some use the wrong building materials, but whether the building erected on the foundation will survive in the final judgment (vv. 13–15). The "work" that is destroyed on the day of judgment is not the particular building materials that some have used, but the manner in which the teachers and leaders of the church have built upon the foundation. Paul states, "Each builder must choose with care *how to build on it*. For no one can lay any foundation other than the one that has been laid" (vv. 10–11). Paul's point is not to assert that gold, silver, and precious stones do not burn up, in contrast to wood, hay, and straw: a palace, a temple, a basilica, or a sumptuous villa that are decorated with the most precious materials can be destroyed by fire as well, of course. Paul does not distinguish between valuable and worthless building materials. He contrasts "buildings" that will be vindicated on the day of judgment with "buildings" that will be condemned by God. Paul warns the congregation in Corinth that there are leaders and teachers whose work will not be acknowledged by God. It will vanish on the day of judgment. The targets of this solemn warning are Corinthian believers who employ secular criteria in their effort to ascertain the value of the contributions of Paul, Peter, Apollos, and other apostles and teachers.[23]

Paul asserts that the fixation of some Corinthian leaders on the secular values of rhetorical brilliance and party loyalties represents a "building" that ignores the foundation of Jesus (3:11) the crucified Messiah (2:2) and it will burn up on the day of judgment. The purpose of the examination by fire is not punishment,[24] destruction[25] or purification,[26] but the manifestation of the quality of the work of those who have been involved in building the church. The "work of each builder" (v. 13) is not the "works" (plural) of the (moral) behavior of the individual believers; rather, it is the "work" (singular) of those who are responsible

---

22. Diodorus Siculus, *Bibliotheca Historica* 20.65.1, refers to huts used by the military that were constructed of straw (reed) and hay (grass) and eventually destroyed by fire.

23. Cf. Kuck, *Judgement and Community Conflict*, 181.

24. As in Jude 7; Rev 18:8; 19:20; 21:8.

25. As in Matt 3:10; 13:40, 42, 50; Heb 10:27.

26. As in 1 Pet 1:7.

for the life of the congregation.[27] The "work" that will be examined is the contribution to the upbuilding of the church. The criterion of the examination is the faithfulness of the teachers with regard to the foundation, the message of Jesus the crucified and risen Messiah and Lord. This work encompasses both the proclamation of the Christian message to unbelievers, and the teaching of the Christian message before believers whose faith continuously needs consolidation and invigoration. Both types of "construction work" need to be in compliance with the foundation, which is Jesus Christ. The proclamation of Jesus the crucified and risen Savior must be central in mission and evangelism as well as in the regular meetings of the believers. Paul is confident that the work of those who safeguard the centrality of Jesus in mission and evangelism, in preaching and in teaching, and in the everyday behavior of the believers, will endure now and in the future of God's Judgment.

THE CHURCH IS GOD'S "TEMPLE"

The description of the church as God's "temple" (3:16–17; cf. 6:9) is Paul's third metaphor.[28] The hope for a perfect temple in the last days characterizes the Old Testament and Second Temple Jewish literature.[29] Paul reminds the Corinthian believers of his earlier teaching, passed on during the time when he worked in the city as a missionary: "Do you not know that you are God's temple and that God's Spirit dwells in you?" (3:16). The Christian believers in Corinth are God's temple and therefore they are the holy place of the presence of God's Spirit, i.e., of God himself.[30]

27. Cf. 1 Cor 9:1 where Paul describes the church in Corinth as "my work in the Lord."

28. In the Gospels, the Greek term *naos* refers to the Jerusalem temple (e.g., Matt 23:16–17; Mark 14:58; Luke 1:9; John 2:19). In Acts 7:48, Stephen emphasizes that God does not live in temples made with human hands. John uses the term *naos* for the heavenly sanctuary (Rev 3:12; 7:15; 11:1, 2, 19; 14:15, 17; 15:5, 6, 8; 16:1, 17; 21:22).

29. The basic text is Ezekiel 40–48; cf. also Ezek 37:26–27; Isa 44:28; Tob 14:5; *Jub.* 1:17, 29; 4:24–25; *1 En.* 90:28–29; 91:13; *Sib. Or.* 3:290; 1QM II, 3; VII, 11; 11QTemple XXIX, 8–10. The Qumran Community understood itself as the true Israel and described its identity in terms of the "sanctuary of Aaron," the "house of truth in Israel," the "most holy place for Aaron;" cf. 1QS V, 4–7; VIII, 4–10; IX, 3–9; XI, 8; 1QH VI, 24–28; 4QFlor I, 2–3; CD III, 18–IV, 10. Cf. Klinzing, *Die Umdeutung des Kultus in der Qumrangemeinde*, 50–93; cf. Gärtner, *The Temple and the Community in Qumran.*

30. Studies on the metaphor of the church as temple include McKelvey, *New Temple*; Marshall, "Church and Temple"; Müller, *Gottes Pflanzung—Gottes Bau—Gottes Tempel*; Lanci, *New Temple for Corinth*; Beale, *Temple*, 245–68; Hogeterp, *Paul and God's Temple.*

This theological reality of the congregation of believers is contradicted by the behavior of those who evaluate the teachers of the church on the basis of the secular criteria of contemporary rhetoric, pledging allegiance to individuals (1:12; 3:4) while forgetting that the effective power of the gospel is not connected with rhetorical stratagems but with the power of God himself whose Spirit convinces people to believe in Jesus, the crucified Messiah (1:18—2:5).

First, the reference to the temple does not focus on the building but on the worship that characterizes the "building." Claudius, who was emperor from AD 41 to 54,[31] rejected petitions of provincial cities to build a temple in which he would be venerated.[32] Paul's description of the church as temple thus accords to the congregation of believers in Jesus Christ a dignity that the reigning emperor rejects for himself. The apostles and the teachers of the church build a "temple" that belongs to God and in which Jesus Christ is worshiped.

Second, the church can be described as "God's temple" because God is present in the fellowship of the followers of Jesus through his Spirit (v. 16). The presence of the promised Spirit of God in the congregation of believers[33] explains why they are God's messianic temple.[34] The presence of God's Spirit is connected with the effective reality of Jesus' death on the cross as the place of God's atoning presence (cf. Rom 3:25). This is precisely why the proclamation of "Jesus Christ, and him crucified" is fundamental. As Jesus' death on the cross atones for sins, God's gracious presence is a reality for those who believe in Jesus Christ and who have thus received the Holy Spirit. The congregation of believers in Jesus Christ is God's temple in the sense that it is here that God is graciously present.

Third, Paul ends his exposition of the nature of the church in 1 Corinthians 3 with a warning for the teachers who are active in the work of "building" the church in Corinth that Paul had started and Apollos had continued (3:17). If they persist in using secular values in the work in the church, they will destroy the church. The teachers

---

31. Paul evangelized in Corinth in AD 50–51, and he wrote 1 Corinthians in AD 54.

32. Cf. Witulski, *Kaiserkult in Kleinasien*, 46–49.

33. Cf. 1 Cor 6:19; 12:13; 2 Cor 13:5; Rom 8:9; Gal 6:1; Eph 1:17; cf. Acts 2.

34. Important is the Old Testament notion of God or God's *shekhina* dwelling among his people; cf. Exod 25:8; 29:45–46; 40:34–35; Lev 26:11; Num 5:3; 35:34; 1 Kgs 6:13; 8:10–11; Isa 8:18; Ezek 37:27; Zech 8:3; Ps 74:2; 135:21).

who want to mold the church in agreement with the secular values of the urban elites of the Greco-Roman world tolerate and even promote quarrels, competition, and divisions. They do not build the church. They destroy the temple that God is building and that belongs to God. The announcement, "God will destroy that person" (v. 17) is an urgent warning. In antiquity, the desecration of a temple was severely punished, often by death.[35]

THE CHURCH IS THE "BODY" OF CHRIST

The regular meetings of the Corinthian believers were more often than not characterized by individual Christians monopolizing the worship services with their contributions. The main culprits were believers who passed on prophetic messages and who spoke in unlearned languages. Before Paul provides specific guidelines on how to deal with these matters, he begins in 12:1–31 with an emphasis on the unity of the church that controls the diversity of gifts and ministries of the individual church members. This extended discussion focuses on an exposition of the metaphor of the body: "For just as the body is one and has many members, and all the members of the body, though many, are one body, so it is with Christ . . . Indeed the body does not consist of one member but of many . . . Now you are the body of Christ and individually members of it" (12:12, 14, 27). The phrase "body of Christ" refers here not to the physical body of Jesus who died on the cross,[36] but to the local congregation of believers in Jesus Christ.[37] The concept of the "body of Christ" takes up a metaphor that was widely known at the time.[38] The metaphor of the body was used for the concept that in nature, a social organism forms a unity. Three nuances of this idea can be distinguished. First, each member of an organism possesses a different value. This is the point that Menenius Agrippa emphasizes when he compares society with a human

---

35. Cf. Herodotus, *Historiae* 8.35–38. In the Jerusalem temple, Greek and Latin inscriptions, installed on the wall at regular intervals, warned Gentiles on penalty of death against passing into the inner court where the laws of purification were rigorously kept (Josephus, *Jewish War* 5.193–94; 6.124–26; *Jewish Antiquities* 15.417). Cf. Bahat, "Herodian Temple," 52.

36. Thus in 1 Cor 10:16; Rom 7:4; cf. 1 Cor 11:24, 27.

37. See 1 Cor 10:17; 12:12, 27; Rom 12:4–5. Cf. Robinson, *Body*; Schweizer, *Church as the Body*; Yorke, *Church as the Body*; Lee, *Paul, the Stoics, and the Body of Christ*.

38. Mitchell, *Paul and the Rhetoric of Reconciliation*, 158–60; Dunn, *Theology of Paul*, 550–51.

body in order to resolve the strife between the aristocratic patricians and the plebeians, arguing that the "active members" have no right to revolt against the apparently "idle belly."[39] The various members of the body have different roles to fulfill. Second, the body is more important than the individual members of the body, i.e., the unity of the organism is more important than the individual human being. Third, the body has a hierarchical structure in which the head controls the individual members of the body, i.e., the leadership is supreme. Another trajectory of the use of the metaphor of the body related the body to the notion that the members of a social organism are related to each other. This application of the metaphor is frequent in treatises on political ethics.[40]

Paul's comparison of the local congregation of believers with a human body includes nuances of both models of the metaphor of the body in ancient literature. On the one hand, Paul emphasizes that the congregation of believers is *one* body. On the other hand, he insists that the individual members of the congregation are related to each other and that they are of equal rank. As Paul discusses the various activities and ministries in the congregation, he asserts that the diverse functions of the individual members do not establish a diverse quality rating or hierarchy—they all belong to the same body, whether they are foot or hand, ear or eye.

First, Paul begins his discussion in 12:12–31 with the assertion that the believers who belong to the congregation constitute a unity (vv. 12–14). As a human body constitutes one single entity even though it consists of many diverse members, "so it is with Christ" (v. 12). This means that all who believe in Jesus Christ, whether they are Jews or Greeks, slaves or free, have received the one Spirit and have been incorporated into one body (v. 13). The congregation consists of people with diverse ethnic or social backgrounds (v. 14).

Second, Paul explains this reality with the metaphor of the human body (vv. 15–26). He uses two "quotations" of speaking body parts (vv. 15–16) and two rhetorical questions the answer to which is obvious (v. 17). Paul first explains the self-evident unity of the human body, whose various organs have different tasks, none of which is dispensable. It would be a ridiculous notion if a foot were to declare, "Because I am not

---

39. Dionysius of Halicarnassus, *Antiquitates romae* 6.86. For an explanation of this passage, cf. Lee, *Paul, the Stoics, and the Body of Christ*, 31–34.

40. Cf. Plato, *Respublica* 462c–d.

a hand, I do not belong to the body," or if an ear were to affirm, "Because I am not an eye, I do not belong to the body." A body is a complete, living organism only when it consists of a plurality of members with diverse functions that all depend on each other. Paul affirms that the assignment of the tasks of the various organs has been arranged by God the Creator (v. 18), and repeats the interrelatedness of the unity and the diversity of the human body (vv. 19–20). With two further "quotations" of speaking body parts—now it is the eye and the head that declare that the hand and the feet are expendable—Paul demonstrates the absurdity of the desire for self-sufficiency of individual members of the body (v. 21). The fact that we treat the ostensibly less honorable members of our body (the sexual organs) with particular care illustrates the self-evident unity of the members of a human body (vv. 22–24a). The reference to the more respectable and the less honorable members of the human body prompts Paul to reassert God's sovereignty with regard to the assignment of the tasks of the body's organs (vv. 24b–26).

Third, Paul introduces the application of the metaphor of the human body to the Christian believers (vv. 28–31) with the fundamental assertion that the congregation in Corinth is "the body of Christ" and that the individual believers are members of this body (v. 27). He then proceeds to apply the metaphor of the body to the Corinthian church and to the various gifts, services, and activities of the individual believers (v. 28). The list of spiritual gifts and functions that are practiced in the congregation refers to apostles, prophets, teachers, deeds of power, gifts of healing, forms of assistance, forms of leadership, and speaking in various kinds of unlearned languages. This list is followed by eight rhetorical questions that enumerate again these spiritual gifts and functions (vv. 29–30). Paul makes the obvious point that not all believers have all these gifts and functions. He emphasizes the individuality and the essential equality of the believers and their various gifts, functions, and activities. He concludes that the Corinthian believers should strive for "the greater gifts" (v. 31), i.e., they should be consistently and continuously devoted to exercising and exhibiting those gifts that contribute most directly to the edification of all believers in the congregation.[41]

---

41. Note the emphasis on intelligibility in 14:1–25. There is no space to discuss the gifts of the Spirit more extensively; cf. Carson, *Showing the Spirit*; Fee, *God's Empowering Presence*, 158–75, 187–97, 886–95; Turner, *Holy Spirit*.

Fourth, Paul links the unity of the local congregation to the work of the Holy Spirit. When the Corinthian believers were converted they received the Spirit who "immersed" them into a body, which thus constitutes an organic unity (v. 13). The term that I translate as "immersed" represents the Greek term *baptizō*, which does not *mean* "to baptize"[42] but "to dip, to plunge, to immerse." In Greek literature, the term *baptizō* is used for a person who drowns, for a ship that sinks, for clothes drenched with water, for bread soaked in wine. Used as a metaphor, the term *baptizō* can describe a person who is over head and ears in debt, a person who is getting into deep waters.[43] Paul emphasizes that when people are converted to faith in Jesus Christ, the Spirit "immerses," i.e., incorporates, them into the body of Christ, which is the congregation of believers. This means that the unity of the congregation is not a *goal* of Christian activity (a goal some may regard as naive or utopian). Rather, the unity of the church is a *reality* that has been established by the Holy Spirit, by the effective presence of God himself. God's sovereignty is not just significant in the creation of the church as a unified organism. It is also significant for understanding and accepting the diversity that characterizes this unity. God "created" the individual believers when they came to faith in Jesus Christ. He has given each believer a distinct role and function within the community of the believers, whose ordered structure as a body with many members corresponds to his sovereign will (v. 18). Paul is convinced that when Christians understand the nature of the *ekklēsia* as body of Christ, and when they realize their role within that body, they will not tolerate dissension because they will care for each other (v. 25).

Fifth, the metaphor of the human body and its members illustrates Paul's conviction that the one Spirit provides the Christian believers with various gifts that complement one another and are to be used for the edification of the church. We misunderstand the metaphor of the church as the body of Christ if we deduce the nature of the church from the exis-

---

42. The English term "baptize" is a word that transliterates the Greek term *baptizō* when reference is made to the initiatory rite of Christian water baptism. A transliteration is not a translation.

43. Cf. Liddell et al., *Lexicon*, 305. Specialized meanings common in New Testament and later Christian texts are "to wash ceremonially for purpose of purification" and "to use water in a rite for purpose of renewing or establishing a relationship with God (= to baptize)"; cf. Bauer et al., *Lexicon*, 164; E. J. Schnabel, "The Meaning of βαπτίζειν in Greek, Jewish, and Patristic Texts," *Filologia Neotestamentaria* (2011) forthcoming.

tence of the risen and glorified Christ in heaven.[44] The glory of the body of the risen Christ in heaven does not establish the glory of the church as the body of Christ on earth. On the contrary, Paul argues that the raison d'être of the congregation as the body of Christ is to serve others, not self-service, the proclamation of the gospel in the world, not isolation from the world. Claims that the existence and the mission of the church are "incarnational" find no support in the exposition of the nature of the church as the body of Christ. The reality of Jesus' incarnation is not continued in an "incarnational" mission of the church. The metaphor of the "body of Christ" does not signify that the church extends Jesus' incarnation through time.[45] The life and ministry of the church is not "incarnation" because there was only one true incarnation, which took place when Jesus was born in Bethlehem, a reality that certainly has ongoing consequences for the world but a historical reality that cannot be repeated—and a historical reality that must not be dissolved into a theological chiffre that we may employ as we think best. The analogy of the metaphor "body of Christ" is not to the body of Jesus who was born in Bethlehem, who died on a cross on Golgotha, and who was raised from the dead on the third day. Rather, Paul's metaphor of the body of Christ expounds the analogy between the physiological reality of the human body whose diverse members constitute a unitary oneness and the theological reality of the congregation of believers whose diversity must not be allowed to dissolve or diminish the unity of God's people. Paul fights for the unity of the church. At the same time he fights for the consolidation of the life and ministry of the individual believers. Paul knows that the church cannot safeguard her unity if the functions of the individual Christians are diminished or repressed. The unity of the church is both genuine and effective only when the leaders of the congregation help the individual believers to fulfill their calling, in accordance with the gifts, talents, and vocations that God has given through the Spirit.

Sixth, Paul's repeated emphasis in 12:7, 25 and in his exposition of the gifts of the Spirit in 14:1–40 is focused on the need for edification. Whatever gifts of the Spirit the individual believer possesses and whatever his or her function in the congregation is, followers of Jesus

---

44. This is a misunderstanding that theologians connected with the World Council of Churches have promulgated; for a critique, cf. Käsemann, "Theological Problem," 116–17.

45. As argued again, recently, by Yancey, "Ongoing Incarnation," 72.

know that their gifts complement each other, and they are consistently concerned that they use their gifts for the benefit of their fellow believers. The purpose of the diversity of the gifts of the believers and the purpose of the unity of the church is the continued upbuilding of the congregation. The unselfish concern for one's fellow believers constitutes the controlling criterion for the use of one's particular ministry in the congregation. It is thus not surprising that Paul expounds the concept of love as the decisive principle that must govern the behavior of Christians (13:1–13). Paul can use the same benchmark for the behavior of all believers precisely because they are all members of the congregation as the *one* body of Christ, and because all genuine Christians are governed by the *one* Spirit. Love is therefore the "still more excellent way" (12:31).

Seventh, the exposition of love as the fundamental criterion of Christian behavior in 13:1–13 begins with the argument that the gifts of the Spirit do not save in God's final judgment (vv. 1–3). It is only God's love, manifesting itself in the life of the followers of Jesus, that saves the believer from being "nothing" or gaining "nothing." Those spiritual gifts and activities that are the "greater" gifts and ministries correspond most clearly to the nature of love that insists not on its own way but seeks to serve the interests of the neighbor (vv. 4–7). Paul ends his exposition of love by pointing out that despite the wealth of the gifts of the Spirit, our present experience of God's salvation remains fragmentary, compared with the future glory of God's unmitigated presence (vv. 8–12).

THE LIFE OF THE CHURCH: THE MEETINGS OF THE LOCAL CONGREGATION

The evidence in 1 Corinthians allows us to draw up the following profile of the meetings of the followers of Jesus in Corinth. First, the believers seem to have met on *the first day of every week* (16:2),[46] i.e., on Sundays. Paul advises the Corinthian believers to put aside money for the collection for the Christians in Jerusalem on the first day of every week. They also could do this at home. However, the early evidence for Christian

---

46. In 1 Cor 16:2 the term *sabbaton* does not mean "sabbath" (i.e., Saturday), as is evident from the use of the ordinal number *mia* ("first"). In the LXX the term *sabbaton* usually describes the "sabbath," i.e., the seventh day of the week, but sometimes it designates the "week" (Ps 47:1 LXX; cf. also Mark 16:9; Luke 18:12). As the "week" was unknown in the Greco-Roman world, it is evident that Paul presupposes knowledge of the Jewish calendar in the Corinthian church. On the calendar, cf. VanderKam, "Calendar."

meetings on the first day of the week[47] makes it plausible that Paul's comment reflects the tradition of regular meetings on the first day of the week.[48]

Second, the congregation in Corinth *met in the private house* of Gaius (Rom 16:23), probably one of the more eminent men in the city.[49] The reference to occasions on which the whole congregation comes together (1 Cor 14:23) implies that there were times when the Corinthian believers came together in smaller groups that were quite possibly also regarded as *ekklēsiae*.[50]

Third, an important element of the Christian meetings was *singing*.[51] When the Corinthian believers met, they sang psalms, hymns, and songs. In 1 Cor 14:26 Paul mentions a *psalmos* (usually translated as "hymn"); in Col 3:16 and Eph 5:19 he mentions besides *psalmoi* also *hymnoi* (hymns) and *odai pneumatikai* (spiritual songs [of praise]). The term *psalmoi* describes in the LXX the psalms of the Psalter, sometimes the singing accompanied by the music of stringed instruments.[52] There is no reason to doubt that when Paul uses the term *psalmoi* in Col 3:16 and Eph 5:19 he refers to the singing of the Old Testament psalms. Since in 1 Cor 14:26 the term *psalmos* introduces other activities in the meetings of the church, it is plausible to take it here as a general reference to the singing of the believers, which included the psalms of Scripture and new Christian hymns and songs of praise.[53] When a believer "has

47. *Epistle of Barnabas* 15:9; Justin, *First Apology* 67; Pliny, *Epistulae* 10.96.

48. Cf. Bauckham, "The Lord's Day," 230–33.

49 He could accommodate Paul, and he probably supplied Tertius, perhaps his slave, as the secretary to whom Paul dictated his letter to the Roman Christians, cf. Rom 16:22–23. On the house churches, cf. Branick, *House Church*; Gehring, *House Church and Mission*.

50. Banks, *Paul's Idea of Community*, 32.

51. Contrary to the loose language of contemporary evangelicals, the singing of Christian songs (or, more narrowly still, of praise songs) should not be identified with "worship." On Christian worship, cf. Peterson, *Engaging with God*; Carson, ed., *Worship by the Book*.

52. For the latter, cf. Ps 147:1 (LXX 146:1); note the instruments mentioned in Ps 150:3–5.

53. New Testament scholars identify the following texts as early Christian hymns: Luke 1:46–55; 1:68–79; Rom 8:31–39; 1 Cor 13:1–13; Phil 2:6–11; Col 1:15–20; 1 Tim 3:16; 1 Pet 2:21–24; Rev 5:9–10, 12, 13; 11:15, 17–18; 15:3–4. The reconstruction of these hymns is disputed, and more recently some have questioned the description of these texts as hymns, preferring terms such as elevated prose or rhythmic prose; cf. Kennel, *Frühchristliche Hymnen?*; Brucker, *"Christushymnen" oder "epideiktische Passagen"?*

a hymn" and brings it to the congregational meeting (14:26), he or she evidently has composed a new Christian hymn at home and sings it before the assembly, presumably teaching it to the other believers so that everyone can participate.

Fourth, another regular element was *teaching*. The word *didachē* in 14:26 means "teaching" or "instruction."[54] The term implies the systematic reflection on God's word, which would have included the exposition of the Scriptures, of the words of Jesus, and of the teachings of the apostles.

Fifth, some believers passed on *prophetic messages*. Paul speaks of "revelation" (14:26), a word that describes the content of prophetic speech. Early Christian prophecy describes the reception and declaration of revelation conveyed as revealed truth that provided guidance, exhortation, or remonstration, whether for the church or for individuals.[55] According to 14:29–33, other believers had to examine both the content and the claim to authority of the prophetic message.

Sixth, the followers of Jesus shared *communal meals*. When Paul discusses the problematic behavior of some believers during the Lord's Supper (11:17–34), he presupposes that the Christians are sharing a meal during their meetings. The most plausible reconstruction[56] assumes that the believers brought their own food to the private house in which the congregation met. Everyone consumed the food that he or she had brought, with the result that the wealthier believers shamed the poor believers who had to watch how they ate their larger and more sumptuous portions. Paul exhorts the wealthier believers to share their food with the poor Christians. In other words, he urges them to have a "pot luck" dinner (which was not unknown in antiquity)[57] so that everyone would have enough to eat. This reconstruction assumes that the blessing of the

---

54. NRSV translates "lesson," NASB "a teaching," TNIV "a word of instruction."

55. Cf. Forbes, *Prophecy and Inspired Speech*, 229.

56. Cf. Hofius, "Herrenmahl und Herrenmahlsparadosis"; Klinghardt, *Gemeinschaftsmahl und Mahlgemeinschaft*, 286–301; Winter, *After Paul Left Corinth*, 143–52.

57. Cf. Xenophon, *Memorabilia* 3.14.1: "Whenever some of the members of a dining-club brought more meat than others, Socrates would tell the waiter either to put the small contribution into the common stock or to portion it out equally among the diners. So the high batteners felt obliged not only to take their share of the pool, but to pool their own supplies in return; and so they put their own supplies also into the common stock. And since they thus got no more than those who brought little with them, they gave up spending much on meat."

bread that served as the remembrance of Jesus' broken body took place at the beginning of the meal, while the blessing of the cup in remembrance of Jesus' shed blood took place at the end of the meal (perhaps before the dessert). In 11:34 Paul distinguishes between private meals at home where people satisfy their appetites, and the congregational meals whose main purpose was fellowship.

Seventh, the Christians in Corinth *collected money for other congregations* (16:2–4; cf. 2 Cor 8–9; Rom 15:26).[58] The reasons for this collection that Paul organized, evidently in all the churches that he had established, are varied. The collection was to alleviate the economic hardship of the Judean Christians (2 Cor 8:13–15). It demonstrated the fellowship between Paul's mission and the Christians in Jerusalem, and it demonstrated the central importance of the church in Jerusalem (Rom 15:26–27). The delegation of Christians that took the money to Jerusalem illustrated the equality of Jewish believers and Gentile believers; some see a connection with the Jewish expectations of a pilgrimage of the nations to Zion in the last days.[59] Although this is possible and perhaps plausible, there is no evidence that the Corinthian believers collected money for their own needs.

THE LIFE OF THE BELIEVERS
AND THE LOGIC OF THE GOSPEL

Some have suggested that the life of the church in Corinth (and in Pauline churches) was improvised, as fixed church structures did not come into view. It is certainly correct that Paul does not emphasize the internal order or organization of the church. However, the reason for Paul's personal intervention in areas of church discipline (5:1–13; 6:1–11) and the order of the congregational meetings (14:1–33) was not a lack of organization but the fact that the church leadership in Corinth evidently had failed to address and solve the existing problems. It seems that they either lacked the courage to address problems caused by wealthy members of the church (e.g., 5:1–13; 11:17–34), or, in the case of elders who belonged to the wealthy elite, they were part of the problem and thus could not be part of the solution. For Paul, three realities are normative

---

58. Cf. McKnight, "Collection"; Joubert, *Paul as Benefactor*; Schnabel, *Early Christian Mission*, 2:959–61.

59. Cf. Isa 2:2–5; 14:30, 32; 60–61; 66:10–24; Mic 4:1–3; Zeph 3:9, 12.

for the life of believers: the gospel of Jesus Christ, the goal of the edification of the church, and the Scriptures.

First, the *normative significance of the gospel of Jesus, the crucified and risen Messiah and Lord* is the central theme in Paul's discussions of the Corinthians' problems. Jesus' life, death, and resurrection have established the new covenant (11:25). The reality of the new covenant means that the assembly of the followers of Jesus, whether Jews or Gentiles, elite or slave, rich or poor, have been constituted as God's people. Jesus Christ has been sacrificed as "our" paschal lamb (5:7). The Israelites in the desert are "our" ancestors (10:1). While those who belong to "Israel according to the flesh" (10:18) eat meat that has been offered in temple sacrifices, the believers in Jesus belong to God's new covenant people[60] who do not eat in temples. Once the believers recognize that both the existence and the life of the congregation is determined by the good news of Jesus who is the crucified Messiah and thus the wisdom from God (1:18—2:5), they will not allow the rhetorical praxis of contemporary orators to control the manner in which the church evaluates their missionaries, teachers, and preachers (1:1—4:21). Once they grasp what it means that Jesus Christ is "our paschal lamb" who has been sacrificed (5:7), they will be eager to "clean out the old yeast,"[61] i.e., they will have the courage to discipline a church member who persists in serious sinful behavior, no matter what his social position may be (5:1–13). When they realize that they have been washed, sanctified, and justified "in the name of the Lord Jesus Christ and in the Spirit of our God" (6:11), they will refrain from initiating legal proceedings against fellow believers (6:1–11). Once a believer understands that he is a member of Christ's body and a temple of the Holy Spirit (6:15, 19), he cannot possibly contemplate joining himself to a prostitute (6:12–20). When believers comprehend that they are called "to lead the life that the Lord has assigned, to which God called" them (7:17), they will not allow convictions concerning the proximity of Jesus' second coming and concerning the time of crisis that precedes this climactic event to uniformly control the behavior of Christians (7:1–40). Once they understand that Jesus Christ has died for all (8:11), they will not jeopardize the salvation of new converts who are

---

60. Cf. Gal 6:16 for the phrase "the Israel of God" describing both Jewish and Gentile Christians.

61. In preparation for the celebration of the festival of Passover, the Israelites had to clean out any old yeast that was in the house (Exod 12:15).

weak. And once they understand the significance of their union with Jesus Christ (10:16–17), they will refrain from accepting invitations to banquets in pagan temples since Christians cannot be partners of pagan deities and their demonic reality (8:1—10:32). Once Christian men and women understand their respective positions "in the Lord" (11:3, 11), they will neither flaunt their prominent position in society in the meetings of the believers nor will they behave as if they are unmarried (11:1–16). When wealthy believers understand what they celebrate when they come together with other believers, sharing a meal and remembering the death of Jesus (12:23–26), they will not ignore the material needs of the poor (6:17–34). When Christians understand that the confession "Jesus is Lord" is possible only on account of the power of the Spirit who convinces people of the truth of the gospel (12:3), particular activities in the congregation such as prophecy and speaking in unlearned languages will not be allowed to divide the church (12:1—14:40). And if believers understand what happened in Jesus' resurrection from the dead (15:3–5), they believe that there will be a future resurrection of the body, and they will not be deceived concerning the eternal significance of what we do with our human bodies (15:1–58; esp. 15:33–34). The normative significance of the gospel of Jesus Christ is evident in quotations of sayings of Jesus that Paul regards as authoritative; 7:10 (cf. Mark 10:11–12); 9:14 (cf. Luke 10:7 par. Matt 10:10); 11:23–25 (cf. Mark 14:22–25 par. Luke 22:14–23; Matt 26:26–29).[62] While Paul alludes to sayings of Jesus in other letters also,[63] it is only in 1 Corinthians that we have explicit quotations of dominical sayings.

Second, the *normative significance of the edification of the church* is the central criterion in Paul's discussion of gifts of the Spirit. The slogan "I have no need of you" (12:21–26) indicates that some Christians in Corinth were eager to ostentatiously show off their spiritual gifts, evidently with the goal of amplifying their status and prestige in the congregation. Paul argues that what is of primary significance is the edification of the church as the body of Christ, not the activity of an individual believer in the congregational meetings (12:1–30). This concern

62. Wenham, *Paul*, 144–47, 156–59, 192–93, 242–49.

63. Allusions to sayings of Jesus in 1 Corinthians have been detected in 1:19–21, 24–25 (cf. Matt 11:25–27 par. Luke 10:21–22); 1:23 (cf. Matt 7:24–27 par. Luke 6:47–49); 4:1–2 (cf. Luke 12:42); 9:1–14 (cf. Matt 10:1–10); 13:2 (cf. Matt 17:20; 21:21; Mark 11:23).

corresponds with self-sacrificial love that aims at the welfare of fellow believers (13:1–13). Speaking in an unlearned language (glossolalia) is indeed a gift of the Holy Spirit (12:10, 28), a gift that serves the praise of God (14:2). If this gift is exercised in the public venue of the congregational meeting without translation into the vernacular (specifically into Greek, which everyone in the Corinthian church would have understood), the words that are spoken remain unintelligible and thus cannot benefit the other members of the church who are present, not to speak of unbelievers who may be attending the worship service (14:2, 6–12). Paul rejects the notion that worshipers edify themselves in the meetings of the congregation (14:4). He insists that glossolalia must be translated if it is practiced in the congregation meetings, since otherwise the other believers are not edified (14:13–19, 27–28). When believers focus on their own spiritual experience, they are like children who are naturally self-absorbed (14:20). Mature believers are less concerned about themselves than they are about the edification of their fellow believers and about the conversion of unbelievers who are present (14:1–25).

Third, the *normative significance of the Scriptures* is evident in the frequent quotations[64] of and allusions[65] to the Old Testament. The two main vices that Paul deals with in 1 Corinthians—sexual immorality (chs. 5–7)[66] and idolatry (chs. 8–14)[67]—were regarded as typical of pagans in Jewish moral teaching, which was based on the (Old Testament) Scriptures. The vice list in 5:11 describes six types of sinners with whom genuine followers of Jesus should have no social contact. As Paul quotes the Deuteronomic expulsion formula "Drive out the wicked person from among you" (5:13), the inclusion of the greedy, idolater, reviler, drunkard, or robber, after the opening reference to the sexually immoral, is explained by the list of sins that Deuteronomy associates with an expulsion formula.[68] When Paul discusses Israel's failures in 10:7–8, he

64. Explicit quotations are 1 Cor 1:19, 31; 2:9; 3:19, 20; 6:16; 9:9, 10; 10:7; 14:21; 15:45, 54–55; cf. also 2:9b; 9:10. On Paul's quotations in 1 Corinthians, cf. Stanley, *Paul and the Language of Scripture*, 185–215.

65. The allusions to Old Testament texts include 1 Cor 5:7–8; 8:4; 9:13; 10:5, 18–22; 11:7–9; 14:25; 15:25. For a full treatment of the quotations and allusions, see Ciampa and Rosner, "1 Corinthians"; for the following point, see ibid., 695–96.

66. Cf. May, *Body for the Lord*.

67. Cf. Newton, *Deity and Diet*; Cheung, *Idol Food in Corinth*; Fotopoulos, *Food Offered to Idols*.

68. For sexual immorality, cf. Deut 22:21–22, 30; for idolatry, cf. Deut 13:1–5;

ties these two vices to their Old Testament background with the quotation of Exod 32:6.

Paul's main focus is the concentration on theological foundations that provide principles whose application will solve the various problems in the congregation. Paul is convinced that the Corinthian believers will be able to address their problems if and when they orientate their behavior by the gospel of Jesus Christ, if and when they comprehend their connectedness with the person, life, death, and resurrection of Jesus Christ, if and when they realign their priorities with the goal of the edification of the church as the growing body of Jesus Christ, and if and when they grasp the effective reality of God in the presence of the Holy Spirit.

FOR FURTHER STUDY

Banks, Robert. *Paul's Idea of Community: The Early House Churches in Their Historical Setting*. Rev. ed. Peabody, MA: Hendrickson, 1994.

Cerfaux, Lucien. *The Church in the Theology of Saint Paul*. New York: Herder, 1959.

Fee, Gordon D. *God's Empowering Presence: The Holy Spirit in the Letters of Paul*. Peabody, MA: Hendrickson, 1994.

Ferguson, Everett. *The Church of Christ: A Biblical Ecclesiology for Today*. Grand Rapids: Eerdmans, 1996.

McKelvey, R. Jack. *The New Temple: The Church in the New Testament*. Oxford: Oxford University Press, 1969.

Roloff, Jürgen. *Die Kirche im Neuen Testament*. Grundrisse zum Neuen Testament 10. Göttingen: Vandenhoeck & Ruprecht, 1993.

Schweizer, Eduard. *The Church as the Body of Christ*. Richmond: John Knox, 1964.

Turner, Max M. B. *The Holy Spirit and Spiritual Gifts Then and Now*. Carlisle: Paternoster, 1996.

Winter, Bruce W. *After Paul Left Corinth: The Influence of Secular Ethics and Social Change*. Grand Rapids: Eerdmans, 2001.

17:2–7; for people giving false testimony, cf. Deut 19:16–19; for drunkenness (of a rebellious son), cf. Deut 21:18–21; for robbery, cf. Deut 24:7. Cf. Rosner, *Paul, Scripture and Ethics*, 68–70.

BIBLIOGRAPHY

Bahat, Dan. "The Herodian Temple." In *The Cambridge History of Judaism*. Vol. 3, *The Early Roman Period*, edited by W. Horbury et al., 38–58. Cambridge: Cambridge University Press, 1999.

Banks, Robert. *Paul's Idea of Community: The Early House Churches in Their Historical Setting*. Rev. ed. Peabody MA: Hendrickson, 1994.

Bauckham, Richard J. "The Lord's Day." In *From Sabbath to Lord's Day: A Biblical, Historical and Theological Investigation*, edited by D. A. Carson, 221–50. Grand Rapids: Zondervan, 1982.

Bauer, Walter, et al. *A Greek-English Lexicon of the New Testament and Other Early Christian Literature*, edited by F. W. Danker. 3rd ed. Chicago: University of Chicago Press, 2000.

Beale, Gregory K. *The Temple and the Church's Mission: A Biblical Theology of the Dwelling Place of God*. NSBT 17. Downers Grove, IL: InterVarsity, 2004.

Branick, Vincent P. *The House Church in the Writings of Paul*. Zachaeus Studies New Testament. Wilmington, DE: Glazier, 1989.

Brucker, Ralph.'*Christushymnen*' oder '*epideiktische Passagen*'? *Studien zum Stilwechsel im Neuen Testament und seiner Umwelt*. FRLANT 176. Göttingen: Vandenhoeck & Ruprecht, 1997.

Carson, Don A. *Showing the Spirit: A Theological Exposition of 1 Corinthians 12–14*. Grand Rapids: Baker, 1987.

———, ed. *Worship by the Book*. Grand Rapids: Zondervan, 2002.

Cheung, Alex T. *Idol Food in Corinth: Jewish Background and Pauline Legacy*. JSNTSup 176. Sheffield: Sheffield Academic, 1999.

Ciampa, Roy E., and Brian S. Rosner. "1 Corinthians." In *Commentary on the New Testament Use of the Old Testament*, edited by G. K. Beale and D. A. Carson, 694–783. Grand Rapids: Baker, 2007.

Dunn, James D. G. *The Theology of Paul the Apostle*. Grand Rapids: Eerdmans, 1998.

Fee, Gordon D. *God's Empowering Presence: The Holy Spirit in the Letters of Paul*. Peabody, MA : Hendrickson, 1994.

Ferguson, Everett. *The Church of Christ: A Biblical Ecclesiology for Today*. Grand Rapids: Eerdmans, 1996.

Forbes, Christopher B. *Prophecy and Inspired Speech in Early Christianity and Its Hellenistic Environment*. WUNT Second Series 75. Tübingen: Mohr Siebeck, 1995.

Fotopoulos, John. *Food Offered to Idols in Roman Corinth: A Social-Rhetorical Reconsideration of 1 Corinthians 8:1–11:1*. WUNT Second Series 151. Tübingen: Mohr Siebeck, 2003.

Fujita, Shozo. "The Metaphor of Plant in Jewish Literature of the Intertestamental Period." *JSJ* 7 (1975) 30–45.

Gärtner, Bertil. *The Temple and the Community in Qumran and the New Testament*. Cambridge: Cambridge University Press, 1965.

Gaventa, Beverly R. "Mother's Milk and Ministry in 1 Corinthians 3." In *Theology and Ethics in Paul and His Interpreters*, FS V. P. Furnish, edited by E. H. Lovering and J. L. Sumney, 101–13. Nashville: Abingdon, 1996.

Gehring, Roger W. *House Church and Mission: The Importance of Household Structures in Early Christianity*. Peabody, MA: Hendrickson, 2004.

Gemünden, Petra von. *Vegetationsmetaphorik im Neuen Testament und seiner Umwelt. Eine Bildfelduntersuchung*. NTOA 18. Freiburg: Universitätsverlag; Göttingen: Vandenhoeck & Ruprecht, 1994.

Höcker, Christoph. "Architect." In *Brill's New Pauly*, edited by H. Cancik and H. Schneider, 1:999–1002. Leiden: Brill, 2002.

———. "Building Trade." In *Brill's New Pauly*, edited by H. Cancik and H. Schneider, 2:810–17. Leiden: Brill, 2003.

———. "Construction Technique." In *Brill's New Pauly*, edited by H. Cancik and H. Schneider, 3:730–40. Leiden: Brill, 2003.

Hofius, Otfried. "Herrenmahl und Herrenmahlsparadosis. Erwägungen zu 1Kor 11,23b–25." In *Paulusstudien*, 203–40. Tübingen: Mohr Siebeck, 1994.

Hogeterp, Albert L. A. *Paul and God's Temple: A Historical Interpretation of Cultic Imagery in the Corinthian Correspondence*. Leuven: Peeters, 2006.

Joubert, Stephan. *Paul as Benefactor: Reciprocity, Strategy and Theological Reflection in Paul's Collection*. WUNT Second Series 124. Tübingen: Mohr Siebeck, 2000.

Käsemann, Ernst. "The Theological Problem Presented by the Motif of the Body of Christ." In *Perspectives on Paul*, 102–21. London: SCM, 1971.

Kennel, Gunter. *Frühchristliche Hymnen? Gattungskritische Studien zur Frage nach den Liedern der frühen Christenheit*. WMANT 71. Neukirchen-Vluyn: Neukirchener Verlag, 1995.

Kitzberger, Ingrid. *Bau der Gemeinde: Das paulinische Wortfeld* οἰκοδομή/(ἐπ) οἰκοδομεῖν. FzB 53. Würzburg: Echter, 1986.

Klinghardt, Matthias. *Gemeinschafts-mahl und Mahlgemeinschaft: Soziologie und Liturgie frühchristlicher Mahlfeiern*. TANZ. Tübingen: Francke, 1996.

Klinzing, Georg. *Die Umdeutung des Kultus in der Qumrangemeinde und im Neuen Testament*. SUNT 7. Göttingen: Vandenhoeck & Ruprecht, 1971.

Kraus, Wolfgang. *Das Volk Gottes. Zur Grundlegung der Ekklesiologie bei Paulus*. WUNT 85. Tübingen: Mohr Siebeck, 1996.

Kuck, David W. *Judgement and Community Conflict: Paul's Use of Apocalyptic Judgement Language in 1 Cor 3:5–4:5*. NovTSup 66. Leiden: Brill, 1992.

Lanci, John R. *A New Temple for Corinth: Rhetorical and Archaeological Approaches to Pauline Imagery*. Studies in Biblical Literature 1. New York: Lang, 1997.

Lee, Michelle V. *Paul, the Stoics, and the Body of Christ*. SNTSMS 137. Cambridge: Cambridge University Press, 2006.

Liddell, Henry George, et al. *A Greek-English Lexicon*. Edited by Peter G. W. Glare. 9th ed. with Revised Supplement. Oxford: Clarendon, 1996.

Marshall, I. Howard. "Church and Temple in the New Testament." *TynBul* 40 (1989) 203–22.

May, Alistair Scott. *The Body for the Lord: Sex and Identity in 1 Corinthians 5–7*. JSNTSup 278. London/New York: T. & T. Clark International, 2004.

McKelvey, R. Jack. *The New Temple: The Church in the New Testament*. Oxford: Oxford University Press, 1969.

McKnight, Scot. "Collection for the Saints." In *Dictionary of Paul and His Letters*, edited by G. F. Hawthorne et al., 143–47. Downers Grove, IL: InterVarsity, 1993.

Mitchell, Margaret M. *Paul and the Rhetoric of Reconciliation: An Exegetical Investigation of the Language and Composition of 1 Corinthians*. Louisville, KY: Westminster/ John Knox, 1992.

Müller, Christoph G. *Gottes Pflanzung—Gottes Bau—Gottes Tempel. Die metaphorische Dimension paulinischer Gemeindetheologie in 1 Kor 3,5–17*. Fuldaer Studien 5. Frankfurt: Knecht, 1995.

Newton, Derek. *Deity and Diet: The Dilemma of Sacrificial Food at Corinth*. JSNTSup 169. Sheffield: Sheffield Academic, 1998.

Peterson, David. *Engaging with God: A Biblical Theology of Worship*. Leicester: Inter-Varsity, 1992.

Richardson, Peter. *Building Jewish in the Roman East*. Waco: Baylor University Press, 2004.

Robinson, John A. T. *The Body: A Study in Pauline Theology*. 2nd ed. Philadelphia: Westminster, 1977.

Roloff, Jürgen. "ἐκκλησία." In *Exegetical Dictionary of the New Testament*, edited by H. Balz and G. Schneider, 1:410–16. Grand Rapids: Eerdmans, 1990–1993.

———. *Die Kirche im Neuen Testament*. Grundrisse zum Neuen Testament 10. Göttingen: Vandenhoeck & Ruprecht, 1993.

Rosner, Brian S. *Paul, Scripture and Ethics: A Study of 1 Corinthians 5–7*. Grand Rapids: Baker, 1999.

Schnabel, Eckhard J. *Early Christian Mission*. 2 vols. Downers Grove, IL: InterVarsity, 2004.

———. "The Meaning of βαπτίζειν in Greek, Jewish, and Patristic Texts." *Filologia Neotestamentaria* (2011) forthcoming.

Schneider, Rolf M. "Marble." In *Brill's New Pauly*, edited by H. Cancik and H. Schneider, 8:281–91. Leiden: Brill, 2006.

Schweizer, Eduard. *The Church as the Body of Christ*. Richmond: John Knox, 1964.

Shanor, Jay. "Paul as Master Builder: Construction Terms in First Corinthians." *NTS* 34 (1988) 461–71.

Stanley, Christopher D. *Paul and the Language of Scripture: Citation Technique in the Pauline Epistles and Contemporary Literature*. SNTSMS 69. Cambridge: Cambridge University Press, 1992.

Turner, Max M. B. *The Holy Spirit and Spiritual Gifts Then and Now*. Carlisle: Paternoster, 1996.

VanderKam, James C. "Calendar." In *The New Interpreter's Dictionary of the Bible*, edited by K. D. Sakenfeld, 1:521–27. Nashville: Abingdon, 2006.

Wenham, David. *Paul: Follower of Jesus or Founder of Christianity?* Grand Rapids: Eerdmans, 1995.

White, L. Michael. *The Social Origins of Christian Architecture*. 2 vols. Valley Forge: Trinity Press International, 1996–1997.

Williams, H. H. Drake. *The Wisdom of the Wise: The Presence and Function of Scripture within 1 Cor. 1:18–3:23*. AGAJU 49. Leiden: Brill, 2001.

Winter, Bruce W. *After Paul Left Corinth: The Influence of Secular Ethics and Social Change*. Grand Rapids: Eerdmans, 2001.

Witulski, Thomas. *Kaiserkult in Kleinasien*. Göttingen: Vandenhoeck & Ruprecht; Fribourg: Academic, 2007.

Yancey, Philip. "Ongoing Incarnation." *Christianity Today*, 8 January 2008, 72.

Yorke, Gosnell L. O. R. *The Church as the Body of Christ in the Pauline Corpus: A Reexamination*. Lang: University Press of America, 1991.

7

Heaven Can't Wait

The Church in Ephesians and Colossians

CURT NICCUM

WITHIN THE NEW TESTAMENT, Ephesians and Colossians offer perhaps the most matured view of the church. At the very least they
represent a major turning point in Pauline ecclesiology.[1] The church is
no longer a semi-autonomous gathering of believers in a specific locale.
She is universal. More than that, she inhabits the very realms of heaven
itself. The church now lives and acts at the cosmic level.

Such an elevated perspective deserves substantial treatment, but, as
Joachim Gnilka aptly notes, any treatment of ecclesiology in Ephesians
alone nearly demands a commentary.[2] How much more so with the
inclusion of Colossians? Obviously one chapter cannot do the subject
justice, yet overlooking the contributions of these letters in a book of
this nature would be a mistake. These epistles provide a window through
which one can glimpse the contours of a burgeoning late first-century
ecclesiology in Asia Minor—one that greatly contributed to subsequent

---

1. Schmidt, "ἐκκλησία," 512, summarizes the general consensus saying, "Erst in
diesen Briefen wird eine *besondere Kirchenlehre* vorgetragen" ("Within these letters a
peculiar ecclesiological doctrine is expressed for the first time," emphasis his). Houlden
argues otherwise in "Christ and Church in Ephesians."

2. Gnilka, "Kirchenmodell," 162.

self-definitions of the church catholic. Therefore, this chapter briefly surveys their important ecclesiological landscape.[3]

THE BODY POLITIC

At their most basic level the Asian letters perceive the church to be a political entity. They label her a "kingdom" and a "body." She submits to one Lord, but surprisingly this title seldom occurs absolutely, outside of the Household Codes. Instead, the church's leader is better known as the Christ, the Anointed One of Jewish expectation.

The Church as Israel

The church therefore understands herself to be "Israel," although this is more tacit than explicit. That designation occurs only once in this corpus (Eph 2:2), but language reserved for Israel in the Old Testament permeates both letters. In Ephesians, those who have received the Spirit participate in the "promises," the "inheritance," and are a people for God's "own possession" (1:12–14). Those formerly alienated from citizenship in "Israel," God has now made "fellow citizens" (2:19). Rather than disobedient children, objects of God's wrath, these beloved "children" are recipients of God's benefaction (1:5; 2:1–5; 5:1–2, 8–10). Gentile believers in Colossae are the "chosen" (3:12) and the spiritual "circumcision" (2:9–12).

In both letters, believers are enumerated among the "holy."[4] They also populate the "kingdom," but Ephesians and Colossians make the connection between Christ and Israel even more explicit by expanding the expected formula. Not just the kingdom of God, the church constitutes the kingdom "of Christ and God" (Eph 5:5) and "of his beloved Son" (Col 1:13).

---

3. For various reasons, critical issues will not be explored in this chapter despite their significance for the task. The fundamental presuppositions are that these letters come from the pen of Paul and/or a Paulinist and reflect knowledge of Asian Christianity as it existed in the last half of the first century. For this perspective and a convenient summary of other positions, see Hoehner, *Ephesians*, 2–61, and his extensive bibliography. One may also consult Roon, *Authenticity of Ephesians*, and Cross, ed., *Studies in Ephesians*, especially the articles by Sanders, "Case for the Pauline Authorship," and Nineham, "Case against Pauline Authorship."

4. See the discussion of Cerfaux, *Church in the Theology of St. Paul*, 118–20.

At the heart of this identification with God's historic people stands ἐκκλησία (*ekklēsia*). For good reason interpreters posit that Christians adopted this word because of its theological significance in the Septuagint (LXX). There it often translates קָהָל (*qahal*), especially in phrases like "the *assembly* of Israel" and "the *assembly* of the Lord." But in the undisputed letters, Paul primarily reserves ἐκκλησία for individual congregations. Although occasionally expressing a broader understanding, especially when looking back on his previous violence against "the church" (1 Cor 15:9; Gal 1:13; Phil 3:6), references to individual gatherings of the saints prevail.[5] Even when Paul sends a letter to a larger region or refers to other groups, he opts to speak of "churches" rather than "the church."[6]

Yet Ephesians and Colossians regard ἐκκλησία as a universal entity, infusing the word with its most pregnant meaning. From a certain perspective, this collective sense imitates the LXX even more than its normal application in Paul. But it cannot be the sole catalyst for this change. If anything, it results from the cosmic Christology produced in response to the Colossian heresy.[7] The church, swept up by Christ into the fullness of everything, can hardly be limited in space and time (1:15–20).[8] This more realized eschatology, undoubtedly helped along by the word's biblical precedent as a signifier of Israel's national and religious identity, made ἐκκλησία most suitable for encompassing the whole. This becomes, therefore, the ultimate expression of unity and continuity with the salvation history of God's people, the Jews.

Much less pervasive but no less important is the concept of the church as "bride."[9] Marriage as a metaphor for relations between God

---

5. See Schmidt, "ἐκκλησία," and Dunn, *Theology of Paul*, 537–43. Dunn also argues that Paul's references to persecuting the "church of God" refer to the Jerusalem congregation (pp. 539–41).

6. 1 Cor 4:17; 11:16; 14:33; 16:1, 19; 2 Cor 8:1; Gal 1:2, 22. Categorizing Ephesians as a circular letter, therefore, offers no help in explaining its universal perspective, *contra* Hoehner, *Ephesians*, 112.

7. Dunn, *Colossians and Philemon*, 94–97; Gnilka, "Kirchenmodell," 164–65; and Perkins, "God, Cosmos and Church Universal," 766–68.

8. Colossians does recognize individual congregations (4:15–16).

9. See Minear, *Images of the Church*, 54–56, and Sampley, *One Flesh*, 34–51. Paul employed this metaphor in 2 Cor 11:2, but applied it only to a single congregation. On additional differences, see Schnackenburg, "Tauflehre," 182. This adaptation of the biblical theme found in Ephesians, if not already known by the churches in Asia Minor, quickly cemented itself in that region. The picture of Christ as bridegroom and

and his people has its roots in the Old Testament. Most notably Hosea 1–4 and Ezekiel 16 portray God as the loving husband of an ever unfaithful Israel. The Household Code of Ephesians takes up this theme, with Jesus standing in as the groom precisely because he *left* his heavenly parentage to *cling* to his spouse, Israel, by joining her in the *flesh* (5:31–32, reading the incarnation into Gen 2:24). As a result of this union, Israel, too, finally comes to share in the characteristics of her betrothed—she is now radiant, holy, and blameless.

Two other metaphors, temple and planting, have connections to Israel. At the end of Ephesians 2, the author envisions Jewish and Gentile believers coming together as stones erected into a dwelling place for God's Spirit. The Old Testament offers a few antecedents for viewing the aggregate of the faithful as a spiritual temple, but this theme grew more popular in the intertestamental period.[10] Of course Paul employed the metaphor too, and Ephesians follows his adaptation more than any other. As an apostle, Paul lays a foundation, which is none other than Jesus Christ (1 Cor 3:10–12; see also Rom 15:20). Ephesians assigns the same function to all apostles and prophets. In light of Messianic speculation about certain Old Testament texts, it makes Christ's role more distinct; he has become the "cornerstone."[11]

While the church is never fully described as a plant, botanical language tends to appear within contexts of the church as a building or body, thereby producing mixed metaphors. For example, the church is "rooted" in (Eph 3:17; Col 2:7) as well as "founded" (Ephesians) or "built" (Colossians) upon Christ.[12] Paul conjoins both pictures in 1 Cor 3:1–17, but clearly transitions from one metaphor to the other (v. 9). The references to both baptism and the temple in the immediate context provide additional parallels with Ephesians and Colossians, but these

---

church as bride plays a significant role in the Fourth Gospel, Revelation, and other early Christian works from the area.

10. Cf. Isa 54:11–17; 1QS VIII, 4–10 and IX, 6. Although definitely rare as a descriptor of the church in the New Testament, this, too, has remarkable parallels in other Asian literature, including 1 Pet 2:4–8 and Rev 21:9–21.

11. See Isa 28:16 and Ps 118:22. First Peter 2:4–8 may attest to an early catena of such passages. Because of the reference to the foundation and perhaps the context of stumbling (expressed only in 1 Peter), "cornerstone" rather than "capstone" is the better translation.

12. See also 1QS VIII 4–5. In a different context, the Colossians bear fruit and grow in good works (1:6 and 10).

may be coincidental. Certainly the biblical comparisons of Israel to a vine underlie both (see, for example, Isa 5:1–7 and Psalm 80).

It is one thing to equate the church with Israel, but what does that actually mean? Does the "church" replace "Israel," with God stripping ethnic Jews of all prior benefits? Or do Gentile believers enter into a previously established and divinely privileged nation? The Asian letters fit somewhere in the middle, but Ephesians 2 requires something closer to the latter.[13]

One of the distinctive lexical features of Ephesians 2 is the number of its συν– (*sun-* indicating *joint* action or status) compounds. These occur in the midst of a discussion about how Gentiles previously were alienated from Israel (rather than from God!). Once outsiders due to their associations with the demonic realms (2:1–5), they have become united (2:5–7) in the resuscitation (συνεζωοποίησεν), resurrection (συνήγειρεν), and glorification (συνεκάθισεν) of the Jewish Messiah, who embodies his people.[14] Once estranged because of their distance from Israel's polity (τῆς πολιτείας τοῦ Ἰσραήλ), they have become fellow citizens (συμπολῖται), having been joined together (συναρ–μολογουμένη) and built up with (συνοικοδομεῖσθε) Israel (2:19–22). The author then recapitulates this discussion by identifying the mystery of the gospel with Gentile believers attaining status as fellow heirs (συγκληρονόμα), fellow members of the body (σύσσωμα), and fellow partakers (συμμέτοχα) of the promises (3:6). Each triad presumes a quantifiable group to which the Gentiles are unexpectedly joined.[15]

But Israel itself does not remain unchanged; it too has been transformed. The Jewish author of Ephesians lumps himself in with those who, before Christ's arrival, were dead in their trespasses ("we" 2:5 versus "you" 2:2). Jews also stood in need of regeneration and reconciliation. As a result, certain aspects of the Jewish religion undergo renewal.

In effect, Christ's crucifixion destroys the Jerusalem temple, or at least its obstructions to universal access. On the grounds of the Herodian complex a dividing wall separated the Court of the Gentiles from the

13. The concentration of this language in Ephesians has placed it at the forefront of post-Holocaust debates about what stance the modern church should take toward Israel. For the two extremes, see Lindemann, *Aufhebung*; and Barth, *People of God*; Barth, "Conversion and Conversation."

14. Eph 1:10, 22–23; 2:16; 3:6; 4:4, 13–16; 5:23–32; Col 1:18, 21–25; 2:19.

15. *Pace* Lindemann who regards Ephesians as annulling Paul's presentation in Romans 11 (*Aufhebung*, 253), and Talbert, *Ephesians and Colossians*, 91–94.

temple proper. Along this balustrade warnings detailed how trespass-
ers would summarily be executed.[16] According to Acts 21, certain Asian
Jews, seeing Paul offering sacrifices at the altar, wrongly concluded that
he had escorted a Gentile traveling companion, Trophimus of Ephesus,
past this barrier. The ensuing riot culminated in Paul's arrest, detention,
and eventual appearance before the royal tribunal in Rome. Ephesians
alludes to this event (see also 3:1, where the author indicates his chains
were on the Asians' behalf) only to proclaim that barrier now null and
void. Jesus lowered himself to raze that wall (Eph 2:14).

The larger pericope (vv. 11–22), filled with cultic language, argues
further that believers in Christ, both Jews and Gentiles, now have unre-
stricted access. This "new and improved" Israel enjoys full participation
(προσαγωγή) with the Presence of God, as God constructs them into
a new Holy of Holies (ναός).

Parallel to this reconstruction of the temple in Ephesians is the redefinition of circumcision found in Col 2:11–13. The ritual previously
performed "by hand" and "in the flesh" now has a spiritual counterpart
or fulfillment in baptism (see below).

Whether either book presents a supersessionist point of view,
i.e., the church completely replaces the current or a future temple in
Jerusalem, is doubtful. First, the implied audience consists of Gentiles
from a Pauline heritage for whom the physical temple and circumcision
played no role. Second, earlier Jewish literature describes the people of
Israel as a temple and idealizes circumcision without assuming an end
to their physical realities.[17] Renewal does not necessarily require a cessa-
tion of those divine gifts granted to the Jews in the past.

But the treatment of the Law in these letters poses a particular problem for such a position. Ephesians claims that the Law of commands with
decrees (τὸν νόμον τῶν ἐντολῶν ἐν δόγμασιν) required removal for
the integration of Gentiles into the church (Eph 2:15). Colossians likewise has those decrees (τὸ . . . χειρόγραφον τοῖς δόγμασιν) nailed
to the cross (Col 2:14). This sounds dogmatic and incapable of any other
interpretation than the complete abrogation of the Mosaic Law.[18]

---

16. See Josephus's description in *Ant.* 15.11.5 (15.417) and *J.W.* 5.5.2 (5.194). Photos
of the actual warnings can be found on the internet.

17. See especially 1QS V, 4–6 and VIII, 4–8 where the assembly is described as a
"temple" and inward "circumcision."

18. So Lincoln, *Ephesians*, 141–43, and Hoehner, *Ephesians*, 368–81.

Some have attempted to alleviate the harsh impact of these passages by limiting reference to just the ritual law or to those commands specifying separation from pagans, but these face insurmountable problems. They anachronistically reduce "the Law" to the 613 commands (or fewer). Second, they require creating categories of commands unknown in Judaism and early Christianity. Third, the Law is against "us," so it opposes Jews just as much as Gentiles.

Still, a complete annulment of the Law cannot be in question. The transformation of "circumcision" and "temple" works only if Torah remains authoritative. Both letters also cite or allude to each portion of the Tanakh as Scripture.[19] Greater still is the citation of a "command" bearing full weight in Eph 6:2 (see also Col 3:20)!

Paul himself may offer a solution to this conundrum. While recognizing that the Law is good, holy, righteous, and spiritual (Rom 7:12–14), he believes the power of sin on the would-be disciple subverts its purposes.[20] Through Christ, sin is neutralized, and those who place their faith in him submit to and fulfill the Law, but as it exists in the ideal, spiritual realm (Rom 8:1–4). Where Paul argues this, however, he clearly identifies this ideal Law, as in Rom 8:1 ("the Law of the Spirit of life in Christ") and Gal 6:2 ("the Law of Christ"), but no direct parallel occurs in either Ephesians or Colossians. This is especially surprising in the latter where the Platonic dichotomy of shadow and substance opens the door for a heavenly counterpart to the Law.

Despite the lack of any explicit identification of a "spiritual" Law, Ephesians and Colossians may still follow the same trajectory. This would explain the negative assessment of the Law with its decrees (νόμου . . . ἐν δόγμασιν) in contrast to the positive evaluation of the command with its promise (ἐντολὴ . . . ἐν ἐπαγγελίᾳ) in Eph 2:15 and 6:2. This fits well with the eschatological emphasis on "promise" in the letter and particularly the remark that Gentiles were estranged from the covenants of "promise" (Eph 1:13; 2:12; 3:6). In Colossians the distinction drawn between physical and spiritual (ἀχειροποιήτῳ) circumcisions seems to imply a heavenly counterpart to the handwritten (χειρόγραφον) Law.

19. If any distinction exists, it is now that the Tanakh must be interpreted Christologically. The midrash on Psalm 69 and interpretation of Gen 2:24 provide examples of how this worked (see Eph 4:7–10 and 5:31–32). Note also the adaptation of the Shemaʿ (4:4–6).

20. On ancient Jewish perceptions of Torah, including Paul's, see Davies, *Paul and Rabbinic Judaism*, and Sanders, *Paul and Palestinian Judaism*.

However this is to be settled, the letters clearly assume Judaism has changed. In this sense one cannot conclude that Asian Christianity saw or was encouraged to see itself as part of or related to Judaism at large.[21] Instead, Ephesians and Colossians stand midway between the church as Israel, with Gentile branches receiving their nourishment from the patriarchal trunk (Rom 11), and the church as a "third race."[22] Of the various contemporary interpretations circulating, the restored Israel of Luke-Acts offers the closest parallel.

The Church as the Body

In contrast to the biblical formulations above, the "body" language of Ephesians and Colossians is more at home with popular philosophical conversations about societal structure and participation.[23] Considering Paul's fondness for this construction, its appearance in Ephesians and Colossians seems natural. Similarities with the corporeal metaphors in Romans 12 and 1 Corinthians 12 include the interdependence of all parts, the impartation of spiritual gifts, and the ultimate goal of corporate edification. But again these letters push the familiar into new territory. Both Ephesians and Colossians now apply "body" to the universal

---

21. *Pace* Barth, *People of God*, 11–49.

22. *Pace* Lincoln, "Church and Israel." For the "third race" see *Epistle to Diognetus*, and Aristides the Athenian, *Apologia* 2. Ephesians refers to all of the Jewish privileges identified by Paul in Rom 9:4–5 *except for* the patriarchs. Perhaps they are to be presumed with the references to "the promises" or "the covenants."

23. For a summary and analysis of the political understanding of "body," see Lee, *Paul, the Stoics, and the Body of Christ*, 29–102, and Dunn, *Theology of Paul*, 548–52. George van Kooten argues that σῶμα (*sōma*) in Colossians reflects classical discussions and Stoic physics regarding the cosmos (van Kooten, *Cosmic Christology*, see especially 11–58). For "body" as expressing Jewish corporate personality, see Best, *One Body in Christ*, especially 115–26. To some extent all of these converge in Ephesians and Colossians. The human is a microcosm of the political system, which itself is a microcosm of the universe. Thus the church as body of Christ has both political (body as *polis*) and anthropological (one, new human subsumed "in Christ") implications as well as cosmological application. For different political understandings of "church" and "kingdom," see Blumenfeld, *Political Paul*, 95–119. A Jewish origin for σῶμα (body) in Ephesians cannot be totally eliminated. The prevalence of "new creation" in the book and the singular importance of the Genesis story where the Spirit animates an otherwise lifeless Adam could explain much. It is plausible that this secular, political context was filtered through this fundamental Jewish narrative and Christian appropriations of it.

church rather than the local congregation, and set apart Christ as its head.

Ephesians takes this one step further by merging the body and temple imagery (Eph 2:21). Paul's statement in 1 Cor 6:19 that a person's body is the temple of the Holy Spirit provides a possible antecedent for this combination. Two things militate against this: (1) Paul speaks of individual disciples, not the local congregation nor the church at large,[24] and (2) where Paul clearly discusses the church/congregation as the temple (1 Cor 3:10–17), he makes no mention of the body. A more plausible point of origin is Jesus' prediction, "Destroy this temple and in three days I will raise it up again." This works especially for the Johannine version (John 2:13–22) where the author explicitly connects the temple and Jesus' body (John 2:21).

THE COSMIC COMMUNITY

The church definitely attains new heights in Ephesians and Colossians. Not only do these epistles view the church holistically, the church exists on a completely different plane: believers have been seated at the right hand of God (Eph 2:6; Col 3:1). Their lives are hidden in the glorified Christ waiting to be revealed (Col 3:1–4). The church participates in the victorious triumph of Christ over the spiritual powers (Col 2:15) and proclaims God's manifold wisdom to those same powers (Eph 3:10).

In many ways this resembles realized eschatology. The uneasy tension between the "now" and "not yet" found in Paul appears to have resolved itself into a present reality. But this is capable of other interpretations. Although the church has a cosmic presence, its day-to-day life is mundane. Furthermore, certain aspects of future eschatology continue to be emphasized. The Holy Spirit seals believers for the coming age and serves as an "earnest" of the inheritance yet to come (Eph 1:13–14). The current times are evil, awaiting ultimate transformation (Eph 5:15–16). An ongoing battle among the spiritual powers must result in victory and peace (Eph 6:10–15). Most of all, Christ has yet to appear (Col 3:4).

What, then, explains this modified perspective? Life in Asia Minor included a fear of the unseen spiritual realms that could affect daily life. On one end of the spectrum folk placated the gods (religion) and on the other end manipulated those powers (magic). Not surprisingly,

---

24. See Gundry, *Sōma in Biblical Theology*, 76.

Ephesians connects the believers' former conduct to these uneasy associations with their invisible malefactors (Eph 2:1–4).[25]

In this light the universal and cosmic scope of the church aims to dispel the fears of former pagans still wrestling with their past. Solidarity with Christ, who conquered the demonic realms, and community with his people, who share his Spirit, should inspire confidence. Because all things come to a head in Christ, both in and outside the church, Asian believers need fear nothing.[26]

CHURCH PRACTICES

Both Ephesians and Colossians describe activities of the church in some detail. The vast majority of these relate to daily social interaction. The author of Ephesians, for example, contrasts the former life lived under the sway of demons with that under the lordship of Jesus Christ and the power of the Holy Spirit. Thus the one who used his hands to steal from others instead works with those same hands to feed others (Eph 4:28). Colossians presents the same picture, although also marking certain parameters. Extremes like asceticism and ecstatic experiences have no value for and perhaps no place in the spiritual life (Col 2:16–19). The difference between "us" and "them," both theologically and practically, is night and day (Eph 5:8–14).

In addition to general guidelines for life in this world, the letters discuss other activities unique to the Christian community. These include prayer, assemblies, singing, baptism, and exercising spiritual gifts.

Prayer

Disciples actively engage in prayer, both private and communal. Its foundational role for Asian Christianity becomes clear at the beginning and end of each letter. Ephesians and Colossians follow contemporary conventions by including petition to deity as each letter's second element. In contrast to usual Greco-Roman practice, however, the opening invocations are much longer and more impassioned (Eph 1:3–23 and Col 1:3–8). At the end of Ephesians, prayers constitute the sole human contribution to spiritual warfare and the safeguarding of Paul and other

25. See Arnold, *Ephesians: Power and Magic*, and Arnold, *Colossian Syncretism*.

26. For additional treatment, see Cerfaux, *Church in the Theology of St. Paul*, 289–397.

disciples (Eph 6:18–20). Colossians reiterates the need for a community dedicated to petition (Col 4:2–4). Significantly, prayers also occur in places not dictated by epistolary custom (i.e., Eph 3:14–21) and play a role in the paranetic sections.

Apparently these communities had a repertoire of prayer, all with Jewish antecedents. Beyond the thanksgiving formulae one discovers benedictions and doxologies. A *berakhah* opens Ephesians (1:3–14).[27] As is customary, this benediction expresses the deeds of God by means of participle phrases: "who blessed . . . (v. 3), predestined . . . (v. 5), and revealed to . . . his people" (v. 9). A reference to praising God's glory, roughly equivalent to the *chatimah*, closes the prayer (v. 14).[28]

Of considerable importance is the doxology, which consists of four distinct parts. In its shortest form it includes: (1) to him/God, (2) be glory/honor, (3) forever, (4) Amen. Only the first three elements can be expanded (Eph 3:20–21, for example). The fourth element marks a communal response and is therefore static. By embedding this prayer in the text, the author invites his audience to affirm verbally its truths and to join together in worship. Whereas the other prayers might merely reflect private devotion, the doxology requires the gathering of a worshipping community.

Assembly

Unfortunately the letters provide no specific details about these assemblies. They may have been a natural byproduct of writing. In other words, the arrival of a letter might precipitate a gathering, rather than having it read during a regularly scheduled meeting. Due to the high illiteracy rate in the ancient world, every correspondence would require public recitation for all intended recipients to receive the message. Still, the author's charge to the Colossians to read the letter sent to the Laodiceans (Col 4:16), and especially the *Sitz im Leben* of the doxology, make better sense if gatherings happened with regularity. How frequently they occurred or on what day(s), the letters understandably do not state.[29]

27. Although atypical for Paul, this occurs also in 2 Cor 1:3–7, but without a subsequent thanksgiving formula.

28. For information on these and other early prayers, see Deichgräber, *Gotteshymnus*, and Heinemann, *Prayer in the Talmud*.

29. Perhaps the reading of these letters at a time when Scripture was normally recited contributed to the early perception of Paul's epistles as Scripture (cf. 2 Pet 3:16).

Singing

Both letters exhibit a developed hymnody, but the passages traditionally adduced in support offer the least valuable evidence. The collocation of "hymns," "psalms," and "spiritual songs" (Eph 5:19//Col 3:16), far from specifying three categories of early Christian music, reflect instead the idiomatic stacking of synonyms to circumscribe a whole. This literary device envelops all spiritual music without distinction.

More information is forthcoming, thankfully. Familiarity with the Psalms is apparent. Ephesians alludes to or cites them without preamble (Eph 1:22 and 4:8). The letters also attest to the churches' own creative and artistic expression of their faith. Already they sing hymns to Christ as to a god. The poetic fragment in Col 1:15–20 probably belongs to this genre, whether created or edited by the author. In Ephesians, music also reflects on or accompanies Christian ritual. With some confidence scholars have associated the poetic content of Eph 5:14 with baptism.[30] Colossians and Ephesians evince the rapid development of material designed specifically for Christian celebration.

Neither letter provides much information about the mechanics of church music. Indeed, in both expanded discussions (Eph 5:18–20// Col 3:16–17) music belongs to the larger Christian experience. "Being filled with the Spirit" and "always giving thanks" suggest an environment beyond the formal gathering. And Colossians sandwiches its exhortation with (1) letting the "word" of Christ dwell richly and (2) doing all in "word" and "deed" in the Lord's name, far exceeding the scope of a corporate assembly.

Baptism

Baptism has a special place of prominence in Ephesians and Colossians.[31] Much of the material reworks previously existing traditions. For example, the widely attested depiction of baptism as a "new creation" recurs in

---

30. See Schnackenburg, "Tauflehre," especially 160–66. Surprisingly, Ephesians quotes the hymn with the same citation formula used to introduce Scripture (see διὸ λέγει in Eph 4:8)!

31. See Dahl, "Concept of Baptism." In stark contrast to baptism, the Eucharist appears nowhere in these epistles. Its absence from Colossians is understandable, considering the general focus of that letter, but the omission of any hint of the common, unifying meal in Ephesians is not. Its failure to make the list of the "Seven Ones" (Eph 4:4–6) presents a challenge to the church's long history of holding to two sacraments.

both letters.[32] Through baptism one exchanges an earthly humanity for a heavenly one.[33] One thus becomes re-created in God's true image (Eph 4:24//Col 3:10) and sealed by the Holy Spirit for the day of redemption (Eph 1:13–14; 4:30).

Colossians incorporates baptismal instruction familiar from Paul's writings (1 Cor 12:13; Gal 3:26–28; Col 3:9–11). Since these texts span a timeframe of decades and occur in disparate letters addressing different communities with distinct problems, they must belong to an established formula. That all three passages occur within baptismal contexts suggests the phrasing originated in or for that particular setting. Its purest and perhaps earliest form likely occurs in Gal 3:28—"Neither (οὐκ) Jew nor (οὐδέ) Greek, neither (οὐκ) slave nor (οὐδέ) free, nor (οὐκ) male and (καί) female." The third pair, male *and* female, comes straight from Genesis 2:24 and provides an additional link between baptism and new creation.[34] Colossians alters the basic content by adding "barbarians and Scythians" and inexplicably omitting references to gender.

Ephesians and Colossians also offer fresh perspectives on and new material for baptism. First, the link between baptism and Christ's death, burial, and resurrection becomes stronger. Those "buried with Christ" in baptism are also "made alive with," "raised with," and "seated with" him at the right hand of God (Eph 2:6–8//Col 2:12–13).[35] Although nothing yet suggests a practice of baptizing only on Sundays or Easter, these letters lay the foundation for that development.

Second, unique to Colossians is the *qal wahomer* comparison of baptism to circumcision. If circumcision, a ritual performed by human hands that removes a small part of the flesh, indicates membership in the old covenant, how much more then baptism, a ritual ultimately performed by Christ that removes the entire person, assures one's place in the new (Col 2:9–12). Third, the rhythmic interlude in Eph 5:14 celebrates baptism as the point at which one becomes endowed with the

---

32. See Minear, *Images of the Church*, 105–35.

33. See Tannehill, *Dying and Rising*, 47–54.

34. This also occurs in 1 Cor 7:1–24, with each section ending with a tag about position and God's calling: male-female (vv. 1–17), Jew-Greek (vv. 18–20), slave-free (vv. 21–24). Paul may have truncated this in 1 Cor 12:13 to avoid further misunderstandings by certain women in that community; see Wire, *Corinthian Women Prophets*, 137–38.

35. Ephesians, however, does not explicitly state "that the believer participates in Christ's death" (Tannehill, *Dying and Rising*, 48).

Spirit and empowered by Christ to live apart from those tainted by sin and the demonic realms. While the concept has parallels in other early Christian literature, the composition of poetry specific to the initiatory rite marks a notable advancement in the liturgy of the church.

The most striking evidence for baptism's importance is its inclusion among the "Seven Ones," an early creed (Eph 4:4–6). Originally, each grouping began with a member of the Trinity: Spirit, Lord, and God. Because of the ecclesiological focus of the letter, "one body" moves to the front of the first set that also includes "hope" and "Spirit." Although one might expect a collocation of baptism with the Spirit, here it belongs with "one Lord" and "one faith," perhaps influenced by the earliest Christian baptismal confession, "Jesus is Lord." This creed reworks the Shema' (Deut 6:4), Israel's classic expression of monotheism, which only further highlights the esteem in which the community held baptism.

Exactly how baptism was administered in these churches remains unclear because the letters presume knowledge of and participation in the rite. Still, certain things can with differing degrees of probability be deduced. As expected with the unqualified use of βαπτίζειν, it took place in water, as the parallel with the wedding bath suggests (Eph 5:26).[36] In conformity with the earliest Christian practice, this appears to have been by immersion. Being "buried" and "raised" with Christ (Col 2:12; cf. Eph 5:14), although perhaps figurative, have significantly greater meaning if believers had visibly been conformed to the Passion story through baptism. The age of baptizands remains open. Colossians does connect baptism with circumcision, but it is an issue of efficacy, not age.

Spiritual Gifts

Ephesians and Colossians depict a community led by the Spirit.[37] All have been sealed by the Spirit. All have received the Spirit as an eschatological guarantee. The church interestingly can also grieve the Spirit.

In vanquishing the spiritual forces opposed to humanity Jesus bestows gifts upon "each one" of his people (Eph 4:7–8). Following close on the discussion of church unity, this literally extends the creed (vv. 4–6). As the Godhead and church are "one" so also each "one" (ἑνί) receives

36. The Fourth Gospel again provides close parallels, cf. John 13:10 and 15:3.

37. Eph 1:13, 17; 2:18, 22; 3:5, 16; 4:3–4, 23, 30; 5:18; 6:17–18. Among the Pauline letters, Ephesians has the highest concentration of references to the Holy Spirit.

spiritual blessings. The Spirit thus empowers both the unity and diversity of the church.

But this extension also serves as a transition to the next topic—the church that has, but must laboriously maintain, the *unity of the Spirit* (4:3), must also strive towards a *unity of the faith* (4:13). Verse 11, then, does not restrict the work of the Spirit to a select handful. Instead, and completely consistent with the understanding of spiritual gifts as intended for the edification of the church elsewhere (Romans 12; 1 Corinthians 12; 1 Peter 4), these gifts provide a specific benefit to the Spirit-filled community. They apply primarily to the goal of attaining the unity of faith. In other words, these teaching gifts are first and foremost a gift to the church for the purpose of moving its members toward the full stature of Christ and works of service (vv. 12–13).[38]

Application of these gifts to a very specific context neither highlights them as more important than any other charism nor identifies the recipients as clergy set apart from laity. Indeed, it is anachronistic to view these gift holders as office holders. While later Christianity will limit the descriptor "apostle" to the Twelve, with Paul somewhat unnaturally appended, Ephesians and Colossians hardly understand the term in this fashion; "apostles" are tradents of the newly revealed mystery. This is more akin to Paul's understanding (Rom 16:7 and Gal 1:19; although one could argue he further limits "apostle" to one who has visibly encountered the resurrected Lord and thereby received unique insight into the meaning of the gospel, cf. 1 Cor 9:1–2 and 15:3–8, especially v. 7). The "prophets," too, play a similar role as special agents of revelation.[39]

On the other hand, the "apostles and prophets" constitute the foundation of the church (Eph 2:20; 3:5). Not only does this distinguish them from those who exercise the other teaching ministries mentioned in 4:11, the manner of reference seems to fit best a quantifiable group; apostles and prophets exist (or existed), but none will be added to their number.[40] At the same time, the implied author as apostle exhibits no heightened view of apostleship. He, as all others, has simply received a gift from God (δοθεῖσαν, Eph 3:2, 7; 4:7, 11; Col 1:25) and employs it in service to others (διάκονος, Eph 3:7; 4:12; Col 1:23–25).

38. So Hoehner, *Ephesians*, 538–47; cf. Gnilka, "Kirchenmodell," 176–83.

39. Because of their inclusion among those currently receiving spiritual gifts from the exalted Christ, the prophets of the biblical tradition are not in view here.

40. Best, *One Body*, 163–64, thinks otherwise.

Why then do "apostles and prophets" stand at the head of the list? A supposed step towards "early Catholicism" seems highly unlikely and historically implausible. Some evidence, including references within Ephesians, suggests that, in contrast to evangelists, shepherds, and teachers who educate within individual congregations, apostles and prophets have obligations to the church universal. The very designation "apostle" (one sent out) implies as much. Many prophets also had itinerant ministries.[41]

As for the teaching gifts granted to local communities, the concept of office or hierarchy remains foreign. "Evangelist," "shepherd," and "teacher" describe functions; they do not serve as titles. The use of "shepherd" rather than "overseer" or "elder" appears to reflect a time when terminology for congregational leaders remained in flux. Later hierarchical distinctions between elders and bishops are unknown in Ephesians. In subsequent generations Christianity would compartmentalize the active work of the Spirit and reserve it for properly ordained clergy, but Ephesians neither reflects this nor offers a model for it.

The order of gifts betrays intentionality, but the importance therein should not be read in hierarchical terms. Most likely the order reflects the author's understanding of the relative importance of each of these roles for the task at hand—the education of the church. Even here, and this is critical, the teaching of the church does not center upon a body of doctrine. The core of the church's faith can easily be summarized by creedal statements. The church's teaching concerns practical living. These letters still see education in terms of mentorship rather than catechesis or classroom instruction. The end is a transformed life rather than an acknowledgment of a set of tenets defined as orthodoxy.

CONCLUSION

What then can be said of the Asian church? It views itself first and foremost as Israel. But the church is also distinct, for it alone possesses the Holy Spirit and proclaims that Jesus is the Jewish Messiah of promise who is to be confessed as "Lord," even by Gentiles. This resulted in modi-

---

41. Schnackenburg, *Schriften zum Neuen Testament*, 279–80, includes evangelists in this category. Cf. Dunn, *Theology of Paul*, 540–41, who assigns each to the congregation. The two perspectives are not necessarily incompatible, as apostles and prophets could serve as missionaries (for the universal church), establishing, and thus serving in, congregations (individual churches).

fications to interpretation and practice: Scripture requires Christological exegesis, even the Shema'. Baptism exceeds circumcision in power and significance. The temple stands on the newer foundation of "apostles and prophets" and offers access to all.

Yet Ephesians and Colossians represent a community some years after its inception. Christians have become comfortable enough to establish their own liturgical elements including creedal and hymnic material celebrating Christ and ritual. Even if certain aspects retain a considerable portion of their Jewish content, such as the *berakhah*, the church now has placed its stamp of ownership on everything.

Finally, in anxious anticipation of the end and in response to the daily fears of the unseen forces of evil, the church now understands itself in cosmic proportions. No congregation stands alone; each is incorporated into a larger whole that itself constitutes the body of Christ—the Creator of all things and the Head of the church. To God be the glory in the church and in Christ Jesus throughout all generations forever . . .

BIBLIOGRAPHY

Arnold, Clinton. *The Colossian Syncretism: The Interface between Christianity and Folk Belief at Colossae.* WUNT Second Series 77. Tübingen: Mohr Siebeck, 1995.

———. *Ephesians: Power and Magic.* SNTSMS 63. Cambridge: Cambridge University Press, 1989.

Barth, Markus. "Conversion and Conversation: Israel and the Church in Paul's Epistle to the Ephesians." *Int* 17 (1963) 3–24.

———. *The People of God.* JSNTSup 5. Sheffield: JSOT, 1983.

Best, Ernest. *One Body in Christ.* London: SPCK, 1955.

Blumenfeld, Bruno. *The Political Paul.* JSNTSup 210. Sheffield: Sheffield Academic, 2001.

Cerfaux, Lucien. *The Church in the Theology of St. Paul.* Freiburg: Herder & Herder, 1959.

Cross, F. L., ed. *Studies in Ephesians.* London: Mowbray, 1956.

Dahl, Nils. "The Concept of Baptism in Ephesians." In *Studies in Ephesians: Introductory Questions, Text- and Edition Critical-Issues, Interpretation of Texts and Themes,* by Nils Dahl et al., 413–39. WUNT 131. Tübingen: Mohr Siebeck, 2000.

Davies, W. D. *Paul and Rabbinic Judaism.* 4th ed. Philadelphia: Fortress, 1980.

Deichgräber, Reinhard. *Gotteshymnus und Christushymnus in der frühen Christenheit: Untersuchungen zu Form, Sprache und Stil der frühchristlichen Hymnen.* SUNT 5. Göttingen: Vandenhoeck & Ruprecht, 1967.

Dunn, J. D. G. *Colossians and Philemon.* Grand Rapids: Eerdmans, 1996.

———. *The Theology of Paul the Apostle.* Grand Rapids: Eerdmans, 1998.

Gnilka, Joachim. "Das Kirchenmodell des Ephesebriefes." *Biblische Zeitschrift* 15 (1971) 161–84.

Gundry, R. H. *Sōma in Biblical Theology with Emphasis on Pauline Anthropology.* SNTSMS 29. Cambridge: Cambridge University Press, 1976.

Heinemann, Joseph. *Prayer in the Talmud.* Studia Judaica 9. Berlin: de Gruyter, 1977.

Hoehner, Harold. *Ephesians: An Exegetical Commentary*. Grand Rapids: Baker, 2002.

Houlden, J. L. "Christ and Church in Ephesians." *Studia Evangelica* 6 (1973) 267–73.

Lee, Michelle. *Paul, the Stoics, and the Body of Christ*. SNTSMS 137. Cambridge: Cambridge University Press, 2006.

Lincoln, Andrew. "The Church and Israel in Ephesians 2." *CBQ* 49 (1987) 605–24.

———. *Ephesians*. WBC 42. Dallas: Word, 1990.

Lindemann, Andreas. *Die Aufhebung der Zeit*. SNT 12. Gütersloh: Gerd Mohn, 1975.

Minear, Paul. *Images of the Church in the New Testament*. Louisville, KY: WJKP, 2004.

Nineham, D. E. "The Case against Pauline Authorship." In *Studies in Ephesians*, edited by F. L. Cross, 21–35. London: Mowbray, 1956.

Perkins, Pheme. "God, Cosmos and Church Universal." *SBLSP* 39 (2000) 752–73.

Sampley, J. Paul. *'And the Two Shall Become One Flesh': A Study of Traditions in Ephesians 5:21–33*. SNTSMS 16. Cambridge: Cambridge University Press, 1971.

Sanders, E. P. *Paul and Palestinian Judaism*. Philadelphia: Fortress, 1977.

Sanders, J. N. "The Case for the Pauline Authorship." In *Studies in Ephesians*, edited by F. L. Cross, 9–20. London: Mowbray, 1956.

Schmidt, K. L. "ἐκκλησία." *TWNT* 3:512–30.

Schnackenburg, Rudolf. "'Er hat uns mitauferweckt': Zur Tauflehre des Epheserbriefes." *Liturgisches Jahrbuch* 2 (1952) 159–83.

———. *Schriften zum Neuen Testament*. Munich: Kösel, 1971.

Talbert, Charles. *Ephesians and Colossians*. Paideia. Grand Rapids: Baker, 2007.

Tannehill, Robert. *Dying and Rising with Christ*. Töpelmann: Berlin, 1967.

Van Roon, A. *The Authenticity of Ephesians*. Leiden: Brill, 1974.

Van Kooten, George. *Cosmic Christology in Paul and the Pauline School*. WUNT Second Series 171. Tübingen: Mohr Siebeck, 2003.

Wire, Antoinette. *The Corinthian Women Prophets*. Minneapolis: Fortress, 1990.

8

"In the Churches of Macedonia"

Implicit Ecclesiology in Paul's Letters
to the Thessalonians and Philippians

JEFFREY PETERSON

PAUL'S LETTERS TO THE churches in Thessalonica and Philippi include little thematic reflection on the nature of the communities addressed, especially those to Thessalonica.[1] The letters rather address specific issues in the life of Paul's converts that are of concern to him: the churches' relationship with him (1 Thess 1–3; 2 Thess 2:13—3:5; Phil 1:3–26; 4:10–19), moral conduct in the community (1 Thess 4:1–12; 2 Thess 3:6–15; Phil 1:27—4:9;), the return of Christ and its implications (1 Thess 4:13—5:11; 2 Thess 2:1–12), and perseverance amid opposition and hostility (1 Thess 3:1–4; 2 Thess 1:4–10; Phil 1:27–30), among others. Yet throughout, the letters are informed by an understanding of the nature of the fellowship into which Paul had initiated these Macedonians. Indeed, the letters reveal that Paul had sought to impart a sense of this already in the initial instruction that he offered at the founding of each church, as one might expect. At a minimum, some promised benefit from entering the association into which Paul invited prospective con-

---

1. This essay treats 2 Thessalonians as a genuine letter of Paul, for substantially the reasons offered by Malherbe, *Thessalonians*, esp. 364–70, 379–463.

verts was needed to motivate the break with the converts' past that this association demanded.

This chapter will attempt to identify the ecclesiological convictions largely implicit in 1 and 2 Thessalonians and Philippians. The concern is primarily with the understanding of the church that informs Paul's exhortation in the letters, rather than with the Macedonians' own sense of what their societies meant, though as a good pastor Paul is concerned throughout with the latter. The letters to Thessalonica and to Philippi will be surveyed independently of each other, but as 2 Thessalonians expands on concerns introduced in the first letter, its evidence will be treated in connection with 1 Thessalonians.

ECCLESIOLOGY IN THE THESSALONIAN CORRESPONDENCE

Paul opens 1 Thessalonians with perhaps the most striking ecclesiological expression found in either of his letters to this church, addressing the letter "to the assembly of the Thessalonians by God the Father and the Lord Jesus Christ" (τῇ ἐκκλησίᾳ Θεσσαλονικέων ἐν θεῷ πατρὶ καὶ κυρίῳ Ἰησοῦ Χριστῷ, 1:1).[2] The use of the *nomen gentilicium* Θεσσαλονικέων (also in 2 Thess 1:1) rather than the usual designation of the recipients by reference to the city or region is striking; Paul addresses not "the assembly/church [of God] in Thessalonica" but "the assembly of the Thessalonians" (τῇ ἐκκλησίᾳ Θεσσαλονικέων, 1 Thess 1:1).[3] The language evokes the classical more than the biblical associations of the word usually translated "church" (ἐκκλησία), suggesting the civic assembly of a Greek *polis*, as though Paul's relatively few converts constituted the gathering of freeborn citizens in Thessalonica.[4] Yet this

---

2. Except as otherwise indicated, translations of the New Testament herein are the author's, usually with consultation of at least the RSV.

3. Donfried, "Assembly," 139.

4. Meeks describes the passage as a near-parody of the civic language (*First Urban Christians*, 108). Somewhat similarly, Paul sometimes refers to his churches as provinces of the Roman Empire, not merely as "the church in Thessalonica/Philippi/Corinth" but by synecdoche *as* "Macedonia" or "Achaia" (cf. Rom 15:26; 2 Cor 9:2). Donfried's conclusion that the word ἐκκλησία in 1 Thess 1:1 evokes no "developed sense of Christian ecclesiology" ("Assembly," 140) stands in tension with his observation that the Thessalonian assembly recognizes itself as "in fellowship with all the churches *of God*, including those in Macedonia, Achaia, and Judea" (p. 150, italics original). Donfried further presupposes that Paul had told his converts nothing about the ἐκκλησία while

assembly exists through divine initiative, "by God the Father and the Lord Jesus Christ" (ἐν θεῷ πατρὶ καὶ κυρίῳ Ἰησοῦ Χριστῷ, 1 Thess 1:1).[5] Paul presently makes it clear that his mission was the instrument through which God called "the assembly of the Thessalonians" together (1 Thess 1:5–6; 2:4, 13).

The report of Paul's prayers of thanksgiving assures the letter's audience that they are "beloved of God" and the objects of his "choice" (τὴν ἐκλογὴν ὑμῶν, 1 Thess 1:4), as evidenced by the divinely empowered character of the Pauline mission and the Thessalonians' reception of its message (1 Thess 1:5–6). Paul subsequently elaborates that the Thessalonians received their message as not merely human, but as "a word of God, who [or "which"] is at work in you believers" (1 Thess 2:13). The Thessalonians' joy in responding to the Pauline gospel in spite of the "distress" (θλῖψις) that attended their conversion was divinely motivated as well by God's Holy Spirit (1 Thess 1:6). The Thessalonians' entry into this assembly involved an exclusive commitment to the "living and true God," the one God of Israel's faith, and a concomitant abandonment of the "idols" that characterized the worship of pagan gods

---

he was in the process of forming it. Perhaps the point depends on the sense one gives to "developed."

5. The locative construction of ἐν θεῷ πατρί here and in 2 Thess 1:1 suggested by the translation "in God the Father" (RSV, NIV, NRSV) would be without parallel elsewhere in the Pauline corpus, whereas Paul uses ἐν τῷ θεῷ with instrumental force at 1 Thess 2:2 (Malherbe, *Thessalonians*, 99). An instrumental construction also yields the most satisfactory sense for ἐν τῷ θεῷ in Eph 3:9 and Col 3:3. The appended καὶ κυρίῳ Ἰησοῦ Χριστῷ in 1 Thess 1:1 does not argue against this interpretation, as (1) ἐν κυρίῳ Ἰησοῦ [Χριστῷ] (distinct from the simple ἐν Χριστῷ, usually understood in a locative sense) is used instrumentally in 1 Thess 4:1 (cf. διὰ τοῦ κυρίου Ἰησοῦ in 4:2) and evidently also in 2 Thess 3:12; and (2) ἐν Χριστῷ Ἰησοῦ has an unambiguously instrumental force in 1 Cor 4:15 (ἐν γὰρ Χριστῷ Ἰησοῦ διὰ τοῦ εὐαγγελίου ἐγὼ ὑμᾶς ἐγέννησα) and a number of other uses of the expressions invite, or at least admit of, an instrumental construction (e.g., θεὸς ἦν ἐν Χριστῷ κόσμον καταλλάσσων ἑαυτῷ, 2 Cor 5:19). Donfried curiously argues that the "interpretation of ἐν as incorporative [i.e., locative] presupposes and includes the instrumental sense, viz., the incorporation into God and Christ is because of what God accomplished in and through [the] life, death, and resurrection of Jesus Christ" ("Assembly," 143 n. 20). If one accepts the less problematic instrumental sense, there seems to be no need to retain the locative sense as well.

(1 Thess 1:9).[6] This involved a distressing break with their former associates and ways of life.[7]

The common life of this recently formed assembly is imbued with spiritual and moral qualities that Paul celebrates from the opening of the letter, recalling the Thessalonians' "work of faith and labor of love and perseverance in the hope of our Lord Jesus Christ" (1 Thess 1:3). The recollection of the Thessalonians' abandonment of pagan cults and reorientation of their lives towards "enslavement to God" (δουλεύειν θεῷ, 1 Thess 1:9) also likely alludes to the moral life, as the metaphor of slavery appears repeatedly in Romans in this connection (Rom 6:6, 16–20, 22; 7:6).[8] The first of these uses in Romans appears in the context of a reminiscence of baptism (Rom 6:6; cf. 6:3–4), which heightens the parallel with the recollection of conversion in 1 Thess 1:9.[9]

The chastity required of converts in Paul's founding instruction ("just as we have previously told you and attested," 1 Thess 4:6) and urged afresh in 1 Thess 4:3–8 is a corollary of the Thessalonians' exclusive commitment to Israel's God. In the Jewish Scriptures and the literature of the Second Temple, sexual impurity ranked alongside idolatry as a pervasive sin that defined pagan culture. It was for these sins, which "polluted the land," that the Canaanites had been driven out from before the Israelites.[10] In renouncing the sexual impurity associated with pagan society and embracing the "holiness" (ἁγιασμός, 1 Thess 4:3, 7) required to live in covenant with Israel's God (cf. Leviticus 18), the Thessalonians expressed their commitment to the one Deity to whom they turned in response to Paul's preaching. The Holy Spirit that inspired their joy at conversion (1 Thess 1:6) also empowered their holiness (1 Thess 4:8).

Paul's conduct supplied his converts with a visible model for the moral life to which his gospel called them. Having alluded to the character he and his co-workers modeled when initially present among the

---

6. For the expression "the living God" as designating the covenant God of Israel, see Goodwin, *Paul*, esp. 113–15 on 1 Thess 1:9–10.

7. Malherbe, *Thessalonians*, 127–28.

8. Ibid., 120.

9. On the argument of Romans as an elaboration on the instruction Paul offered in connection with conversion, see Peterson, "Extent of Christian Theological Diversity," 9–10.

10. For a full discussion of this tradition as it relates to the early Christian mission to Gentiles, see Bauckham, "James, Peter, and the Gentiles," esp. 92–96.

Thessalonians ("such [people] as we were among you for your benefit," 1 Thess 1:5), Paul commends them for becoming "imitators of us and of the Lord" from the time that they joyfully received the word despite tribulation (1 Thess 1:6). In 1 Thess 2:1–12 Paul elaborates on the aspects of his conduct that supplied his converts a moral exemplar, citing his courage and steadfastness in the face of opposition (2:2), desire to please God rather than humans (2:4, 6), rejection of flattery and greed (2:5, 10), and renunciation of apostolic privilege in favor of tender care for the Thessalonians (2:7, 11), specifically his ceaseless labor so as not to burden the community with his needs (2:9; cf. 1 Cor 9:12, 15).[11] The last of these aspects of Paul's conduct provides the basis of his appeal to the Thessalonians, already in his initial teaching (καθὼς ὑμῖν παρηγγεί λαμεν, 4:11) to "work with your own hands . . . so that you may behave in a well-ordered way to those outside and have need of nothing" (4:11–12), which Paul recalls in his appeal concerning the fraternal love of Christians (φιλαδελφία) in 4:9–12. That the love in view is a matter not merely of feeling but also of action is suggested by the sequence of thought from vv. 9–10a to vv. 10b–12. The Thessalonians are presently engaged in loving "all the brothers in all Macedonia" (4:10a), and the exhortation to "abound the more" in this (4:10b) leads on to the charge to order their own affairs, working with their hands so as to be in need of nothing (4:11–12). In light of Paul's concrete explication elsewhere of love in terms of hospitality (Phlm 4–7, 12, 20b), one may detect a reference to the welcome of visiting Christians here.[12]

The letters present the Thessalonian church as a community with strong internal bonds, most poignantly indicated by the grief occasioned when members of the community died (1 Thess 4:13). Among other indications of this, its members regard the ties that bind them as familial. Paul addresses the audience of the letter as ἀδελφοί (brothers[and sisters]) with remarkable frequency in the Thessalonian correspondence.[13]

---

11. For the antitheses in this passage as clarifying through contrast Paul's exemplary traits of character, rather than responding to charges of base conduct lodged against Paul by the Thessalonians or opponents from outside, of which the letter otherwise betrays no trace, see Malherbe, *Thessalonians*, 153–56; Lyons, *Pauline Autobiography*, 191–201.

12. Malherbe suggests a reference to hospitality in 1 Thess 4:10 without reference to the parallel in Philemon (*Thessalonians*, 245).

13. Thirteen uses of the vocative in 1 Thessalonians (as noted in ibid., 109–10), seven in 2 Thessalonians.

Whatever Paul's reasons for stressing kinship language in the letters, the address presupposes that the letters' recipients so regarded one another. As Paul's initial address is to the Thessalonians as "brothers [and sisters] beloved by the Lord" (1 Thess 1:4), it is reasonable to suppose that their fraternal consciousness was related to the newfound filial relationship to the God of Israel into which Paul had initiated them, to which the opening references to God "the Father" allude (1 Thess 1:1, 3). The characterization of their response to Paul's preaching in terms of their expectant posture towards Jesus the Son of God (1 Thess 1:10) supports the conjecture that, like the Galatians, the Thessalonians had experienced their Christian initiation as adoption by the Father through spiritual and ritual union with Jesus his Son (cf. Gal 3:26–28, 4:6). Paul assumes such a consciousness also among the Roman Christians (Rom 8:14–15), suggesting that this understanding of initiation was widespread in the first Christian generation.[14] The Thessalonians' sense of connection to members of the Christian community was not limited to Christians in their locality. In addition to Paul and the Lord (1 Thess 1:6), the Thessalonians have modeled their conduct on "the churches of God that are in Judea in Christ Jesus" (1 Thess 2:14), to whom they eventually sent alms (2 Cor 8:1–5), and they exhibit love for "all the brothers in all of Macedonia" (1 Thess 4:10).[15] Nor can they have imagined the parousia as an event that would embrace only their community (1 Thess 4:15–17).

This sense of belonging was not only theoretical but was also experienced in occasions of intimate Christian fellowship. The conclusion of 1 Thessalonians, with its solemn adjuration that the letter be "read to all the brothers and sisters" (1 Thess 5:27) presupposes a gathering of the community so that this reading can take place. The letter also presupposes that the Thessalonians regularly engage in mutual exhortation (5:11, 14) and inspired worship, including prophetic speech (5:19–20). Finally, the community's life includes shared meals, about which Paul gave instruction on his initial visit (2 Thess 3:10). The propensity of some Thessalonians to live off of the community's resources requires Paul to revisit repeatedly the precept that "if anyone is unwill-

14. Malherbe appropriately appeals in this connection to Paul's adaptation of traditions of Jewish proselytism but does not consider the specifically Christian form that Paul's "proselytism" likely took (ibid., 110).

15. For this aspect of Paul's formation of his converts, see Meeks, "Circle of Reference."

ing to work, neither shall he eat" (1 Thess 5:14; 2 Thess 3:6–15). The most likely setting for such intimate fellowship among the Thessalonian church was a communal banquet such as Paul describes at some length (owing to Corinthian abuses) in 1 Corinthians 11–14.[16] Doubtless the observance of this early Christian institution was less sumptuous among the Thessalonians than among the Corinthians (cf. 1 Cor 11:21–22; 2 Cor 8:1–2), but nonetheless the context fostered close personal contacts between members. Indeed, the intimacy of the meal context, and the associations of banqueting with debauchery, may supply the occasion for Paul's concern that one member of the community not wrong another in the matter of marriage and sexual purity (1 Thess 4:6).[17]

Like other Pauline churches, the Thessalonian community was overseen by recognized leaders who guided the community's life in Paul's absence.[18] At the conclusion of the exhortation in 1 Thessalonians, Paul appeals to the members at large to "recognize those who labor among you and stand before you in the Lord and admonish you" (1 Thess 5:12), turning thereafter to those responsible for this admonition (1 Thess 5:14). The verses that follow address the responsibilities of those exercising leadership in the community, as is first suggested by the exhortation, not merely not to repay anyone evil for evil, but to "see that" no one does (ὁρᾶτε, v. 15), the language suggesting the function of oversight.[19] An oversight function is suggested as well by the brief instructions for communal worship (1 Thess 5:19–22), in which those addressed have the responsibility not to "quench the Spirit" or (concretely) "scorn prophecies," but instead should "test all things [said]" and distinguish the good

16. See the informative discussion by Smith, *From Symposium to Eucharist*, 173–217.

17. On sexual immorality associated with banqueting, see ibid., 35–36, 42. Bauckham's observation that, apart from marriage, sharing a meal was the most intimate form of association in antiquity is crucial to appreciating the importance of table fellowship in early Christianity (Bauckham, "James, Peter, and the Gentiles," 124).

18. This contention runs counter to the influential thesis of Rudolf Sohm and Hans von Campenhausen that the Pauline churches began as egalitarian communities operating under the free inspiration of the Spirit, but it can claim impressive exegetical support; see esp. Campbell, *Elders*, 97–140. By way of summary, "the emergence of more formalized leadership was not a development contrary to the Pauline legacy, and . . . it was inherent from the start in the household setting of the earliest congregations" (125).

19. The rendering "See that none *of you* repays" in the RSV and NRSV introduces a democratizing note absent in the Greek, a fault that the NIV avoids with "Make sure that nobody pays back wrong for wrong."

from the bad. Such a structure of leaders responsible for the nurture of the community and members obliged to recognize them for these efforts is attested also in 1 Cor 16:15–16 and Phlm 1–2, 4–7, where it is clear that Stephanas and Philemon exercise leadership in virtue of their service as sponsors of a house church. The same may be concluded for the unnamed residential leadership of the church in Thessalonica.[20]

The Thessalonian Christians share a common eschatological destiny. Their initial response to Paul included coming to anticipate the risen Christ's return from the heavens to deliver them from impending divine wrath (1 Thess 1:10). Paul refers to the Lord's advent only incidentally before the major discussions of chaps. 4–5, assuring the Thessalonians that they will provide the occasion for his boasting and joy on that day (2:19–20; cf. 2 Cor 1:14), praying that they will be holy and blameless at the coming of the Lord (3:11), and reminding them that the Lord will execute justice in matters of sexual impurity (4:6).[21] The discussion of deceased Christians (4:13–18) centers on an eschatological scenario in which all those who have awaited Christ's return are assembled together with him and with one another, the dead as well as the living. Paul's purpose is to forestall the Thessalonians' grieving (1 Thess 4:13) and to encourage them in consoling one another (1 Thess 4:18), but the ground of this consolation is the hope that they and all the faithful "will always be with the Lord."

The pericope concerning the time of the Lord's return (1 Thess 5:1–11) takes the eschatological concerns of the Thessalonians (vv. 1–3) as the occasion for renewed moral exhortation (vv. 4–11), the image of the "day of the Lord" (v. 2) inspiring first the contrast between the Thessalonians as "children of light and children of the day" and others who are "of the night or of darkness" (vv. 4–7), and then the exhortation to prepare for the day of the Lord as for the "day" of battle (v. 8). Here Paul returns to the themes that opened the letter. The metaphorical

---

20. Campbell, *Elders*, 120–25.

21. This warning, recalled from Paul's founding visit (καθὼς καὶ προείπαμεν ὑμῖν καὶ διεμαρτυράμεθα, 1 Thess 4:6), is plausibly related to the statements in Galatians and 1 Corinthians that the sexually immoral "shall not inherit the kingdom of God," presented in both passages as an element of Paul's initial instruction (explicitly in Gal 5:21, καθὼς προεῖπον ὅτι οἱ τὰ τοιαῦτα πράσσοντες βασιλείαν θεοῦ οὐ κληρο–νομήσουσιν; implicitly in 1 Cor 6:9, οὐκ οἴδατε ὅτι ἄδικοι θεοῦ βασιλείαν οὐ κλ–ηρονομήσουσιν). Thus, while 1 Thess 4:6 does not specify the time of God's judgment "regarding all these matters," we may assume that eschatological judgment is in view.

equipment for the Thessalonians' battle consists of faith, hope, and love (v. 8; cf. 1:3), and they are assured that their future will lead not to wrath but to deliverance through the Lord Jesus Christ as purposed by God (v. 9; cf. 1:4, 10).

Rather than calming the Thessalonians' eschatological anxiety, Paul's reminder that the day of the Lord "is coming like a thief in the night" (1 Thess 5:2) seems only to have agitated them further. The most satisfactory explanation of the situation that Paul addresses in 2 Thess 2:1–15 is that the Thessalonians interpreted 1 Thess 5:2 as predicting an extremely imminent parousia.[22] The common interpretation of 2 Thess 2:2 as referring to a spurious Pauline letter is doubtful on lexical grounds. It requires that the preposition διά bear a different sense in its fourth appearance in the phrase μήτε διὰ πνεύματος μήτε διὰ λόγου μήτε δι' ἐπιστολῆς ὡς δι' ἡμῶν than in its first three (cf. NRSV, "either by spirit or by word or *by* letter, as though *from* us"). The verse appeals to the Thessalonians to be disturbed "neither by a [prophetic] spirit nor by a [spoken] word nor by a letter, as though by us" (i.e., "as though we should be the source of your disturbance"). For the common interpretation to be correct, the phrase should conclude μήτε δι' ἐπιστολῆς ὡς ὑφ' ἡμῶν ("neither through a letter as though [written] by us"). The concluding greeting (2 Thess 3:17), while more emphatic than other comparable ones (cf. 1 Cor 16:21; Col 4:18), need only have the function of offering a visible commendation of the teaching contained in the letter and so reassuring its anxious recipients, rather than also distinguishing this authentic letter from a spurious one in circulation.[23] The teaching itself, recalling Paul's initial instruction (2 Thess 2:5), briefly rehearses the events that must be accomplished before the parousia (2:3–12), including general apostasy and the deception of many by the "lawless one" (NRSV).

The coda to this discussion of the Lord's coming (2 Thess 2:13–17) contrasts those who will be deceived by the lawless one with the Thessalonians, and can stand as a concise summary of the ecclesiology of these letters. Paul reassures the Thessalonians that God has chosen

22. Malherbe, *Thessalonians*, 416.

23. Malherbe's scenario of an annotated copy of 1 Thessalonians (*Thessalonians*, 430) is not impossible, but neither does it seem necessary to account for the greeting of 3:17; oral teaching based on Paul's letter would cause just as much trouble, and a letter stating Paul's position and signed emphatically would be just as useful in correcting the misinterpretation.

them for eschatological salvation, to be accomplished by the sanctification of his Spirit and their fidelity to the truth (2:13). It is to this end that he called them through Paul's preaching that they might ultimately share in Christ's glory (2:14). If they will adhere to the traditions they have received from Paul, whether in person or by letter, the Lord Jesus and God the Father will comfort and strengthen them "in every good word and deed" (2:15–17).

ECCLESIOLOGY IN PHILIPPIANS[24]

Philippians is addressed not to "the church of God in Philippi," nor yet to "the assembly of the Philippians," but to "all the saints in Christ Jesus who are in Philippi, with the overseers and servants" (Phil 1:1). This evokes the theme of sanctification and includes in the address the house-church leadership that came into view at the conclusion of 1 Thessalonians (cf. Phlm 1–2).[25] The report of Paul's prayers (1:3–11) includes thanksgiving for the Philippians' "fellowship" (κοινωνία, 1:5) in the gospel, and this theme of joint participation of the church with Paul recurs throughout the letter. Thus, both in his imprisonment and in his defense and confirmation of the gospel, the Philippians are Paul's "fellow partakers in grace" (συγκοινωνούς μου τῆς χάριτος, 1:7). The unity to which Paul urges the Philippians in order to fulfill his joy (2:2) is predicated on "fellowship in the Spirit" (κοινωνία πνεύματος, 2:1), among other things. As for the Thessalonians, Paul offers himself as an exemplar for the Philippians (3:15a), specifically in his desire to experience "the fellowship of Christ's sufferings" (τὴν κοινωνίαν τῶν παθημάτων αὐτοῦ, 3:10), being conformed to Christ's death that he might also attain to the resurrection from the dead (3:11). The Philippians, to whom it has "been granted for the sake of Christ . . . to suffer" (ἐχαρίσθη τὸ ὑπὲρ Χριστοῦ . . . πάσχειν, 1:29) have thereby "become [Paul's] fellow participants in affliction" (συγκοινωνήσαντές μου τῇ θλίψει, 4:14). Their recent gift (4:10) continues their unique position among Paul's churches

24. This sketch of the letter's ecclesiology is based in part on my brief commentary, "Philippians." Among recent commentaries, I have found most helpful Bockmuehl, *Philippians*, and Fee, *Philippians*, which afford a full introduction to the secondary literature.

25. See Campbell, *Elders*, 123–25, who suggests that the Philippian "overseers and servants" likely include the members named in the letter: Epaphroditus, Syntyche, Euodia, and Clement.

in that they alone have "shared in the matter of giving and receiving" (ἐκοινώνησεν εἰς λόγον δόσεως καὶ λήμψεως, 4:15). Paul's report on the way his imprisonment has served to advance the preaching of Christ (Phil 1:12–26) makes concrete the Philippians' "partnership in the gospel" (1:12–18), and his account of the alternatives of life or death that constrain him in his circumstances (1:19–26) grants them partnership in his imprisonment (cf. 1:7) and in the distress (θλῖψις, cf. 4:14) he is experiencing. The church is thus a fellowship of suffering and grace, in which the Philippians "share the same contest" as Paul (τὸν αὐτὸν ἀγῶνα ἔχοντες, 1:30), sharing in both his sufferings for Christ and the hope of resurrection.

Turning to exhortation in 1:27, Paul introduces one of the letter's principal ecclesiological metaphors. These residents of a Roman colony bearing the name of a Macedonian king who conquered Greece—no strangers to politics—are urged to "exercise [their] citizenship in a manner worthy of the royal proclamation [gospel] of Christ" (ἀξίως τοῦ εὐαγγελίου τοῦ Χριστοῦ πολιτεύεσθε, Phil 1:27). The image recurs explicitly at 3:20, where the "city-state" to which Paul and the Philippian Christians owe allegiance is said to "subsist in the heavens" (ἡμῶν γὰρ τὸ πολίτευμα ἐν οὐρανοῖς ὑπάρχει), from which they expect a Savior, the Lord Jesus Christ, even as the Thessalonians awaited his descent from heaven to rescue them from wrath.[26] In Gal 4:26, Paul names the heavenly city to which Christians owe allegiance as "the Jerusalem above" (ἡ δὲ ἄνω Ἰερουσαλήμ), describing the city in terms of ancient political rhetoric as "free" (ἐλευθέρα) and "our mother" (ἥτις ἐστὶν μή τηρ ἡμῶν), a marked contrast to "the present [earthly] Jerusalem, for she is in slavery with her children" (τῇ νῦν Ἰερουσαλήμ, δουλεύει γὰρ μετὰ τῶν τέκνων αὐτῆς, Gal 4:25). Paul's declaration in Phil 3:3 (discussed below) may presuppose the Philippians' familiarity with such an identification of the heavenly *civitas*.[27]

26. On the political connotations of Paul's language in Phil 1:27–30 and 3:20–21, see Bryan, *Render to Caesar*, 82–90.

27. The image appears also in Rev 21:1–2, likely in common dependence with Paul on a traditional Christian exegesis of Isaiah 65–66. In the prophetic text, the new heavens and new earth are conjoined with the dwelling of God's people in Jerusalem (65:17–19; 66:22–23), but the house the Judeans have built for God and the sacrificial worship conducted there are treated with some disdain (66:1–3), and the promise is held out that God will "create" Jerusalem anew (בוֹרֵא, Isa 65:18 MT). First-century interpreters might well have understood this re-creation in terms of the descent of the heavenly Jerusalem to supersede the earthly.

The essential quality urged on the Philippians as citizens of God's heavenly commonwealth likewise reflects a political trope. Evoking the quest for the harmony of the *polis* and the horror of faction in Athens and the Roman Republic, Paul appeals for the Philippians' unity in faithfulness to the gospel, even in the face of opposition (1:27b–28; 2:2). In concrete terms, this involves the willingness to lower oneself and forego one's own interests to mind the interests of others (2:3–4). Paul is uncharacteristically direct in this regard later in the letter, mentioning by name two who have struggled alongside him in the gospel, Euodia and Syntyche, to whom he now appeals to "be of the same mind in the Lord" (4:2–3, NRSV).

The great exemplar of the manner of life Paul commends to the Philippians is the *princeps* of the heavenly commonwealth, the Lord Jesus Christ (2:6–11), whose earthly sojourn involved the descent from subsistence in the form of God to assume the form of a slave among humans, and then the further descent to suffer the form of execution reserved for slaves and enemies of the Roman order of which the city of Philippi was an agent. The pivot of the Christological passage is the "therefore" (διό) that opens v. 9: it is on account of Christ's self-abasement that God exalted him and granted him divine honors anew ("the name that is above every name," i.e., YHWH, v. 9).[28] Yet the climax of the passage preserves Paul's emphasis on Christ's humility as well, for even in his triumph, the universal acclamation "Jesus Christ is Lord!" redounds "to the glory of God the Father" (v. 11).

The introduction to this magnificent passage (2:5) urges the readers to find their unity by sharing in the mind of Christ, as exhibited in his selfless descent, and in his continuing to act for the glory of God the Father rather than his own glory even after the exaltation with which he was rewarded.[29] In the section following the Christological passage, Paul characterizes the Philippians, himself, and his co-workers in terms

---

28. See Bauckham, "Worship of Jesus," 128–39.

29. The RSV's curious rendering of this verse, "Have this mind among yourselves, which is yours in Christ Jesus," reflects the uneasiness of many exegetes influenced by Lutheran theology with the *imitatio Christi* as an organizing category for the Christian life (notably Käsemann, "Critical Analysis.") In favor of the interpretation followed in the text, see Bockmuehl, *Philippians*, 122–25, who would refine the NRSV rendering slightly and translate "Have this mind in you which *is* in Christ Jesus," rather than "was." The recognition above that Christ's humility continues through v. 11 supports this translation.

that echo Christ's example and so offers glimpses of what a church sharing in the mind of Christ looks like on the ground (2:12–3:1a). Thus,
the Philippians are to continue the obedience they have always practiced (2:12; cf. 2:8).[30] The God who exalted Christ (2:9) is at work in
the Philippians as well (2:13). Paul is in the process of "being poured
out as a libation over the sacrifice and offering" (2:17, NRSV) of the
Philippians' "faith(fulness)" (a word Paul closely associates with "obedience," cf. Rom 1:5), even as Christ suffered the death of the cross, and
by order of the same Roman imperium. Unlike others, Timothy seeks
not his own interests (2:21; cf. 2:4) but those of the Philippians (2:20)
and of Jesus Christ (2:21), in whose mind he and the Philippians are to
share (cf. 2:5). Epaphroditus, dispatched by the Philippians to minister
to Paul by conveying the church's gifts (4:18), fell ill and drew near "to
the point of death" (μέχρι θανάτου, 2:30) in the course of discharging
this responsibility, even as Christ was obedient "to the point of death"
(μέχρι θανάτου, 2:8). The church is thus a community in which the
faithful, sharing in the mind of Christ, "work out their own salvation"
(2:12) in selfless acts of service for those in need, as God works in them
for his good purpose (2:13).

The most explicit ecclesiological declaration to be found in
Philippians appears in Phil 3:3, following a warning about those urging
circumcision on Gentile converts (2:2): "we are the circumcision, who
worship by the Spirit of God and boast in Christ Jesus and put no confidence in the flesh." Similarly in Romans, Paul insists that true circumcision is a matter of a heart (i.e., a will) capable of keeping God's law (Rom
2:26–29). He further affirms that God's purpose for sending Christ in
the likeness of sinful humankind (cf. Phil 2:7) was to make this theoretical possibility a reality, "so that what the Torah justly demands might be
fulfilled among us who walk not in accordance with the flesh, but in
accordance with the Spirit" (Rom 8:3–4). Finally, he presents the confession of Jesus as Lord in response to the preaching of Christ as the path
to salvation (Rom 10:6–10), and he argues from Scripture that this path
is for Jews and Gentiles alike, linking the promise of Isa 28:16 that "No
one who trusts on him shall be put to shame" with that of Joel 2:32 (LXX
3:5) that "Every one who calls on the name of the Lord [Jesus] shall be

---

30. The RSV "as you have always obeyed [God]" is superior to the NRSV "just as
you have always obeyed *me*," as the personal pronoun is lacking in Greek, and supplying
it weakens the parallel with Christ's obedience to *God* in 2:8.

saved" (Rom 10:11–13).[31] It is unlikely to have escaped the notice of an exegete of Paul's acumen that four verses earlier Joel records the promise of God's Spirit poured out on "all flesh," and it may be that in the manner of other Jewish interpreters he expected the more alert members of his audience to recall the context, as Luke certainly did (Acts 2:17–21). The Christian community is the eschatological Israel of God (cf. Gal 6:16) gathered around the Messiah Jesus by the free outpouring of his Spirit rather than by ancestral right. Paul's Gentile converts in Philippi, as in Galatia, should resist any pressure to become nationalized citizens of "Israel according to the flesh" (cf. 1 Cor 10:18) but should rather accept the status that God has accorded them along with Jews like Paul who have acknowledged Jesus as Messiah.[32]

Following the declaration in Phil 3:3, Paul sketches his example of renunciation of advantage for the sake of knowing Christ (3:4–11) and progress towards full participation in his death and resurrection (3:12–14) before appealing to the Philippians to join together in imitation of his example of steadfastness (3:15–17; 4:1) while marking those earthly-minded "enemies of the cross" who do not share the Philippian Christians' heavenly citizenship (3:18–21). After appeals for unity among the church's leaders (4:2–3) and for joy, prayer, and peace among all (4:4–7), Paul concludes his ethical appeal by commending a series of notably Hellenistic-tinged virtues (4:8) and renewing his appeal to imitation as an assurance of divine blessing (4:9). The letter concludes by strengthening the ties that bind Paul and the Philippians together. Paul's grateful acknowledgement of the church's assistance (4:10–18), his assurance that God will supply the Philippians' needs (4:19–20), the exchange of greetings (4:21–22), and his participation in the church's worship through the wording of a benediction (4:23) reinforce the bonds that unite Paul and the Philippians as citizens of God's heavenly polity.

---

31. For κύριος in Rom 10:13 as referring to Jesus rather than God the Father, see Dunn, *Romans 9–16*, 617.

32. The question of supercessionism, understandably prominent in theological discussion since the Holocaust and ever more so in an increasingly pluralist environment, is largely anachronistic when addressed to Paul. The Jewish apostle Paul, who acknowledged Jesus as the Messiah of Israel along with other Jews living mostly in Jerusalem before 70 CE, was no more a "supercessionist" than the authors of the sectarian documents preserved at Qumran. He was a member of a Messianist sect of Judaism that came to accept Gentile converts on the basis of its interpretation of Israel's Scriptures.

CONCLUSION

The view of the church that emerges from the Thessalonian and Philippian letters is of a closely knit religious society exclusively devoted to the God of Israel and gathered in the name of Jesus through the work of his apostle Paul, who has modeled for his converts the life that is pleasing to God. The members of this society celebrate the salvation they have received through the work of Christ and the gift of his Spirit, which has given them a spiritual kinship with people throughout the Mediterranean world who share these commitments, but also involves them in tension with their pagan neighbors. They seek to live in virtue and harmony with one another under the guidance of Paul and the local leadership and to assist those in need while living in expectation of the return of Christ to begin the messianic age in earnest and reorder the world to the glory of his God and Father.

BIBIOGRAPHY

Bauckham, Richard. "James, Peter, and the Gentiles." In *The Missions of James, Peter, and Paul*, edited by Bruce Chilton and Craig Evans, 91–142. NovTSup 115. Boston: Brill, 2005.

———. "The Worship of Jesus in Philippians 2:9–11." In *Where Christology Began*, edited by Brian J. Dodd and Ralph P. Martin, 128–39. Louisville, KY: WJKP, 1998.

Bockmuehl, Markus. *The Epistle to the Philippians*. BNTC. Peabody, MA: Hendrickson; Grand Rapids: Baker, 1998.

Bryan, Christopher. *Render to Caesar: Jesus, the Early Church, and the Roman Superpower*. Oxford: Oxford University Press, 2005.

Campbell, R. Alastair. *The Elders: Seniority within Earliest Christianity*. Edinburgh: T. & T. Clark, 1994.

Donfried, Karl Paul. "The Assembly of the Thessalonians: Reflections on the Ecclesiology of the Earliest Christian Letter." In *Paul, Thessalonica, and Early Christianity*, 139–62. Grand Rapids: Eerdmans, 2002.

Dunn, James D. G. *Romans 9–16*. WBC 38B. Dallas: Word, 1988.

Fee, Gordon D. *Paul's Letter to the Philippians*. NICNT. Grand Rapids: Eerdmans, 1995.

Goodwin, Mark. *Paul, Apostle of the Living God: Kerygma and Conversion in 2 Corinthians*. Harrisburg, PA: Trinity Press International, 2001.

Käsemann, Ernst. "A Critical Analysis of Philippians 2:5–11." *JTC* 5 (1968) 45–88.

Lyons, George. *Pauline Autobiography: Toward a New Understanding*. SBLDS 73. Atlanta: Scholars, 1985.

Malherbe, Abraham J. *The Letters to the Thessalonians: A New Translation with Introduction and Commentary*. New York: Doubleday, 2000.

Meeks, Wayne A. "The Circle of Reference in Pauline Morality." In *Greeks, Romans, and Christians: Essays in Honor of Abraham J. Malherbe*, edited by David L. Balch, Everett Ferguson, and Wayne A. Meeks, 305–17. Minneapolis: Fortress, 1990.

———. *The First Urban Christians: The Social World of the Apostle Paul*. New Haven: Yale University Press, 1983.

Peterson, Jeffrey. "The Extent of Christian Theological Diversity: Pauline Evidence." *ResQ* 47 (2005) 1–12.

———. "Philippians." In *The Transforming Word: One-Volume Commentary on the Bible*, edited by Mark W. Hamilton, 965–71. Abilene, TX: Abilene Christian University Press, 2009.

Smith, Dennis E. *From Symposium to Eucharist: The Banquet in the Early Christian World*. Minneapolis: Fortress, 2003.

9

Ecclesiology in the Pastoral Epistles

CHRISTOPHER R. HUTSON

T HE PASTORAL EPISTLES (PE) present themselves as letters from an aged Paul[1] to his "young" delegates Timothy and Titus, aimed at preparing the next generation of youthful ministers to carry on the traditions.[2] Not all scholars are convinced that the same author wrote all three letters,[3] but assuming that the same author produced all three,[4] the PE seem to reflect an ecclesiological situation that has moved from the charismatic leadership of the first generation to a third or fourth generation focused on perpetuating a consolidated body of tradition (2 Tim 2:2).[5] This tradition is referred to as "the faith" (1 Tim 1:19; 3:9; 4:1, 6; 5:8; 6:10, 21; 2 Tim 2:28; 3:8; Titus 1:13) or "the deposit" (1 Tim 6:20; 2 Tim 1:12). The PE do not explain the basic tenets of the Christian faith so much as presume them. Instead, these letters focus on practi-

---

1. Although the author calls himself "Paul," there are good reasons to think this might be a pseudonym. Arguments may be found in any critical commentary or introduction, e.g., Holladay, *Critical Introduction*, chap. 20. I shall refer to the author as Paul to respect his self-identification while leaving open the likelihood of pseudonymity. On the characterization of Paul as an old man, see Malherbe, *"Paulus Senex."*

2. Hutson, "My True Child," also argues that the portrayal of the protégés as youthful does not fit into the career of the historical Paul and suggests that the addressees have been fictionalized, perhaps by a disciple of Paul late in the first century.

3. Aageson, *Paul*, 3–5; Johnson, *Writings*, 430; Prior, *Paul the Letter Writer*; Murphy-O'Connor, "2 Timothy Contrasted."

4. Hutson, "My True Child," 33–60.

5. See MacDonald, *Pauline Churches*; Aageson, *Paul*.

164

cal matters of Christian leadership, which is why they are so often cited on matters of church polity. But we must understand polity questions within larger theological and historical contexts. This essay will consider (1) what the PE say about the theological origin and mission of the church, (2) what the letters reflect about the social and historical circumstances that shaped them, and in light of these factors (3) what the letters say about church organization and polity.

THEOLOGICAL CONTEXT

The PE presume a body of doctrine defined by a previous generation to be passed on intact to future generations. At several places Paul quotes what appear to be creedal or hymnic[6] statements summarizing the contents of this doctrine that, taken together, provide a framework for understanding the theological assumptions undergirding the instructions in the PE. I shall discuss these statements in the order that they appear in the canonical texts. Each statement deserves a lengthy discussion, but space permits only a glance at the essential points as they pertain to ecclesiology.

1 Timothy 1:15

This statement is embedded in the thanksgiving prayer (1 Tim 1:12–17) within the letter opening (1:3–20):

> Christ Jesus came into the world to save sinners.

This statement is the first of five "faithful sayings" in the PE, of which we shall include three in this survey.[7] It is not poetic, but the label "faithful saying" does suggest that it was an established element of

---

6. I use the adjectives "creedal" and "hymnic" to avoid debate about whether any given instance is quoting a traditional creed or hymn. On the difficulties of precise identification of such "preformed traditions," see Yarbrough, *Paul's Utilization*, 17–57. In any case, these summaries of core beliefs are presumed as grounds for the exhortations in the letters. One might compare the philosophical distinction between *dogmata* or θεωρετική (core beliefs) and παραίνεσις (application to specific cases), on which see Seneca, *Epistulae morales* 94–95; Hadot, *Philosophy*, 59–61; Hutson, "My True Child," 300–302.

7. It is unclear whether the "faithful saying" mentioned at 3:1 refers to what precedes in 2:15 or to what follows in 3:1, but neither verse expresses core Christian doctrine. The "faithful saying" at 4:8–9 is more paraenetic than doctrinal and so does not fit within the purview of this essay.

Christian tradition. The prayer identifies Paul as "foremost" of sinners and the example *par excellence* of all who would come after and "believe in him [Jesus] to eternal life." This prayer thus characterizes the church as a community of believers in Christ who have been saved from sin to eternal life. That is, the community has an ethical dimension in the present and is oriented toward an eschatological future.

1 Timothy 2:5–6

This saying appears following the letter opening in the first section of ethical exhortation in the letter body:

> For God is one,
> And one is the mediator between God and humans,
> The human Christ Jesus,
>> Who gave himself as a ransom for all,
>> The testimony when the times were right.

This dense Christological statement echoes Pauline themes: Christ as "mediator" (cf. Paul's reference to Moses in Gal 3:19–20; and Christ as mediator in Heb 8:6; 9:15; 12:24); as a "human being" (cf. Paul's relatively low Christology in Rom 1:3); as a "ransom" (not from foreign domination, as in Luke 24:21, but from immoral conduct, as in Titus 2:14; 1 Pet 1:18; cf. Rom 3:24; 8:23); and as a "testimony" (shorthand reference to the crucifixion, as in 1 Cor 1:6; 2 Tim 1:8).[8] But all of this is presumed without explanation.

This statement turns on the *Shema* ("God is one," paraphrasing Deut 6:4). Such a blunt assertion of monotheism pushes in the direction of God's universal concern for all peoples, because if there is only one God, then that God is the creator of all peoples and interested in their

---

8. The last line of this creedal statement has been understood in various ways. Some ancient scribes altered the last line of the poem to read, "*whose* [or *about whom*] testimony *was given* when the times were right" (D*FG), or alternatively, "Who gave himself as a ransom for all *and* a testimony when the times were right" ()*). I understand τὸ μαρτύριον ("the testimony") as accusative, functioning as appositional to ἑαυτόν ("himself"), renaming the direct object of the participle ὁ δούς ("the one who gave"). Thus, "himself as a ransom for all" expresses the content of the "testimony" that Jesus gave. So Jesus' crucifixion was his "testimony." For a similar understanding, see Fiore, *Pastoral Epistles*, 61. Even if one understands 6b to refer to *God's* testimony (e.g., Witherington, *Letters and Homilies*, 216), the content of the "testimony" remains Jesus' death.

welfare.[9] Paul also makes this connection when he paraphrases "God is one" in Gal 3:20, as a part of an argument from "the gospel proclaimed beforehand" in Gen 12:3, namely that, "in you will *all* the nations be blessed." So here, the creed moves from the *Shema* to the claim that Christ Jesus "gave himself a ransom for *all*." This supports the exhortation to pray "for *all* who are in positions of authority" (2:2), because "God our Savior wants *all* humans to be saved" (2:3–4).

A major point for ecclesiology, then, is that Christianity is not the exclusive domain of any nation or ethnic group, but that the God of *all* people has acted through Christ for the redemption of *all* people. So also, "The grace of God has appeared, bringing salvation to *all*" (Titus 2:11), and Timothy's ministry is that of an evangelist (2 Tim 4:5).

1 Timothy 3:16

This passage is a hymnic summary of the Christ story, the gist of "the truth" (3:15):

> Who appeared in flesh,
>> Was justified in spirit,
> Appeared to angels,
>> Was proclaimed among the nations,
> Was believed on in the world,
>> Was taken up in glory.

Like 1 Tim 2:5–6, this hymn tells the Christ story in theological shorthand ("appeared," "justified," "proclaimed," "taken up"). "Among the nations" and "in the world" reinforce the universal scope of Christ's mission, and this point is reflected also in the expression "the living God" (3:15), a stock element in Jewish preaching to Gentiles.[10]

This hymn comes in the context of the first explicit mention of the "church" (ἐκκλησία, 3:15) in the PE, here described as the "household of God." The phrase "pillar and foundation" (3:15)[11] evokes the architectural imagery of 1 Cor 3:10–17 but with a shift of focus. In 1 Corinthians, the foundation is Jesus Christ (3:11), the edifice is the community of believers (3:9, 16–17), and the construction crew consists of apostles

---

9. On the trajectory from monotheism toward universalism in Jewish thought, see Kaminsky and Stewart, "God of All the World"; Kogan, *Opening the Covenant*, 231–46.

10. Acts 14:15; 1 Thess 1:9; 2 Cor 3:3. And see Goodwin, *Paul*, 94–108.

11. On ἑδραίωμα as "foundation," see Hanson, *Studies*, 5–7.

and evangelists ("co-workers," 3:9; "architect," 3:10; "builders," 3:10, 12, 14). But in 1 Timothy, the church does not stand *on* the foundation of the truth but *is itself* the foundation of truth, the pillar that upholds the truth, the keeper of the "mystery of piety" (3:16) that is summarized in this hymn.[12] This is a high ecclesiology: the church is the repository of the correct tradition about Christ on which the community of believers is built. Thus the church's tradition about Christ pre-exists the New Testament. The church created the New Testament and interprets it.[13]

In this regard, we may notice how often Timothy and Titus are exhorted to remember what they have been taught. The doctrine has been given to them as a "deposit" to "guard" (1 Tim 6:20; 2 Tim 1:14) and to pass on to the next generation (2 Tim 2:2).

The image of the church as "household of God" (1 Tim 3:15) is thematic in the PE,[14] in which household metaphors regularly describe Christian leaders. Indeed, household concerns characterize the only other two passages in which the word ἐκκλησία occurs in the PE. First, the role of an overseer is analogous to that of the head of a household (1 Tim 3:5); and second, the church functions as a surrogate family to care for the needs of "real widows" (1 Tim 5:16). This household imagery is ethical in nature, illustrating how members of the community relate to one another.

1 Timothy 6:15–16

This is another creedal statement, in the form of a doxology:

> The blessed and only sovereign,
>> The King of kings, and Lord of lords,
> The only One who has immortality,
>> Who dwells in unapproachable light
> Whom no human has seen, or is able to see,
> To whom be honor and might forever, amen.

12. Ephesians 2:20–22 presents a mediating position. Hanson, *Studies*, 5–20, argues for a Christological reading of 1 Tim 3:15, which is theologically engaging, but it extends the metaphor beyond the text.

13. By contrast, in challenging Roman ecclesiastical authority, the Reformers developed a high view of Scripture that the Bible somehow precedes and governs the church (Calvin, *Institutes* 1.6–8). For a critique of such a view, see Allert, *High View*, esp. 67–130.

14. Verner, *Household of God*, 83–186.

This doxology reasserts the universal sovereignty of God, who claims authority over *all* kings and lords. Again, any ecclesiology oriented to national or ethnic identity risks denying the universal sovereignty of God. Paul calls to witness the Creator "God who gives life to *all* things" (6:13), again drawing out the universalizing implications of monotheism ("the only One").

In the immediate context, Timothy is a "man of God" (6:11, a designation for a prophet, 1 Sam 2:27; 1 Kgs 13:1), who has been "called" to "eternal life" (6:12). That is, his mission has an eschatological orientation, "until the epiphany of our Lord Jesus Christ" (6:14). Further, Timothy has "made the good confession before many witnesses" (6:12), which could refer to his baptism[15] but more likely refers to his ordination.[16] In the larger context, Timothy is to "teach and exhort" (6:2) and to repudiate anyone who "teaches otherwise" and does not give attention to "the sound words about our Lord Jesus Christ and the teaching that is in accordance with piety" (6:3). That he is to "keep the commandment unspotted, unimpeachable" (6:14) points again to his role in the church, the repository of correct doctrine.

2 Timothy 1:9–10

This is a hymnic passage that summarizes the gospel as a demonstration of the "power of God" (1:8):

> Who saved us
> > And called us with a holy calling
> Not according to our works,
> > But according to his own purpose and grace,
> Which was given to us in Christ Jesus before times eternal,
> > But is now manifested through the epiphany of Christ Jesus
> our Savior
> Who destroyed Death
> > And brought to light life and immortality through the gospel.

---

15. Marshall, *Pastoral Epistles*, 661, thinks the context reflects baptismal language and finds no contemporary parallel for a confession in an ordination. Cf. also Johnson, *Letters to Timothy*, 307.

16. Bassler, *1 Timothy, 2 Timothy, Titus*, 113–14, points out that "many witnesses" were associated with Timothy's ordination in 2 Tim 2:2 (cf. 1 Tim 4:14), that the PE nowhere mention baptism but are concerned with ordination, just as here ("man of God"), and suggests that early ordination liturgy may have included elements of baptismal liturgy. Cf. also Fiore, *Pastoral Epistles*, 122–23.

This text affirms the origins of the Christian community ("us") in the eternal plan of God, brought to fruition in the work of Christ. The "epiphany of Christ" refers to the incarnation ("now manifested"). The resurrection of Jesus "destroyed death" (cf. 1 Cor 15:20–28; Rom 6:8–9). The eternal plan of God called into existence a community of people who are no longer under the tyranny of death (cf. Romans 6–7; 1 Cor 15:24–26) but oriented toward life eternal (cf. Rom 12:1–2).

The text summarizes the message to which Paul was "appointed a herald and apostle and teacher" (2 Tim 1:11). His apostolic commission is to tell this story, even though he suffers for doing so (1:12). But he exhorts Timothy to "share in suffering for the gospel" (1:8). The story that called the church into existence is counter-cultural, a threat to the powers that be, and Christian teachers who proclaim it may find themselves under attack.

2 Timothy 2:11–13

This is yet another poetic creedal statement depicting life in the community ("we, us") and identified as one of the "faithful sayings" in the PE:

> For if we suffer with him, we shall also live with him;
>> If we endure, we shall also reign with him;
> If we deny him, he will deny us;
>> If we are unfaithful, he remains faithful,
>>> For he cannot deny himself.

In the context, Paul summarizes "my gospel" as a story about the suffering and resurrection of Jesus. His mission to proclaim this is the reason he suffers in "chains as a criminal" (2 Tim 2:9). Nevertheless, his mission remains paramount: "I endure everything for the sake of the elect, so that they may find salvation" (2:10). In other words, Paul's devotion to Christ compels him to work for the interests of the community, even against his own immediate interest. This poem suggests that suffering and endurance are not reserved for apostles and teachers but characterize the Christian community as a whole. The suffering of Christ called the community into existence, and their suffering "with" Christ gives a distinctive shape to the community. Yet they endure because of their eschatological hope that they will "live with . . . reign with" Christ (cf. Rom 6:1–14).

Titus 3:4–7

This is one of the "faithful sayings" and the final creedal statement in the PE:

> But when the kindness and philanthropy of God our Savior
> appeared,
>> Not out of works that we did in righteousness, but according
> to his own mercy,
> He saved us through a washing of regeneration
>> And a renewal of the Holy Spirit
> Which he poured out upon us richly
>> Through Jesus Christ our Savior
> So that, having been justified by his grace,
>> We might become heirs in accordance with hope of eternal life.

Here again, what God did through Christ is formative for a community ("we, us") that is oriented toward an eschatological future ("eternal life"). The community is characterized by a "washing of regeneration" (baptism) and the presence of the Holy Spirit. Through Christ, we have been "justified" or "made righteous." Those who were once "foolish, disobedient, deceived, slaves to various passions and desires, spending time in evil and deceit, despicable, hating one another" (3:3) have now become "believers in God" who "care for good works" (3:8). In other words, life in this community is characterized by ethical transformation.

To summarize, these creedal statements reflect four overarching ideas about the church. First, the church is a community formed by belief in the death and resurrection of Jesus Christ as the turning point of the ages, with the result that members reorient their lives toward the eschaton. Second, this reorientation is an ethical transformation from lives that are self-serving to lives that are self-sacrificial, both in terms of their care for one another and for the sake of the church's mission. Third, the call and acts of God are universal in scope, and therefore the mission of the church is evangelistic and universal. Fourth, the church is the repository of correct teaching about Jesus, and so the function of Christian leaders is to teach the tradition about Christ and to equip others to do the same.

HISTORICAL CONTEXT

The statements about church organization and polity that are often drawn from the PE should be understood in light of the historical circumstances that shaped them. What was happening that commended these particular instructions? The letters reflect three different types of problems that put polity concerns into perspective (a) factionalism within the community of believers, (b) social criticism from without, and (c) official persecution.[17]

Factionalism within the Christian Community

The PE contain several explicit references to rival teachers within the community. In 1 Timothy we read that "certain ones" should not "teach other doctrines" (1:3; cf. 6:3), have "swerved" and "turned aside" (1:6; 6:20), and have "shipwrecked the faith" (1:19), among whom are Hymenaeus and Alexander. In Titus, we read of "many disorderly . . . especially those of the circumcision, whose mouths must be stopped, who are upsetting whole households by teaching what they ought not" (1:10–11), whom Titus is to "reprove unceasingly" (1:13). In 2 Timothy also, "all who are in Asia have abandoned me, among whom are Phygelus and Hermogenes" (1:15); rivals have rejected Paul's authority, whose "word spreads like gangrene, among whom are Hymenaeus and Philetus" (2:17); "Demas has abandoned me" (4:10); and "Alexander the bronze smith did me much harm" (4:14).

These explicit references to rival teachers may be supplemented by a number of apparent allusions to known or anticipated instances of believers straying from the healthy doctrine (1 Tim 6:3–5; 2 Tim 2:16, 23; 3:5–9; 4:3–4), of factionalism within the community (1 Tim 2:8; 2 Tim 2:14, 23–24; Titus 3:10), of challenges against the authority of Paul or his delegates (1 Tim 2:7; 4:12), and of the need to refute rival teachers (1 Tim 5:1, 19; Titus 3:10–11).

Thus the PE reflect rival teachers who, having rejected Pauline authority, are promulgating other doctrines and vying for followers. The content of the false doctrine(s) is tantalizingly unclear. One may see in "Jewish myths" (Titus 1:14; cf. 1 Tim 1:4) and "those who want to be teachers of Torah" (1 Tim 1:7) evidence of some sort of controversy with Judaism or Jewish Christianity. But the text also quotes Epimenides as "one of their own" (Titus 1:12), indicating that some rivals were Gentile

---

17. I adapt the method of Sumney, *Identifying Paul's Opponents*, 95–113; Sumney, *Servants of Satan*, 13–32, who distinguishes explicit references from allusions and affirmations in reconstructing historical contexts. See also Hutson, "My True Child," 198–213, 356–62.

Christians, and it is possible that the Jewish Christian author is combating Gentile converts who have wildly misconstrued Torah. Conflicts about "myths and genealogies" (1 Tim 1:4) may or may not have been related to arguments about marriage and dietary restrictions (1 Tim 4:3). It is not necessary to assume some sort of proto-Gnosticism behind the "knowledge falsely so-called" (1 Tim 6:20), though such a reading is possible. And finally, the controversy concerning the resurrection (2 Tim 2:18) may or may not be related to any dispute mentioned in the other two letters. In sum, the author of the PE does not identify his rivals' doctrines clearly or engage them in theological argument. Debates about whether the opponents were Jewish Christians or Gnostics or some amalgam of the two fail to reckon with the possibility that the PE reflect more than one intra-Christian conflict.[18]

What is important is that various sorts of controversies are liable to arise from time to time. In the PE, apostasies are associated with the "last days" (1 Tim 4:1; 2 Tim 3:1; cf. 4:3), which fits with the eschatological orientation of the church noted above. Essential for Christian leaders will be the ability to recognize departures from "sound doctrine" and so to protect and pass along the central tenets of the faith to the next generations.

But rival Christian teachers are not the only opponents in view in these letters. The PE are engaged with opposition on at least two other fronts, both outside the community.

Social Criticism from Outsiders

Inasmuch as Christianity was a new religion, outsiders often viewed it as strange, deviant, or even subversive. Pagans alleged outlandish goings on among Christians in general, with obvious misunderstanding of the Christian practices of ἀγάπη, "holy kiss," and "eating the flesh of Christ" and "drinking his blood."[19] Of course, charges of moral profligacy were easy to make against any group that was new, foreign, or

---

18. Sumney, *Servants of Satan*, 253–302; Brown, *Churches the Apostles Left Behind*, 39.

19. Tacitus, *Ann.* 15.44, accused the Christians of crimes; Pliny, *Ep.* 10.96.7, found them an "unrestrained, perverse superstition"; and Fronto, *apud* Minucius Felix, *Octavius* 9.5–6, gave a graphic report of cannibalism and orgies. On pagan misunderstandings of and allegations against Christians, see Grant, "Charges of Immorality," 161–70; Wilken, *Christians*.

simply misunderstood. Jews and Epicureans, for example, were prime candidates for suspicion. The PE give reason to believe that outsiders suspected the Christian community of such things as disrupting the order of households, of promoting aberrant behavior among women, and possibly even of subverting the government.[20]

The PE make several references to outside critics of the Christian community. Instructions regarding Christian leaders show concern for "outsiders" (1 Tim 3:7); "the opponent" who engages in "reviling" (1 Tim 5:14); "antagonists" (2 Tim 2:25); "those who speak against" Christianity (Titus 1:9); and "the one from the opposition" (Titus 2:8).

In light of these explicit references to outsiders, a number of passages seem to allude to similar concerns for how the community appeared to the wider society. The PE anticipate possible criticism from outsiders concerning the character and behavior of their leaders (1 Tim 3:2–13; 2 Tim 2:23–26; Titus 1:5–16), of women (1 Tim 2:9–15; 2 Tim 2:6–7; Titus 2:3–5), of slaves (1 Tim 6:1–2; Titus 2:9–10), and concerning support for the government (1 Tim 2:1–2).[21] Indeed, much of the moral exhortation in the PE makes sense in terms of outsider criticism. The paraenetic style of the PE is well suited to this concern, since paraenesis functions to foster the honor that accrues to a good reputation and to avoid the shame that accrues to a bad reputation.[22]

The concern for reputation in the PE is both defensive and offensive: to deflect attacks against what would appear to outsiders as a deviant religion, and to enhance evangelistic opportunities. The ability of Christian leaders to distinguish between good and bad teachers in terms of their behavior will also be essential. This is so because outsiders will not be concerned about the fine points of Christian doctrine; rather, they will be attracted or repelled by the ethical behavior of Christian leaders. Interestingly, this concern about social criticism is found throughout

20. On the PE as response to social criticism from outsiders, see MacDonald, *Legend*; MacDonald, *Pauline Churches*, 160–202.

21. First Timothy 2:1–2 echoes a stock theme of Jewish apologetics. Since Jews were criticized by pagans for failure to sacrifice to the emperor, Philo, *Flaccus* 48–50, took pains to point out that Jews did pray *for* the emperor.

22. "The paraenetic letter: Always be an emulator, dear friend, of virtuous men. For it is better to be well spoken of when imitating good men than to be reproached by all while following evil men" (Ps-Libanius, *Epistolary Styles* 52, translated in Malherbe, *Ancient Epistolary Theorists*, 75). See also Fiore, *Personal Example*.

1 Timothy and Titus and all but disappears in 2 Timothy. In 2 Timothy we meet another type of outside opposition.

Official Opposition

In 2 Timothy we find almost none of the social critique of 1 Timothy and Titus,[23] although we do find government opposition. Paul is a prisoner (2 Tim 1:8) in chains (1:16), imprisoned as a wrongdoer (2:9), who has already faced one trial (4:16). Furthermore, he has a history of persecution in Antioch, Iconium, and Lystra (3:11), apparently referring to events recounted in Acts 13–14. There we read about persecution from "devout women of high standing and the leading men of the city" (Acts 13:50). Similarly in Iconium, Paul's mission generated anger from both Gentiles and Jews "along with their rulers" (Acts 14:5). Likewise in Lystra, "the Jews" persuaded "the crowds" to stone Paul (14:19). It appears that what began as a doctrinal dispute within the synagogue in Antioch grew into a public furor that rolled from town to town feeding on popular resentments and attracting the notice of the civil authorities.

One source of official opposition to Christianity may have been their resemblance to voluntary associations (*collegia* or θίασοι). We need not assume that Christians or Jews organized their churches or synagogues as *collegia*,[24] but we should expect that outsiders perceived churches as such.[25] Even a superficial resemblance could be a basis for official harassment, given Roman suspicion of *collegia* as breeding grounds for sedition.[26] For example, as governor of Bithynia in the early second century, Pliny could not even get permission to start a fire brigade in Nicopolis precisely because of fear of sedition.[27] Thus it is hardly

---

23. Second Timothy 3:6 seems to allude to disruption of households mentioned in Titus 1:11.

24. On the "godfearers" inscription from Aphrodisias, which indicates a third-century *collegium* affiliated with a synagogue, see Reynolds and Tannenbaum, *Jews and Godfearers*, 28–38; Tannenbaum, "Jews and God-Fearers"; White, *Texts and Monuments*, 2: no. 64, esp. nn. 41–42. On synagogues as *collegia*, see Smallwood, *Jews under Roman Rule*, 133–38; Richardson, *Building Jewish*, 111–221; Gruen, *Diaspora*, 24–26, argues that the synagogues were not *collegia* but were treated as such by Rome.

25. Peregrinus made himself a θιασάρχης of a Christian community (Lucian, *Peregrinus* 11). Similarly synagogues were sometimes treated as *collegia* (Josephus, *Ant.* 14.215).

26. Suetonius, *Julius* 42.3 (possibly Josephus, *Ant.* 14.215); Philo, *Flaccus* 4.

27. Pliny, *Letters* 10.33–34.

surprising that Jews in Asia Minor under the late Republic and early Empire had to petition repeatedly for special concessions on a number of religious practices, including permission to hold regular Sabbath meetings.[28] Such stories shed light on how pagan authorities might have (mis-) understood early Christian churches, including the official persecutions reflected in 2 Timothy.

Recognition of this third source of opposition helps to sharpen the point of Paul's final exhortation in 2 Tim 3:1—4:8. The passage begins with a dire warning that in the last days "perilous times will come" (3:1). The immediate peril is the rival teachers operating within the community (3:1–9, 13; 4:3–4), but their operation is hardly Christian. They have a "form of piety (εὐσέβεια)," a buzzword that was important in Roman imperial propaganda and that the PE redefine in Christian terms (4:12; cf. 1 Tim 2:2; 3:16; 4:7–8; 5:4; 6:3, 5–6, 11; Tit 1:1; 2:12). Also, the allusion to Jannes and Jambres (3:8) would be consistent with state opposition, since those two magicians belonged to Pharaoh.[29] And references to persecutions in 3:11 call to mind the stories in Acts in which Paul was persecuted not only by local synagogue leaders but also by "leading men" of Antioch (Acts 13:50), and "rulers" of Iconium (Acts 14:5). Furthermore, although Paul is a prisoner (1:8) who has already faced one hearing (4:16), his confidence in the "appearance and kingship" of Christ (4:1; cf. 4:8), the "Righteous Judge" (4:8; cf. 4:1), highlights his lack of similar confidence in the appearance and kingship of the earthly ruler on whose judgment seat he is being "poured out as a libation" (4:6).

The picture that emerges from 2 Timothy, then, is that the opposition no longer stems from mere rivalry within the community or social criticism from neighbors. It seems that outsider criticism has provoked government intervention. In 1 Timothy and Titus, there is an effort to thwart rival teachers, whose methods and manners are disruptive and

28. Sardis (Josephus, *Ant.* 14.235; 259–21); Ephesus (14.225–27; 262–64); Laodicea (14.241–43); Miletus (14.244–46); and Halicarnassus (14.256–58). See Smallwood, *Jews under Roman Rule*, 120–43; Barclay, *Jews in the Mediterranean*, 259–81.

29. Exodus 7:11 does not name the magicians who opposed Moses, but legends about Jannes and Jambres circulated widely among Jews in antiquity (CD 5.17–19; *Targum of Ps.-Jonathan* on Exod 1:15; 7:11) and also among Gentiles, (e.g., Pliny, *Natural History* 30.2.11; Apuleius, *Apology* 90). The *Book of Jannes and Jambres* survives only in fragmentary form and is of uncertain date, but at least it bears witness to the popularity of the tale. Though these texts usually emphasize that Jannes and Jambres were magicians, they served in the court of Pharaoh.

troublesome. There is also a call for the community leaders to adopt exemplary lifestyles that would deflect criticism. But now, if outsiders fail to distinguish among competing Christian groups, the pressure is turned up considerably, and this calls for a different kind of response. Paul alludes to his own suffering (2 Tim 1:12) and steadfastness unto death (4:6–8), and he calls Timothy to follow his example as a fellow sufferer (1:8; 2:3). The time will come for the ultimate test of Timothy's mettle.

Although there are no explicit references to official persecution in Titus or 1 Timothy, there is a possible allusion in 1 Tim 2:1–7, where we find an exhortation to pray for the political authorities "that we may lead a quiet and peaceable life." In the context of 1 Timothy, this could be read as an expectation that the authorities might intervene to quell social criticism from outsiders, as a Roman tribune took Paul into protective custody in Jerusalem (Acts 21:27–36). But in the context of the PE as a group, this passage makes sense as a prayer that the authorities themselves will not add to the unofficial harassment from neighbors.

To summarize, in the PE, factionalism within the community undermines the role of the church as guarantor of correct doctrine about Christ, while social criticism and official persecution constitute threats to the church's ability to carry out its evangelistic mission to all people. We should expect, therefore, that issues concerning church polity in the PE will be shaped by the need to mitigate these threats so that the church can fulfill its mission.

POLITY QUESTIONS

Older commentators tended to use the PE as a kind of Rorschach test for church polity, various verses functioning like inkblots onto which they projected their own ecclesiastical traditions.[30] More recent interpreters have been more circumspect, yet there is not clear consensus on how to resolve a number of ambiguities.

---

30. On the history of polity debates, see Ferguson, "Church Order"; Burtchaell, *From Synagogue to Church*, 1–190.

Leadership Roles

Discussions of church polity in the PE debate whether these letters reflect two offices (overseers/elders and deacons)[31] or three (overseers, elders, and deacons),[32] or some intermediate stage of development.[33] Further, they debate what first-century social structures serve as the best analogies for understanding the PE. From Jewish society, interpreters have suggested analogies from synagogues[34] and the Dead Sea Scrolls community,[35] while from Greco-Roman society they have suggested analogies from voluntary associations (*collegia*)[36] and households.[37] Among these, the household has won widest support, as explicit household language is most pervasive in the PE, but one cannot rule out possible additional influences from other social structures. The precise organization of the churches reflected is difficult to ascertain, because, apart from instructions to Timothy and Titus themselves, the PE say little about what various Christian leaders are actually supposed to *do*. The matter is also complicated by the fact that the letters have different addressees in different geographical locations that may reflect different organization among the Christian communities in Ephesus (1–2 Timothy) and Crete (Titus). It will be helpful, then, to list the leadership roles mentioned in these letters before we address some of the ambiguities that have fueled debate.

---

31. "Overseers and deacons" (*1 Clem.* 42:4–5); "overseer" and "presbyter" used interchangeably (*1 Clem.* 44:1–5; 47:6; 57:1; Clement of Alexandria, *Who Is the Rich Man?* 42); "presbyters and deacons," (Polycarp 5.3).

32. Ignatius, *Magn.* 6.2; *Trall.* 2.2–4; 3.1; *Phld.* preface; *Smyrn.* 12.2; Polycarp 6.1; and possibly Hermas, *Vis.* 3.5.1, which lists apostles, overseers, teachers (= teaching elders?), and deacons. Aageson, *Paul*, 122–56, shows that, on ecclesiastical organization, the PE are closer to Ignatius than *1 Clement*.

33. Young, *Theology*, 97–121; Marshall, *Pastoral Epistles*, 512–21; Aageson, *Paul*, 127–31.

34. Burtchaell, *From Synagogue to Church*, 272–338; Meeks, *First Urban Christians*, 80–81. On organization of ancient synagogues, see Burtchaell, *From Synagogue to Church*, 201–71; Schürer, *History of the Jewish People*, 2:423–39.

35. Brown, *Priest and Bishop*, 34–43, 65–72; Thiering, "*Mebaqqer* and *Episkopos*." On the organization of the Dead Sea Scrolls communities, see Schürer, Vermes, et al., *History of the Jewish People*, 2:575–85.

36. Judge, "Social Pattern," 27–34; Meeks, *First Urban Christians*, 77–80.

37. Verner, *Household of God*; Meeks, *First Urban Christians*, 75–77; Campbell, *Elders*; Osiek and MacDonald, *A Woman's Place*.

OVERSEER (1 TIMOTHY 3:1–7; TITUS 1:7–9)

The Greek term ἐπίσκοπος (overseer)[38] was used in both Jewish and Greek literature for various positions of responsibility and direction. In the PE, the overseer is analogous to a head of household (1 Tim 3:4–5), but we should not press that analogy too far, as if an overseer has the absolute authority of a Roman *paterfamilias*. On the contrary, the church in the PE is God's household (1 Tim 3:15), and the "overseer" is a "steward" or "household manager" (οἰκονόμος, Titus 1:7). A household manager was a slave with management responsibility but was not himself the head of household.

Both 1 Timothy and Titus emphasize the overseer's character and reputation. The qualities of a good overseer begin with "irreproachable" (1 Tim 3:2) and end with "a good testimony from outsiders" (3:7). These concepts bracket the paragraph, indicating that all of 3:1–7 deals with how the overseer's life should be such that outsiders will acknowledge his exemplary character. In this context, the rationale, "lest he fall into condemnation and a snare of the slanderer" (διάβολος, 3:6) seems to refer to a human critic rather than the devil.[39]

The overseer's duties are to "care for the church of God" (1 Tim 3:5) and "attend to the faithful word that is in accordance with the teaching, so as to be able to exhort with the sound teaching and to refute the opponents" (Titus 1:9; cf. "apt to teach," 1 Tim 3:2). Thus, the overseer exercises moral authority derived from an ethical reputation, adherence to established doctrine, and effective persuasion and dissuasion.

DEACONS (1 TIMOTHY 3:8–13)

Like the overseer, the deacons (διάκονοι) must have an excellent reputation for conduct and character, but their duties are not spelled out. Elsewhere in the New Testament, the word root (διάκονος, "servant;" διακονέω, "serve;" διακονία, "service") is either literal, serving food (Acts 6:1, 2; Luke 4:39; 12:37; Rom 15:31; etc.) or metaphorical, ministry of the word (Acts 6:4; 1 Cor 3:5; Eph 3:7; etc.). The latter seems to be more in view here, in that deacons are to be grounded in "the mystery of

---

38. I avoid the traditional translation "bishop" in order not to impose later hierarchical polity onto the text.

39. The word διάβολος clearly refers to human "slanderers" in 1 Tim 3:11; 2 Tim 3:3; Titus 2:3. On the "slanderer" in 1 Tim 3:6–7, see MacDonald, *Pauline Churches*, 167; Young, *Theology*, 101.

the faith" (3:9) and Timothy himself will be a good διάκονος (1 Tim 4:6) precisely in his role as a teacher (cf. 2 Tim 4:5; 1 Tim 1:12).

Deacons apparently included women, according to 1 Tim 3:11. This understanding of the passage is ancient,[40] though later interpreters have tended to assume that the verse refers to the wives of deacons.[41] The latter interpretation seems to derive from the unwarranted assumption that women did not serve in ordained, ecclesial functions in Pauline churches.[42] Women deacons are known in the New Testament (Rom 16:1–2), and women deacons would be consistent with the roles of "real widows" in 1 Timothy 5 (see below).[43] Even if in some times and places women deacons were restricted from carrying out every duty assigned to their male counterparts, there is no reason not to read this verse as referring to women deacons.

The relationship between deacons and overseer is not specified, though deacons may have been assistants to the overseer, much as a synagogue was led by a "chief of synagogue" (rosh hakneset ‏ראש הכנסת‎ = ἀρχισυνάγωγος, Acts 13:15; 18:8) who was assisted by a "minister" (hazan ‏חזן‎, variously represented in Greek as νεώκορος; ὑπηρέτης, Luke 4:20; Acts 13:5; or διάκονος).[44] In this capacity, it is worth comparing Timothy as a "server" to Paul in Acts 19:22. In any case, this is how Hippolytus understood the relationship in the third century.[45]

Elders (1 Timothy 5:17–25; Titus 1:5–6)

According to Campbell, "elders" (πρεσβύτεροι) did not designate an office in ancient Judaism but a status of prestige based on seniority and reputation.[46] The passing reference to their role in the ordination of Timothy (1 Tim 4:14) could be explained that way. And yet the PE seem

40. For example, the commentaries of John Chrysostom and Theodore of Mopsuestia.

41. For example, the commentaries of Aquinas, Calvin, and Erasmus.

42. Against this assumption, see Hutson, "Laborers in the Lord."

43. Women deacons are mentioned in Pliny, Letters 10.96.8 (early second century); Apostolic Constitutions 8.19–20 (fourth-century text compiled from earlier sources).

44. On the hazan, see m. Shabbath 1:3; m. Sukkah 4:4; m. Tamid 5:3. On synagogue leaders, see Schürer, Vermes et al., History of the Jewish People, 2:433–39; Burtchaell, From Synagogue to Church, 240–49.

45. Hippolytus, Apostolic Tradition 9.

46. Campbell, Elders, 20–66.

to refer to some elders, at least, who functioned in an official capacity. Like the overseer and deacons, elders must have impeccable reputations (Titus 1:6; 1 Tim 5:19–21, 24–25), they "preside" (προΐστημι, 1 Tim 5:17; cf. 3:4, 12), "labor in word and teaching" (5:17), are subject to disciplinary procedure (5:19–21), and are ordained (5:22). For teaching elders there is a financial honorarium (1 Tim 5:17–18). On the relation between elders and overseer, see below.

WIDOWS (1 TIMOTHY 5:3–16)

Often overlooked among leadership roles in the PE are the "real widows." Apart from chauvinistic assumptions, this neglect may be because the widows are clearly "enrolled" (1 Tim 5:6) as recipients of charitable assistance from the common funds (5:3–8). Nevertheless, the qualifications for "real widows" (5:9–10) are remarkably similar to those for overseer and deacons. And the apparent mention of women deacons (1 Tim 3:11; cf. Rom 16:1) suggests that the "real widows" are enrolled as assistants in the ministries of the church. Indeed, we hear of just such ministries of widows in various churches early in the second century.[47]

Relation between Overseer and Elders

The relation between overseer and elders in the PE is not clear. On the one hand, some have read these as synonymous terms, mainly because they seem to be used interchangeably in Titus 1:5–9, but also because of the similarity in the desired qualities and the teaching functions of the two roles.[48] Others read them as two distinct roles, noting that ἐπίσκοπος always appears in the singular in the PE, whereas πρεσβύ–τεροι is usually plural when it refers to leadership roles.[49] Also, it is curious that elders are not mentioned in 1 Timothy 3 but they do appear in chapter 5 along with instructions about older men and women in general (5:1) and widows (5:3–16). The references to disciplinary action

47. Ignatius, *Smyrn.* 13:1; *Pol.* 4–5; Tertullian, *The Veiling of Virgins*, 9.2; *Prescription against Heretics* 3; cf. Thurston, *Widows*; Bassler, "Widows' Tale"; Davies, *Revolt of the Widows*.

48. So Calvin, *Commentary* on Titus 1:5; Meier, "*Presbyteros*," argues on the basis of 1 Tim 5:19, where πρεσβύτερος appears in the singular, and Titus 1:6, where there is already a shift to the singular (τίς ἐστιν ἀνέγκλητος) *before* the supporting argument regarding an ἐπίσκοπος.

49. So Ignatius, *Magn.* 6.1–2; *Trall.* 2–3, in which bishop and deacons outrank elders.

in 5:1–2 and 5:19–25 frame the chapter and blur the distinction between any "elder" man or woman in the community and the subsets of "real widows" and "teaching elders," who receive financial support for their service.

The PE reflect an early stage of institutionalization, though the precise details are unclear. Campbell distinguishes elders and overseer in the PE by arguing that elders "preside" (προΐστημι) over house churches (1 Tim 5:17), whereas an overseer is an elder "at the city-level" (κατὰ πόλιν,[50] Titus 1:8) who oversees the elders of the various house churches, having demonstrated his ability by "presiding well over his own house" (1 Tim 3:4).[51] Here we might compare the role of the *mebaqqer* (מבקר, literally "pastor," but usually rendered "overseer," or "guardian") in the Dead Sea Scrolls. The Damascus Document provides guidelines for a "*mebaqqer* of the camp" over each local community, but also a "*mebaqqer* of all the camps" (CD 14.8–9) who presides over joint assemblies. Alternatively, Trebilco argues that the elders were simply seniors, some of whom served in teaching and administrative roles as overseers and deacons.[52] Given the uncertainties, one should be cautious about using the PE as a strict organizational template for congregational or ecclesiastical polity.[53]

Paul, Timothy, and Titus in the PE

The question of the degree of institutionalization reflected in the PE leads to the question of the roles of Timothy and Titus in these letters. Christian tradition since at least the fourth century has identified Timothy as the first bishop of Ephesus and Titus the first of Crete,[54] but is this a projection of later Christian hierarchy onto the PE? In favor of reading Timothy and Titus as bishops are considerations that Timothy is to adjudicate charges against elders (1 Tim 5:17–18), and both Timothy and Titus ordain elders (1 Tim 5:19–25; Titus 1:6). Both engage in various teaching functions (1 Tim 1:3; 2:7; 4:6, 11; 6:2, 17; 2 Tim 4:2; Titus

---

50. Understanding κατὰ πόλιν as indicating a relationship, "with respect to" (BDAG κατὰ B.6–7).

51. Campbell, *Elders*, 196–200.

52. Trebilco, *Early Christians*, 447–57; Meier, "*Presbyteros*."

53. For similar conclusions, see Marshall, *Pastoral Epistles*, 170–81; Johnson, *Letters to Timothy*, 220–23.

54. Eusebius, *Hist. eccl.* 3.4.6.

2:1; 3:1), and guard against heresies (1 Tim 1:3–11; 4:1–5, 7; 2 Tim 3:1–9; Titus 3:9–10). Timothy is to protect the sound doctrine he learned from Paul (1 Tim 6:14, 20; 2 Tim 1:13–14; 3:10–17) and pass it to the next generation of teachers (2 Tim 2:2). It is not hard, then, to see how Timothy and Titus have served as models for monarchical bishops through the centuries.

On the other hand, Timothy and Titus are not called "overseers" in the PE. Timothy is a διάκονος (1 Tim 4:6; 2 Tim 4:5). Both Timothy and Titus follow directives from Paul (e.g., 1 Tim 1:3, 18; 4:6, 7, 11–16; 5:23; 6:20; 2 Tim 2:14; 4:9; Titus 1:6), and Paul projects his own teaching through them to the churches in Ephesus and Crete ("I exhort," 1 Tim 2:1; "I want," 2:8; "I command," 6:13). Also, Paul expects to visit Timothy soon with further instruction (1 Tim 3:14; 4:13). Further, both Timothy and Titus are characterized as youthful (1 Tim 4:12; 5:1–2; 2 Tim 2:22; Titus 2:6–8). On the whole then, the model for a monarchical bishop in the PE would not be Timothy or Titus but Paul, who projects his apostolic authority through his delegates.[55]

Qualifications of Leaders

The PE say little about what the various leaders *do,* focusing instead on personal qualities of honesty, integrity, self-control, and hospitality. The lists in 1 Timothy 3 and 5 are not exhaustive checklists but suggestive guidelines for the kind of character leaders should exemplify. The lists are functional: the conduct of Christian leaders must be not only exemplary for insiders but recognizably and undeniably good to outsiders, especially to those who are suspicious or critical of a religious movement that is new, outlandish, or threatening.

For example, the qualification "husband of one wife" (1 Tim 3:2, 12) stresses the importance of marital fidelity, but it reflects a category that does not operate in modern, Western culture. For this reason, it has been a source of much confusion, leading to misunderstandings that the overseer and deacons must be married or must be male.

First, the same expression appears in 1 Timothy 5:9 but inverted as "wife of one husband" and applied to widows. In that context, it is obviously not a requirement that the widow be married.[56] Second, this ex-

---

55. So Johnson, *Letters to Timothy,* 137–42; Trebilco, *Early Christians,* 447.

56. It is ironic that many Christians would disqualify Jesus himself from leadership in their churches on the grounds that he was not married. Celibate Christian leadership should be appreciated, not denigrated.

pression makes no sense as a specification that the overseer and deacons must be male. After all, 1 Tim 3:11 seems to recognize women deacons. Further, when applying the same qualification to widows, it would make no sense to exclude a destitute elderly man from financial assistance on the basis that he could not be "wife of one husband." The language in each case probably reflects what was typical of first-century society—overseers of most organizations were male, and widows were much more common than widowers. So this qualification is not intended to require marriage or to impose a gender restriction.

The phrase "husband of one wife" reflects the Greco-Roman romantic ideal of life-long devotion to a single spouse even beyond that spouse's death.[57] Romans called a widow who never remarried *univira* ("one-man-woman"), but the ideal could apply to any man or woman who maintained life-long devotion to a single mate. There was no social stigma in remarrying, but the one who opted for celibate devotion to the deceased spouse was admired as a paragon of self-control and marital fidelity, likely to be celebrated in story and song. This qualification, then, emphasizes the importance of marital fidelity and sexual chastity, qualities that even hostile outsiders would recognize and admire. Read in this way, this qualification makes sense as one element of a whole list of similar qualifications. The PE stress high ethical ideals for Christian leaders, because they help deflect social criticism from outsiders.

CONCLUSION

The Pastoral Epistles are important sources for understanding the emerging shape of the (post-) Pauline church. It would be a mistake to insist that these letters present a precise model for church polity or to insist on particular titles or ecclesiastical structures. The PE can, however, serve to provide a theological orientation for church polity. That is, regardless of the specific ecclesiastical tradition one follows in terms of church organization, it will always be important to see how that organization is related to the theological origin and purpose of the church.

57. Propertius, *Elegies* 4.11; Livy, *History of Rome* 10.23; Xenophon of Ephesus, *Anthia and Habrocomes* 4.3; Jdt 8:4; 16:21–23; Luke 2:36–37. For early Christian interpretations of the phrase, see Clement of Alexandria, *Strom.* 3.12.82; Tertullian, *To His Wife* 1.7. For discussion of the *univira* in ancient social contexts, see Dixon, "Sentimental Ideal"; Treggiari, *Roman Marriage*; Fantham et al., *Women in the Classical World*, 232, 276. And for discussion of the idea in this passage, see Spicq, *Épitres Pastorales*, 430, 533.

Theologically, the church is an eschatologically oriented community shaped by belief in the death and resurrection of Jesus Christ. The shape of the church is ethical, not political, as believers are transformed from self-serving to self-sacrificial people, who care for one another and for the spread of the gospel. The church proclaims that story universally and without partiality. And the church is the repository of correct teaching about Jesus.

Historically, the communities of believers reflected in the PE were shaped by internal doctrinal controversies, as well as by pressures and persecutions from outsiders who misunderstood them. Of these two, our author is more concerned about the latter, and this leads him to emphasize the behavior of church leaders, which must be exemplary so as to deflect hostility that comes from non-Christians.

In light of these theological and historical factors, Christian leaders are to understand and teach the correct doctrine about Christ, to equip others to do the same, and to correct those who teach otherwise. But if they are to be effective, they must hold themselves to the highest ethical standards. Anything less will compromise their ability to carry out the evangelistic mission of the church.

FOR FURTHER STUDY

Aageson, James W. *Paul, the Pastoral Epistles and the Early Church.* Peabody, MA: Hendrickson, 2008.

Burtchaell, James Tunstead. *From Synagogue to Church: Public Services and Offices in the Earliest Christian Communities.* Cambridge: Cambridge University Press, 1992.

Campbell, R. Alistair. *The Elders: Seniority within Earliest Christianity.* New York & London: T. & T. Clark, 1994.

MacDonald, Margaret Y. *The Pauline Churches: A Socio-Literary Study of Institutionalization in the Pauline and Deutero-Pauline Writings.* Cambridge: Cambridge University Press, 1988.

Meier, J. P. "*Presbyteros* in the Pastoral Epistles." *CBQ* 35 (1973) 323–45.

Trebilco, Paul. *The Early Christians in Ephesus from Paul to Ignatius.* Grand Rapids: Eerdmans, 2008.

Verner, David C. *The Household of God: The Social World of the Pastoral Epistles.* SBLDS 71. Atlanta: Scholars, 1983.

Young, Frances. *The Theology of the Pastoral Letters.* Cambridge: Cambridge University Press, 1994.

BIBLIOGRAPHY

Aageson, James W. *Paul, the Pastoral Epistles, and the Early Church*. Peabody, MA: Hendrickson, 2008.

Allert, Craig D. *A High View of Scripture? The Authority of the Bible and the Formation of the New Testament Canon*. Grand Rapids: Baker Academic, 2007.

Barclay, John M. G. *Jews in the Mediterranean Diaspora: From Alexander to Trajan*. Berkeley: University of California Press, 1996.

Bassler, Jouette M. *1 Timothy, 2 Timothy, Titus*. ANTC. Nashville: Abingdon, 1996.

———. "The Widows' Tale: A Fresh Look at 1 Tim 5:2–16." *JBL* 103 (1984) 23–41.

Brown, Raymond E. *The Churches the Apostles Left Behind*. Mawhah, NJ: Paulist, 1984.

———. *Priest and Bishop*. Mawhah, NJ: Paulist, 1970.

Burtchaell, James T. *From Synagogue to Church: Public Services and Offices in the Earliest Christian Communities*. Cambridge: Cambridge University Press, 1992.

Campbell, R. Alistair. *The Elders: Seniority within Earliest Christianity*. New York & London: T. & T. Clark, 1994.

Davies, Stevan L. *The Revolt of the Widows: The Social World of the Apocryphal Acts*. Carbondale, IL; Southern Illinois University Press, 1980.

Dixon, Susanne. "The Sentimental Ideal of the Roman Family." In *Marriage, Divorce, and Children in Ancient Rome*, edited by B. Rawson, 99–113. Oxford: Clarendon, 1991.

Fantham, Elaine, et al. *Women in the Classical World: Image and Text*. New York: Oxford University Press, 1995.

Ferguson, Everett. "Church Order in the Sub-Apostolic Period: A Survey of Interpretations." *ResQ* 11.4 (1968) 225–48.

Fiore, Benjamin. *The Function of Personal Example in the Socratic and Pastoral Epistles*. Rome: Biblical Institute, 1986.

———. *The Pastoral Epistles: First Timothy, Second Timothy, Titus*. SP 12. Collegeville: Liturgical, 2007.

Goodwin, Mark J. *Paul: Apostle of the Living God: Kerygma and Conversion in 2 Corinthians*. Harrisburg,VA: Trinity Press International, 2001.

Grant, R. M. "Charges of 'Immorality' against Various Religious Groups in Antiquity." In *Studies in Gnosticism and Hellenistic Religions*, edited by R. van den Boeck and M. J. Vermaseren, 161–70. Leiden: Brill, 1981.

Gruen, Erich S. *Diaspora: Jews amidst Greeks and Romans*. Cambridge, MA: Harvard University Press, 2002.

Hadot, Pierre. *Philosophy as a Way of Life*. Trans. M. Chase. Oxford: Blackwell, 1995.

Hanson, A. T. *Studies in the Pastoral Epistles*. London: SPCK, 1968.

Holladay, Carl R. *A Critical Introduction to the New Testament*. Nashville: Abingdon, 2005.

Hutson, Christopher R. "Laborers in the Lord: Romans 16 and the Women in Pauline Churches." *Leaven* 4.2 (1996) 29–31, 40.

———. "My True Child: The Rhetoric of Youth in the Pastoral Epistles." PhD diss., Yale University, 1998.

Johnson, Luke Timothy. *The First and Second Letters to Timothy*. AB 35A. New York: Doubleday, 2001.

———. *The Writings of the New Testament*. Rev. ed. Minneapolis: Fortress, 1999.

Judge, E. A. *The Social Pattern of Christian Groups in the First Century*. Some Prolegomena to the Study of the New Testament Ideas of Social Obligation. London: Tyndale,

1960; Repr. in *Social Distinctives of the Christians in the First Century: Pivotal Essays by E. A. Judge*, edited by D. M. Scholer, 1–56. Peabody, MA: Hendrickson, 2008.

Kaminsky, Joel, and Anne Stewart. "God of All the World: Universalism and Developing Monotheism in Isaiah 40–66." *HTR* 99.2 (2006) 139–63.

Kogan, Michael S. *Opening the Covenant: A Jewish Theology of Christianity*. New York: Oxford University Press, 2008.

MacDonald, Dennis R. *The Legend and the Apostle: The Battle for Paul in Story and Canon*. Philadelphia: Westminster, 1983.

MacDonald, Margaret Y. *The Pauline Churches: A Socio-Literary Study of Institutionalization in the Pauline and Deutero-Pauline Writings*. Cambridge: Cambridge University Press, 1988.

Malherbe, Abraham J. *Ancient Epistolary Theorists*. Atlanta: Scholars, 1988.

———. "*Paulus Senex*." *ResQ* 36 (1994) 197–207.

Marshall, I. H. *The Pastoral Epistles*. ICC. New York: T. & T. Clark, 1999.

Meeks, Wayne A. *The First Urban Christians: The Social World of the Apostle Paul*. New Haven, CN: Yale University Press, 1983.

Meier, J. P. "*Presbyteros* in the Pastoral Epistles." *CBQ* 35 (1973) 323–45.

Murphy-O'Connor, Jerome. "2 Timothy Contrasted with 1 Timothy and Titus." *RB* 98 (1991) 403–18.

Osiek, Carolyn, and Margaret Y. MacDonald. *A Woman's Place: House Churches in Earliest Christianity*. Minneapolis: Fortress, 2006.

Prior, Michael. *Paul the Letter Writer and the Second Letter to Timothy*. JSNTSup 23. Sheffield: JSOT Press, 1989.

Reynolds, Joyce M. and Robert Tannenbaum. *Jews and Godfearers at Aphrodisias*. Cambridge: Cambridge Philological Society, 1987.

Richardson, Peter. *Building Jewish in the Greek East*. Waco: Baylor University Press, 2004.

Schürer, Emil. *The History of the Jewish People in the Age of Jesus Christ (175 B.C.–A.D. 135)*. Vol 2. Revised by G. Vermes et al. Edinburgh: T. & T. Clark, 1979.

Smallwood, E. Mary. *Jews under Roman Rule from Pompey to Diocletian: A Study in Political Relations*. 2nd ed. Leiden: Brill, 1981.

Spicq, C. *Les Épîtres Pastorales*. 4th ed. Paris: Gabalda, 1969.

Sumney, Jerry L. *Identifying Paul's Opponents: The Question of Method in 2 Corinthians*. JSNTSup 40. Sheffield: Sheffield Academic, 1990.

———. "*Servants of Satan*," *False Brothers and Other Opponents of Paul*. JSNTSup 188. Sheffield: Sheffield Academic, 1999.

Tannenbaum, Robert. "Jews and God-Fearers in the Holy City of Aphrodite." *BAR* 12.5 (1986) 54–57.

Thiering, B. "*Mebaqqer* and *Episkopos* in the Light of the Temple Scroll." *JBL* 100 (1981) 59–74.

Thurston, Bonnie Bowman. *The Widows: A Women's Ministry in the Early Church*. Minneapolis: Fortress, 1989.

Trebilco, Paul. *The Early Christians in Ephesus from Paul to Ignatius*. Grand Rapids: Eerdmans, 2008.

Treggiari, Susan. *Roman Marriage: Iusti coniuges from the Time of Cicero to the Time of Ulpian*. Oxford: Clarendon, 1993.

Verner, David C. *The Household of God: The Social World of the Pastoral Epistles*. SBLDS 71. Atlanta: Scholars, 1983.

White, L. Michael. *The Social Origins of Christian Architecture*. Vol. 2. *Texts and Monuments for the Christian* Domus Ecclesiae *in its Environment*. HTS 42. Valley Forge: Trinity Press International, 1997.

Wilken, R. L. *The Christians as the Romans Saw Them*. New Haven, CN: Yale University Press, 1984.

Witherington, Ben III. *Letters and Homilies for Hellenized Christians* Vol. 1. *A Socio-Rhetorical Commentary on Titus, 1–2 Timothy and 1–3 John*. Downers Grove, IL: IVP Academic, 2006.

Yarbrough, Mark M. *Paul's Utilization of Preformed Traditions in 1 Timothy*. LNTS 417. New York: T. & T. Clark, 2009.

Young, Frances. *Theology of the Pastoral Letters*. Cambridge: Cambridge University Press, 1994.

10

Left Behind?

The Church in the Book of Hebrews

CYNTHIA LONG WESTFALL

INTRODUCTION

IN THE CHRISTIAN COMMUNITY, the phrase "left behind" immediately brings to mind the best-selling novels about the "pre-trib" rapture and the earth's last days, or we may even remember Hal Lindsey's *Late Great Planet Earth* and the surge of interest in prophecy in the 1970s.[1] However, there is nothing about a pre-tribulation rapture in the book of Hebrews. In this case, "left behind" refers to the fear that, when the church moves forward and pursues spiritual goals, someone might not make it. This is one of the author's primary concerns in the book of Hebrews. Most of us will be familiar with the stern warnings in Hebrews about apostasy and sinning willfully, but the author's concern is primarily expressed in pleading for vigilant pastoral concern by all the members of the church for all the others.

It is interesting that most New Testament theologians find very little to say about the ecclesiology in Hebrews.[2] Partly, this is because

1. Hal Lindsey's eschatological theories in *Late Great Planet Earth*, published first in 1970, have been popularized recently in the thirteen novels published between 1996 and 2007 in the "Left Behind" series by Jerry B. Jenkins and Tim LaHaye.

2. See, for example, Marshall, *New Testament Theology*, 625, under the subheading "People of God"; Ladd, *Theology of the New Testament*, 631–33, has some information

some have certain categories that serve as lenses for searching the text, and others come to Hebrews with theories about the nature of the text that may prevent them from recognizing the author's engagement with and concern for the church. They search for corporate identity and note that the "familiar" metaphor of the church as the body of Christ is "missing" (though the metaphors of the church as Jesus' house and the people of God as a city receive extensive development). They look for ecclesial organization such as church offices, information on the rite of baptism or baptismal formulas, references to the Lord's Supper, evidence of liturgical creeds, references to the public reading of Scripture, and instructions on the order of worship in formal services, and find Hebrews surprisingly uninformative with little to add to their categories.[3] Furthermore, there is a theory popular among scholars that the writer of Hebrews thinks of the church as a group of people like nomads, so he has no concept of church organization.[4] Because we do not know the author or the recipients of Hebrews, and it does not begin like a letter, some believe that Hebrews is a theological essay written to the church at large to be read by anyone, which causes them to miss the information and clues about the context. As in all research, you tend to find what you are looking for.

The approach to identifying the theology of the church in Hebrews begins with discussing what we can know of the circumstances of the church community (the recipients) and the identity of the author, as well as the general message of Hebrews, which provide a context for understanding any information. The most relevant feature in the context is

---

subsumed under the subheading "The Christian Life"; see also Donelson, *From Hebrews to Revelation*, 7–34, where there is very little that he can identify as ecclesiology.

3. For example, Guthrie states, "On the theme of worship within the early community there is again very little in this epistle, surprisingly so in view of the cultic background of the whole" (Guthrie, *New Testament Theology*, 779). Yet the climax of the middle section involves meeting God in the Holy of Holies (10:19–22) and in chapter 12, the believers' entire existence is framed as worship in terms of priestly service.

4. E. Käsemann has been very influential in promoting the theory of the people of God as a nomad group in the book of Hebrews in *The Wandering People of God*. Guthrie follows Käsemann's lead: "We may say that the writer has no concept of the church as an ecclesiastical organization. He thinks only of a group of people, like nomads, with no settled abode in this life" (Guthrie, *New Testament Theology*, 779). However, the issues of ecclesiastical organization were already shared information if the believers were second generation Christians. The author states that he does not wish to discuss what they already know.

the author's anticipation of an impending crisis. Most of his approach to the church is driven by his desire to help them in their time of need. Therefore, the ecclesiology of Hebrews is practical and largely found in the commands. The author specifically calls the believers to participate actively in Christian community. The presence of the believers in community is addressed pragmatically and imaginatively. The community's appropriate relationship to their past and present leaders receives some focus. The importance of maintaining the doctrinal confession is highlighted, and the necessity of growth and investment back into the church community is considered to be imperative. However, the most distinctive feature of the ecclesiology in Hebrews is how carefully and consistently the author stresses the responsibility of vigilant pastoral care for everyone in the community as they move forward spiritually in response to their crisis.

THE CIRCUMSTANCES AND MESSAGE TO THE CHURCH

The Identity of the Author and Church in Hebrews

We do not know the identity of the author or the recipients of Hebrews—that information may have been lost already by the end of the first century.[5] However, we can glean evidence from the text that is highly informative about both, and this provides some context for understanding the information and teaching about the church.

The author is a Hellenist Jew who claims that he received the gospel from the apostles who were eyewitnesses of Jesus' teaching and life (2:3–4).[6] He appears to have received a more advanced Hellenist education than the other New Testament authors, with the possible exception

---

5. *First Clement*, probably the oldest Christian document apart from the New Testament writings, attests to the Epistle of Hebrews in Rome ca. 96, but the Latin West contested Pauline authorship without offering an alternative.

6. The author of Hebrews used terminology that indicated apostolic testimony from the twelve, which included being an eyewitness of Jesus' ministry (Acts 1:21–22), and, according to Paul, signs wonders and miracles (2 Cor 12:12). What was heard was "confirmed to us by those who heard [the Lord]. God also testified to it by signs, wonders and various miracles and gifts of the Holy Spirit, distributed according to his will." While Apollos is the most popular candidate according to scholars, this is hardly the description that one would expect of him—his teaching came first from the baptism of John and the Old Testament, and then from Priscilla and Aquila (Acts 18:24–26). It is also unlikely that Paul would have described the gospel that he preached as derivative in this way.

of Luke—his Greek and writing style are excellent.[7] He also demon-strates knowledge of Paul's teaching and he may well be associated with the Pauline network, since, at the time of writing, he hopes to visit the church with "our brother Timothy" who has recently been released from prison (13:23). The author knows the church and knows its past. He writes to the church with warmth, passion, concern, and authority as a leader who is absent during a crucial time.

The letter is addressed to a specific Jewish Christian community or house church that is the second generation after the apostles.[8] In the same way as the author, they received the gospel from apostolic eye-witnesses (2:3–4), and those leaders who first preached the gospel to them have already died (13:7).[9] They have been Christians for some time. They have been given an adequate foundation in the basics of the faith, and they have received enough teaching to have become teachers themselves (5:11—6:3). The author knows that in the past, the Christian community has suffered persecution that involved public abuse and hu-miliation as well as imprisonment and property seizure (10:32–34). He is highly complimentary about the way they stood their ground when they suffered, how they had a positive attitude about their losses, their bravery when they publicly supported others under attack, and how they sympathized with the prisoners. However, he makes it clear that none of them was martyred at that time (12:4). He also commends their actions

7. Scholars are generally agreed that the author of Hebrews was a well-educated Hellenist Jew because of the high quality of the Greek and the sophistication of the style, which combines Greek rhetorical techniques and traditional rabbinic methods. This places the book of Hebrews among the documents of early Jewish Christianity. The book is considered by G. A. Deissmann to be the earliest example of "Christian artistic literature" (Deissmann, *Light from the Ancient Near East*, 243–44).

8. This assertion is based not only on the knowledge of the Old Testament, Jewish institutions, and rabbinic exegesis that the readers must bring to the text, but on the fact that the central extended argument demonstrating Jesus' priesthood and involving the primary Jewish institutions answers Jewish questions—it would not be relevant to a Gentile audience that needed help in a crisis. However, scholars are divided on the ethnic composition of the church community. See Ellingworth's arguments for mixed Jewish and Gentile readers (Ellingworth, *Hebrews*, 24–26). He states that the evidence does not absolutely require an exclusively Jewish readership.

9. The terminology that the readers received the gospel from "those who heard" and had it confirmed by "signs, wonders and miracles" indicates that this church received the gospel from eyewitnesses who were qualified to be apostles and had died by the time the letter was written (see n. 6). This would suggest that the readers lived in an area that was the focus of the mission to the Jews led by Peter.

in general and the help that they have consistently provided for other Christians (6:10–11).

The Crisis the Church Was Facing

Things have changed for the church. Now, for example, though their good works continue, the author needs to urge the readers to remember those in prison and to be sympathetic (13:2). But even more important, they have become lax in their commitment to the things they have been taught (2:1–4; 5:12), and evidence a significant failure to thrive in response to new teaching (6:1–8)—instead of growing they need to be taught the basics all over again (5:12). Furthermore, at this point their problems appear to have come to a head.[10] The author indicates that they are at a time when they need help (4:16). In their time of need, the author is afraid that they are in danger of drifting or falling away from the confession (2:1–4; 6:1–8), becoming lazy in moving forward or hardhearted in not responding to God's voice (3:7–19; 6:12), or losing confidence and shrinking back in the presence of God (10:35–39). They must be warned about the dangers of continuing to sin (10:26); they appear to be at odds with their leadership (13:7) and some are deserting the community in their time of need (10:25). The church is in a state of crisis.[11] The readers are compared to the Israelites in the wilderness generation, and the author shows that they are in danger of hardening their hearts to what Jesus is saying to them in their time of crisis just like the Israelites did with Moses (3:1–17).

There are many kinds of crises churches face that can involve this kind of behavior. Some scholars believe that the readers are experiencing second generation lethargy, in which they have failed to adequately adopt the faith of the first generation, or their expectation of an imminent *parousia* has been disappointed and is no longer sustaining their level of commitment. Many believe that the recipients are experiencing

---

10. For further discussion of how the world of the recipients was falling apart, see Lane, *Hebrews 1–8*, lxi; Lane, "Hebrews: A Sermon in Search of a Setting," 16.

11. Two possibilities for the looming crisis involve a confrontation with the Roman Empire: the recipients could be in Rome facing persecution, or in an area close to Palestine facing the invasion of the Roman army at the time of the Great Jewish Revolt and the destruction of the temple. See Westfall, "Running the Gamut," 20–21. The fact that the message of salvation came directly from multiple apostolic witnesses (2:3) would favor an area close to Palestine.

loss of status and honor, so that they are tempted to revert to Judaism.[12] Others believe that the recipients were facing persecution and martyrdom or some other life-threatening crisis. While Hebrews may offer help in each of these circumstances, certain features in the text suggest that the readers are indeed facing a life-threatening situation and they are literally scared to death.[13]

The text suggests that the crisis the readers are facing involves possible death and exile. After opening with a description of how Jesus is God's ultimate messenger or apostle, the author introduces Jesus' high priesthood, which is based on his identity with humanity. In this introduction, Jesus' death is said to accomplish two purposes: to destroy the devil who holds the power of death, and to free people who are held in slavery to the fear of death (2:14–15). Therefore, the problem of death and the fear of death is highlighted as a relevant concern and Jesus is introduced as meeting that human need (2:16). In chapter 11, the readers are motivated by examples of obedient endurance while experiencing alienation and the reversals of expectation.[14] The actions and achievements of faith compose a strange and rather dark list. Death and suffering permeate the list and sojourning in exile is highlighted. The chapter climaxes with a graphic description of various sufferings that range from torture and violent death to abject poverty and homelessness (11:35a–38). One may conclude that the readers are being encouraged against a lethal danger that can either kill them or render them without homes or possessions.[15] But it is still on its way. As the author says, "In

12. Hughes, *Hebrews*, 10–11. That the primary theme is Christ's superiority, the intent is apologetic, and the danger is reverting to Judaism have achieved the status of presuppositions among some scholars. See, for example, Brown's critique of A. Vanhoye in *Introduction to the New Testament*, 691: "Too formal an approach may be in danger of divorcing Heb from the clear apologetic goal that it seeks to achieve by stressing the superiority of Christ." Therefore, Hebrews is often perceived as a polemic against Judaism, but it lacks polemic overtones. See, for example, Attridge, "Paraenesis in a Homily," 220–21. This is not to say that the institutions of Judaism such as the temple, the covenant, and the high priesthood are not relativized in Hebrews.

13. For further discussion of the crisis that the readers were facing, see Westfall, "Running the Gamut," 20–21.

14. For the aspects of death that dominate ch. 11, see Westfall, *Discourse Analysis of Hebrews*, 256–57.

15. The sojourning theme in Hebrews has led some, following Käsemann, to assert that "the Christian community is viewed almost entirely as the wandering people of God" (Guthrie, *New Testament Theology*, 778; see also Strecker, *Theology of the New Testament*, 616–20). One might as easily say the community is viewed as the dead

your struggle against sin, you have not *yet* resisted to the point of shedding your blood" (12:4).

The Message to the Church in Its Time of Crisis

The author of Hebrews has a practical message for the church that is relevant for a Christian community in this kind of severe need and under such threat. Many think of Hebrews as primarily theological and didactic teaching about the person of Christ, or an apologetic that proves that Christianity is better than Judaism. However, it is actually an exhortation to a particular church, supported and equipped by teaching about how Jesus is the apostle of our faith and our great high priest, and how believers share in his holy calling (3:1). The author wants the church to do three things in order to endure the coming pressure: to hold on to their confession, to draw near to the presence of God, and to move forward spiritually. These three things are repeated prominently throughout the discourse in the hortatory subjunctive commands.[16] "Let us hold on to the confession" occurs three times (2:4; 4:14; 10:23), and "Let us draw near to God" occurs four times (4:16; 10:22; 12:28; 13:12). The command "Let us move forward" is repeated five times with a variety of metaphors that involve forward movement (4:1, 11; 6:1; 10:25; 12:1). These commands combine the two concepts of pursuing goals and the pastoral ministry of every believer.[17] While the command to draw near to God is at the heart of the text and supported by much of the teaching on Jesus' priesthood, the covenant, tabernacle, and sacrifices,

---

people of God—the view of this paper is that the themes of sojourning, reversal, suffering, and death represent the threat they face, rather than the characterization of the church. This has been a relatively stable community (though under pressure) for at least two generations, with leaders and members that share an identity and a history. The "nomad" element is either completely metaphorical, or more likely, it projects the future—a community that is on the verge of extinction.

16. This is the key to the structure of Hebrews. See Westfall, *Discourse Analysis of Hebrews*, 297–301 for a summary of these patterns.

17. See, for example, the discussion on the meaning of the rest in Hebrews in ibid., 132, which concludes, "The goal is the 'heavenly calling' in 3:1. It is 'maturity' in 6:1. It is the 'promises' in 6:12 and chapter 11. It is the ministry goal of 'love and good works' in 10:24. It is the goal of the race in 12:1 that is specified as peace and sanctification in 12:14. It is presence in the heavenly Jerusalem and the festival assembly in 12:22–24. In each of these references, there is a collocation of achieving a goal with a corporate or pastoral concern. The rest has a present and eschatological reality."

the pastoral element in the command to move forward makes it of particular interest for a discussion of the theology of the church.

CALL TO CHRISTIAN COMMUNITY DURING CRISIS

Throughout Hebrews, the significance of the local church and the importance of the commitment of the individuals in it to each other are both explicit and implicit. Presence is an obvious requirement that is usually assumed in the rest of the New Testament. But in Hebrews, presence is also extended to the historic people of God, the universal church and the heavenly assembly. The believer is also asked to maintain a connection to the leadership, holding on to their common foundation, and personal growth that secures an investment back into the community.

Presence

The primary vital component of presence is the church community's meeting together. As some have noted, Hebrews is the only place in the New Testament that actually tells people to go to church. In 10:24–25, the author commands: "Let us consider how to stimulate one another to love and good deeds, not abandoning meeting together as some are in the habit of doing, but exhorting one another—and all the more as you see the day drawing near." The mutual concern and care for other believers has to take place in the context of gathering together. Furthermore, the sense here is to "pay close attention to each other,"[18] especially in terms of how to motivate each other forward. It is similar to several other commands in Hebrews to "look" to make sure that no one has an unbelieving heart, that no one misses the grace of God, that bitterness does not develop, and that no one is sexually immoral or godless (3:12; 12:15, 16). There is a consistent concern that believers give time and attention to study each other so they can understand how to effectively stimulate and exhort the other members. The author is fighting against the tendency to isolate and insulate oneself from the community during times of stress and crisis—we should reverse that tendency and even increase our care, commitment, and presence in the face of all kinds of catastrophe and pressure that will culminate in eschatological upheaval.[19]

18. See Johnson, *Hebrews*, 259.

19. As Attridge, *Hebrews*, 291, writes: "The urgency of the summons is underlined by the final, eschatological notice."

Hebrews also portrays the historic people of God as present participants and witnesses in the community's struggle. In chapter 11, the author provides examples of how faith operated with individuals in the pre-history, early history, conquest, and post-conquest history of Israel. At the end of chapter 11, the author explains that these people who exercised faith did not receive the promises because "God planned something better for us, so that they would be made perfect only together with us" (11:40). Therefore, the Old Testament saints experienced sojourning, reversal, suffering, death, and/or at the very least unfulfilled hope, and have waited in anticipation for this very time when the promises would be fulfilled for all of God's people. The result of God's plan is not unfair treatment, but more of an essential unity where all the people of God from the past and present are perfected together in Christ. Therefore, Hebrews maintains an essential continuity between the people of God under the old and the new covenants.[20] Even more, the faithfulness of the readers is required for this completion. In 12:1, the writer portrays the individuals in chapter 11 as a cloud of witnesses in an athletic stadium surrounding the readers who are located on a track running a race, which represents responding to life's challenges with faithful actions. Therefore, the Jewish ancestors that compose the people of God are cast as both athletic role models and fans in the sense that they have run their race, they are currently witnessing and encouraging the church community, and they have a stake in the church's success.

The presence of the struggling community responding to life's challenges in a stadium full of sports fans from Israel's past is placed in a bigger context in chapter 12. The race is an event included in a heavenly festival assembly in 12:22: "You have come to Mount Zion, to the heavenly Jerusalem, the city of the living God. You have come to thousands of angels, to a festival assembly, to the church of the first born whose names are written in heaven. You have come to God, the judge of all, to the spirits of the righteous ones who are made perfect, and to Jesus, the

20. As Guthrie says, the people of God are the spiritual successors of the faithful Israelites (Guthrie, *New Testament Theology*, 778). There is discontinuity between covenants and access to God, but continuity between the communities of the people of God. Ellingworth finds a tension between the Hebrews view of salvation history and emphatic statements of discontinuity found elsewhere (Matt 3:9; John 8:44; Rom 9:6). He suggests that the context of Hebrews reflects neither the parting of the ways between Christianity and Judaism reflected in John, nor the preoccupation with the Gentile mission shown by Paul (Ellingworth, *Hebrews*, 69).

mediator of a new covenant and to the sprinkled blood which is speaking better than Abel's blood" (12:22–24). This is a composite picture or a crowded stage that includes all other faithful beings in celebration.[21] The Father, Jesus, all the leaders who shared the word of God with the readers, the Old Testament saints, and the spiritual beings that have been mentioned in the discourse are present in the gathering.[22] The significance of this vision is that the struggling church community's faithful response to life's challenges is literally embedded in the unseen reality of the universal church and the heavenly assembly. This is where they really exist, and the church's presence and location in the heavenly celebration endows every mundane action with a priestly significance.

Relationship with Leadership

While the group's relationship to the church's leadership is by no means a dominant theme, it is a concern and focus at the end of the epistle. Amid a string of short commands, the readers are told to remember their leaders who spoke the word of God to them and consider the outcome of their life and imitate their faith (13:7).[23] The conscious continuity with and importance of the past is characteristic of the epistle. As Lane says, "The formulation ['to speak the Word of God'] indicates that the leaders were a link in the chain of tradition that accounted for the reliable transmission of the message of salvation to the audience" (cf. 2:3).[24] The

21. Many assert that this is an eschatological future vision (see Lane, *Hebrews 9–13*, 465; Michel, *Hebräer*, 460 n. 2; Koester, *Hebrews*, 550–51; Peterson, *Hebrews and Perfection*, 160–66). However, the fact that it is a present reality is shown by the blood of Jesus speaking to them in the present (corresponding with "today if you hear his voice"), whom they must not resist. In addition, the kingdom in 10:22–24 is depicted in contrast to the shaking in the future (10:26–27).

22. "God had planned something better for 'us' so that only together with 'us' would they be made perfect." Now the participants from chapter 11 are perfected and located in the anticipated city in joyful assembly together with the readers. This also forms cohesive ties with the theme of the perfection of Christ and his followers. Finally, Jesus is described in terms that evoke the entire central section with the references to his role as mediator of the new covenant and to his sprinkled blood. As in 12:1–2, the author depicts the readers as located spatially in a heavenly location in the presence of the heavenly hosts, the faithful, God the judge, and Jesus the mediator and sacrifice who is in the process of speaking to them" (Westfall, *Discourse Analysis of Hebrews*, 280).

23. The author chooses a broad term for leadership (ἡγουμένοι) that applies collectively to the people who played a key role in the life of the early community, rather than the technical word for officials. See Lane, *Hebrews 9–13*, 526.

24. Ibid., 527.

model of their lives at their death provided an example of the important connection between faith and outcome for the believers during their crisis. In the epistle's closing, the author focuses on the present leaders of the church and includes himself with them.[25] He exhorts the church to obey their leaders and submit to their authority (13:17). In contrast, the leaders are commended rather than exhorted—the author believes that they are watching over the church in a way that shows they are accountable to God. He asks the believers to make the leaders' job a pleasure rather than a burden. In the benediction, Jesus Christ is described as the as the great Shepherd of the sheep, which metaphorically binds him to the leaders (13:20). The author's closing personal concern is for the recipients to align themselves in an appropriate and mutually supportive relationship with their leadership. It is a final plea for connection and continuity with the Christian community.

Maintain the Common Foundation

As noted above, part of the importance of remembering the leaders is due to their role as a link in the chain of tradition that insured the reliable transmission of the message that Jesus first announced (2:3). The author clearly believes that an important part of belonging to the community involves maintaining that confession they received. The exhortation to hold on to the confession is part of the primary message of Hebrews (2:1; 4:14; 10:23), and the author is afraid that without paying careful attention to the message, the readers will drift away (2:1). The author describes some of the elements of the common foundation that the members share in 6:1–5. The common foundation includes the basic teachings about Christ (6:1–2) and experiences that come with initiation into the Christian community (6:4–5).[26] Many studies of the church in the New Testament are interested in locating references to baptism and

---

25. Ellingworth, *Hebrews*, 703, states: "The author probably identifies himself as one of the leaders of this church (cf. vv. 17–18), so he addresses the readers as 'you' here."

26. Leaving the elementary teaching in 6:1–2 is equivalent to not rebuilding the foundation that consists of teaching and praxis. The foundation is further qualified by a series of six genitive phrases: of repentance from dead works, and of faith in God, of teachings about baptisms, of laying on of hands, and of the resurrection from the dead, and of eternal judgment. There is a second list in 6:4–6, which is a negative example of one who forsakes the experiences of the believer who joins the community. The experiences are a list of five aorist participial phrases: The first four describe the believer's initiation into the Christian community and the fifth depicts falling away.

the Lord's Supper. While there are probable references to baptism in 6:2 and 10:22–23, and a possible though improbable reference to the Lord's Supper in 13:9–10, the author does not elaborate on the basic doctrines and ecclesial practices that they all share. He only stresses the importance of maintaining them. If one abandons the elementary teachings about Christ and walks away from the community, they will not be able to find an alternate road to repentance. An alternate path of repentance would require shaming and crucifying Jesus all over again on a different foundation—it's not going to happen (6:6).[27]

Growth and Investment in the Church Community

According to the author of Hebrews, it is not enough for the believers only to maintain the confession together. Spiritual nurturing and information in the community never produce a static state. The believers are meant to respond by growing in both knowledge and application. Each individual is meant to be trained eventually to discern good from evil, and to be able to teach the community. However, members of the church have failed to respond well to the teaching they have been given, so that the author of Hebrews metaphorically accuses them of being hard of hearing. Instead of maturing, they need to have the basics repeated all over again—they have actually regressed (5:11–14). The author warns them with a metaphor about the farmland that receives rain. If the land produces a crop that is useful for the owners, it is blessed by God. If the land unnaturally produces thorns and thistles, it is worthless, in danger of being cursed, and will eventually be burned (6:7–8). Hebrews gives a number of exhortations and metaphors that illustrate and expand how the believer is to respond to teaching in a way that is "useful" to God and the community. Ultimately, on the basis of the teaching about Jesus' high priesthood, the believers are urged to follow him into the Holy of Holies in the heavenly tabernacle as priests (10:19–22). Their priestly responsibilities and privileges are to access and serve God with their lifestyle, praise, and good works, which include loving each other, exercising hospitality, and caring for believers who are abused, suffering, and in prison (12:28—13:16).[28]

---

27. See Westfall, *Discourse Analysis of Hebrews*, 154–55 for a more complex analysis of 6:4–8.

28. See ibid., 283–91.

PASTORAL CARE IN A TIME OF CRISIS

The call to the believers to growth is part of one of the three major themes in Hebrews, the one that includes exhortations to the community to move forward spiritually toward goals. The commands are: "Let us enter the rest" (4:1, 11), "Let us press on to maturity" (6:1), "Let us consider how to stimulate each other to love and good works" (10:25), and "Let us run the race" (12:1).[29] However, pastoral care is manifested in concern for every believer as the church moves forward spiritually—this insistence that all members exercise pastoral care is the most dominant ecclesial theme in Hebrews. This is particularly interesting in view of the pervasive individualism in North American Christianity. We may tend to read the passages about goals individualistically, particularly since the author does not hesitate to use imagery drawn from athletic competition.[30]

Let Us Enter the Rest

The call to enter the rest (4:1, 11) represents the concrete goal of the exhortations: it is the realization of God's promises and the believers' eternal inheritance.[31] The metaphor is based on the comparison between the situation of the Israelites of the wilderness generation and the readers. When they faced their crisis, the Israelites hardened their hearts against God's command and consequently failed to enter the land of

29. Ibid., 132: "One of the puzzles of Hebrews is determining exactly what is signified by the phrase 'entering the rest.' Certainly its meaning is constrained by the literary context, which includes the diverse references to rest in the Old Testament as well as the references to rest in the extra-biblical literature. However, its meaning is complemented and expanded by certain occurrences of the hortatory subjunctive in the following context." See n. 17.

30. For example, Guthrie says, "Although the major exhortations emphasize individual responsibility, the OT background forbids any individualizing of believers apart from the community" (Guthrie, *New Testament Theology*, 779). This is a misreading of the text, and a failure to see that when the author says "none of you" instead of "you" (sg.), it places a direct focus on mutual accountability, which is clear from the surrounding contexts as well. Nevertheless, Guthrie recognizes that the author "everywhere assumes the corporate nature of God's people" (Guthrie, *New Testament Theology*, 778–79).

31. As Strecker, *Theology of the New Testament*, 616, states succinctly. This description helps process the "already-not-yet" nature of the discussion on rest, where "we who have believed enter the rest" (4:2), but at the same time, the believers are urged to make every effort to enter the rest (4:1, 11).

Canaan, that is, they failed to enter God's rest from their wanderings. In 3:7, the author applies a command in Psalm 95 directly to the readers: "Today, if you hear his voice, do not harden your hearts as you did in the rebellion!"[32] But when the author further applies it to the church, the focus is placed on concern for others:

> Watch out, brothers and sisters, that none of you has a sinful, unbelieving heart that falls away from the living God. But encourage one another daily as long as it is called "Today," so that none of you will be hardened by sin's deception. (3:12–13)

Again, in the face of crisis, the people are called primarily to pay close attention to each other's spiritual state. There is a clear and present danger for everyone in the community while the window of opportunity to respond to God is open. They are called to be committed to each other so much that they are in place to encourage each other every day. The object is mutual encouragement towards the goal.[33]

Similarly, at the conclusion of the unit, the congregation is supposed to be terrified at the prospect of losing anyone as the community responds as a group to God's voice and moves forward: "Therefore, let us be afraid, that since the promise of entering his rest is open, any one of you might seem to come short of it" (4:1). Based on Israel's example and the parallels between their situations, there is a good chance that some of them may not make it. However, there is no theology of moving with the movers or looking for a few good men. No one can be left behind.[34]

---

32. It is fascinating that the Holy Spirit is clearly depicted as speaking directly to the church throughout Hebrews by the repetition of "today if you hear his voice" (3:15; 4:7), and at the climax of the epistle, Jesus' blood is speaking: "See to it that you do not refuse the one who is speaking!"

33. The metaphor "rest" is defined as resting from work in the same way that God rested from his work. This involves relaxation after completion rather than inertia. The connection with the rest of entering Canaan also evokes the alleviation of distress and the meeting of needs through the attainment of a goal. It is also connected to participation in the Sabbath celebration of spiritual completion. Therefore, entering the "rest" involves the idea of "people on their way to a divine goal" (Westfall, *Discourse Analysis of Hebrews*, 130; quoting Attridge, *Hebrews*, 114).

34. When the theme is repeated in 4:11, the focus is shifted to individual effort and responsibility, which is also necessary for a community to succeed: "Therefore, let us make every effort to enter that rest so that no one may fall in the same pattern of disobedience." The communal concern is still there, but is secondary.

Let Us Press On to Maturity

The command to press on to maturity is accompanied arguably by the most disturbing and discouraging section of Hebrews, which is the warning against apostasy that allows no return to repentance. One may well ask how Hebrews 6 can be pastoral. However, the pastoral intent in this passage is clear in its purpose, the reverse psychological motivation for the readers to see themselves as teachers of the community, and the frank pastoral affirmation after the harsh warning in 6:9–12. The author is preparing the readers to respond as a group to the new information about Jesus as a great high priest according to the order of Melchizedek, by pressing on to maturity. This teaching is central to the author's purpose for the letter, because it will ultimately equip the readers to find the face of God in a powerful way in their time of crisis (4:16; 6:19–20; 10:19–22). The author thinks that they desperately need this.

In 5:11–14, the author says the readers are slow to learn and needed to be taught the basics again, even though they should be teachers by this time. According to deSilva, "the author rouses the hearers once more to attention and hopes to impel them forward in their investment in the Christian group through an appeal to the emotion of shame."[35] They are meant to come away wanting to live up to the author's expectations and become teachers of the community.

The readers need to take their choices seriously. The two alternatives to growth are falling away or not growing and producing garbage. If they do not move forward as a group in response to the teaching, they will go backwards, and going backwards during a time of crisis can be disastrous, as the example of the Israelites shows. But the author shifts to encouragement in 6:9: "But we are convinced of better things in your case, loved ones, things that accompany salvation, even though we speak to you like this." The author bases his confidence on their history of work and love for God shown by helping people. He restates the goal to move on to maturity by urging each one of them to make every effort to make their hope sure—the intended effect is motivation for the group's mutual growth.

35. deSilva, *Perseverance in Gratitude*, 219.

Let Us Consider How to Stimulate Each Other to Love and Good Works

After a long didactic section that offers an extensive proof of the high priesthood of Christ, as a conclusion in 10:19–22 the author urges the readers to follow Jesus into the Holy of Holies as consecrated priests. He then repeats the command to hold on to the confession in 10:23. Subsequently he introduces the final section of Hebrews with another command to pursue spiritual goals. The command in 10:24 introduces the last section of Hebrews, which focuses on how the readers share in Jesus' heavenly calling. It paraphrases or restates the discourse theme of "let us move forward" by replacing the goal of the rest or spiritual maturity with a goal of mutual stimulation to love and good works. With this command, the author has explicitly included the pastoral, ethical, and service-oriented concerns that support the first two commands. The third section develops the theme of the readers' pastoral and ethical service, which is their heavenly calling, and which is reflected by the increase in commands to the readers.

Let Us Run the Race with Endurance and Faith

The exhortation to run the race could easily be taken as an individualistic command, but closer scrutiny reveals an intense pastoral concern at the conclusion of the unit in 12:12–17. As mentioned above, the exhortation to run the race in 12:1–2 involves responding to life's challenges with faithful actions. Running the race takes place in the presence of the cloud of witnesses from chapter 11 who are presumably cheering from the stands. The race is run by fixing our eyes on Jesus who is the author and finisher of our faith. In 12:3–11, the author redefines the suffering and dishonor that the readers are experiencing as discipline, training, or conditioning for the race, with the goal of the formation of character evidenced in righteousness and peace.

The unit concludes with three second person plural commands to strengthen weak hands and limbs (12:12), to make level paths (12:13), and to pursue the goals of peace and holiness as a runner presses toward the finish line of a race. The command to strengthen weak hands and limbs shows a direct concern for the weakest members, such as those who are exhausted and discouraged.[36] Furthermore, the author urges the

---

36. Lane, *Hebrews 9–13*, 426. This pastoral concern for the disabled is explicit in the source of 10:12 in Isa 35:3–6: "Strengthen the feeble hands, steady the knees that give

readers to make level paths "so the lame may not be disabled, but rather healed." In the passage that sounds the most competitive, the author urges the readers to build "wheelchair accessible paths" so that no one will be left behind in the race.

The third command continues the athletic imagery of the race with the word "pursue" (διώκετε), which is associated with the pursuit of a goal in a race or in figurative language. The readers are urged to pursue the goals of peace and holiness. But they pursue the goals by looking carefully at each other to make sure that no one falls short of the grace of God, that no bitter root springs up, and that no one is immoral or godless like Esau. This refers to virtually anyone who is pulled off track. It is a directive "to exercise vigilant concern for each member of the house church."[37] Someone who falls short of the grace of God is representative of the apostasy that the author fears. It involves unbelief, carelessness, and a conscious rejection of grace. They are to watch out for bitterness in each other, because that is the source of trouble and it "defiles many" in the sense that it poisons the community. However, the most focus is placed on the possibility that someone may be immoral or godless. It is like Esau selling his inheritance for a pot of stew, because immorality and godlessness sell everything of spiritual value for a very cheap return. Once more, the author stresses the seriousness of these choices at defining moments.

CONCLUSION

The book of Hebrews has a wealth of information on the relationship between the individual and the community. Much of our Western spirituality is individualistic and it is common to read Hebrews in terms of an individual believer's responsibility and privilege. After all, I myself have said that Hebrews is about the priesthood of the believer.[38] However, if

---

way; say to those with fearful hearts, 'Be strong, do not fear; your God will come, he will come with vengeance; with divine retribution he will come to save you.' Then will the eyes of the blind be opened and the ears of the deaf unstopped. Then will the lame leap like a deer, and the mute tongue shout for joy" (NIV).

37. Lane, *Hebrews 9–13*, 451.

38. See Westfall, *Discourse Analysis of Hebrews*, 289, 295. In finding the identity and function of the priesthood of the believer in the climax and conclusion of Hebrews, I frame it as the point or focus of the discourse.

that means that we think Hebrews teaches us that we should approach God independently, we have it wrong.

While most or all of us can relate to the deep need to see the face of God while under pressure, it is important to recognize that Hebrews is written to help a church community as it faces a life-threatening crisis. As I write this conclusion, two recent catastrophes still dominate the news: the cyclone in Myanmar and the earthquakes in China. In the case of Myanmar, the predictable after-effects have been more damaging than the storm itself. Whole communities have been decimated. Comparable tragedies have been caused by war and famine. The Hebrews community stood in the path of a crisis of this kind of magnitude, whether they were casualties of war or victims of persecution. Comparable to the Essenes and the Dead Sea Scrolls community, the Hebrews community did not survive the crisis to communicate the information about the document.

The message of Hebrews tells the community how as a group under pressure they must hang on to the confession, move forward spiritually, and draw near to God in their time of need—the theological teaching about Jesus supports that message and equips them to do all three activities. The author urges each believer to maintain a vital connection to the people of God and the leaders. Maintaining the doctrinal confession of the faith is also essential, especially during a time of crisis or change. It is a group effort and determines the identification of the community—you cannot walk away from the confession and the community and claim to have a relationship with Christ. Furthermore, blessing from God in the form of teaching and resources must produce growth in terms of maturity, righteousness, and the enhanced spiritual capacity to serve the church community. This is a solemn charge for students, academics, and scholars in biblical studies. Finally, we are all called to mutual pastoral care in the faith community, particularly in difficult circumstances, crises, or times of change. We need to be attentive to each other's spiritual state and needs in a way that is healthy, healing, and nurturing.

BIBLIOGRAPHY

Attridge, Harold W. *Hebrews*. Hermeneia. Philadelphia: Fortress, 1989.

———. "Paraenesis in a Homily: The Possible Location of, and Socialization in, the 'Epistle to the Hebrews.'" *Semeia* 50 (1990) 211–26.

Brown, R. E. *An Introduction to the New Testament*. New York: Doubleday, 1997.

Deissmann, G. A. *Light from the Ancient Near East*. Translated by L. R. M. Strachar. Grand Rapids: Baker, 1978.

deSilva, David A. *Perseverance in Gratitude: A Socio-Rhetorical Commentary on the Epistle "to the Hebrews."* Grand Rapids: Eerdmans, 2000.

Donelson, Lewis R. *From Hebrews to Revelation: A Theological Introduction*. Louisville, KY: Westminster John Knox, 2001.

Ellingworth, Paul. *Commentary on Hebrews*. NIGTC. Grand Rapids: Eerdmans, 1993.

Guthrie, Donald. *New Testament Theology*. Downers Grove, IL: InterVarsity, 1981.

Hughes, P. E. *A Commentary on the Epistle to the Hebrews*. Grand Rapids: Eerdmans, 1977.

Johnson, Luke Timothy. *Hebrews*. NTL. Louisville, KY: Westminster John Knox, 2006.

Käsemann, E. *The Wandering People of God: An Investigation of the Letter to the Hebrews*. Translated by R. A. Harrisville and I. L. Sandberg. Minneapolis: Augsburg, 1984.

Koester, Craig R. *Hebrews: A New Translation with Introduction and Commentary*. AB. New York: Random House, 2001.

Ladd, Eldon. *A Theology of the New Testament*. Grand Rapids: Eerdmans, 1993.

Lane, William L. *Hebrews 1–8*. WBC. Dallas: Word, 1991.

———. *Hebrews 9–13*. WBC. Dallas: Word, 1991.

———. "Hebrews: A Sermon in Search of a Setting." *SWJT* 28 (1985) 13–18.

Lindsey, Hal. *The Late Great Planet Earth*. Grand Rapids: Zondervan, 1970.

Marshall, I. Howard. *New Testament Theology: Many Witnesses, One Gospel*. Downers Grove, IL: InterVarsity, 2004.

Michel, O. *Der Brief an die Hebräer*. 6th ed. Göttingen: Vandenhoeck & Ruprecht, 1966.

Peterson, D. G. *Hebrews and Perfection: An Examination of the Concept of Perfection in the "Epistle to the Hebrews."* Biblical Interpretation Series 48. Cambridge: Cambridge University Press, 1982.

Strecker, Georg. *Theology of the New Testament*. Translated by M. Eugene Boring. Louisville, KY: Westminster John Knox, 2000.

Westfall, Cynthia Long. *A Discourse Analysis of the Structure of Hebrews: Relationship between Form and Meaning*. London: T. & T. Clark, 2005.

———. "The Hebrew Mission: Voices from the Margin?" In *Christian Mission: Old Testament Foundations and New Testament Developments*, edited by Stanley E. Porter and Cynthia Long Westfall, 187–207. Eugene, OR: Pickwick, 2010.

———. "Running the Gamut: Endurance in Resistance—Empire in Hebrews, the General Epistles and Revelation." In *Empire in the New Testament*, edited by Stanley E. Porter and Cynthia Long Westfall, 230–58. Eugene, OR: Pickwick, 2011.

11

The Community of Believers in James

WILLIAM R. BAKER

THIS BRIEF LETTER TO early Christian believers is easy to pass over in a volume on New Testament ecclesiology. In fact, the Epistle of James has been an object of neglect for investigating any kind of theological interest, especially in the Protestant era. However, the early church based two of its seven sacraments on passages in this epistle, a view that continues in the Roman Catholic expression of Christianity today. The sacrament of extreme unction ("last rites") is believed to be established by an interpretation of Jas 5:14, and confession by an understanding of 5:16. However, since Luther's negative characterization of James as "an epistle of straw"[1] and his belief that the book was not apostolic and certainly not of the same rank as Paul's epistles, most Protestant or evangelical theologians have not included it, or included it only summarily, in any discussions of theology, or in volumes or articles on New Testament theology. In the early twentieth century Martin Dibelius put the hammer in the coffin of James by considering it to be such an illogical collection of unconnected sayings that in fact one would have to conclude that James "has no theology" at all, for Dibelius did not believe a single authorial mind framed its ideas.[2] It was more like the Old Testament book of Proverbs than a towering book of theological insight from Paul.

---

1. Luther, *Works*, 35:362.
2. Dibelius, *James*, 21.

More investigation of interpretative models for New Testament books has led to the conclusion for most who study James today that it is by one single author, most likely the brother of Jesus at least in rudiment,[3] who constructed the book with at least holistic assumptions of theology and an overarching framework, however loose, that hold the book together.[4] Thus, theological study of James reveals a consistent understanding of the church. The epistle is categorized appropriately in the vein of Jewish wisdom literature,[5] which plays by different rules than say, the book of Romans. Romans and other writing by Paul epitomize Greek styles of logic and rhetoric.[6] James and other wisdom literature like Proverbs and Ecclesiastes are typical of Eastern styles of philosophical and ethical communication in which logical moves from paragraph to paragraph do not need to be spelled out but are left for the readers to integrate for themselves. The theological assumptions of the author are to be discovered by asking why the author wrote what he did rather than limiting the search to the precise language employed by the author.[7] James must be read on its own, then, and not seen as somehow faulty or inferior in form or theology because of its different style of communication. As Johnson observes, "Throughout the history of interpretation James has been most appreciated theologically when allowed to speak in its own voice."[8]

Because it can be ranked as the earliest epistle of the New Testament, its great value is that it offers a window into the earliest communities of believers more than any other book of the New Testament. This may mean that its theology in general as well as its ecclesiology is underformed and patchy compared to other parts of the New Testament, but nevertheless it will prove no less fascinating in its own way. When one examines the book, a stunning number of standard Christian ideas found in many other New Testament books are missing: the cross, resurrection, justification by faith, the Lord's Supper, the Holy Spirit, spiritual gifts, evangelism, and more.[9] However, this should not deter readers

3. McCartney, *James*, 8–30; Johnson, *James*, 92–93; Davids, *James*, 2–22.

4. Hartin, *James*, 10.

5. Bauckham, *James*, 29–34.

6. Jewett, *Romans*, 23.

7. McCartney, *James*, 67; Davids, *James*, 25.

8. Johnson, *Brother of Jesus*, 242.

9. Chester and Martin, *Letters of James, Peter, and Jude*, 45; Schreiner, *New Testament Theology*, 743.

from appreciating the glimpse of church life among the earliest believers that the book reflects, as well as the assumptions about the church held by James.

DESCRIBING THE COMMUNITY

Historically (Author, Date, Location)

Most likely, James the brother of Jesus is the author of this epistle. Although none of Jesus' brothers and sisters was a believer before the resurrection, James was with the apostles in the upper room awaiting Pentecost (Acts 1:14) and received a personal appearance from the resurrected Jesus (1 Cor 15:7), most likely earlier. Very quickly he became one of the key leaders of the church, ranking with Peter and John (Gal 1:19; 2:9; Acts 12:17), even presiding over the Council of Jerusalem (Acts 15:12–21) in AD 49. He was the leader of the church in Jerusalem until his martyrdom in AD 62 (recorded by Josephus, *Ant.* 20.200–201).

Though James may have penned this epistle later in his ministry,[10] there is much evidence to lead to the conclusion that it was more likely written very early, before AD 49.[11] The main basis for such a view is the completely Jewish perspective of the letter, showing no indications whatsoever that Gentiles are even part of the Christian community. This would seem to be very unlikely if it was written after AD 49 when the whole contentious matter of the conditions for Gentiles to be part of the church was decided. Supporting this conclusion are many facets of the letter. First, when it refers to a gathering of believers in 2:2 this is called a synagogue (συναγωγή, *synagōgē*) rather than a church (ἐκκλησία, *ekklēsia*). Second, in 5:4 God is called "the Lord of Hosts" (Lord Sabaoth), the Greek transliterating a Hebrew word that pictures God leading an army intent on destruction.[12] Third, 2:19 refers to the most basic confession about God, that "God is one," which is the monotheistic foundation of all Jewish thought about God. Fourth, James depends on quotations from the Old Testament, which he assumes his readers know well (Lev

10. Chester and Martin, *Letters of James, Peter, and Jude*, 48; Tasker, *James*, 31.

11. McCartney, *James*, 8–31, considers many views at length to come to the conclusion that it was written early, by James, the brother of Jesus. See also Moo, *James*, 9–25; Johnson, *James*, 121; Hartin, *James*, 21–24; Bauckham, *James*, 21; Wall, *Community of the Wise*, 9.

12. The phrase is also found in the LXX of Isa 5:9. See McCartney, *James*, 234, and Brown, Driver and Briggs, *Lexicon*, 838–39.

19:18 in 2:8; Exod 20:13–14 in 2:11; Gen 15:6 in 2:23; Prov 3:34 in 4:6). The author also assumes they know the stories of Abraham (2:21–23), Rahab (2:25), Job (5:11), and Elijah (5:17, 18). Finally, however we understand it, he addresses his letter in 1:1 "to the twelve tribes scattered among the nations," the most Jewish description of any audience in the New Testament.

Perhaps James intends his opening depiction of the audience to include "in spirit" all Jews living outside of Palestine.[13] Certainly, this is its normal function, Jews believing that God had dispersed them throughout the nations as punishment for disobedience but also to be seeds for bringing knowledge of the one, true God to the world. The only other use of "dispersion" to refer to an audience is 1 Pet 1:1, which describes its readers as "dispersed" throughout most regions of Asia Minor. First Peter's target audience is mostly Gentile Christians, who are the new people of God (2:9–10).[14] Most likely the added description as "twelve tribes" restricts James's immediate reference to Jewish Christians as its target audience.[15] The early date and other Jewish features of James also ground this view. In addition, despite some minority views that hold that James originally was directed only to Jews, not Christians,[16] the epistle provides ample evidence that it is addressed to Christians, including references to Jesus by name (1:1; 2:1), as Lord (5:14, 15), an indirect reference to his name (2:7),[17] dependence on Jesus' teaching (5:12,[18] among many examples), and anticipation of the return of Jesus (5:7–8).

Good reasons exist to restrict the audience to an even more narrow community of early Jewish believers, Jewish Christians "dispersed" from Jerusalem by persecution. First, Acts 11:19 mentions Jerusalem believers being "dispersed as far as Phoenicia and Cyprus" and also Antioch, "telling the message only to Jews" during the time of "persecution in connection with Stephen." This was also about the time that King Herod executed James the brother of John and arrested many Christians, in-

---

13. Bauckham, *James*, 14.

14. Davids, *Peter*, 8. However, Jobes, *1 Peter*, 23, and Achtemeier, *1 Peter*, 50, consider the audience to be mixed, Gentile and Jewish.

15. Achtemeier, *1 Peter*, 16.

16. Massebieau, "L'épître de Jacques"; Spitta, *Der Brief des Jakobus*, 1–13.

17. Baker, "Christology."

18. For a full account of passages that connect James and the Synoptic Gospels, see Davids, *James*, 47–48; Bauckham, *James*, 93–107; McCartney, *James*, 50–51.

cluding Peter (Acts 12:1–4). Second, James demonstrates that it has a specific community of believers in mind at numerous points, but especially in 2:6–7, 3:1, 4:1–3, and 5:9, where knowledge of specific incidents regarding their community is displayed.[19]

This conclusion means that James is addressing a community or communities, many of whom once lived in and around Jerusalem, where he was the principle leader and teacher. They are former members of the Jerusalem Christian community about whom he has some knowledge as a starting point for many of his exhortations.[20] They possibly live in regions just beyond Palestine but not deep into Gentile territory to the west. Since the martyrdoms of Stephen and James the brother of John are considered to be in the late 30s or early 40s, and James is writing before AD 49, much of the author's audience may have left Jerusalem within the last five years. Probably other Jews in the regions to which they were dispersed had become Christians too. They considered themselves Jews who believed in Jesus.

Characteristics/Problems

Despite the general moral tone of the letter that could apply to anyone, the specific community to which James directs his epistle has an identity, and the people addressed are in a situation to which his teaching is directed for their benefit and improvement. On the whole, his teaching comes across as scolding people who are young or immature in their faith, who grasp the rudiments of faithfulness to God and Christ, but who need to be pushed to grasp deeper understanding and grow up.

CONFLICTED

The best way to describe James's community of readers is that they are conflicted. They have confessed loyalty to Christ but they are not living out the impact of this in their lives very well. James comes up with a unique word to describe this problem. First in 1:8 and later in 4:18 he calls them "double-minded" (δίψυχος, *dipsychos*) or "double-souled," a word unique to the New Testament and unattested in Greek literature prior to James.[21] James uses this word to describe individuals who act

---

19. Laws, *James*, 7.

20. Moo, *James*, 23–25; Bauckham, *James*, 14–16; Hartin, *James*, 26–27.

21. McCartney, *James*, 94; Davids, *James*, 74; Marshall, "Δίψυχος"; Porter, "*Dipsychos*."

inconsistently, who are uncertain, split down the middle in terms of their allegiance. James epitomizes such people as blaming God for the troubles in their lives and for the sins they commit (1:13). They fail to be obedient to God's teaching to control their tongues and to live out their faith acting in love toward the poor (2:1–26). They are drawn into coveting the pleasures of the world at the expense of their relationship with God (4:1–4). They fail to trust God for the future (4:13–17). They are grumbling against each other (5:9).

Contrasting this picture of confliction stands God, whom James dramatically characterizes as "one" in 2:19. He is whole and complete, integrated in word and deed, consistently operating out of love and respect for all. He is the exact opposite of James's community of readers and is thus the ideal to which they are to aspire. Their spiritual confliction is negatively affecting their relationship with God, with others both inside and outside the church, and even within their own individual selves (4:1–4).

Thus, it may be draw from this that James's assumption about the ideal church is that it should be whole and complete like God and not filled with individuals who are in spiritual conflict. They should be a community of people who trust in God, care about one another, and who live out the radical truth of God's love for them shown in Christ. This challenges the immature, partially formed community to become mature, and should inform our understanding of what the church today should become.

POOR

The community of believers James addresses is for the most part economically poor. Land, both in Palestine and elsewhere, especially in rural areas, was controlled by a few wealthy landowners upon whom most everyone else was dependent for their livelihood.[22] James tends to cast the rich in the most negative light possible, depicting them as using their social and monetary advantage in the court system against the poor (2:6) and by doing so blaspheming the name of Christ (2:7). In these cases, the Christians are identified as among the poor. The same is true in 5:1–6, which describes the terrifying punishment of the rich for cheating and abuse of the poor. However, it may be that at least a small

---

22. Davids, *James*, 30–31; Hartin, *James*, 27.

portion of the community is not so poor.[23] Some of the rich typified in
1:9–11 as condemned could in fact "glory in their humiliation" and thus
stand outside the general nature of the proverbial-like illustration. The
merchants planning to expand their business without consideration of
God's will may only be an illustration but could typify some of James's
community of readers. Also, James does use as an illustration the atten-
dance of a very wealthy individual in an assembly of believers. Finally,
James also suggests that some outside of their community are even
poorer than themselves, such as the widows and orphans in 1:27 and the
poor man who is pictured entering into the assembly in 2:2.

Being poor was a social and economic hardship for most of James's
community of readers. Their life was difficult, not because they were
persecuted as Christians, but because, like all poor people of their day,
they suffered at the hands of the rich. Their poverty also impinged upon
their prayer, causing them to be selfish when praying to God (4:3) as
well as quarrelsome with one another (4:1–2; 5:9). As a church, James
counsels them to repent of their hedonistic desires and selfishness (4:4–
10) and patiently trust that Christ will come and put things right (5:8).
Those in the ideal church will forsake selfishness and embrace patience
with one another and trust in God. James also teaches in 1:9–11 that,
rather than seeing poverty and hardship as harmful to believers in the
church and wealth as a blessing from God, they should view poverty as
a distinct advantage spiritually that will help them to fully depend on
and trust in God. And in one sense, everyone is poor before the Lord
because of our sin.

Harassed from Without

The community James addresses does not appear to be coping very well
with pressure coming from a number of different sources in their lives.
This is evident from the opening concern of the epistle. Certainly, the
advice in 1:2 for them to embrace difficult situations as opportunities
to develop spiritual maturity can apply to any circumstance, whether
caused by some sort of harassment by nonbelievers, difficulty with other
believers, or simply troubling matters that occur during the course of a
person's lifetime. James shows concern that any difficulty in life could
upset their spiritual integrity and trust in God. It may also demonstrate
the hollowness of their faith in that they move quickly to blaming God

23. Moo, *James*, 24.

for their trouble, even their own sin (1:13). Their faith should be durable and grow stronger throughout the course of life, no matter how difficult life becomes.

Difficulty from outside the Christian community is coming from rich landowners. As noted earlier, this is not likely occurring because they are Christians, and so the word persecution is not the appropriate description. It is happening because the vast majority of the believers in James's community are poor (along with probably 90 percent of the population).[24] The poor in all societies are routinely mistreated and taken advantage of by the wealthy. James 2:6 says they "abuse you" (NASB) or "exploit you" (NIV), and notes in particular rich people's manipulation of the civil court system to take advantage of the poor, saying the rich are "dragging you into court."

The wealthy land owners are not only exploiting the poor—and the believers along with them—in the courts, they are also cheating them out of their due wages. James 5:1–6 describes the wealthy as withholding deserved pay from the day laborers who work in their fields. They do this selfishly, James says, to line their own overflowing pockets. The vehement denunciation and pronouncement of gruesome punishment upon these doomed people is based upon the Jewish law in Deut 24:14–15 (and Lev 19:13) that demands day laborers be paid at the end of each day's work. It also warns that God himself will hear the desperate cries of the helpless poor and act in certain judgment (cf. Amos 8:3).

In response to this trouble with the rich people in their lives, James urges patient endurance from his community of readers. They need to hold firmly to the truth that the Lord will one day come and swiftly turn the tables on the unscrupulous rich and judge them mercilessly in that coming eschatological day (5:8).

Distressed from Within

Some of the distress in the lives of James's readers comes from within the Christian community. This is evident first in James 2:4, which seems intended to hold the community accountable for making "distinctions

---

24. Hartin, *James*, 27; Davids, *James*, 41–47, 159; Baker, *Personal Speech-Ethics*, 135–36. Ropes, *James*, 255, and Laws, *James*, 169, take the term "murder" literally. However, the context and the ample association of various sorts of speech sins such as slander with bloodshed and murder make a literal application unwarranted. See Lev 6:3; Ps 14:4; Prov 10:6, 11, 18; 12:6; Ezek 22:9; Sir 8:16; 26:5; 28:8–11, 19–21; 1QH V, 7, 10–11.

among yourselves" (NASB) or having "discriminated among yourselves" (NIV). This seems to be the very purpose for the dramatic illustration in 2:2–6 regarding the wealthy and influential person visiting their assembly who is fawned over and the person in rags who is treated with disdain. James's point with the illustration is not to suggest they are doing that literally, since the illustration is poignantly hypothetical. Rather, James must think they are guilty within their community of favoring some over others based on a variety of superficial traits in a whole host of circumstances. To do so, 2:1 and 2:8 state, is to ignore the clear standard of Christ who accepted poor and rich alike equally into relationship with him, an attitude that is based on the standard of God in the Old Testament. In the Gospels, Jesus is shown time and time again accepting all. To treat others based on superficial traits is also to break the "law" of Christ to love your neighbor as yourself (Matt 22:38). James warns them severely not to continue this type of behavior.

More evidence that the believing community is stressed from within comes in 4:1–4. Here the charge is leveled against at least some in the community of being corrupted by the world in such a way that their lives are dominated by desiring pleasure. This leads them into conflict with others in the community. James pictures this in such deplorable terms as battles, wars, and even murder. While this almost certainly refers to verbal assaults,[25] it is considered severely harmful and divisive. James even speaks of envy between believers. Those who are conducting themselves this way are also insulting God with their selfish demands in prayer. Rather than being selfish and being driven by demonic influence, James advocates that true believers in the church nurture traits of wise living, like purity and gentleness (3:13–18). However, the chief characteristic among these is living peacefully and advocating peace. Behind this, James reveals his idea of a true church as being dominated by peace and not division or selfishness.

The issue of controlling the tongue is raised as a recurrent concern in James and is likely a known problem for the community of readers as well as a broad problem for people in general. This concern is first articulated in a memorable proverb in 1:19: "Let everyone be quick to hear, slow to speak, slow to anger." Control over speech is pivotal to building positive relationships with people by not saying things one will

---

25. McCartney, *James*, 207; Hartin, *James*, 107; Johnson, *James*, 277; Wall, *Community of the Wise*, 197.

later regret. A few verses later, in 1:26, control over speech is elevated as the litmus test for the value of any religious community, obviously including those who are Christians. James 3:1–12 contains an intense litany against the evils of the uncontrolled tongue as an agent of ultimate evil in people's lives, producing incalculable damage to everyone and everything, including the speakers themselves. In 4:11–12 slandering other believers is not just sinning against those slandered, it is an offense against God himself from whom law comes. It is failing to carry out the Christian law of loving one's neighbor that Jesus gave as the essence of all law. In 5:9, believers in this community are told not to complain about one another, with a warning that for such things they will be accountable when Christ returns as judge. Finally, in 5:12, believers are told not to add any oaths to support the honesty of their speech. Their words should be valued as true based on their own personal integrity, character, and commitment as believers.

James, then, portrays the ideal church as consisting of people who live in peace and harmony with one another and who demonstrate Jesus' teaching of love to the neighbor. This should be true certainly in their speech habits. However, their speech habits are viewed as a window into all their other behavior.

Not Living Out the Law of Jesus

One of the most well known features of the Epistle of James is its adamant position, worked out in 2:14–26, that the faith of true believers must be complemented by behavior that demonstrates their faith to all. The community of James's readers is not doing this very well, thus the general consensus that they should be characterized as immature. However, the real key to James is to understand on what basis Christians are expected to live out their faith. Reference to law a couple of times and even the quotation of two of the Ten Commandments (2:11) makes it easy to think that what James has in mind is Old Testament law. This would fit nicely into the early Jewish-Christian perspective of the entire letter.

However, when James's references to law are examined a different result comes into view, that the law James has in mind consistently is the law Jesus taught as the summation of all law: love your neighbor as yourself. This makes sense if for no other reason than that this epistle is peppered with teaching based on Jesus' teaching as found in the Gospels, most particularly Matthew's Sermon on the Mount, which contains a version of this principle.[26] Other reasons emerge from specific passages in James.

In 1:25 "the perfect law, the law of liberty" (NASB) describes the law that Christians are supposed to live out and not simply give lip service to. The word "perfect" (τέλειος, *teleios*) might make one think of the Old Testament law, since Jews did view it this way. However, "liberty" (ἐλευθερία, *eleutheria*) seems an odd way to describe this or any law, since laws by definition are restrictive. This term is used again in 2:12 to describe the law Christians are to live out. This time, however, 2:8 provides a parallel term and even pinpoints the "law" in mind. Here, it is called "the royal law" and then Lev 19:18 is quoted specifically as being this "law." There is no denying that James is quoting the Old Testament here, but the real question is, why is he quoting it? The only plausible answer is that he does so because of the central position this principle holds in Jesus' teaching. Only Jesus elevates this law from oblivion; only Jesus explains why James would call it royal. Jesus is the king and this law is the central tenet of his kingdom. Finally, 4:12, after charging that believers who slander other believers are judging the law in 4:11, indicates what "law" James points to with one choice word: "neighbor." Surely readers are expected to connect this word with 2:8 and "Love your neighbor as yourself." Thus, James expects the church to adopt Jesus' principle of loving one's neighbor and to do so both in their behavior and their speech. This love is to be demonstrated among the believers and toward those outside the church as well.

Practices and Leadership of the Community

The Epistle of James does not depict in much detail the practices of the early Christian community that makes up its audience. The most complete is the teaching about prayer and teachers. Though brief, what it says about confession, the lordship of Christ, the service of elders, and the responsibility everyone has to minister to one another is fairly revealing about this early Christian community's view of church.

---

26. Moo, *James*, 32, 112.

PRAYER

From the extensive discussion of prayer in the Epistle of James, we can conclude that prayer must have been a vital aspect of the believing community to whom the Epistle of James is directed. The comments that involve prayer are sprinkled throughout the letter and cover a wide variety of issues. Some of these are corrections and chastisement for how some are practicing prayer. Others are reminders of how prayer should actively be utilized within the community.

The opening concern in 1:2–8 about how believers cope with the variety of difficulties that may come their way in life assumes that prayer is intertwined with how they deal with these things. Certainly they should ask God for help in the difficult decisions that must be made during these times. James assumes they know that God is more than willing to provide them the wisdom they need if they will only ask. But they need to believe that he can and will help them. They need to believe, not just at that moment, but consistently, demonstrating a life that trusts God thoroughly through all the ups and downs, and not questioning God's faithfulness or promises. They cannot be double-souled (2:8). Otherwise, God will find it difficult to get through their barrier of doubt to communicate guidance and wisdom at the worst times when they need him most. The communication between them and God needs to follow a well-worn path so that it may operate smoothly when life brings the most trying situations.

James 4:3 is one of the few places in Scripture that provides a reason why prayers are sometimes not answered. Here it pinpoints the matter of the motives of the one who prays. Probably a wide variety of "wrong motives" might be involved. However, this passage highlights selfish envy that motivates people to ask for things to give them pleasure. Such worldly desires are outside the scope of God's interest. They reveal a hollow kind of believer lacking in spiritual depth. As Jesus shows in his model prayer, believers always need to be seeking to understand their place and their concerns in God's overall plan (Matt 6:10—"your kingdom come, your will be done"). Prayer is not to be used as a self-serving tool. Those who offer self-serving prayers, James says in what follows in 4:4–10, need to repent and come before God in humility.

James 4:13–17 addresses the acceptable and unacceptable manner for believers to plan for the future. Basically, the point, not unlike the point in 4:3, is that God's should be taken into account. To plan and not consider God is not wise. It insults God, coming across as the epitome of boastful, arrogant selfishness. Though James uses the example of merchants planning to expand their markets, this is an example from which all can learn regarding their own lives and how they look ahead. They need to pray to God for wisdom and ask whether what they are planning will fit in with God's overall plans.

James 5:13–18 emphasizes the power of prayer within the context of a believing community. This power is embodied especially in those who lead the community, but James makes it a point of emphasis that anyone truly devoted to Christ can accomplish amazing things by prayer. When citing Elijah, who stopped and started the rain, as an example of this, Jas 5:17 stipulates that he was a person "just like us" (NIV). Prayer can heal those who are seriously ill (5:14–15). Anointing the sick with oil is mentioned incidentally as a symbol of consecration to the Lord accompanying the prayer.[27] This was a custom of the early church.[28] The emphasis is on the effectiveness of the prayers of those who are devoted to Christ, elders being examples not only of those who represent the whole community and their corporate devotion but also examples of individuals who stand out in their wisdom, experience, and commitment to Christ. However, 5:16 encourages each member of the believing community to be praying on behalf of others in need, mentioning illness specifically, and says that they should expect this to be very effective.

Although the paragraph emphasizes prayer focused on those who are sick, it opens in 5:13 by encouraging believers to pray in all situations. When life is difficult, believers should pray, probably for wisdom as emphasized earlier. But when life is at the other end of the spectrum and they are being blessed by God, they should praise him. The fact that

27. McCartney, *James*, 244–45; Davids, *James*, 194; Moo, *James*, 241.

28. As Moo, *James*, 239, notes, the Western church continued to anoint the sick with oil for centuries until this was designated the sacrament of extreme unction performed by priests in AD 852. This action was based upon this passage and Mark 6:13, where Jesus sends out the twelve to anoint the sick with oil in conjunction with healing them. James demonstrates that the early church followed this instruction of Jesus. James may also be motivated to mention the application of oil because it was a traditional Jewish medicinal remedy for the sick, as McCartney, *James*, 253, notes, and can be seen in Isa 1:6, Jer 8:22, and Luke 10:34. However, Moo, *James*, 242, is on target when he concludes that anointing with oil in 5:14 is intended to picture a "physical action with symbolic significance."

the passage notes that they should "sing songs" suggests what is in mind is some type of corporate community gathering, perhaps for worship.[29]

So, James expects the Christian community to be a praying community. Prayer must be properly motivated toward serving God in the best way possible and not motivated by selfish wants. Prayer should serve the needs of the community, especially those who are hurting. Prayer should recognize the blessings of God in one's life.

CONFESSION

James includes confession as a vital aspect of the Christian community. He does not appear to be introducing a new practice for believers. Rather, he is reinforcing the value of a common practice among Christians. James 5:16 is linked to the last sentence of 5:15 with the inferential conjunction "therefore" (*oun*), indicating that forgiveness of sin in this passage may not be the result of the elders' prayers only but also the result of the person who is ill confessing sin.[30] Confession of sin, then, is advocated in 5:16 as a preventative measure for good health and as a positive spiritual action aiding in the healing of ailments. But it is not just confession that is emphasized. James also encourages Christian communities to practice intercessory prayer for the physical and spiritual well-being of one another. James does not imply that all physical ailments are connected to personal sin but rather that they might be.[31] Thus, regular personal confession and intercessory prayer are both advanced as aiding in the spiritual and physical well-being of believers and of the community as whole.

The long-standing practice in the church of ministers making hospital calls a priority in their ministries extends from this early practice of elders visiting the sick in James. This is an important practice to continue. The focus of the visits should move to the spiritual condition of the patients as much as possible, especially for those who are seriously ill. Perhaps they have a regret they need to share and confess and opportunity should be provided for this to happen. Opportunity for shar-

---

29. McCartney, *James*, 252.

30. Moo, *James*, 205.

31. Davids, *James*, 194. A possible relationship between illness and sin is found also in Mark 2:5; John 5:14; 9:2–3; 1 Cor 11:30. However, John 9:1–5 suggests this is not always the case.

ing intimately with others within the life of the church should also be a priority in line with James's advocacy of mutual confession.

LORDSHIP OF JESUS/BAPTISM

The Epistle of James does not mention baptism specifically. However, it both assumes and specifically reminds believers that they live under the Lordship of Christ. First, James refers to Jesus as Lord twice, directly in 1:1 and 2:1 and by inference in 5:7, 8, 14, and 15.[32] James 2:7 reminds readers that the rich "blaspheme the excellent name that has been invoked over you" (NRSV).[33] In this instance "the name" would certainly refer to the name of "Jesus" to whom they have in some public way committed themselves as Lord. He is now their owner.[34] This phrasing probably refers to his name being formally pronounced over them when they were baptized.[35] This corresponds to the fact that the New Testament converts in Acts are described as being baptized in the "name of Jesus" or in the "name of the Lord Jesus" (Acts 2:38; 8:16; 10:48; 19:5; note also Hermas, *Sim.* 9.16.3). This also makes sense if those who are part of James's community are Jewish. They are not converting from paganism or leaving Judaism. They are identifying with Jesus as the promised Jewish Messiah.

THE SERVICE OF TEACHERS, ELDERS, AND OTHERS

Corresponding to the likelihood that the Epistle of James reflects life in a very early Christian community, the leadership roles depicted are few. Most stressed is the teacher, the role with which the author himself identifies. However, as we have already seen, elders are functioning as well. In addition, all the members of the community are expected to disciple one another if the situation calls for this.

32. Baker, "Christology," 47–57.

33. The NIV has "to whom you belong" and the NASB has "by which you have been called." The Greek phrase is τὸ ἐπικληθὲν ἐφ᾽ ὑμᾶς (*to epiklēthen eph' hymas*). Note the doubled use of ἐπι (*epi*) as a compound with the verb and as a preposition. Taking the accusative, it means "upon" or "over."

34. Johnson, *James*, 226; McCartney, *James*, 143; Moo, *James*, 109; and Wall, *Community of the Wise*, 118, affirm, however, that the ownership being depicted is now of Jesus rather than God (as it would have been for Israel in the Old Testament: 2 Chr 7:14; Isa 43:7; Jer 14:9). These scholars are hesitant to affirm that the situation as described in James assumes a baptismal scene.

35. Davids, *James*, 113; Laws, *James*, 104; Hartin, *James*, 121; and Dibelius, *James*, 141, are more certain that James is assuming a baptismal scene.

All of 3:1–18 is aimed at members of the community who want to be teachers but who need to consider far more deeply what is expected. For James, teachers are not just dispensers of information. They are role models who are to exemplify a life of controlled behavior that engenders peace and harmony in the community.[36] James focuses on control of speech as the most revealing barometer of this quality and devotes most of his comments to the dangers of uncontrolled speech and the enormous difficulty people have in controlling their speech. Those who can do so demonstrate that they are "able to bridle the whole body as well" (3:2, NASB). This does not mean they are sinless but just that they are mature believers. It means also that they may be viewed as among the wise of the community. James 3:13–18 extols this wisdom as amounting to "good behavior," a humble attitude, and peacemaking.

James assumes believing communities will have a number of teachers but is adamant that each one must be qualified. They should also be aware that teachers "will be judged more strictly" (3:1), assuming that God is the judge as in 4:12, and James includes himself in this warning. Nothing more is explained as to why. However, the influence teachers have on the behavior and attitudes of the rest of the community is huge. Poorly behaved teachers can have catastrophic influence on their communities well out of proportion to their numbers.

The Epistle of James describes elders in only one function in the community: ministering to those who are seriously ill (5:14). They are to be available to visit them, pray for their healing, anoint them with oil, and, if needed, encourage confession of sin. As noted previously, the oil is likely a symbol of consecration and not central to the task. The emphasis is on the power of their prayers. How these individuals become elders, or how else they might function in the community, is not mentioned. That elders function as community leaders probably reflects the Jewish context of James, but it is significant that this community structure shows up so early in church history. Were the elders teachers? Probably, but James does not connect the two.

The Epistle of James does not leave all the pastoral care and discipleship to the elders and teachers. The last two verses of the epistle, 5:19–20, are intriguing because they make everyone in the community

---

36. This correlates with the conclusion that James should be viewed as wisdom literature. See Bauckham, *James*, 30–31; Johnson, *James*, 27–28; Perdue, "Paranesis," 250–52.

responsible for the spiritual well-being of the others. If anyone notices a fellow believer "straying from the truth," they are urged to talk to the one straying and find out what is going on. They are to do everything they can to bring that person back into the center of the community. The way they are straying may not be doctrine but lifestyle, given James's accent on behavior throughout the epistle. How are they to bring this person back? Presumably they will do this by going to them, listening, talking, and providing them with good reasons not to remain outside the community of believers.

The Epistle of James, then, provides extensive warning to teachers and potential teachers regarding the seriousness of this role in the church. Likewise, its emphasis on the pastoral role of elders to the sick supports this continuing ministry role in the life of the church. Finally, its provocative last two verses deputize everyone in the church to take action to help those they recognize to be moving away from commitment to Christ and the community. This is not the exclusive responsibility of the leaders. In this way James democratizes serving the church.

CONCLUSION

The author of the Epistle of James is most likely Jesus' brother, writing before AD 49 to believers who had once been part of the Jerusalem church. He does not write out his thoughts about the church in any direct way. However, what he says about other matters reveals a very well formed idea of what the ideal church should be like.

First, the ideal church consists of people who whole-heartedly trust in God. Second, people in the church who are economically challenged develop an even closer spiritual relationship with God. Third, those who are treated unfairly are patient and believe that God will balance the scales one day. Fourth, they treat one another with respect and work toward harmonious relationships among all. Fifth, they live by Jesus' teaching to love their neighbors. Sixth, they develop a deep and ongoing relationship with God that allows them to pray genuinely regarding their needs and the needs of others, both in private and when gathered in community. Seventh, they confess their sins to God regularly, especially when they are in trauma. Eighth, people in the church have pledged publicly their loyalty to Jesus, probably by being baptized. Ninth, teachers control their speech, elders visit the sick, and all believers seek out and disciple fellow-believers who are wavering in their faith for whatever reason.

BIBLIOGRAPHY

Achtemeier, Paul. *1 Peter*. Hermeneia. Minneapolis: Fortress, 1996.

Bauckham, Richard. *James*. New Testament Readings. New York: Routledge, 1999.

Baker, William R. "Christology in the Epistle of James." *EvQ* 74 (2002) 47–58.

———. *Personal Speech-Ethics in the Epistle of James*. WUNT. Tübingen: Mohr Siebeck, 1995.

Brown, Francis, S. R. Driver, and Charles A. Briggs. *Hebrew and English Lexicon of the Old Testament*. Oxford: Clarendon, 1907.

Chester, Andrew, and Ralph Martin. *The Theology of the Letters of James, Peter, and Jude*. New Testament Theology. New York: Cambridge University Press, 1994.

Davids, Peter. *Commentary on James*. NIGTC. Grand Rapids: Zondervan, 1982.

———. *The First Epistle of Peter*. NICNT. Grand Rapids: Eerdmans, 1990.

Dibelius, Martin. *James*. Revised by Heinrich Greeven. Translated by Michael Williams. Hermenia. Philadelphia: Fortress, 1976.

Hartin, Patrick. *James*. SP. Collegeville, MN: Liturgical, 2003.

Jewett, Robert. *Romans*. Hermeneia. Minneapolis: Fortress, 2007.

Jobes, Karen. *1 Peter*. BECNT. Grand Rapids: Baker, 2005.

Johnson, Luke Timothy. *Brother of Jesus, Friend of God*. Grand Rapids: Eerdmans, 2004.

———. *The Letter of James*. AB. New York: Doubleday, 1995.

Laws, Sophie. *A Commentary on the Epistle of James*. London: Adam and Charles Black, 1980.

Luther, Martin. *Luther's Works*. American Edition. 55 vols. Edited by H. T. Lehman. St. Louis: Concordia, 1955–76.

Marshall, Sophie. "Δίψυχος: A Local Term?" *Studia Evangelica* 6 (1973) 348–51.

Massebieau, L. "L'épître de Jacques, est-elle l'oeuvre d'un chrétien?" *RHR* 32 (1895) 249–83.

McCartney, Dan. *James*. BECNT. Grand Rapids; Baker, 2009.

Moo, Douglas. *The Letter of James*. PNTC. Grand Rapids: Eerdmans, 2000.

Perdue, Leo. "Paranesis and the Epistle of James." *ZNW* 72 (1981) 250–52.

Porter, Stanley. "Is *Dipsychos* (James 1:8; 4:8) a 'Christian' Word?" *Bib* 71 (1990) 469–98.

Ropes, J. H. *The Epistle according to St. James*. ICC. Edinburgh: T. & T. Clark, 1916.

Schreiner, Thomas. *New Testament Theology*. Grand Rapids: Baker, 2008.

Spitta, Friedrich. *Der Brief des Jakobus*. Göttingen: Vandenhoeck & Ruprecht, 1895.

Tasker, R. V. G. *General Epistle of James*. TNTC. Grand Rapids: Eerdmans, 1957.

Wall, Robert. *Community of the Wise: The Letter of James*. Valley Forge, PA: Trinity Press International, 1997.

12

Called to Be Holy

Ecclesiology in the Petrine Epistles

ALLEN BLACK

FIRST PETER

IN RECENT YEARS 1 Peter has begun to receive the attention from scholarship that it richly deserves.[1] This short book of five chapters is one of the most powerful books in the New Testament.[2] It addresses Christians in ancient Asia Minor who were suffering for their faith and seeks to encourage them in holiness and good deeds as they interact within their households (often led by non-Christians), within their Christian communities, and within the hostile society around them.

First Peter's Pastoral Purpose

Peter sums up the book's purpose in 5:12: "Through Silvanus, whom I consider a faithful brother, I have written this short letter to encourage you and to testify that this is the true grace of God. Stand fast in it."[3]

1. See the survey of scholarship in Horrell, *1 Peter.*

2. Luther. *Peter and Jude*, 10, described 1 Peter as "one of the grandest [letters] of the New Testament, and it is the true, pure gospel." Marshall, *1 Peter*, 12, says, "if one were to be shipwrecked on a desert island and allowed to have only one of the New Testament letters as a companion, then 1 Peter would be the ideal choice, so rich is its teaching, so warm its spirit, and so comforting its message in a hostile environment."

3. All citations are from the NRSV unless otherwise indicated. I accept the letter's

226

He writes in the sixties of the first century to persecuted Christians to encourage them to stand firm in their faith.[4] Earlier interpreters often thought of this persecution as state sponsored, but there are no references in the book to state sponsorship. There are, however, references to severe trials: for example, 1:6 "even if now for a little while you have had to suffer various trials," and 4:12 "do not be surprised at the fiery ordeal that is taking place among you to test you." The book of Acts and the letters of Paul provide examples of the kinds of persecution Peter may have had in mind. Many of the persecutions Peter speaks of seem to have been social: 2:12 "they malign you as evildoers" or 3:16 "when you are maligned, those who abuse you for your good conduct in Christ." These attitudes may be illustrated by the comments of Tacitus who described Christians as "a class hated for their abominations" and called Christianity "a deadly superstition . . . hideous and shameful"; by Suetonius, who described Christians as "a class of men given to a new and wicked superstition"; or by Pliny, the Roman governor of Bithynia, who described Christianity as "a perverse and extravagant superstition."[5] Peter wrote for Christians who found it difficult to be faithful, and he sought to build them up.

First Peter's contributions to New Testament ecclesiology emerge in the context of this pastoral purpose. It is due to its pastoral purpose that 1 Peter makes major contributions to a biblical theology of the church. John Elliott, perhaps the pre-eminent 1 Peter scholar of our time, strikingly states: "In fact, even though the term *ekklēsia* ("assembly," "church") itself is not used in 1 Peter, this letter is one of the most ecclesiological writings of the New Testament."[6] The reason for this is that Peter sees *community* as a central feature in his effort to encourage

---

claim to be written by Peter the apostle, perhaps with Silvanus serving as an amanuensis. For arguments for and against these conclusions see Michaels, *1 Peter*, lxii–lxvi; and Feldmeier, *First Letter*, 32–39.

4. A date in the sixties is almost universally accepted among those who accept apostolic authorship, although Michaels, *1 Peter*, lvii–lxi, argues that Peter lived into the eighties.

5. Tacitus, *Annals* 15.44.2–8; Suetonius, *Life of Nero* 16.2; Pliny, *Epistle* 10.96. For translations and discussions of all three texts, see Ferguson, *Backgrounds*, 593–95. See the excellent discussion of the situation of 1 Peter by Feldmeier, *First Letter*, 3–13.

6. Elliott, *Conflict, Community, and Honor*, 42. Cf. Achtemeier, *1 Peter*, 36: "Although the word ἐκκλησία is absent from the text of our letter, it is clear from the letter's contents that the Christian community is of central importance."

these Christians to stand firm in a society in which they are estranged and mistreated. As Elliott observes, "In the response and strategy of 1 Peter, the stress upon community is a major one."[7] It is as a community of faith that they can persevere.

Images of the Church in 1 Peter

Peter's ecclesiological contribution appears fundamentally in a set of images, predominantly metaphors, that he uses to portray the church. These images may be divided according to whether they emphasize the community's (1) relationship with God, (2) internal relationships with each other, or (3) external relationship to the surrounding culture.

IMAGES OF THE CHURCH'S RELATIONSHIP TO GOD

The images that emphasize the community's relationship with God include the church as the elect, the called, God's people, God's flock, the priesthood, the temple, and the reborn. The first word Peter uses in the Greek text to describe his recipients is the word *eklektos*, "chosen" or "elect," which is then modified at the beginning of v. 2 with the phrases "according to the foreknowledge of God the Father, by the sanctifying work of the Spirit, to obey Jesus Christ and be sprinkled with his blood."[8] Peter's readers are portrayed as a community selected by God, set apart by the Spirit, and sprinkled by the blood of Christ. All of this setting apart is said to lead to obedience to Jesus Christ. Peter does not speak here of an individualistic election, but of a corporate one.[9] The idea of the church as the community of the elect surfaces again in 1 Pet 2:4, 9–10; and 5:13. Just as Peter says in the greeting that election leads to obedience, in 2:9 he says that being a "chosen race" should lead them to "proclaim the mighty acts of him who has called you out of darkness into his marvelous light." And in 2:4–5 a similar point is made if one reads the verb for "building up" in v. 5 as an imperative, as in the NRSV, so that the point is that the chosen ones should "*let [them]selves be built into a spiritual house, to be a holy priesthood, to offer spiritual sacrifices acceptable to God through Jesus Christ.*" Peter is appealing to the readers to recognize their chosen status and to let it affect the way they live.

---

7. Elliott, *Conflict, Community, and Honor*, 42.

8. NASB95.

9. Witherington, *1–2 Peter*, 68.

Closely related to the concept of election is the notion of being called (from *kaleō*; 1 Pet 1:15; 2:9, 21; 3:9; 5:10). First Peter 2:9 clearly brings these concepts together: "But you are a *chosen* race, a royal priesthood, a holy nation, God's own people, in order that you may proclaim the mighty acts of him who *called* you out of darkness into his marvelous light." As in the case of those who are elect or chosen, Peter emphasizes that those whom God has called are called for a purpose: "as he who called you is holy, be holy yourselves in all your conduct" (1:15); "in order that you may proclaim the mighty acts of him who called you out of darkness into his marvelous light" (2:9); "For to this you have been called, because Christ also suffered for you, leaving you an example, so that you should follow in his steps" (2:21); "Do not repay evil for evil or abuse for abuse; but, on the contrary, repay with a blessing. It is for this that you were called" (3:9).

The notions of election and calling are important elements in 1 Peter's ecclesiology. The church is a body of people chosen and called by God. As such it must be holy; it must be obedient to Christ; it must proclaim the mighty acts of God; it must offer spiritual sacrifices; it must be willing to suffer. It was called for these purposes, and it has the ultimate chosen One as its example (1 Pet 1:17–21; 2:21-25; 3:17—4:2). These portraits of the community are used to stir the community to faithfulness.

First Peter 2:9-10 is rich in metaphorical description of the Christian community. It is arguable that the keys to these verses and to much of the imagery in 1 Peter are the images in v. 9 of "a chosen race" and "God's own people," along with what Peter says in 2:10, with its allusion to Hosea: "Once you were not a people, but now you are God's people." These statements apply to Peter's Christian, predominantly Gentile, readers, language formerly reserved for Israel. From 1:1 to the implication of the reference to Babylon in 5:13, Peter transfers the imagery of Israel to his readers.[10] The Christian community in Asia Minor is now the Diaspora (1:1), which is under the rule of Babylon (5:13). They are now God's "chosen race" (2:9) and "God's people" (2:9-10). As I observed above, they are now the elect, the chosen ones,

---

10. One modern scholar who thinks Peter writes for a predominantly Jewish Christian audience is Witherington, *1-2 Peter*, 24-25. Most modern scholars believe the audience is predominantly Gentile, including Horrell, *1 Peter*, 47-48, and Michaels, *1 Peter*, xlv–xlvi.

of God. Achtemeier is so impressed by use of the language of Israel for the Christian community that he argues "Israel as a totality has become for this letter the controlling metaphor in terms of which its theology is expressed."[11] Once again, Peter's purpose is pastoral. As the chosen race, as God's own people, as those who were not a people but are now God's people, who had not received mercy, but have now received mercy, Peter's readers are called to "proclaim the mighty acts of him who called you out of darkness and into his marvelous light" (2:9), "to abstain from the desires of the flesh that wage war against the soul" (2:11), and "to conduct [them]selves honorably among the Gentiles" (2:12).

Another image Peter uses for the Christian community in relationship to God is that of a flock of sheep. In 2:25 he says "you were going astray like sheep, but now you have returned to the shepherd and guardian of your souls."[12] In 5:2–3 he encourages elders to "tend the flock of God that is in your charge . . . be examples to the flock." And in 5:4 he speaks of Christ as "the chief shepherd." Of course this imagery of God's people as a flock of sheep is common in the Old Testament.[13] It is used there, as it is used in 1 Peter, to comfort God's people and to exhort those who are in charge of shepherding them. It is another case of Peter taking the language of Israel and using it to build up the Christian community.

In 1 Pet 2:9 Peter also applies another metaphor to the church that had been used for Israel. He declares the church to be "a royal priesthood" (basileion hierateuma). It has been argued that the adjective "royal" should be translated as a noun so that we get two descriptions, "a royal residence, a priestly community." However, this view destroys the parallelism between "a royal priesthood" and the preceding and following phrases in the series in v. 9: "a chosen race" (genos eklekton) and "a holy nation" (ethnos hagion), both of which contain a noun and an adjective. Furthermore, the phrase "a royal priesthood," followed as it is by "a holy nation," is clearly based on the LXX of Exod 19:6: "And you shall be for me a royal priesthood and a holy nation" (. . . basileion hierateuma kai ethnos hagion).[14] This is what God said to Israel at Sinai and in 1 Peter those descriptions are transferred to the Christians of Asia Minor. A royal priesthood is a priesthood in service to the king. In 2:5 Peter

11. Achtemeier, 1 Peter, 69.

12. Cf. Isa 53:6, "All we like sheep have gone astray."

13. E.g., Ps 23; 28:9; 78:52; Isa 40:11; Jer 13:17; 50:6; Ezek 34:6–8, 31; Mic 7:14.

14. Pietersma and Wright, Septuagint; Rahlfs and Hanhart, Septuaginta.

describes his readers as a "holy priesthood" (*hierateuma hagion*), who are to "offer spiritual sacrifices acceptable to God through Christ Jesus."

It has been a common Protestant doctrine that Peter's teaching about Christians being a priesthood supports the idea of the priesthood of every believer as opposed to the designation of certain individuals as priests. Although there is no New Testament warrant for a separate Christian priesthood, this use of the two verses commonly cited in 1 Peter may be questioned because of their Old Testament roots. When God declared the nation of Israel a "royal priesthood" in Exod 19:6 he did not thereby designate each Israelite a priest in such a way as to rule out a specially designated priesthood. Peter is reiterating the same language in a similar manner.[15] He is declaring the Christian community to be a priesthood in a corporate sense.

As a royal priesthood Peter's readers are to serve their king, who is Christ. As a holy priesthood they are "to offer spiritual sacrifices acceptable to God through Jesus Christ" (v. 5), a metaphor for a holy and sacrificial life. Feldmeier rightly observes that the idea of speaking of sacrifices in a spiritual sense is already present in the Old Testament, e.g., Ps 51:17 ("The sacrifice acceptable to God is a broken spirit") and Ps 141:2 ("Let my prayer be counted as incense before you, and the lifting up of my hands as an evening sacrifice.")[16]

All of these images and metaphors for relationship to God are tied together by the idea of transferring the language of Israel to the church: the Christians are now the elect, the called, God's people, God's flock, and a royal/holy priesthood. One other image also comes from a similar transferal, but is not used metaphorically in the same way in the Old Testament: the spiritual house metaphor introduced in 2:4. Elliott sees this metaphor as the controlling metaphor for 1 Peter's ecclesiology.[17] In 2:4–8 it is introduced in the context of the stone imagery, found in other portions of the New Testament but usually with a Christological application (e.g., Mark 12:10–11; Acts 4:11; Rom 9:33; cf. Eph 2:19–22). The Christological application observes that Christ is the headstone or cornerstone. Peter extends this metaphor in a manner similar to Eph 2:19–22 to state that Christians are the other stones that make up the building

15. Cf. Achtemeier, *1 Peter*, 165.

16. Feldmeier, *First Letter*, 136 n. 6. Cf. also his references to 1QS IX, 3–5; X, 6; 4QFlor III, 6–7.

17. Elliott, *1 Peter*, 418.

that is God's "spiritual house" (2:5). It is a matter of debate whether Peter is speaking of a metaphorical temple or simply the household, that is, (although the modern connotations may be misleading) the family of God. But the references to the priests and sacrifices suggest Peter has the temple in mind.[18] The house where the priests offer their sacrifices is the temple. Peter says that Christians are metaphorically stones in God's temple, and as such they must be holy.[19]

The house metaphor is taken up again in 4:17, where a reference to the temple is again likely.[20] The Old Testament frequently portrays judgment beginning at the temple (see especially Ezek 9:6; also Mal 3:1–5). The notion that these Christians were living stones in the spiritual house of God is used to build them up and encourage them to faithful service. In 4:17 it is used as a warning concerning judgment: "the time has come for judgment to begin with the household [that is, temple] of God."

One metaphor Peter exploits for the community's relationship with God that does not have its roots in Israel and the Old Testament is the metaphor of new birth.[21] This metaphor is found elsewhere in the New Testament (John 3:3–5; 2 Cor 5:17; Titus 3:5–6; 1 John 3:9; 5:1–4). In 1:3–5 Peter blesses God for giving the readers a "new birth" into a living hope and an inheritance that is kept in heaven. In 1:23 he reminds them that they have been "born anew" through the word of God. And in 2:2 he urges them to act like "newborn infants" and long for the pure, spiritual milk that leads to salvation.

Peter uses this image to urge his readers on to faithful living. The living hope and inheritance of 1:3–5 and the following verses lead to the exhortations to holiness and faithfulness beginning in 1:13. First Peter 1:23 provides the warrant for the exhortations of 1:22 ("love one another deeply from the heart") and of 2:1 ("Rid yourselves, therefore, of all malice, and all guilt, insincerity, envy, and all slander"). And 2:2 provides warrant and design for longing for the pure, spiritual milk. The imagery

---

18. See the arguments given by Achtemeier, *1 Peter*, 158–59. The chief proponent of simply "house(hold)" is Elliott, *1 Peter*, 414–18.

19. In the Old Testament Israel is not called a temple, but Best, *1 Peter*, 102, argues that the Qumran community viewed itself as a new temple.

20. Achtemeier, *1 Peter*, 315–16.

21. Feldmeier, *First Letter*, 127, does find the new birth metaphor in Hellenistic Judaism: Philo, QE II,46, and Asenath's conversion to Judaism in *Jos. Asen.* 8.11.

of new birth continues to be one of the most powerful metaphors for a large sector of modern Christianity (i.e., evangelicalism).

AN IMAGE OF INTERNAL RELATIONSHIPS IN THE CHURCH

If we turn our attention to relationships within the Christian community, Peter basically uses one metaphor, that of being brothers and sisters in a family. This image appears in 1 Pet 1:22 ("so that you have a sincere love for your brothers"), 2:17 ("Love the brotherhood of believers"), 3:8 ("love as brothers"), 5:9 ("your brothers throughout the world are undergoing the same kinds of suffering"), and 5:12 (Silas, whom I regard as a faithful brother").[22] As the NIV translation clarifies, Peter expresses this notion with what his culture regarded as a generic use of male terminology, a usage that does not communicate in the same way in English in many circles today. But the basic idea of the fictional kinship should not be lost, as it is in translations such as "so that you have sincere love for each other" (1:22), "love your fellow believers" (2:17), or "your fellow believers throughout the world are undergoing the same kind of sufferings" (5:9).[23] For Peter, the notion of using familial imagery is an important part of encouraging the faith and holiness of his readers. The "kiss of love" encouraged in 5:14 may also be a part of this familial imagery, since this kiss was "normally practiced within the family."[24]

Peter does not use a variety of metaphors to describe the relationships within the Christian communities of Asia Minor, but in a situation of persecution, strengthening internal relationships in the churches is a significant aspect of the letter. Every chapter contains exhortations emphasizing aspects of Christians' relationships to each other, such as mutual love, humility, service, and hospitality:

> Now that you have purified your souls by your obedience to the truth so that you have genuine mutual love (NIV: love for your brothers), love one another deeply from the heart. (1:22)

22. NIV.

23. TNIV. The NRSV has better gender neutral alternatives for 2:17 ("Love the family of believers") and 5:9 ("your brothers and sisters in all the world are undergoing the same kinds of suffering").

24 Achtemeier, *1 Peter*, 355–56, "The employment of such a kiss, normally practiced within the family, but also as a gesture of greeting between friends, served to emphasize the point that all Christians were to regard themselves as members of the Christian family."

Rid yourselves, therefore, of all malice, and all guile, insincerity, envy, and all slander. (2:1)

Love the family of believers. (2:17)

Finally, all of you, have unity of spirit, sympathy, love for one another (NIV: love as brothers), a tender heart, and a humble mind. (3:8)

Above all, maintain constant love for one another, for love covers a multitude of sins. Be hospitable to one another without complaining. Like good stewards of the manifold grace of God, serve one another with whatever gift each of you has received. (4:8–10)

And all of you must clothe yourselves with humility in your dealings with one another, for "God opposes the proud, but gives grace to the humble." (5:5)

In churches that are embattled from the surrounding culture, it is vital that these Christians come together in love and support each other. So Peter constantly reiterates this theme.

IMAGES OF THE CHURCH IN RELATIONSHIP TO THE WORLD

The third area of consideration, that of relationships to the surrounding culture, is vitally important to Peter since he is writing to encourage these believers in a situation of suffering at the hands of that culture. Here the basic metaphor is "foreignness."[25] Returning to the opening lines of 1 Peter, we find the next two Greek words after "chosen" are related metaphorical descriptions that Troy Martin believes form the controlling metaphor of 1 Peter.[26] The first of these two words, *parepidēmoi*, may be translated "strangers in the world"[27] or "exiles."[28] The second, *diaspora*, may be translated "scattered"[29] or, more technically "Dispersion,"[30] to show that it was a technical term among the Jews that referred to Jews who were scattered outside of Palestine (cf. John 7:35). The concepts are overlapping in sense because both were used to refer to people who were away from their homeland. Similar thoughts occur in 1:17 ("live in rev-

---

25 On the use of the word "foreignness" see especially Feldmeier, *First Letter*, 13–17.

26. Martin, *Metaphor and Composition*, 144.

27. NIV. This paraphrastic translation brings out the term's metaphorical meaning.

28. NRSV.

29. NIV.

30. NRSV.

erent fear during the time of your exile [*paroikia*]") and 2:11 ("Beloved, I urge you as aliens [*paroikoi*] and exiles [*parepidēmoi*] to abstain from the desires of the flesh that wage war against the soul"). All three terms—exile, alien, and Dispersion—refer to people who are living as foreigners. The traditional understanding of these terms is that Peter is describing Christians as "strangers in the world" (the NIV translation) because their true citizenship is in heaven (cf. Phil 3:20).

This understanding has been challenged by John Elliott, who has been followed by a number of others. Elliott argues that in 2:11 "aliens" [*paroikoi*] refers to "the stranger who resides longer or permanently in a place different from that of his or her origin and hence is a *resident alien*," but "exiles"[31] [*parepidēmoi*] refers to "the *temporary visitor*, the *transient* stranger who, as a traveler passing through, has no intention or opportunity to establish permanent residence."[32] He takes these terms as applying literally to some of the believers in Asia Minor. Then, "[t]he experience of many as actual strangers and resident aliens provided an existential basis for the depiction of all believers as strangers and resident aliens in a metaphorical sense."[33] These terms are thus literally true of some Christians in Asia Minor and metaphorically of all. But Elliott denies that the metaphor is understood by Peter in what he calls a "cosmological" sense, that is, that Christians are strangers on earth because their home is in heaven. He says that for Peter it is purely a "social" metaphor of not having a home in Greco-Roman society.[34]

Elliott's distinction between "aliens" [*paroikoi*] and "exiles" [*parepidēmoi*] is questionable. In v. 1 the term *parepidēmoi* alone is used, and in 1:17 *paroikia* is used alone, both seemingly referring to all of Peter's addressees. In addition, the background of the LXX texts in which Abraham and David call themselves both "an alien" (*paroikos*) and "an exile" (*parepidēmos*) using exactly these terms (Gen 23:4; Ps 38:13 = MT Ps 39:12) suggests that Peter is not making a significant distinction between these two words.[35] But this is not the major problem with Elliott's position.

---

31. Elliott, *1 Peter*, 312–13, does not accept the word "exile" as a suitable translation of the Greek term.

32. Ibid., 458–59.

33. Ibid., 482.

34. Ibid.

35. Chin, "Heavenly Home," 110.

The major issue concerns whether the traditional understanding of 1 Peter is correct, that he envisions a "cosmological" metaphor that Christians are strangers in the world because they belong elsewhere. Certainly there are other New Testament texts that use this foreignness theme metaphorically of Christians living in exile on earth away from their home in heaven. The clearest such text is Heb 11:13–16:

> All of these died in faith without having received the promises, but from a distance they saw and greeted them. They confessed that they were strangers and foreigners (*parepidēmoi*) on the earth, for people who speak in this way make it clear that they are seeking a homeland. If they had been thinking of the land that they had left behind, they would have had opportunity to return. But as it is, they desire a better country, that is, a heavenly one. Therefore God is not ashamed to be called their God; indeed, he has prepared a city for them.

In Hebrews the idea is that the Old Testament faithful were metaphorically exiles on the earth in the sense that their homeland was "a heavenly one." James 1:1 uses the Dispersion idea metaphorically to describe his Christian readership: "James, a servant of God and of the Lord Jesus Christ, to the twelve tribes in the Dispersion." The idea of heaven as the Christian's real home is found (without the term exile or alien) in Phil 3:20: "But our citizenship is in heaven and it is from there that we are expecting a Savior, the Lord Jesus Christ." A second-century example of the use of *paroikos* in a metaphorical manner is found in an excerpt from Diognetus 5.5: "They live in their own countries, but only as aliens (*paroikoi*)."[36]

First Peter does not make a metaphorical meaning for "exiles," "aliens," and "Dispersion" unquestionable in the manner of Hebrews or Diognetus—therefore the modern debate has arisen.[37] However, the traditional (and probably still the majority) view[38] that Peter is using these terms as spiritual metaphors for those whose homeland is heaven still seems the most appropriate in the light of Hebrews, Paul, and early Christian usage. This understanding of 1:1 fits well with 1:3–4, which focuses on the "homeland" these exiles await while living in their cur-

---

36. Ibid., 109.

37. Primarily brought about by the work of John H. Elliott.

38. So, e.g., Michaels, *1 Peter*, 116; Achtemeier, *1 Peter*, 223–24; Best, *1 Peter*, 110; Chin, "Heavenly Home," 110–12.

rent Dispersion: "By his great mercy he has given us a new birth into a living hope through the resurrection of Jesus Christ from the dead, and into an inheritance that is imperishable, undefiled, and unfading, kept in heaven for you."

Peter's purpose in framing his readers' lives as lives of *exile as aliens in a Diaspora* is to help them to live faithfully in the face of suffering. In 1:17 he says, "If you invoke as Father the one who judges all people impartially according to their deeds, live in reverent fear during the time of your exile." They are to remember that in their homeland they have a Father who will judge both them and those who now mistreat them. They are to fear this Father, not their current opponents. And in 2:11–12 he says,

> Beloved, I urge you as aliens and exiles to abstain from the desires of the flesh that wage war against the soul. Conduct yourselves honorably among the Gentiles, so that, though they malign you as evildoers, they may see your honorable deeds and glorify God when he comes to judge.

They are to maintain holiness and not succumb to those desires that will take them off the path to their homeland, and they are to conduct themselves in such a way as to lead to the conversion of their opponents, that they too may rejoice at the coming of the Father.

Baptism and Church Leadership

Beyond all of these images, 1 Peter makes contributions to ecclesiology with comments on baptism and on church leadership. In a brief but significant statement about baptism, Peter makes a type-antitype comparison between Noah's ark in which a few were saved through water and baptism that now saves believers. But he is clear that he does not have in mind salvation by removing dirt from the body, but by the *eperōtēma* of a good conscience toward God. What is more difficult is what Peter means by an *eperōtēma*. The NIV translates this as "the pledge of a good conscience toward God."[39] The NRSV translates it as "an appeal to God for a good conscience."[40] As Schreiner suggests, the emphasis on receiving salvation through baptism in the immediate context probably favors

---

39. Achtemeier, *1 Peter*, 269–72.

40. Schreiner, *1, 2 Peter, Jude*, 195–97. Both Achtemeier and Schreiner have excellent discussions of the alternatives.

the NRSV approach and the notion that "believers at baptism ask God—on the basis of the death and resurrection of Christ—to cleanse their conscience and forgive their sins."[41]

First Peter 5:1–5 addresses elders whom Peter instructs to "shepherd" and "oversee" the churches in Asia Minor. He indicates that they had significant authority in the churches ("exercising the oversight" v. 2; the warning "do not lord it over those in your charge" v. 3). He may also imply some were paid for their service ("not for sordid gain" v. 3). Peter's exhortations to elders are also a part of his pastoral purpose in connection with the sufferings of the churches in Asia Minor. This is highlighted by the "therefore" (*oun*) at the beginning of 5:1, which connects his exhortation to the comments about suffering that precede it.[42] It is in view of these circumstances that these churches need this kind of leadership at this time.

SECOND PETER

Second Peter addresses an entirely different set of circumstances. Peter wrote it in anticipation of his death, presumably in the mid sixties.[43] He is no longer addressing an occasion of persecution, but rather one involving the rise of heresy. The threat is not from without, but from within. It is the rise of false teaching and immoral living by those who still share in the feasts of the Christian community (2:13).

Nearly all scholars believe that 3:1, "This is now, beloved, the second letter I am writing to you," refers back to 1 Peter and therefore indicates that 2 Peter is written to the same audience as 1 Peter.[44] However, Davids rightly suggests that "the hypothesis of the same readership has to assume itself to establish itself."[45] Without the presumption of a late first/early second century pseudepigrapher, there is not a compelling

---

41. Schreiner, *1, 2 Peter, Jude*, 197.

42. The NRSV misses the point in translating *oun* as "now" and the NIV leaves it out altogether. See the NASB95: "Therefore, I exhort the elders among you . . ."

43. For substantial reasons, more scholars consider 2 Peter pseudepigraphical than any other New Testament letter in which the author is named in the greeting. However, I ultimately agree with Gene Green that "we may reasonably affirm that Simeon Peter, the apostle, authored the book" (150). See his discussion in *Jude and 2 Peter*, 139–50. Cf. also the even-handed discussion in Davids, *2 Peter and Jude*, 123–30, 145–49.

44. See, e.g., the list in Schreiner, *1, 2 Peter, Jude*, 369 n. 7.

45. Davids, *2 Peter and Jude*, 259.

argument that the letter referred to in 3:1 should be 1 Peter rather than a lost letter written to whatever group Peter is writing in 2 Peter. The audience of 2 Peter is uncertain.

The contribution of 2 Peter to ecclesiology is not nearly as significant as that of its counterpart. There is a small overlap. Second Peter 1:3 declares that the community has been called (*kaleō)* by God and 1:10 speaks of the community's calling (*klēsis*) and election (*eklogē*), using cognates of the terms used in 1 Peter. Peter is still concerned about how these concepts work out in godly living (1:4–9), one of the major emphases of 2 Peter.

He also continues to use the idea of fictional kinship to describe relationships in the Christian community: Christians are brothers and sisters in a family. Second Peter 1:7 encourages the faithful to "brotherly kindness" (*philadelphia*).[46] In 1:10 he exhorts his audience as "brothers and sisters" (*adelphoi*) and in 3:15 he speaks of Paul as "our beloved brother Paul."

The Threat of False Teaching

Peter's concern for the community in 2 Peter is primarily expressed over against the false teaching that threatens it. The nature of the false teaching is notoriously difficult to define. Peter excoriates them for both doctrinal and moral issues. Second Peter 2:1 describes the opponents as "false teachers . . . [who] . . . secretly introduce destructive heresies . . ."[47] The primary doctrinal error Peter emphasizes is their scoffing concerning the second coming (3:3–6, 9). Their moral problems can be characterized by words like "licentiousness," "lawlessness," "unrighteousness," and "ungodliness." Specifically, we find references to "their licentious ways" (2:2), "the ungodly" (2:5, 6), "the licentiousness of the lawless" (2:7), "their lawless deeds" (2:8), "the unrighteous" (2:9), "the godless" (3:7, the same word translated "ungodly" in 2:5–6), and "the lawless" (3:17). Specific sins Peter designates include greed (2:3, 14–15), arrogance (2:10, 12), and sexual immorality (2:10, 14).

It is problematic to associate these heretics with any known group. The idea that the heretics are Gnostics does not have as many proponents now as in the past, with good reason since 2 Peter's opponents do

---

46. The NIV translation. The NRSV's "mutual affection" loses the kinship dimension.
47. NIV.

not demonstrate a cosmic dualism, and Gnostic systems did not promote skepticism toward the second coming based on its delay.[48] Perhaps the most popular recent suggestion is Neyrey's proposal that these heretics find their roots in Epicureanism.[49] It is true that there is some similarity between popular (ancient and modern) (mis)conceptions of Epicureanism and the heresy of 2 Peter. The Epicurean denial of divine judgment was believed to lead to flagrant immorality.[50] One could argue that in a similar fashion the heretics' denial of the second coming and the judgment to follow led to a flagrant immorality. However, such beliefs need not necessarily be tied to Epicureanism *per se* and the Epicureans would not endorse a doctrine of creation (cf. 2 Pet 3:4).[51] All links to any known group are tenuous.

A Call to Godliness

Regardless of our inability to specifically define the false teachers, for Peter the key issue is that in contrast to the heretics the community must be godly (1:3, 6–7; 2:8, 11) and righteous (2:5, 7, 8, 21) because Christ is coming back and God will exercise judgment and reward the godly and punish the ungodly (3:7–14; cf. 2:3–10, 12–13, 21). In 2 Peter this ecclesiological call for godliness is not a matter of dealing with outside forces as in 1 Peter. It is a matter of resisting the false teachers within the Christian community, those who had "escaped the defilements of the world through the knowledge of our Lord and Savior Jesus Christ" (2:20) and "known the way of righteousness" (2:21), but have now "turn[ed] back from the holy commandment that was passed on to them" (2:21) as "The dog turns back to its own vomit" or "The sow is washed only to wallow in the mud" (2:22). And yet these persons are still present in the

---

48. Bauckham, *Jude, 2 Peter*, 156–57.

49. Neyrey, *2 Peter, Jude*, 122–28. Those sympathetic to Neyrey include Bauckham, *Jude, 2 Peter*, 156; Horrell, *Peter and Jude*, 139.

50. E.g., Lactantius, *Divine Institutions* 3.17, as cited by Neyrey, *2 Peter, Jude*, 123–24: "If any chieftain of pirates or leader of robbers were exhorting his men to acts of violence, what other language could he employ than to say the same things which Epicurus says: that the gods take no notice; that they are not affected with anger or kind feeling; that the punishment of a future state is not to be dreaded, because the souls die after death, and there is no future state of punishment at all." Green, *Jude and 2 Peter*, 157, observes that Lactantius and others reflect popular viewpoints and not true Epicurean doctrine.

51. Green, *Jude and 2 Peter*, 156–57.

community's feasts (2:13) and are enticing others into their beliefs and lifestyles (2:14). Peter reveals a lack of ecumenicity toward this group of so-called brothers and sisters. He is more interested in maintaining the holiness and godliness of the church.

Peter's reference to the heretics "reveling in their dissipation while they feast with you" certainly refers to meals eaten together in the ancient church and possibly meals that were in the context of the Lord's Supper.[52] In a parallel text Jude 12 describes the meals they share as "love feasts." First Corinthians 11 indicates that the Lord's Supper was eaten in the context of a meal. But the information in 2 Peter and Jude is scant. We only know that the heretics were blemishes on the community meals.

CONCLUSION: HOLINESS AND GODLINESS IN GOD'S FAMILY

Neither of Peter's two letters uses the word church. However, both of them, especially the first, contribute to the ecclesiology of the New Testament. Both treat the church as a community of people chosen and called by God to live in holiness (especially 1 Peter) and godliness (especially 2 Peter). First Peter issues this call against the pressures of pagan forces outside the community, 2 Peter against heretical forces within. Both summon the community to relate to one another as members of a fictional family. First Peter expands the description of the community's relationship to God to include many images that once belonged to Israel. They are now God's people, God's flock, the priesthood, and the temple. They are also those who have been born again into a new life through God's word. In relationship to the surrounding culture they are described in metaphors of foreignness: exiles, the Dispersion, and aliens. Heaven is their homeland. Peter refers briefly to feasts (2 Pet 2:13) and provides some significant information about baptism (1 Pet 3:20–21) and elders (1 Pet 5:1–5) in early Christianity. But his greatest contributions to New Testament ecclesiology are the great metaphors he provides as sustaining images for the church. These images have power to continue to inspire the contemporary church to greater levels of holiness and godliness.

52. Ibid.

BIBLIOGRAPHY

Achtemeier, Paul J. *1 Peter*. Hermeneia. Minneapolis: Fortress, 1996.

Bauckham, Richard J. *Jude, 2 Peter*. WBC 50. Waco, TX: Word, 1983.

Best, Ernest. *1 Peter*. NCBC. Grand Rapids: Eerdmans, 1982.

Chin, Moses. "A Heavenly Home for the Homeless: Aliens and Strangers in 1 Peter." *TynBul* 42 (1991) 96–112.

Davids, Peter H. *The Letters of 2 Peter and Jude*. PNTC. Grand Rapids: Eerdmans, 2006.

Elliott, John H. *1 Peter*. AB 37B. New York: Doubleday, 2000.

————. *Conflict, Community, and Honor: 1 Peter in Social-Scientific Perspective*. Eugene, OR: Cascade, 2007.

Feldmeier, Reinhard. *The First Letter of Peter*. Translated by Peter H. Davids. Waco, TX: Baylor University Press, 2008.

Ferguson, Everett. *Backgrounds of Early Christianity*. 3rd ed. Grand Rapids: Eerdmans, 2003.

Green, Gene L. *Jude and 2 Peter*. BECNT. Grand Rapids: Baker Academic, 2008.

Horrell, David G. *1 Peter*. New Testament Guides. London: T. & T. Clark, 2008.

Luther, Martin. *Commentary on Peter and Jude* [1523]. Edited by John N. Lender. Grand Rapids: Kregel, 1990.

Marshall, Howard I. *1 Peter*. IVPNTC. Downers Grove, IL: InterVarsity, 1991.

Martin, Troy W. *Metaphor and Composition in 1 Peter*. SBLDS 131. Atlanta: Scholars, 1992.

Michaels, J. Ramsey. *1 Peter*. WBC 49. Waco, TX: Word, 1988.

Neyrey, Jerome H. *2 Peter, Jude*. AB 37C. New York: Doubleday, 1993.

Pietersma, Albert, and Wright, Benjamin G. *A New English Translation of the Septuagint*. New York: Oxford University Press, 2007.

Rahlfs, Alfred, and Robert Hanhart. *Septuaginta*. Revised ed. Stuttgart: Deutsche Bibelgesellschaft, 2006.

Schreiner, Thomas R. *1, 2 Peter, Jude*. NAC 37. Nashville: Broadman and Holman, 2003.

Witherington, Ben III. *Letters and Homilies for Hellenized Christians*. Vol. 2. *A Socio-Rhetorical Commentary on 1–2 Peter*. Downers Grove, IL: InterVarsity, 2008.

13

The Church in the Apocalypse of John

OLUTOLA K. PETERS

THE LITERATURE THAT ABOUNDS on the nature, character, and function of the church (ecclesiology) inappropriately exhibits an overwhelming concentration on the Gospels and the letters almost to the exclusion of the Apocalypse of John. This might suggest that the Apocalypse of John has nothing to contribute to current discussion on ecclesiology. This is clearly not the case.[1] In fact, the author of the Apocalypse is vitally concerned with what the recipients, namely, the seven churches of Asia Minor, are called to be and do.[2]

Several attempts have been made to identify and discuss particular issues, themes, images, and motifs that point to the nature and function of these churches. This is evident especially in commentaries with an emphasis that attempts to make the message of the Apocalypse of John relevant to the contemporary church.[3] It is also obvious in some of the journal articles that address the character, experience, and destiny of the church in the Apocalypse of John. Notable articles in this regard include

1. It is important to note that the most common word for "church" in the New Testament, ἐκκλησία, appears twenty times in the Apocalypse, nineteen times in the first three chapters and once in the closing chapter. All twenty occurrences of ἐκκλησία in the Apocalypse point to a community or fellowship of believers gathered together in a particular locality.

2. I give ample evidence of this in my book: Peters, *Mandate of the Church*.

3. To mention a few, Caird, *Revelation*; Beasley-Murray, *Revelation*; Mounce, *Revelation*; and Beale, *Revelation*, in which Beale underscores the necessity and value of reading the Apocalypse of John for its relevance to the churches of Asia Minor.

"St. John's Portrait of the Church in the Apocalypse," in which Aune simply singles out symbolical depictions of the church to discuss the character and functions of the church, and "La mission prophétique de l'Église dans l'Apocalypse johannique," in which Poucouta also focuses primarily on different titles and various images to discuss the character and function of the church in the Apocalypse as that of fulfilling a prophetic mission, and testifying to and reflecting the light of God. These two articles are helpful in citing various symbolic references to the church in the Apocalypse, and also identifying several of the characteristics of the Asian churches. However, their discussions in terms of the nature and functions of the church are limited, as Aune and Poucouta focus primarily on images, symbols, and titles as a basis for treating the various functions and nature of the church.[4] For a well-informed discussion of the portrait of the church, I will give attention to symbolic as well as literal and explicit references to the church in the Apocalypse.

Further research on the character of the church in the Apocalypse is equally lacking in terms of comprehensiveness and cohesion.[5] There appears to be no systematic and comprehensive effort to explore all that the Apocalypse of John calls the church to be and do. Even when several of the characteristics of the church in the book have been identified and discussed in secondary literature, there has been no conscious effort to demonstrate how these characteristics of the church relate to one another. Discussion often focuses on different parts, rather than on the whole of the essence and function of the church in the Apocalypse.[6] A main concern of this chapter, then, in addition to its overall purpose of showing the Apocalypse's unique contribution to our understanding of the New Testament church, is to provide a comprehensive as well as a cohesive understanding of the nature and functions of the church. To satisfy this concern and also to fulfill the purpose of this chapter, attention will be given to a close examination of all the implicit and explicit references to the nature and character of the church in both the letters

4. Minear, *Images*, has identified 96 images and analogies used in the New Testament to refer to the church. Minear's list of symbolic references includes those in the Apocalypse of John.

5. For instance, see Brownlee, "Priestly Character," 224–25; Du Preez, "Mission Perspective"; Bandstra, "A Kingship and Priests."

6. See Peters, *Mandate of the Church*, for a detailed discussion of the comprehensive and cohesive nature of the tasks and functions of the church in the Apocalypse.

and the visions of the Apocalypse of John.[7] Our investigation will start with a consideration of different aspects of the church as a community of believers. This consideration will touch on the witnessing task, redemptive character, and spiritual nature of the church in the Apocalypse. Our enquiry will conclude with the discussion of three of the several designations of the church: as "Royal Priests," "Bride of Christ," and "People of God."

THE CHURCH AS A COMMUNITY

As in other New Testament writings, especially in the Book of Acts and the letters of Paul, the Apocalypse of John portrays the church as a community or fellowship of believers located in different cities (Ephesus, Smyrna, Pergamum, Thyatira, Sardis, Philadelphia, and Laodicea).[8] Each local community has its own life and characteristics and yet they are all well connected with one another in a "common life" that they share together. To all the churches, John sent one book containing a general introduction, identification of the writer and the recipients, and a salutation (ch. 1), seven individual letters (chs. 2 and 3), as well as a series of visions relevant to all the churches and their individual circumstances (chs. 4–22). Each church is marked by its own unique identity, character, relationships, and destiny (as revealed, especially, in the letters addressed to them in chs. 2 and 3). To underscore his "oneness with the community" and "belongingness to the community," John also considers himself a brother (ὁ ἀδελφὸς ὑμῶν)[9] to the members of these local Christian communities, as well as a fellow-participant (συγκοινωνός) in their experience of suffering, membership in the kingdom, and commitment to patient endurance (1:9). In fact, on a day when these churches were gathering together for corporate worship and fellowship,

---

7. There is no attempt here to limit the discussion of the nature and function of the church to the first three chapters of the Apocalypse of John. Both the letters in chapters 2–3 and the visions in the rest of the Apocalypse provide rich materials (literal and symbolic) for our understanding of the church in the book. In this regard, a thorough reading of the Apocalypse with a focus on what the church is called to be and do is helpful.

8. This is a strong emphasis, especially in the letters to the seven churches found in chapters 2 and 3, which are considered to be an integral part of the Apocalypse of John.

9. The concept of the church as a brotherhood is expressed several times in the Apocalypse (6:11; 12:10; 19:10).

John was on the island of Patmos receiving the visions and messages of his Apocalypse. He writes:

> On the Lord's Day, I was in the Spirit, and I heard behind me a loud voice like a trumpet, which said: "Write on a scroll what you see and send it to the seven churches: to Ephesus, Smyrna, Pergamum, Thyatira, Sardis, Philadelphia, and Laodicea. (1:10–11)[10]

As Cabaniss rightly observes concerning John, "In his exile on the Island of Patmos, deprived of the inspiration of common worship with his fellow-Christians, his mind was inevitably drawn to the solemn service he was missing, and in spirit he was joining with his comrades in their prayers, praise and Scripture lessons."[11]

The seven churches of Asia Minor, though in various settings and contexts, are significantly portrayed in the Apocalypse of John as "one community" displaying several aspects of community life, witness, and ministry, to which we now turn our attention.

A Witnessing Community

As a Christian community in its different local contexts, the church in the Apocalypse is called upon to maintain a faithful witness to Jesus (cf. 2:10, 13, 15; 3:4, 10–11; 6:9; 12:11, 17; 20:4). Thus, the church bears the designation "witnesses" (μάρτυρες) as in the Gospel of Luke and the Book of Acts (Luke 24:48; Acts 1:8). Considering the historical context of the Apocalypse of John, which involved both persecution (threatened or actual) and the perversion of the Christian faith, it is not surprising to find a significant emphasis placed by John on both the necessity and nature of faithful witness.[12]

---

10. A majority of scholars would concede that the Lord's Day (τῇ κυριακῇ ἡμέ ρᾳ) refers to the Christian Sunday—the first day of the week, when Christians worshipped their resurrected Lord; see Mounce, *Revelation*, 76; Swete, *Apocalypse*, 13; and Aune, *Revelation 1–5*, 82–85. Stott, "Note," 72–75, notes that τῇ κυριακῇ ἡμέρᾳ gained prominence through the strong emphasis of the early church on the lordship of Christ; on the basis of Christ's resurrection, τῇ κυριακῇ was regarded as a day belonging to Christ. Charles, *Revelation*, 23, also suggests that "the Lord's Day" is in contrast to the days dedicated to the Roman emperor.

11 Cabaniss, "Liturgy-Making Factors," 50. See also Moffatt, *Revelation*, 342; and Kiddle, *Revelation*, 11.

12. It should be noted that the nature of faithful witness in the Apocalypse of John is a controversial issue in scholarship. For some, the witness terminology is simply a juridical metaphor that has been borrowed from the language of the law court by teachers

Apart from the comfort that comes to each church in their distress, there is a challenge to maintain a faithful witness in their own particular context. Sweet puts this well:

> [T]he apocalyptic part [of the Apocalypse] is not so much an attack on the world to encourage the church, as an attack on the church, which is embracing the world—to its own deadly danger, and in betrayal of its true role of convicting the world by its witness, for the world's salvation.[13]

Even in the midst of suffering and the risk of martyrdom, faithful witness for the church of the Apocalypse is sealed by the blood of the saints.[14] A thorough reading of the Apocalypse of John shows significant passages that call the church, implicitly and explicitly, to maintain faithful witness to Jesus in various contexts (cf. 1:5, 9, 12–13, 28; 2:1, 8–10, 12–17; 6:9–11; 11:1–14; 12:10–12; 14:1–5; 20:4-6). It is expected of the church to maintain faithful witness in the context of persecution as well as perversion of faith—enduring persecution with patience (cf. 2:3, 9, 13; 12:11; 14:12), and maintaining purity of teaching and lifestyle (cf. 2:14–15, 20; 3:1; 22:8–9). Of significance then is the connection that faithful witness has to other characteristics and functions of the church. In one particular instance, faithful witness is expressed in the experience of martyrdom, obedience to the word of God, and the refusal to worship the beast (cf. 20:4-6). Obviously, faithful witness in the Apocalypse calls for a comprehensive understanding that embraces more than martyrological nuances and legal terminologies. However, in several examples

---

and writers of both ancient Israel and the early church; for instance, Caird, *Revelation*, 17–18, who provides a description of the "courtroom" context within which the "witness terms" are used in the Apocalypse; Trites, *New Testament Concept of Witness*, 170–71, who draws attention to various legal scenes in the Apocalypse (cf. 12:1–17; 18:20—19:4; 19:11–12; 20:11–12); and Bauckham, *Theology*, 73, for whom the Apocalypse of John contains a "judicial contest" in which Jesus and his followers bear witness to the truth. Finding a connection between the theme of witness and the Apocalypse's dominant concern with truth and falsehood, Bauckham observes that the world is a kind of courtroom in which the issue of who is the true God is being decided. However, for others, "witness" (μαρτυρία) is a martyrological term that implies the sentence of death. For instance, see Brox, *Zeuge und Märtyer*; and Ellingworth, "Marturia Debate," for whom being a "witness" is synonymous with being a "martyr."

13. Sweet, "Maintaining the Testimony of Jesus," 102–3.

14. This may explain the tendency on the part of some to make "witness" synonymous with "martyrdom" in the Apocalypse of John (e.g., Brox, *Zeuge und Märtyer*, and Ellingworth, "Marturia Debate").

provided by John in his Apocalypse, the serious implication that hardship, suffering, and even martyrdom have for faithful witness is apparent. This is true of the following examples:

—Jesus Christ is the archetype of faithful witness, "one who bore witness to the truth from God (cf. John 3:32; 18:37), with special emphasis on his death that followed as a result"[15] (1:5; 3:14).

—John, the author of the Apocalypse, was banished to the island of Patmos because of his witness to Jesus (1:2, 9).

—Antipas was put to death in the city of Pergamum because he did not renounce his faith in Jesus (2:13).[16]

—The slain witnesses are beneath the altar of sacrifice (6:9–11).[17]

—The two witnesses pay the price of death, shame, contempt, and seeming defeat for their faithful witness (11:1–14).

—The victorious witnesses overcame their accuser partly because they did not love their lives so much as to shrink from death (12:10–12).[18]

—The reigning witnesses, prior to their resurrection and elevation to the throne, were beheaded[19] because of their faithful witness to Jesus (20:4–6).

15. Mounce, *Revelation*, 48. Also see Trites, "Μάρτυς and Martyrdom," 79–80, who notes that the reference to the death of Christ (1:5) seems to suggest that "witness" implies death—a point also intimated by some of the other references to ἀρνίον (cf. 5:6, 12; 12:11).

16. While little is known about Antipas apart from the reference in the Apocalypse of John, attempts have been made to cite historical references to Antipas in other ancient writings (cf. Mounce, *Revelation*, 80).

17. The noun θυσιαστήριον, "altar," which is cognate with the verb θυσιάζω, "I sacrifice," appears eight times in the Apocalypse of John (cf. 6:9; 8:3 [2x]; 8:5; 9:13; 11:1; 14:18; 16:7). In Rev 6:9 and 16:7 the noun indicates the place where sacrifice is made, i.e., the altar (cf. Aune, *Revelation 6–16*, 405). However, in other instances, it refers to the altar of incense (8:3, 5; 9:13), or the place of worship (11:1; 14:18).

18. The motif of martyrs conquering through suffering and even death in literature similar to the Apocalypse is well cited and discussed by Aune, *Revelation 6–16*, 702.

19. While it seems extremely unlikely that all the martyrs would have been executed by decapitation, the term used in this context to describe the slain witnesses (πεπελε- κισμένων) is a perfect passive substantival participle from the verb πελεκίζω, meaning "I behead with a πέλεκυς—an axe" (cf. Aune, *Revelation 17–22*, 1086). However, since

The church in her role as a "faithful witness" to Jesus in the Apocalypse of John is faced with various challenges and problems that often reveal her imperfections and vulnerabilities. Of course, this is very true of all the churches of the New Testament, including those in the Book of Acts, and those who received the letters of Paul, Peter, James, Jude, and John. That the church in her current witness to Jesus is not perfect is a strong emphasis in the New Testament documents, including the Apocalypse of John, which anticipates, announces, and celebrates the impending perfection and victory of the church.

Each church of the Apocalypse reveals her own imperfection and vulnerability.[20] The church of Ephesus, which on the one hand is commended for her perseverance and sensitivity to and rejection of unorthodox faith and practice, is also condemned for lacking a significant virtue such as love.[21] The church of Smyrna, while commended for her faithful experience of persecution, and the accompanying poverty, hardship, and suffering, is also challenged to be courageous and faithful in the face of harsher forms of persecution and suffering that may cause her to become unfaithful. The church of Pergamum, which is commended for her faithful witness even to the point of suffering martyrdom,[22] is also condemned for her unfaithfulness by succumbing to non-Christian

---

Christians were known to be killed in ways other than by decapitation (e.g., crucifixion), Beale, *Revelation*, 998, while admitting that only actual martyrs are meant in Rev 20:4–5, notes that τῶν πεπελεκισμένων is figurative for different kinds of execution.

20. This is with the understanding that each church addressed by John is a community made up of different individuals who contribute in different ways to the witness of the local church.

21. In his attempt to tie this criticism of the Ephesian church to the "witness motif," Beale, *Revelation*, 230–31, suggests that the "loss of first love" is not "for one another" nor "for the Lord," but the suppression of spiritual gifts that are necessary for the Christian community's witness to be effective. Thus, losing their first love is tantamount to losing zeal for witness.

22. Antipas is a good example of faithful witness in this local church (2:13). Other faithful witnesses who sealed their witness with martyrdom in the Apocalypse of John include the slain witnesses (6:9–11), the two witnesses (11:1–17), the victorious witnesses (12:11; 15:1–2; 20:1–6), and the saints who bore witness to Jesus (17:6). The "faithful witness" of the church of Pergamum is strongly attested by the statement that she did not deny her faith in Jesus (οὐκ ἠρνήσω τὴν πίστιν μου). Since the terms "confess" (ὁμολογέω) and "deny" (ἀρνέομαι) are frequently used as antitheses in early Christian literature (cf. Matt 10:32–33; Luke 12:8–9; John 1:20; Titus 1:16; 1 John 2:23; Ignatius, *Smyrn.* 5:1–2; *Mart. Pol.* 9:2; *Herm. Sim.* 9.28.4, 7), the church of Pergamum is thus commended for her public confession of faith in Jesus.

influences.[23] (In contrast to those in Ephesus, several in Pergamum were seduced by the teachings of Balaam and the Nicolaitans.) The church of Thyatira, which is noted for a fine expression of love, faith, service, and patient endurance, is also rebuked for her compromise with a woman called Jezebel, who claimed to be a prophetess, and who through her teaching misled the servants of Christ in Thyatira to fornicate and eat meat sacrificed to idols. The church of Sardis, while strongly castigated for deeds not in keeping with appropriate Christian conduct and witness, is also commended for the presence of some who have not soiled their clothes (with the understanding that they have maintained moral and spiritual purity; see 7:13–14; 22:14).[24] The church of Philadelphia, though not rebuked for any act of unfaithfulness or imperfection (in fact commended for her obedience to Jesus and not denying his name),[25] is still warned to remain faithful in light of the second coming of Christ.[26] And the church of Laodicea, receiving no commendation, is chastised for her lukewarm and ineffective witness. Certainly, the church in its present state, according to the Apocalypse of John, is marked by deeds of imperfection. However, as a deterrent, the church is constantly challenged in the Apocalypse to maintain faithful witness to Jesus.

In keeping with the genre of the Apocalypse of John, several symbols are utilized to express as well as promote the faithful witness of the Asian churches. The symbols of "the lampstands," "the temple," and "the open door," have been identified as key to understanding the concept of

23. According to Sweet, *Revelation*, 88, several in Pergamum accommodated themselves to pagan society with its quasi-religious banquets, sexual license, and the adulation of Rome.

24. According to Aune, *Revelation 1–5*, 222, a background reference for the use of this metaphor is Zech 1:1–5, where Joshua the high priest is depicted as wearing dirty clothes (a metaphor for the sins of both the priest and the people).

25. Similar commendations of faithfulness are expressed about the church of Pergamum, which kept the name of Jesus (κρατεῖς τὸ ὄνομά μου) and did not deny the faith of Jesus (καὶ οὐκ ἠρνήσω τὴν πίστιν μου) (2:13). One observes in the Apocalypse of John that keeping the words of Jesus and not denying his name (3:8), keeping the deeds of Jesus (2:26), and also holding forth the name of Jesus and not renouncing his faith (2:13) are common expressions of faithfulness to Jesus. According to Beale, *Revelation*, 286, for the church of Philadelphia not to deny the name of Christ underscores the focus of faithfulness for the church of the Apocalypse of John.

26. Here in Rev 3:11 (as well as 2:25), the motif of the coming of Christ is combined with the theme of faithfulness for the church (cf. Aune, *Revelation 1–5*, 208).

witness in the Apocalypse.[27] Out of these three symbols, the symbol of "the lampstands" is probably the only one specifically concerned with witness. However, attention to each metaphor facilitates our understanding of the contribution each makes to our knowledge of the church as a witnessing community in the Apocalypse of John.

THE LAMPSTANDS

The lampstands (αἱ λυχνίαι) appear seven times as a symbol for the church in the Apocalypse (out of the twelve times the term is used in the New Testament): four times in the inaugural vision of the Apocalypse, where "one like a son of man" stands among the seven golden lampstands, which are identified as the seven churches (1:12, 13, 20); twice in the letter to the church of Ephesus, which is threatened with the removal of its lampstand (2:1, 5); and once in the vision of the two witnesses, who are identified as "the two lampstands" (11:4).

For some commentators, the lampstands of the Apocalypse, with their background in the Old Testament (cf. Exodus 25, 37; Numbers 8; and Zechariah 4), represent the church simply in its role as a "light-bearer." For instance, Poucouta communicates this basic understanding by commenting that the lampstands of the Apocalypse symbolize the mission of the church as reflecting the light of God on earth,[28] maintaining the flame of the divine presence,[29] and making the light triumph over darkness.[30] But she does not spell out what it means for the church of the Apocalypse to serve as "light-bearer." Rather, she simply concludes that in a world full of upheaval, the mission of the church members is that of watchmen, their lamps blazing, staying awake and awaking others.[31] By failing to explore the manner in which the church is to fulfill its mission as a "light-bearer," she leaves the reader wondering about the actual identity and task of the church as symbolized by the golden lampstands of the Apocalypse.

---

27. For instance, see Poucouta, "La mission prophétique de l'Église," and Aune, "John's Portrait," who through their examination of the symbols and portraits of the church in the Apocalypse attempt to define the functions and tasks of the church.

28. Poucouta, "La mission prophétique de l'Église," 49–50.

29. Ibid., 50.

30. Ibid., 51.

31. Ibid., 57.

For other commentators, the lampstands of the Apocalypse, as a symbol of "light bearing," represent the church in its task as a "witness-bearer," since the term lampstand (λυχνία) is also used in reference to the "two witnesses" (11:3–7).[32] It is with this understanding that some commentators equate "light" with "witness" and attempt to demonstrate in the Apocalypse (especially in the letters of chaps. 2–3) what it means for the church to bear witness. Thus both Thomas[33] and Beale[34] point to the likelihood that the prevailing theme of the seven letters is the witness of the seven churches. In particular, Beale makes a notable contribution to the study of the letters of the Apocalypse by demonstrating that all the letters call attention to the different character of the witness of each church. Beale writes:

> [A]ll of the letters deal generally with the issue of witnessing for Christ in the midst of a pagan culture. The churches with problems are all exhorted to strengthen their witness in various ways, and the two churches without problems are encouraged to continue to persevere in the faithful witness that they have been maintaining.[35]

Assuming that the lampstand symbolizes the witness of the church, Beale makes the following observations from the letters regarding each church's witness: The loss of "first love" in the Ephesian church (2:4) "was tantamount to becoming unzealous witnesses,"[36] and the failure of the Ephesian Christians to exercise their call to be a "lamp of witness" (1:5) means ceasing to exist as a church.[37] As for the churches of Smyrna and Pergamum, both of them are commended for their suffering pro-voked by their open witness to their faith in Christ (2:9–10, 13).[38] In the case of the church of Thyatira, the "works" for which they are compli-mented (2:19) are not merely general deeds of "Christian service," but

---

32. That the primary meaning of lampstand is that of witness is indicated in Rev 11:3–7, where the "two lampstands" refer to the "two witnesses" (cf. Beale, *Revelation*, 231, and Aune, *Revelation 6–16*, 612).

33. Thomas, *Revelation 1–7*, 277–78.

34. Beale, *Revelation*, 289.

35. Ibid., 227.

36. Ibid., 230.

37. Ibid., 232.

38. Ibid., 241–42, 246.

"works of persevering witness to the outside world."[39] As for some of the Christians who are castigated in Sardis, the problem with them is their failure to witness to their faith before the unbelieving culture (3:1–2);[40] they suppress their witness by assuming a low profile in idolatrous contexts.[41] With regard to the church of Philadelphia, its commendation for "not denying the name of Christ" (3:8) is an indication of persevering witness.[42] And in the case of the Laodicean church, criticisms are leveled at the church's "innocuous witness" (3:15–17)—a witness that is either non-existent or consistently compromised by participation in the idolatrous Laodicean culture.[43]

Beale's approach to the concept of witness in all the letters to the seven churches tends to be broad and some of his descriptions of the witness of each church appear a bit stretched. However, he certainly confirms the understanding of other commentators that the Apocalypse's use of the term λυχνία (lampstand) "emphasizes the local church in its capacity as a witnessing community."[44] Beale also opens the possibility of discovering the specific content and function of the "witness motif" in the individual letters addressed to the seven churches (the seven lampstands) of the Apocalypse of John. As a "lampstand," each church in her vocation of witness is called upon to hear and respond to the voice of the Spirit with regards to the character of her witness (2:7, 11, 17, 29; 3:6, 13, 22).

THE TEMPLE

In the Apocalypse, there are several symbolic and literal references to a "temple" (cf. 3:12; 7:15; 11:1, 2, 19; 14:15, 17; 15:5, 6, 8; 16:1, 17; 21:22). Of particular interest to our examination of the witness motif in the Apocalypse is the reference to the temple of God in 11:1 and 2 (ὁ ναὸς τοῦ θεοῦ). It is widely held that the temple of God, together with the altar and the worshipers, symbolize "the Christian community who worship God."[45] However, some proceed further to consider the

39. Ibid., 260.
40. Ibid., 273.
41. Ibid., 276.
42. Ibid., 283–86.
43. Ibid., 303.
44. Aune, "John's Portrait," 143.
45. Boring, *Revelation*, 143 (cf. Mounce, *Revelation*, 213, and Aune, *Revelation 6–16*, 597).

temple of God, especially in the context of the vision of the two witnesses (cf. 11:1–14), to be a metaphor for the church's witness.[46]

The attempt to turn the temple of God into a metaphor for witness appears questionable. The temple in the Apocalypse is primarily
associated with the worship motif. Especially in Rev 11:1 and 2, it is
linked with the altar and the worshipers. While it is true that both the
temple and the two witnesses could be identified as the church, they
express complementary and not synonymous roles of the church. The
two witnesses exemplify the witnessing task of the church (11:3–14), but
the temple of God (11:1–2) represents the worship experience of the
church in the context of suffering and oppression. For these reasons,
"the temple of God" should not be considered a "witness metaphor" in
the Apocalypse of John.

The "Open Door"

Following the common interpretation that the "open door" image
(θύρα ἠνεῳγμένη) of 3:8 denotes a great opportunity for missionary
activity,[47] Beale considers the "open door" to be a "witness metaphor"
for the church of Philadelphia.[48] As most commentators agree, the "open
door" metaphor basically speaks of "an opportunity," or "a possibility."
With this understanding, some consider the "open door" to be access to
eschatological salvation—entrance into the messianic kingdom.[49] This
same metaphor is used in Rev 4:1 where John speaks of an open door
in heaven (θύρα ἠνεῳγμένη ἐν τῷ οὐρανῷ); here it simply means
the granting of access, possibility, and opportunity to perceive visions.[50]
In the context of the Apocalypse (cf. 3:8; 4:1), turning the "open door"
imagery into a metaphor specifically for witness is doubtful.

Out of these three metaphors, the lampstands metaphor, used in
reference to the two witnesses (11:3–4) and the seven churches (1:20),
seems to be the only one that contributes to our understanding of the

---

46. E.g., Mounce, *Revelation*, 214.

47. Cf. Ramsay, *Letters to the Seven Churches*, 404; Charles, *Revelation*, 87; and
Caird, *Revelation*, 51.

48. Beale, *Revelation*, 286. For similar use of the "open door" image indicating "witness," Beale cites Acts 14:27; 1 Cor 16:9; 2 Cor 2:12; and Col 4:3.

49. Cf. Beckwith, *Apocalypse*, 480; Kraft, *Offenbarung*, 81; and Roloff, *Revelation*,
61.

50. See Aune, *Revelation 1–5*, 279–82, who provides a comprehensive discussion of
the motif of the "open door" in ancient religious traditions and apocalyptic literature.

witness motif of the Apocalypse of John. As a symbol of witness for each of the seven churches, the lampstand motif illumines the meaning of witness in the issues that are addressed in the letters to the seven churches. Inasmuch as the lampstand metaphor identifies each church as a witness, the tasks for which each church is complimented or condemned in the letters could be considered as functions of the witnessing church. These functions are exemplified in the contexts of both persecution and perversion of faith in the Apocalypse of John.

A Redeemed Community

John's community, the seven churches, is characterized not only by its witnessing task, but also by its redemptive character. In the Apocalypse of John, as well as in other New Testament documents, the redemptive work of Jesus receives a strong emphasis; and as a complement, the sacrifice of Jesus (who is referred to as the "Lamb" in the Apocalypse) is emphasized as that which releases the church from sin and its effects (1:5; 5:9; 7:14; 14:4). In fact, it is through the redemptive work of Jesus, the shedding of the blood, that ultimate victory for the church is guaranteed in the Apocalypse of John. For instance, those who encountered the opposition of the Dragon overcame him by the blood of the Lamb (12:10); those who came out of the great tribulation also had their clothes washed and made white in the blood of the Lamb (7:13–14); and the redeemed 144,000 followers of the Lamb were found to be pure and blameless (14:1–6).

The reference made to Jesus as having loved and loosed (λύσαντι)[51] the church from sin through his blood (1:5) is significant. Implied in this description is the understanding that the church of the Apocalypse is expected to function in ways consistent with what Jesus has done for her. Here then is an instance in the Apocalypse of John where what the church is called to be is tied to what the church is expected to do. So it is not surprising to note this implication in the letters to the seven churches, that the church of Ephesus, a church loved by Jesus (1:5), is later chastised for abandoning its first love for Jesus (2:4);[52] the churches

---

51. The understanding here is that the church is freed/loosed (and not so much washed) from sin. This idea occurs only here in the New Testament and may be derived from Isa 40:2, according to Beale, *Revelation*, 192.

52. This is with the understanding that the "first love" that the Ephesian church abandoned could be a reference to their love for Jesus.

of Pergamum and Thyatira who have been freed from their sin by the blood of Jesus, "the Lamb that was slain," are reprimanded for tolerating sinful activities, including eating food sacrificed to idols and also committing fornication (2:14–15, 20).

In his Apocalypse, John considers the redemptive work of Jesus (the shedding of the blood of the Lamb) to be what has the ability to liberate from the penalty as well as the power of sin. It is for this reason that John mandates the church with a call to holiness that is both implied and explicit in several passages of the Apocalypse (cf. 5:8; 8:3; 11:18; 13:7, 10; 14:12; 16:6; 17:6; 18:20–25; 19:8). Exhortations to purity are given in the commendations and criticisms of the letters (2:6, 14–15, 20–25; 3:4), and are explicit in the contrast between the destiny of the pure and of the immoral in the visions of the Apocalypse (21:1–8; 22:10–15). For the church in the Apocalypse, the call to purity and holiness (in doctrine and life-style) is also John's call for a total separation of the redeemed church from the rest of the society. For instance, eating food sacrificed to idols, tolerated by Paul in some of his letters (Rom 14:1–18; 1 Cor 8:1–13), is considered a sign of unfaithful witness that calls for repentance (Rev 2:14–16, 20–25). Also there is a strong call to the faithful ones, who are known as "God's people," to come out of the vile, detestable, and wicked Babylon that is soon to be destroyed (18:4–5). Whereas Paul admonishes the church to submit to and uphold the Roman government (Rom 13:1–7), the Apocalypse of John sets the redeemed community of God in stark contrast and contradiction to the state. In keeping with the call to holiness, John designates the church as "saints" (ἅγιοι) and communicates in his Apocalypse what it means for the church to be holy (5:8; 8:3; 11:18; 13:7, 10; 14:12; 16:6; 17:6; 18:20, 24; 19:8).

A Community of the Spirit

Another aspect of John's community, the seven churches, is its spiritual character. The special communal relationship that the church enjoys with the Spirit is underscored in the Apocalypse of John.[53] Here in the Apocalypse, the church is not so much portrayed as a community con-

---

53. It should be noted that the phrases "Spirit of God" and "Holy Spirit" never appear in the Apocalypse of John. However, there is the understanding that John's mention of the "Spirit" (1:10; 4:2; 17:3; 21:10), the "Spirit of prophecy" (19:10); and "seven Spirits of God" (1:4; 3:1; 4:5; 5:6) may be in reference to the "Spirit of God" or the "Holy Spirit."

stituted by the Spirit (as in the Book of Acts), but as a community "to whom" and "through whom" the Spirit speaks. The seven messages of the Apocalypse (chaps. 2 and 3) are "what the Spirit says to the churches." Some other parts of the Apocalypse are explicitly uttered as the words of the Spirit (14:13; 22:17). That the Spirit speaks to the church is rightly observed by Bauckham who writes: "the Spirit brings to the churches the powerful word of Christ, rebuking, encouraging, promising and threatening, touching and drawing the hearts, minds, and consciences of its hearers, directing the lives and the prayers of the Christian communities towards the coming of Christ."[54]

Repeatedly, the church is called upon in the Apocalypse of John to hear and respond positively to the voice of the Spirit.[55] The admonition to do so appears significantly in what has been termed "the hearing formula"[56] of the Apocalypse of John. This formula, "let the one who has ears listen to what the Spirit says to the churches" (ὁ ἔχων οὖς ἀκουσάτω τί τὸ πνεῦμα λέγει ταῖς ἐκκλησίαις) occurs eight times in the Apocalypse of John; it indicates a significant aspect of what the church is called upon to be and do. It is used seven times in the second and third chapters of the Apocalypse (2:7, 11, 17, 29; 3:6, 13, 22) in connection with the message to the seven churches and (in an abbreviated form) once in the thirteenth chapter (13:9) in the context of an apocalyptic vision. In the New Testament writings, this formula is certainly not peculiar to the Apocalypse of John. A related formula is combined with the parabolic teaching of Jesus in the Synoptic Gospels (cf. Mark 4:9, 23; Matt 11:15; 13:9, 43; Luke 8:8; 14:35).[57] In some places at least the formula appears to imply an esoteric sense (deeper or hid-

54. Bauckham, "Role of the Spirit," 74.

55. Obedience is one of the themes that features significantly in the Apocalypse of John: benediction is pronounced on those who obey (1:3; 22:7); the church of Sardis is commanded to obey what she has already received and heard (3:3); the church of Philadelphia is commended for her obedience (3:10); several individuals are noted for their obedience to the commandment of God and the words of John's prophecy (12:17; 14:12; 22:9).

56. While Enroth, "Hearing Formula," has termed this "the hearing formula," Aune, *Revelation 1–5*, 150, has called it "a proclamation formula," and Roloff, *Revelation*, 46, has described this as "the summons to listen" or "the call to awakening."

57. Other places where a "hearing formula" is found include the *Gospel of Thomas* 8:21, 24, 63, 65, 96; the *Gospel of Mary* 7:10; 8:16; *Pistis Sophia* I:17, 19, 33, 42, 43; II:68, 86, 87; III:124, 125; and the *Sophia of Jesus Christ* 98, 105, 107 (cf. Enroth, "Hearing Formula," 598).

den meaning), so that what is being said involves highly specialized or abstruse knowledge.[58] However, Enroth, in her discussion of the tradition, background, context, and function of the "hearing formula" in the Apocalypse of John, underscores its paraenetic function.[59] It is in light of this paraenetic function that one sees the relevance of the "hearing formula" to the discussion of the church's relationship and response to the Spirit in the Apocalypse of John.

In its paraenetic function, the "hearing formula" calls the church of the Apocalypse to listen and pay attention.[60] As Enroth notes concerning the usage of the "hearing formula," especially in the letters of the Apocalypse (chaps. 2 and 3), "It underlines what should be heard and how it should be heard and what follows from hearing aright."[61] This, then, is the sense in which the Spirit speaking to the church has "life-giving and life-changing effects,"[62] in keeping with Paul's view of the role of the Spirit in the life of the church. In all seven letters, the "hearing formula" underscores the words of encouragement, comfort, rebuke, warning, and promise. While it punctuates the challenge to maintain faithfulness in two of the letters (2:10–11; 3:8, 10–11), it provides incentives for repentance in five of the letters (2:5–7, 16–17, 20–29; 3:3–6, 19–22).[63] Thus, it highlights repentance as one of the tasks of the church, especially when any of its members (as in the case of the five churches) have failed to maintain their faithfulness.

Even though the "hearing formula" appears in a different form and context in the visionary section of the Apocalypse (13:9),[64] it retains its paraenetic function of calling attention to what should be heard and

58. The esoteric application of the "hearing formula" in all of the New Testament writings, including the Apocalypse of John, is championed by both Dibelius, "Wer Ohren hat zu hören," 461, and Kraft, *Offenbarung*, 58.

59. Enroth, "Hearing Formula," 602.

60. The concern of the author of the Apocalypse for his audience to listen and pay attention is apparent in several of his beatitudes that pronounce benediction on those who hear and respond positively to the words of his prophecy (cf. 1:1–3; 16:15; 22:7, 14).

61. Enroth, "Hearing Formula," 602.

62. Bauckham, "Role of the Spirit," 74.

63. That the "hearing formula" calls each hearer to appropriate the promises and warnings addressed to the churches is well observed by Harrington, *Apocalypse*, 57.

64. Though the word οὖς and the imperative ἀκουσάτω remain unchanged, the participial construction ὁ ἔχων is replaced by a conditional clause εἴ τις ἔχει, and the refrain τί τὸ πνεῦμα λέγει ταῖς ἐκκλησίαις is dropped.

done by the recipients of the Apocalypse. In 13:9, it occurs in connection with the revelation of the Beast's program of worship and the ensuing persecution of the saints who deny him their worship and allegiance (13:1–8). However, the usage of the "hearing formula" in this context does not highlight the call to repentance. Rather, in keeping with its usage in the letter to the church of Smyrna (2:10–11), it underscores the exhortation to the saints to maintain patient endurance and faithful witness, even to the point of death (13:10). In the Apocalypse, then, it is obvious that when the "hearing formula" does not underscore the call to repentance, it stresses the importance of the challenge to the church to maintain faithful witness.

Even though not so explicit, it is implied in the Apocalypse of John that the Spirit also speaks "through" the church. Exploring the communal dimension of the work of the Spirit, Jeske writes the following concerning John and his community of the Spirit:

> The language he chooses to use is that of prophetic discourse, and he conceives of his audience as people equipped with the spirit of prophecy (12:17; 19:10; 22:9). It is as a prophet that John is enabled to proclaim "the word of God and the witness of Jesus," which is the content of the writing itself (1:2) as well as the content of the ministry he shares with his readers (1:9; 12:17).[65]

That the Spirit speaks through the church is implied in John's choice of the two witnessing prophets to symbolize the character and function of the church (11:1–14). This is further implied in John's account of both the Bride of the Lamb and the Spirit, jointly offering an invitation: "a polite entreaty to Jesus to come; and an invitation to participate in redemptive blessing"[66] (22:17). Indeed, if the bride here represents the church, who through the enablement and utterance of the Spirit issues this invitation, Beale is right that "this is another instance in the book [of Revelation] where the Spirit speaks through the entire community of the saints and not just through prophets."[67]

---

65. Jeske, "Spirit and Community," 458.

66. Beale, *Revelation*, 1149.

67. Ibid., 1148.

THE CHURCH AS ROYAL PRIESTS

Another aspect of the church that John portrays in his Apocalypse is the eschatological reality of the church's royal priestly character. Of interest is the combination of the kingship and priesthood of the church in the Apocalypse. According to John in his opening doxology (1:6), the church is to be a kingdom and priests to serve our God. In this context (1:5), John communicates the understanding that the death and resurrection of Christ has established a two-fold office of rulership/kingship and priesthood for himself and the church.[68] Believers, then, have not only been made part of the kingdom of Christ as his subjects, but they have been elevated to the position of kingship to reign with Christ and to share his priestly office. These two privileges, of course, are based on believers' identification with the death and resurrection of Christ.

Here in the Apocalypse, the Kingdom of God, which is inaugurated and announced in the Gospels (Matt 3:2; 13:24–30; Mark 1:14; 4:1–11; Luke 11:14–23), is now consummated and celebrated as part of what the church is called upon to be and do. Similarly, the church, designated as a "priesthood" (cf. 1 Pet 2:9), is now portrayed by John as functioning eternally in that capacity.

In his emphasis on the eschatological royal identity and function of the church, John in his letters to the churches writes about Christ's promises of eschatological reign. To the overcomers in the church of Thyatira, the promise is the gift of "authority over the nations," and the possession of the "morning star" (2:26–28). And to the overcomers in the church of Laodicea, the promise is "to sit on the throne with Christ" (3:21). By way of inference, rulership/kingship in the Apocalypse of John is promised to the overcomers, whose character and function are to be determined by the context in which reference is made to them.[69] In the closing chapters of the Apocalypse, the promise of kingship and reigning with Christ is turned into reality as those who have been slain for their faithful witness enjoy the millennium reign with Christ (20:4–6), and afterwards an eternal reign (22:5). The reality of eschatological reign is celebrated in some of the Apocalypse's hymns of worship in which the reality of the kingdom is affirmed (5:10; 7:15; 11:18; 19:2, 5).

68. Ibid., 192.

69. That overcoming is the basis for inheriting the promises is a strong motif in both the letters and the concluding vision of the Apocalypse (cf. 2:7, 11, 17, 26; 3:5, 12, 21; 21:7; 22:1–5, 12, 14).

Several attempts (often to no avail) have been made by various commentators to discover and discuss quite extensively what it means for the church in the Apocalypse to function as priests.[70] Unfortunately, the Apocalypse (unlike the Book of Leviticus and the Book of Hebrews) has no list of rules and regulations pertaining to the priesthood of the church. Nevertheless, there are a few indications of what the church is called to do as priests. There are two primary functions that stand out: offering prayers coupled with the burning of incense (5:8; 6:10) and rendering worship (19:5, 10).[71] These two primary functions describe the priestly character of the church in the Apocalypse, but in a comprehensive and cohesive manner they also designate the church as Servants of God: to offer worship (αἰνέω) and priestly services (λατρεύω) day and night (7:15; 19:5; 22:3).

THE CHURCH AS THE BRIDE OF CHRIST

Similar to Paul's symbolic view of the church, the Apocalypse designates the church as the Bride (νύμφη)[72] of Christ (cf. 19:9; 21:2, 9; 22:17). However, an added dimension to this imagery is the manner in which John makes the church, the Bride of Christ, virtually synonymous with the image of the Holy City, the New Jerusalem, coming down from Heaven in one of the closing visions of his Apocalypse (21:2–4).[73] This concept of the city, as Minear observes, tends to displace the analogy of the marital relation,[74] which is stressed in Paul's typology of the church as the Bride of Christ (2 Cor 11:2; Eph 5:25–27). However, this may not be the case, since John probably intends his readers to see these two images

70. See Vanhoye, *Priests*, 279–307 for such a listing and discussion. Further comments on the church's royal priestly functions as well as background materials are also found in Beale, *Revelation*, 192–93, and Aune, *Revelation 1–5*, 47–49.

71. Worship is a significant task and character of the church, extensively discussed in Peters, *Mandate of the Church*, 43–75.

72. νύμφη is used here in Rev 21:2 with regards to the church and also in 21:9 and 22:17, but nowhere else in early Christian literature (cf. Aune, *Revelation 17–22*, 1121).

73. The opinion of most scholars is that the New Jerusalem symbolizes the saints (the eschatological people of God). See McKelvey, *New Temple*, 167–76; Holtz, *Christologie der Apocalypse*, 191–95; Gundry, "New Jerusalem." However, others argue that the New Jerusalem does not symbolize the saints. For instance, Schüssler-Fiorenza, *Priester für Gott*, 348–50, argues: (1) the images of the city and the bride are not the same (cf. Rev 21:2); (2) the saints cannot inherit the city and also be the city (Rev 21:7); and (3) the city is where the saints dwell (Rev 21:24–26).

74. Minear, *Images*, 55.

of the church (the Bride and the City) as complementary images of the church (rather than one displacing the other). Here is one of the ways in which the Apocalypse of John enriches our New Testament understanding of the church. John's added dimension enables us to see "the church at the End"[75] in her eternal home (a place described as the Holy City, the New Jerusalem coming down out of Heaven from God). Characteristics of both the Bride and the City, as spelled out in the Apocalypse, certainly provide us with more insights about the future characteristics and functions of the church.

The church as the Bride will be at a marriage supper (19:9), to consummate her special relationship of love and devotion to Christ, the one who is designated as the Lamb in John's Apocalypse. In contrast to another woman in the same Apocalypse (17:1–6), the church as a Bride is "decorated," "adorned" (κεκοσμημένην) for her husband (21:2). While the church, the Bride of Christ, exhibits purity, cleanness, and beauty, this other woman is depicted as impure, adulterous, violent, and wicked. It is said of her that she holds in her hand a golden cup filled with abominable things and the filth of her adulteries (17:4–5). Consequently, she is destined for terrible destruction: she will be brought to ruin, left naked, devoured, and burnt with fire (17:16). Such a negative description of this woman's character and destiny, no doubt, serves as a warning to the church to maintain purity. This warning is reinforced by an explicit mandate to the church to disassociate herself from all that this woman practices and personifies, according to the eighteenth chapter of the Apocalypse. John writes in 18:4: "Come out of her my people, so that you will not share in her sins, so that you will not receive any of her plagues" (ἐξέλθατε ὁ λαός μου ἐξ αὐτῆς ἵνα μὴ συγκοινωνήσητε ταῖς ἁμαρτίαις αὐτῆς, καὶ ἐκ τῶν πληγῶν αὐτῆς ἵνα μὴ λάβητε). The same is true of the contrast between the two cities (Babylon and Jerusalem) that these two women represent. In contrast to Babylon, the great prostitute full of adultery and fornication (cf. 17:4, 5; 18:1–8), the New Jerusalem is morally pure and "decked with virtues"[76] rather than vices. The holy character of the New Jerusalem is further conveyed by the exclusion of impure and wicked individuals from participating in it (21:7–8, 27).

---

75. Bauckham, "Role of the Spirit," 77.
76. Aune, *Revelation 17–22*, 1122.

Obviously, with the images he has chosen to portray the church (the Bride and the City), John shows the contrast between the church and her opponents and adversaries. However, John makes a unique contribution to our understanding of the New Testament church by the contrast that he draws between the present and the eschatological reality of the church. One observes the difference between the church (as the Bride and the Holy City) and the church in her present condition (as described, commended, and chastised in the messages to the seven churches). There is a poignant contrast between what the church is presently and what the church must become in the future. Bauckham captures this contrast very well when he writes:

> Very different were the seven churches addressed in the Apocalypse. The "soiled garments" of Christians at Sardis (3:4) and the "nakedness" of Christians at Laodicea (3:17) contrast with the pure linen of the Bride. The general unpreparedness for the Lord's return at Ephesus, Pergamum, Sardis (2:5, 16; 3:3) contrasts with the Bride's ardent prayer for the Bridegroom's coming. (22:17)[77]

Indeed, John's vision of the church contains both present and future realities. However, it is in anticipation of future realities that the church in her present state must conduct herself. Her present realities should reflect her future glories.

THE CHURCH AS THE PEOPLE OF GOD

In several places, the Apocalypse of John makes it clear that the church is to be designated as the people of God. In 18:4 and 21:3, the word "people" (λαός) appears as a description of the church. Also, in the closing chapters, God fully resides in the Holy City, the New Jerusalem, which symbolizes the church (chaps. 21 and 22). The church, referred to as "my people," is warned to come out of the city of Babylon that is destined for destruction (18:4). However, a significant reference to the church as the people of God is likely found in the representation of the 144,000 in chaps. 7, 14, and 21.

The identity of this redeemed group of 144,000 has occasioned extensive discussion among scholars. Issues involved in the debate include the possible identity of the 144,000 in chapter 14 with the 144,000

---

77. Bauckham, "Role of the Spirit," 78.

who are sealed in 7:1–8, and their relationship to the great multitude that offers worship to God and the Lamb in 7:9–17. Walvoord suggests that this group of 144,000 refers to the nation of Israel.[78] Thus, chapter 7 encompasses two groups of people: the Jews (7:1–8) and the church (7:9–17). This view is problematic since it makes an incorrect and unnecessary division of the people of God.[79] Rather, the two groups should be perceived as one, but with two complementary aspects. In vv. 1–8, John uses Old Testament imagery to speak of the saints as the New Israel (a common phenomenon in the Apocalypse of John), and in vv. 9–17, he enlarges his picture of the saints to include all nations, by speaking of an innumerable multitude.[80]

While most commentators would consider the 144,000 in chapters 7 and 14 to be the same group of people representing the saints of God, there is a tendency on the part of some to adopt a limited view of the 144,000. For instance, Kiddle perceives the 144,000 to be a portion of the church that in the last days is marked out for martyrdom.[81] Charles considers them to be a community of resurrected martyrs.[82] Bauckham regards them as martyrs redeemed from all the nations and offered to God as the firstfruits of the harvest of all the nations, whose reaping is depicted in 14:14–16.[83] However, it must be admitted that to limit the group of 144,000 to a segment of the church is to lose the idea of completeness that John seems to stress in his Apocalypse. The book itself is addressed to the seven Asian churches, with the number seven signifying the completeness of the church. Furthermore, the number 144,000 is used symbolically to speak of wholeness and completeness. In keeping with the symbolic language of the Apocalypse, Mounce observes that "twelve (the number of tribes) is both squared and multiplied by a thousand—a twofold way of emphasizing the completeness."[84] Beale also

---

78. Cf. Walvoord, *Revelation*, 141.

79. That the group in Rev 7:1–8 represents the nation of Israel is rightly rejected by Mounce, *Revelation*, 158; and Sweet, *Revelation*, 151.

80. Cf. Beasley-Murray, *Revelation*, 141.

81. Kiddle, *Revelation*, 136; also see Caird, *Revelation*, 97.

82. Charles, *Revelation*, 2:4.

83. Bauckham, *Climax*, 291–92.

84. Mounce, *Revelation*, 158.

cautions: "to limit the number to a select group of believers dilutes the figurative force of completeness connoted by the number."[85]

There are further reasons to conclude that the number 144,000 symbolizes the whole number of the faithful who worship the Lamb in both chapters 7 and 14: (1) The Apocalypse tends to regard the church as the true Israel (cf. 2:9; 3:9–12); (2) the same number is used in both chapters (7 and 14) for the followers of the Lamb, whose foreheads bear the seal of God; and (3) that the sealing is expressly limited to the 144,000 indicates that there is no distinction to be made between the two groups.[86]

That the 144,000 are described as those who have kept themselves pure from the defilement of women has also occasioned considerable discussion. Kiddle thinks that they should be viewed literally as celibates and virgins.[87] This view certainly leads to an exaltation of celibacy and perhaps to a denigration of marriage and sexual relationships. Charles argues that this description of the 144,000 appeared in the marginal notes of some monkish scribe and was later copied into the text by mistake.[88] This conjecture lacks support in the manuscript tradition. Carrington, taking the words in a figurative sense, and emphasizing the word "defilement," regards the 144,000 as those who have not entered into immoral relations.[89] This elevates sexual purity as the distinctive mark of the redeemed in heaven.[90] Contrary to these views, the non-defilement of the 144,000 with women should be perceived as a symbol of religious fidelity.

The understanding that the purity of the 144,000 is a symbol of religious fidelity originates from several Old Testament texts (cf. 2 Kgs 19:21; Lam 2:13; Jer 3:6; 18:13; Amos 5:2; Hos 2:5). This is a symbolic description of the church kept pure from all defiling relationships with the pagan world system (a significant mandate for the church in John's

85. Beale, *Revelation*, 733.

86. See Swete, *Apocalypse*, 96–97, for a more comprehensive discussion of reasons to adopt a holistic view of the 144,000.

87. Kiddle, *Revelation*, 268. Also see Collins, *The Apocalypse*, 99–100 and *Crisis and Catharsis*, 129–31.

88. Charles, *Revelation*, 9–11.

89. Carrington, *Meaning of Revelation*, 337–40.

90. See Mounce, *Revelation*, 268, for an elaborate discussion and critique of these views of purity and non-defilement from women with regards to the 144,000.

Apocalypse). These 144,000 constitute those who in John's day resisted the seductions of the great harlot Rome with whom the kings of the earth had committed fornication (17:2; cf. 13:7; 14:1–5). Furthermore, they implicitly present a mandate to those who worship the Lamb to maintain purity and holiness (as a mark of faithfulness to the Lamb).

CONCLUSION

Undoubtedly, the deliberations of this chapter lead to the conviction that the Apocalypse of John contributes significantly to the multifaceted view and contextual understanding of the New Testament church. A book that is deemed prophetic, with a focus on things to come (1:1, 3, 19; 10:11; 22:7, 10, 18, 19), is saturated with illuminating and illustrative materials on the nature, character, function, and destiny of the church. While some of these materials are symbolic and implicit, others are literal and explicit references to the church. All together they paint a unique portrait of the church that complements what we find in the rest of the New Testament. As in other New Testament documents, the church of the Apocalypse is a community of believers situated in different local contexts, mandated to maintain the witness of Jesus, redeemed by the blood of Christ, and brought into a special relationship with the Spirit. Also, it is made up of kings, priests, and servants of God/Christ, and it is designated as the Bride of Christ and the People of God.

However, the Apocalypse of John in its presentation of the portrait of the New Testament church (which is in agreement with what we find in the other New Testament documents) also magnifies, highlights, and sheds some light on several features of the portrait of the New Testament church.

While it is true that the witness of the church takes place in a context of perversion and persecution of faith, the Apocalypse of John, like no other document of the New Testament, also stresses the implication of martyrdom for the witnessing church. In fact, a special reward of eternal reign is given to those who seal their faithful witness with martyrdom.

For the Apocalypse of John, the redemptive work of Jesus does much more than release the church from the penalty of sin; it releases from the power of sin in such a way that it promotes the holy character of the church.

In its special relationship with the Spirit, the church is expected to hear and speak the words of the Spirit. According to the Apocalypse of

John, this is the sense in which the Spirit gives life to and through the church. Thus, through the Spirit, the church is called to faithful witness as well as repentance, especially when the church has failed in any of the aspects of what she is called to be and do.

The portrait of the church as royal priests in the Apocalypse of John is with the understanding that priests are freed from sin, and that the redemptive work of Jesus is the basis for kingship and rulership. Rulership itself in the Apocalypse of John is reserved for those designated as overcomers, especially those who suffer martyrdom for the sake of the Lamb. And as for kingship, it is an eschatological reality for the church in the Apocalypse of John.

The Apocalypse of John provides a comprehensive and cohesive list of what the church is called upon to do as servants of God/Christ. The list includes listening to and obeying the words of prophecy, maintaining faithful/orthodox teachings and practices, receiving the seal and mark of God, suffering persecution and even martyrdom, offering worship and priestly activities, and maintaining faithful witness to Jesus.

The church portrayed as the Bride of Christ and the People of God in the Apocalypse of John is with reference not only to what the church is presently, but what the church will become: a holy and perfect people fit for life with God for all eternity.

BIBLIOGRAPHY

Aune, David E. *Revelation 1–5*. WBC. Waco, TX: Word, 1997.

———. *Revelation 6–16*. WBC. Waco, TX: Word, 1998.

———. *Revelation 17–22*. WBC. Waco, TX: Word, 1998.

———. "St. John's Portrait of the Church in the Apocalypse." *EvQ* 38 (1966) 131–49.

Bandstra, A. J. "'A Kingship and Priests': Inaugurated Eschatology in the Apocalypse." *CTJ* 27 (1992) 10–25.

Bauckham, R. *The Climax of Prophecy: Studies in the Book of Revelation*. Edinburgh: T. & T. Clark, 1992.

———. "The Role of the Spirit in the Apocalypse." *EvQ* 52 (1980) 66–83.

———. *The Theology of the Book of Revelation*. New York: Cambridge University Press, 1993.

Beale, G. K. *The Book of Revelation*. Grand Rapids: Eerdmans, 1999.

Beasley-Murray, G. R. *The Book of Revelation*. NCB. London: Oliphants, 1974.

Beckwith, I. T. *The Apocalypse of John*. New York: MacMillan, 1919.

Boring, M. E. *Revelation*. Louisville: John Knox, 1989.

Brownlee, W. H. "The Priestly Character of the Church in the Apocalypse." *NTS* 5 (1959) 224–25.

Brox, N. *Zeuge und Märtyer*. SANT 5. Munich: Kösel, 1961.

Cabaniss, A. "Liturgy-Making Factors in Primitive Christianity." *JR* 23 (1943) 43–58.

Caird, G. B. *A Commentary on the Revelation of St. John the Divine.* HNTC. New York: Harper & Row, 1966.

Carrington, P. *The Meaning of Revelation.* London: SPCK, 1931.

Charles, R. H. *The Revelation of St. John.* ICC. 2 vols. Edinburgh: T. & T. Clark, 1920.

Collins, A. Y. *The Apocalypse.* Wilmington: Michael Glazier, 1979.

———. *Crisis and Catharsis: The Power of the Apocalypse.* Philadelphia: Westminster, 1984.

Dibelius, M. "Wer Ohren hat zu hören, der höre." *Theologische Studen und Kritiken* 83 (1910) 461–71.

Du Preez, J. "Mission Perspective in the Book of Revelation." *EvQ* 42 (1970) 152–67.

Ellingworth, P. "The Marturia Debate." *BT* 41 (1990) 138–39.

Enroth, A. M. "The Hearing Formula in the Book of Revelation." *NTS* 36 (1990) 598–608.

Gundry, R. H. "The New Jerusalem: People, Not a Place." *NovT* 29 (1987) 254–64.

Harrington, W. J. *The Apocalypse of St. John.* London: G. Chapman, 1969.

Holtz, T. *Die Christologie der Apokalypse des Johannes.* Text und Untersuchunge 85. Berlin: Akademie, 1971.

Jeske, Richard L. "Spirit and Community in the Johannine Apocalypse." *NTS* 31 (1985) 452–66.

Kiddle, M. *The Revelation of St. John.* MNTC. London: Hodder & Stoughton, 1940.

Kraft, H. *Die Offenbarung des Johannes.* Tübingen: Mohr-Siebeck, 1974.

McKelvey, R. J. *The New Temple.* Oxford: Oxford University Press, 1969.

Minear, P. S. *Images of the Church in the New Testament.* Philadelphia: Westminster, 1960.

Moffatt, J. *The Revelation of St. John the Divine.* The Expositor's Greek Testament. Grand Rapids: Eerdmans, 1951.

Mounce, R. H. *The Book of Revelation.* Rev. ed. Grand Rapids: Eerdmans, 1998.

Peters, Olutola K. *The Mandate of the Church in the Apocalypse of John.* New York: Peter Lang, 2005.

Poucouta, P. "La mission prophétique de l'Église dans l'Apocalypse johannique." *NRTh* 110 (1988) 38–57.

Ramsay, W. *The Letters to the Seven Churches of Asia.* Grand Rapids: Baker, 1963.

Roloff, J. *The Revelation of John.* Minneapolis: Fortress, 1993.

Schüssler-Fiorenza, E. *Priester für Gott: Studien zum Herrshafts und Priestermotiv in der Apokalypse.* Münster: Aschendorff, 1972.

Stott, W. "A Note on the Word κυριακή in Revelation 1:10." *NTS* 12 (1965–1966) 70–75.

Sweet, J. P. *Revelation.* London: SCM, 1979.

———. "Maintaining the Testimony of Jesus: The Suffering of Christians in the Revelation of John." In *Suffering and Martyrdom in the New Testament*, edited by W. Horbury and B. McNeil, 101–17. Cambridge: Cambridge University Press, 1981.

Swete, H. B. *The Apocalypse of St. John.* London: MacMillan, 1907.

Thomas, R. L. *Revelation 1-7: An Exegetical Commentary.* Chicago: Moody, 1992.

Trites, A. A. "Μάρτυς and Martyrdom in the Apocalypse: A Semantic Study." *NovT* 15 (1973) 72–82.

———. *The New Testament Concept of Witness.* SNTSMS. London: Cambridge University Press, 1977.

Vanhoye, A. *Old Testament Priests and the New Priest according to the New Testament.* Petersham: St. Bede's, 1986.

Walvoord, J. F. *The Revelation of Jesus Christ.* Chicago: Moody, 1966.

Modern Author Index

Scripture and Ancient Sources Index

~

APOCRYPHA

~

OLD TESTAMENT PSEUDEPIGRAPHA

~

DEAD SEA SCROLLS